# The Russian Presidency of Dmitry Medvedev, 2008–12

The term 'Tandem' was used to describe the Putin–Medvedev combination that ruled Russia from 2008 to 2012, when Medvedev was president and Putin prime minister. Many people saw Putin as the real wielder of power, with Medvedev as his puppet. Others, however, saw Medvedev as a visionary, someone who envisioned large scale schemes – even though these schemes have not yet come to fruition. At the same time, many in the West regarded Medvedev favourably, and gave him credit for raising expectations among both the elite and the middle classes in Russia in such a way as to make it difficult for the Russian state to return to its old ways. This book presents a comprehensive survey of the Medvedev presidency, covering all areas including politics, the economy, international relations and social developments. The author concludes that it is still too early to assess Medvedev's achievements definitively.

**J. L. Black** is the Director of the Centre for Research on Canadian–Russian Relations at Laurentian University in Barrie, Ontario, and an Emeritus Professor of Carleton University, Ottawa, Canada.

# Routledge Contemporary Russia and Eastern Europe Series

1 **Liberal Nationalism in Central Europe**
Stefan Auer

2 **Civil-Military Relations in Russia and Eastern Europe**
David J. Betz

3 **The Extreme Nationalist Threat in Russia**
The growing influence of Western Rightist ideas
Thomas Parland

4 **Economic Development in Tatarstan**
Global markets and a Russian region
Leo McCann

5 **Adapting to Russia's New Labour Market**
Gender and employment strategy
Edited by Sarah Ashwin

6 **Building Democracy and Civil Society East of the Elbe**
Essays in honour of Edmund Mokrzycki
Edited by Sven Eliaeson

7 **The Telengits of Southern Siberia**
Landscape, religion and knowledge in motion
Agnieszka Halemba

8 **The Development of Capitalism in Russia**
Simon Clarke

9 **Russian Television Today**
Primetime drama and comedy
David MacFadyen

10 **The Rebuilding of Greater Russia**
Putin's foreign policy towards the CIS countries
Bertil Nygren

11 **A Russian Factory Enters the Market Economy**
Claudio Morrison

12 **Democracy Building and Civil Society in Post-Soviet Armenia**
Armine Ishkanian

13 **NATO-Russia Relations in the Twenty-First Century**
Aurel Braun

14 **Russian Military Reform**
A failed exercise in defence decision making
Carolina Vendil Pallin

15 **The Multilateral Dimension in Russian Foreign Policy**
Edited by Elana Wilson Rowe and Stina Torjesen

16 **Russian Nationalism and the National Reassertion of Russia**
*Edited by Marlène Laruelle*

17 **The Caucasus – An Introduction**
*Frederik Coene*

18 **Radical Islam in the Former Soviet Union**
*Edited by Galina M. Yemelianova*

19 **Russia's European Agenda and the Baltic States**
*Janina Šleivytė*

20 **Regional Development in Central and Eastern Europe**
Development processes and policy challenges
*Edited by Grzegorz Gorzelak, John Bachtler and Maciej Smętkowski*

21 **Russia and Europe**
Reaching agreements, digging trenches
*Kjell Engelbrekt and Bertil Nygren*

22 **Russia's Skinheads**
Exploring and rethinking subcultural lives
*Hilary Pilkington, Elena Omel'chenko and Al'bina Garifzianova*

23 **The Colour Revolutions in the Former Soviet Republics**
Successes and failures
*Edited by Donnacha Ó Beacháin and Abel Polese*

24 **Russian Mass Media and Changing Values**
*Edited by Arja Rosenholm, Kaarle Nordenstreng and Elena Trubina*

25 **The Heritage of Soviet Oriental Studies**
*Edited by Michael Kemper and Stephan Conermann*

26 **Religion and Language in Post-Soviet Russia**
*Brian P. Bennett*

27 **Jewish Women Writers in the Soviet Union**
*Rina Lapidus*

28 **Chinese Migrants in Russia, Central Asia and Eastern Europe**
*Edited by Felix B. Chang and Sunnie T. Rucker-Chang*

29 **Poland's EU Accession**
*Sergiusz Trzeciak*

30 **The Russian Armed Forces in Transition**
Economic, geopolitical and institutional uncertainties
*Edited by Roger N. McDermott, Bertil Nygren and Carolina Vendil Pallin*

31 **The Religious Factor in Russia's Foreign Policy**
*Alicja Curanović*

32 **Postcommunist Film – Russia, Eastern Europe and World Culture**
Moving images of postcommunism
*Edited by Lars Kristensen*

33 **Russian Multinationals**
From regional supremacy to global lead
*Andrei Panibratov*

34 **Russian Anthropology After the Collapse of Communism**
*Edited by Albert Baiburin, Catriona Kelly and Nikolai Vakhtin*

35 **The Post-Soviet Russian Orthodox Church**
Politics, culture and Greater Russia
*Katja Richters*

36 **Lenin's Terror**
The ideological origins of early
Soviet State violence
*James Ryan*

37 **Life in Post-Communist Eastern
Europe after EU Membership**
*Edited by Donnacha Ó Beacháin,
Vera Sheridan and Sabina
Stan*

38 **EU – Border Security**
Challenges, (mis)perceptions, and
responses
*Serghei Golunov*

39 **Power and Legitimacy –
Challenges from Russia**
*Edited by Per-Arne Bodin, Stefan
Hedlund and Elena Namli*

40 **Managing Ethnic Diversity in
Russia**
*Edited by Oleh Protsyk and
Benedikt Harzl*

41 **Believing in Russia – Religious
Policy After Communism**
*Geraldine Fagan*

42 **The Changing Russian University**
From state to market
*Tatiana Maximova-Mentzoni*

43 **The Transition to National Armies
in the Former Soviet Republics,
1988–2005**
*Jesse Paul Lehrke*

44 **The Fall of the Iron Curtain and
the Culture of Europe**
*Peter I. Barta*

45 **Russia After 2012**
From Putin to Medvedev to
Putin – continuity, change, or
revolution?
*Edited by J.L. Black and Michael
Johns*

46 **Business in Post-Communist
Russia**
Privatisation and the limits of
transformation
*Mikhail Glazunov*

47 **Rural Inequality in Divided
Russia**
*Stephen K. Wegren*

48 **Business Leaders and New
Varieties of Capitalism in
Post-Communist Europe**
*Edited by Katharina Bluhm,
Bernd Martens and Vera
Trappmann*

49 **Russian Energy and Security
up to 2030**
*Edited by Susanne Oxenstierna
and Veli-Pekka Tynkkynen*

50 **The Informal Post-Socialist
Economy**
Embedded practices and
livelihoods
*Edited by Jeremy Morris and Abel
Polese*

51 **Russia and East Asia**
Informal and gradual integration
*Edited by Tsuneo Akaha and Anna
Vassilieva*

52 **The Making of Modern Georgia,
1918–2012**
The first Georgian Republic and
its successors
*Edited by Stephen F. Jones*

53 **Digital Russia**
The language, culture and
politics of new media
communication
*Edited by Michael S. Gorham,
Ingunn Lunde and Martin
Paulsen*

54 **Eastern Christianity and Politics in the Twenty-First Century**
*Edited by Lucian N. Leustean*

55 **Punk in Russia**
Cultural mutation from the 'useless' to the 'moronic'
*Ivan Gololobov, Hilary Pilkington and Yngvar B. Steinholt*

56 **Chechnya at War and Beyond**
*Edited by Anne Le Huérou, Aude Merlin, Amandine Regamey and Elisabeth Sieca-Kozlowski*

57 **The Russian Presidency of Dmitry Medvedev, 2008–12**
The next step forward or merely a time out?
*J. L. Black*

'Larry Black's excellent book convincingly demonstrates that Dmitry Medvedev was much more than Vladimir Putin's alter ego, contrary to what was often said in the Western press. It unquestionably helps us to understand why the announcement of his departure in favour of Putin's return to the presidency in the fall of 2011 led to the largest mass demonstrations in Moscow and St. Petersburg since the end of the USSR. Larry Black shows how and why many significant moves introduced by Medvedev, to modernize the economy, to reinforce the rule of law and cope with endemic corruption, did generate high hopes in Russia's new urban middle class for much needed changes. Even if the strong relationship based on personal trust and loyalty between the two leaders allowed for Medvedev's replacement as president and the partial reversal of many of his initiatives, Black is convinced many of these are bound to revive, one way or the other.'

Jacques Lévesque, *Université du Québec à Montréal, Canada*

'This informative and lucid study of Russia between 2008 and 2012 details the challenges that confronted the presidency of Dmitry Medvedev in his efforts to modernize the economic, political, and social life of that vast territory. Larry Black offers much in this account of the four-year Tandem, providing insights not only into domestic developments but also into Russia's relations with neighbouring countries and the West.'

Serge Cipko, *Canadian Institute of Ukrainian Studies, Canada*

'As the Medvedev presidency is receding into history, it continues to puzzle observers of Russian affairs. By providing the first comprehensive account of that period, Larry Black helps us understand the logic of Russia's continuing political evolution, shaped by a complex and ever-changing array of domestic and international factors.'

Sergei Plekhanov, *York University, Canada*

'This is a benchmark assessment of an important transition period in the political, economic and social history of modern Russia. It is highly commended to scholars and students, as it offers unique apolitical insight into the nature of high politics in Russia, 2008–12. This is an indispensable asset to any serious student of Russia's modern progress to finding its place in the world.'

Roger McDermott, *Affiliated Senior Analyst,*
*Danish Institute for International Studies, Copenhagen*

# The Russian Presidency of Dmitry Medvedev, 2008–12

The next step forward or merely a time out?

## J. L. Black

Routledge
Taylor & Francis Group

LONDON AND NEW YORK

First published 2015 by Routledge

2 Park Square, Milton Park, Abingdon, Oxfordshire OX14 4RN
711 Third Avenue, New York, NY 10017

*Routledge is an imprint of the Taylor & Francis Group, an informa business*

First issued in paperback 2017

*British Library Cataloguing in Publication Data*
A catalogue record for this book is available from the British Library

*Library of Congress Cataloging in Publication Data*
Black, J. L. (Joseph Laurence), 1937-
The Russian presidency of Dmitry Medvedev, 2008-2012 : the next step
forward or merely a time out? / J.L. Black.
pages cm. -- (Routledge contemporary Russia and Eastern Europe series ; 57)
Includes bibliographical references and index.
1. Medvedev, D. A. (Dmitrii Anatol'evich) 2. Presidents--Russia
(Federation)--Biography. 3. Politicians--Russia (Federation)--Biography.
4. Russia (Federation)--Politics and government--1991- 5. Russia
(Federation)--Foreign relations. 6. Russia (Federation)--Economic
conditions--1991- I. Title.
DK510.766.M43B53 2014
947.086′3--dc23
2014006350

ISBN: 978-1-138-78191-7 (hbk)
ISBN: 978-1-138-57384-0 (pbk)

Typeset in Times New Roman
by Taylor & Francis Books

# Contents

| | | |
|---|---|---|
| *List of illustrations* | | xi |
| *Preface* | | xii |
| *Acknowledgements* | | xvii |
| *Transliteration and sources* | | xviii |
| *Abbreviations and key terms* | | xix |

**Introduction**                                                               1
*Who was Dmitry Medvedev in 2008?   5*

**1   The Tandem**                                                            11
*The presidency and its power base   12*
*The agenda   15*
*The Tandem in action   15*
*The Tandem – frayed   24*
*Presidential ambitions   26*
*A momentous decision   29*
*Presidential election campaign, 2012   32*
*The aftermath   35*

**2   The Russian Federation: source of strength and
weakness**                                                                      42
*The North Caucasus quicksand   50*

**3   The political cockpit**                                                62
*The legislature   65*
*Voices outside the legislature   69*
*The government   72*
*Preparing for the State Duma election   74*
*The election campaign   78*
*The aftermath   79*

**4   Economic considerations**                                          **91**
*Recession   92*
*World Trade Organization and the Customs Union   97*
*Modernization   98*
*Agriculture   107*
*Energy and the pipeline 'great game'   111*

**5   Themes in foreign affairs**                                         **131**
*War in Georgia   132*
*Ripple effects   137*
*Looking east – toward Beijing   140*
*Looking west – toward Washington   152*
*Defence matters   163*

**6   Society, daily life, and the corruption conundrum**                 **176**
*Social unrest   176*
*Infrastructure   179*
*Natural disasters and other calamities   182*
*Demography and health   183*
*The NGO phenomenon   189*
*The corruption impasse   191*

**Concluding remarks**                                                    **213**

*Appendix*                                                                213
*Bibliography*                                                            219
*Index*                                                                   225

# Illustrations

## Maps

2.1 The North Caucasus (adapted from original created by Peter
    Fitzgerald)                                                          51
4.1 Nord Stream Pipeline (adapted from OpenStreetMap
    contributors)                                                       115
4.2 South Stream Pipeline (adapted from South Stream
    Transport B.V.)                                                     116

## Tables

0.1 State Duma election results, 2 December 2007                          4
1.1 Presidential election results, 2 March 2008                          13
1.2 Presidential election results, 4 March 2012                          35
3.1 Results of the election to the State Duma, 4 December 2011           64
A.1 Levada Centre polls on social issues that most concern Russian
    citizens, 2005–2012                                                 216
A.2 Trust in Russia's basic social and political institutions, October
    2011                                                                217
A.3 Trust in Russia's basic social and political institutions, 2007–2013  218

# Preface

This book is a purposely descriptive and chronological account of Russia during the Medvedev presidency.

Readers may wonder why one would undertake to produce a history of a mere four years out of the middle of Vladimir Putin's 18-year (or more) tenure as Russia's most powerful individual. The reason is simple: Medvedev's presidency marked an opportunity for Russia to take a leap forward in the post-Soviet transition to modern civil statehood. With the political arena apparently stabilized, the components of the Russian Federation outwardly under control and relatively unified in purpose, and the economy booming, it was time to fulfil promises made in the early 1990s. While Medvedev served as an ideal figurehead and spokesman for a change of direction, Putin could keep his hand on the steering wheel as leader of the government from a position somewhat removed from the glare of spotlights.

A lot of things went on simultaneously between the years 2008 and 2012. The task I set for myself here is to provide details of events, organizations and movements as they evolved during this four-year moment of post-Soviet history. Students, specialists and general researchers can look here for information, context and, above all, sequence, enabling them to draw their own conclusions about the matters that interest them the most.

Medvedev had a chance to serve either as an important page-turner in the on-going saga of Russia in transition, or to perform simply as a proxy for Putin. By discovering what happened during his presidency, rather than what could or should have happened, readers can also judge the level of success of Putin's experiment with a stand-in. After lurching from the wild centrifugal forces of the 1990s and the equally dramatic centripetal impetus of Putin's first two terms, it remained to be seen if post-Soviet Russia had steadied enough at the helm to launch itself into the next stage towards modernization.

The book is divided into chapters based on large themes. In Chapter One, 'The Tandem', an unusual form of top down management is described. It is here that we see how Russia was governed from the offices of the President and Prime Minister in a partnership in which the lesser office, Putin's, pulled above its constitutional weight. The second chapter shows how the centre re-shaped its relations with the components of the Federation, expanded the federal presence everywhere, and slowly introduced uniformity to the many subjects of the Constitution. Ever-present dangers faced by the Federation from inside are highlighted in the second part of this chapter. The extremism, separatism and, above all, terrorism – domestic and international – described here set stages for the other chapters, where developments are fashioned in varying degrees by these deliberate sources of chaos.

The political arena and economic considerations take up the fourth and fifth chapters. In the former case, political parties, movements, organizations, and individual activists and their agendas are introduced. Topics discussed in Chapter Five on economics touch everything else in the book and, in fact, could be the basis of a separate monograph. Thus, I have limited the discourse to four overarching themes: the recession, modernization, agriculture, and the energy sector, with notes on certain integrative agencies added, both international (WTO) and domestic (Customs Union).

The same could be said about the chapter on foreign policy, in which Russia's relations with the West, mostly the US, and the East, mostly China, are the two main sections. Overall military strategy, arms control administration, and Russia's uneasy association with NATO are examined here as well, as are the Kremlin's roles in a wide cross-section of international associations. The final chapter provides an overview of certain features in the daily life of Russians and closes with the most corrosive dilemma of all – corruption.

Events and developments in Russia, or any other country for that matter, cannot be compartmentalized under chapter headings easily, nor should they be. For that reason there will be some minor repetitions, and also places where the reader will draw connections intuitively. This is not intended to be an all-inclusive tome; rather, it is intended as a guide to things that changed and things that stayed the same during the four years that Medvedev stood in for Putin – a time of great expectations.

**A word on historical context**

If we take 25 December 1991 as a date for Russians to celebrate the official demise of the Union of Soviet Socialist Republics, then we must also realize how new the current Russian Federation is. It was on that date that USSR President Mikhail Seergevich Gorbachev read his resignation speech over Moscow Central Television, with clear reluctance. He pointed out that the territory of the dying USSR had 'become one of the main strongholds for the transformation of modern civilization by peaceful democratic principles. Peoples and nations have received real freedom of choice in seeking their way of self-determination'.[1] A mere twenty years later, as Dmitry Medvedev's presidency was coming to a close, it still wasn't absolutely clear which path Russians were taking into the future.

The purpose of this short 'word on context' is to provide readers with some notion of where Russians were two decades ago, and how great a leap they had to make to shake their Soviet past.

As Russians looked around on 1 January 1992, they found themselves living in a world that would have been absolutely alien to them a mere few months earlier, and one that would take many more months, perhaps years, for most of them to comprehend and accept as permanent. With the exception of the few years of rapid and extremely confusing adjustments introduced by Gorbachev after 1985, they had all been born, raised, educated and socialized in a USSR that had existed almost without change (except territorially) for their entire lives, the lives of their parents, and perhaps their grandparents.

Until the very late 1980s, the USSR had allowed no freedom of political expression. There were no political parties, never more than one name on a ballot, and no secret ballots. The Communist Party of the Soviet Union (CPSU) was categorized as a public organization, not intended as a vehicle for competition with other such organizations. In fact, by dint of Article Six of the Soviet Constitution, adopted as recently as 1977, the CPSU was,

> The leading and guiding force of the Soviet society and the nucleus of its political system, of all state organizations and public organizations, ... The Communist Party, armed with Marxism-Leninism, determines the general perspectives of the development of society and the course of the home and foreign policy of the USSR, directs the great constructive work of the Soviet people, and imparts a planned, systematic and theoretically substantiated character to their struggle for the victory of communism.

It is true that in 1989 Gorbachev forced the CPSU to relinquish the special status bestowed on it by Article Six, but that was but one of his initiatives that triggered revolutionary changes in thought and practice, and shattered the once omniscient Party's control over all dimensions of Soviet life.

The USSR had no official president until 1990. Instead, the most powerful position in the country was the office of the General Secretary of the Political Bureau of the Central Committee of the CPSU, yet it had no standing in the Constitution.[2] Soviet citizens had no right to own land, no right to free exit from or entry back into their own country, and they carried internal passports (*propiski*) that determined where they could live and work. Although the USSR had exhaustive criminal and civil codes, there was no real rule by law and 'telephone justice' prevailed, i.e., a judge usually ignored the law and simply picked up the phone to get a judgement from his or her Party boss. There was no freedom of religious practice, atheism was a science taught in schools, and a Council for the Office of Religious Cults oversaw most religious affairs. There was absolutely no freedom of the press, and for decades a state censorship bureau (*Glavlit*) determined which subjects were worthy of print, and which subjects were not. Prior censorship had mostly disappeared by the 1980s, but journalists knew very well what they could and could not write and so practiced strict self-censorship. Similar restrictions applied in the worlds of literature, the theatre, film, and other art forms, all of which were subject to guidelines set by CPSU-controlled agencies, such as the Writer's

Union. Even academic research followed dictates set by the CPSU's interpreters of Marxism-Leninism.

Primary and secondary (general) schools were uniform in their curricula and, according to the Education Code, were expected to graduate 'young builders of communism'. To facilitate this end, the schools operated under the principle of *in loco parentis*, that is, they taught behaviour and political thinking along with the three 'Rs'. This practice was known as *vospitanie* or 'upbringing'. The school system was excellent in terms of creating a literate, well-educated society, and at the same time was one that aggressively discouraged imagination and differences of opinion.

The Russian worker had no right to strike or participate in demonstrations and rallies not organized by officialdom. There were no legal private enterprises and until 1987 'profit' was officially termed an artificial measurement of the success or failure of state enterprises. Prices were set on the basis of social need and often had little to do with the cost of producing the particular item; capitalism was deemed exploitive and the first step toward 'imperialism' and war. It was not until 1986 that laws linked salaries to performance. Ironically, the sudden switch to enterprise self-financing, i.e., companies had to make a profit to survive, by dint of a Law on the State Enterprises in 1987 and in effect the next year, forced the CPSU to embark on a rapid and bizarre sequence of unexpected further legislation: allowing bankruptcies, permitting layoffs, then legalizing strikes. As a consequence of these unforeseen ripple effects the entire Soviet economy came to a screeching halt by 1990–91. And newly minted 'capitalists' reaped enormous benefits while millions of workers and professionals lost almost everything.

This last happenstance ensured that other features of the Soviet regime would be the ones remembered most by many citizens of the Russian Federation: there was no unemployment, at least in theory; everyone received a salary ('earned' would be the wrong word) and a pension no matter the unproductive and inefficient nature of their place of work. They enjoyed early retirement (males at 60, females at 55). Everyone had access to free or almost free housing, schooling and medical care; there were no real food shortages after the early 1950s; no fear of crime on the streets, though drunkenness and family violence proliferated. Most importantly, there had been a very high level of social and work security until the late 1980s. Soviet citizens knew what they could and could not do, and simply got on with their lives, with barely a flicker of political consciousness. Political dissidents rightly lionized in the West for their courage in the face of harsh government hostility, were regarded as noisy 'boat-rockers' by the majority of Soviet citizens.

Whether recollections of these latter characteristics of the USSR reveal amnesia or nostalgia among Russians is not the point of this Preface, which is rather that, if we intend to judge Russia's post-Soviet progress, its leaders and its people, we should recall that historical context, no matter how recent, is central to helping explain events as they evolve over time.

How far Russia has come since those Soviet days is an indirect part of our story here. Many of the arguments about Russia's future development heard openly and at length while Medvedev was president would never have seen the light of day during the Soviet era. The four-year period, mid-2008 to mid-2012, provides us with a bit of a 'time out' from the frenetic Yeltsin years, and the driven early Putin years, to assess how far Russia has still to go in its continuing transition towards a modern civil society.

\* \* \*

I would add a few personal words. I travelled to Russia (then the USSR) first in 1970 for further research on a book based on my recently completed dissertation. Those were the days when Brezhnev was still consolidating his power, and changes initiated later by Gorbachev were not yet even dreamed of. I revisited the country many times after that – most recently in 2011 – travelled in almost every Soviet Republic and in Siberia, and came to know people from a wide cross-section of Russian life. I have supervised Russian-born and -educated graduate students in Canada, some of whom returned to their homeland to take up teaching and other posts in the Russian Federation.

My views on what is and has been going on may well clash with those held by some fellow academics and certain cliques in Russia; but I hold to them on the basis of decades of study and continuing conversations with long-standing contacts in Moscow, St. Petersburg, Vladivostok, and elsewhere in that vast country.

## Notes

1 See M.S. Gorbachev, 'Televised Resignation Speech', *USSR Documents Annual, 1991.* Vol. 2: *Disintegration of the USSR*, Gulf Breeze, FL: Academic International Press, 1993, pp. 305–7.
2 The official head of state in the USSR was the chair of the executive committee (Presidium) of the Supreme Soviet. That office-holder was sometimes referred to as 'President', but the title was not official and the position was largely ceremonial.

# Acknowledgements

Thanks are owed to the University Partnership Centre, Georgian College, Barrie, Ontario, for providing the Centre for Research on Canadian–Russian Relations (CRCR) with valuable office space in which materials for this book have been gathered and, along with much else, made available for research and writing.

A debt of gratitude is owed as well to Peter Sowden, Helena Hurd, and the team at Routledge who took this manuscript from a very rough beginning, and brought the project to a successful conclusion. Thanks also to my son, Joseph L. Black, Ph.D., Professor of English at the University of Massachusetts, who helped greatly with the final draft.

# Transliteration and sources

Russian transliteration is based on a modified Library of Congress system, with common-use applications for names and places; for example, soft and hard signs are usually omitted. Endings on Russian names are simplified by using the English-language 'y' instead of the more accurate 'ii' or 'iy' – e.g. 'Dmitrii' will be 'Dmitry'. Most place names are also transliterated according to common usage, e.g. Moscow and not Moskva. Diacritical marks have been deleted in the text, e.g. Udal'tsov is Udaltsov; Triumfal'naya is Triumfalnaya, but not in the endnotes where Russian language references are included.

Although all major citations are referenced in the usual way and Russian sources are cited where appropriate, the endnotes include a number of general, often journalist-like essays in English. These are for quick, first-start reference by readers who do not read Russian and want to pursue a particular subject further. The same can be said of the government and private wire service notations (e.g. Interfax, ITAR-TASS, RIA Novosti, Bloomberg). They are not analytical, but they provide exact dates of information release, context, and sequence to the topic at hand.

# Abbreviations and key terms

| | |
|---|---|
| ABM | Anti-Ballistic Missile |
| AES | Atomic (Nuclear) Energy Station |
| AFP | Agence France-Presse |
| *Apparatchiki* | Officials |
| AP | Associated Press |
| APEC | Asia-Pacific Economic Cooperation |
| ISAF | International Security Assistance Force (NATO in Afghanistan) |
| ASEAN | Association of Southeast Asian Nations |
| ASI | Agency for Strategic Development |
| AVN | *Agentsvo Voennykh Novostei* (Military News Agency, an Interfax service) |
| BBC | British Broadcasting Corporation |
| BMD | Ballistic Missile Defence |
| BNS | Baltic News Service (http.//bns.ec) |
| CDSP | *Current Digest of the Soviet Press* |
| CDPSP | *Current Digest of the Post-Soviet Press* |
| CEC | Central Electoral Commission |
| GECF | Gas Exporting Countries Forum |
| CIS | Commonwealth of Independent States |
| CMTD | Commission for Modernization and Technological Development |
| CNPC | Chinese National Petroleum Corporation |
| CP | Communist Party |
| (CP) | Canadian Press |
| CPRF | Communist Party of the Russian Federation |
| CPSU | Communist Party of the Soviet Union |
| CSTO | Collective Security Treaty Organization |
| CTBT | Comprehensive Test Ban Treaty |
| EAS | East Asian Summit |
| EBRD | European Bureau of Research and Development |
| EDM | *Eurasia Daily Monitor* |
| ESPO | Eastern Siberia Pacific Ocean Pipeline |

| | |
|---|---|
| EU | European Union |
| EurAsEC | Eurasian Economic Community |
| FOM | *Fond 'Obshchestvennoe mnenie'* (Public Opinion Fund, a prominent polling company) |
| FSB | Federal Security Service |
| Gazprom | Gas industry monopoly in Russia |
| GECF | Gas Exporting Countries Forum |
| GLONASS | Global Navigation Satellite System |
| GUAM | Georgia, Ukraine, Azerbaijan and Moldova |
| GUUAM | Georgia, Ukraine, Uzbekistan, Azerbaijan and Moldova |
| IAEA | International Atomic Energy Agency |
| IMF | International Monetary Fund |
| INDEM | Information Science for Democracy, Moscow |
| INSOR | *Institut Sovremennogo Razvitia* (Institute of Contemporary Development) |
| Interfax | Russian International News Group, global |
| Interfax-AVN | Interfax's military news branch (see AVN) |
| JRL | Johnson's Russia List |
| ITAR-TASS | Russian World News Service |
| KGB | Committee of State Security, USSR |
| Kremlin.ru | Russian Federation Presidential website |
| *Krysha* | Protection (literally, 'roof') |
| LDPR | Liberal Democratic Party of Russia (Zhirinovsky's party) |
| MAP | Membership Action Plan (NATO) |
| MFA | Ministry of Foreign Affairs (see also MID) |
| MID | Ministry of Foreign Affairs (see also MFA) |
| MID.ru | Ministry of Foreign Affairs website |
| MN | *Moscow News* |
| MoD | Russian Federation Ministry of Defence |
| MOU | Memorandum of Understanding |
| MVD | *Ministerstvo Vnutrennikh Del* (Ministry of Internal Affairs) |
| NATO | North Atlantic Treaty Organization |
| NDN | National Distribution Network (in Russia, for Afghanistan war) |
| NMD | National Missile Defence System |
| NORAD | North American Air Defence |
| NPP | Nuclear Power Plant |
| NRC | NATO-Russia Council |
| NSA | National Security Agency (USA) |
| NYT | *New York Times* |
| OAO | *Otkrytoe Aktsionernoe Obshchestvo* (Unlimited Joint-Stock Company) |
| OECD | Organization for Economic Cooperation and Development |

| | |
|---|---|
| Oligarchs | Russia's nouveau riche billionaires who bought up state assets in 1990s |
| OMON | *Otryad Mobilniy Osobovo Naznacheniya* (Special Forces within MVD) |
| OPEC | Organization of Oil Exporting Countries |
| OSCE | Organization for Security and Cooperation in Europe |
| PACE | Parliamentary Assembly of the Council of Europe |
| PCA | Partnership and Cooperation Agreement, with the EU |
| PfP | Partnership for Peace (NATO) |
| PGO | Prosecutor General's Office |
| Premier.gov.ru | Russian Prime Minister's website |
| Press-sluzhba | Press Service |
| rbth.ru | Russia Beyond the Headlines |
| RF | Russian Federation |
| RF MFA | Russian Federation Ministry of Foreign Affairs |
| *Rosoboronexport* | Russian Arms Export Agency |
| Rosstat | Russian Bureau of Statistics |
| RP | *Russia Profile* |
| RT | *Russia Today* |
| SCO | Shanghai Cooperation Organization (sometimes ShCO) |
| ShCO | See SCO |
| *Siloviki* | Politically influence (former) members of the Russian military and security agencies |
| SKR | *Sledstvenny Kommitet Rossye* (Russian Investigative Committee) |
| SOVA | Moscow NGO that analyses racism and extremism in Russia |
| SPS | Union of Right Forces Party |
| START | Strategic Arms Reduction Treaty |
| SVR | *Sluzhba Vneshnei Razvedki* (Russian Foreign Intelligence Service) |
| tcm | Thousand cubic feet |
| Tsk KPRF | Central Committee of the CPRF |
| UN | United Nations |
| UNSC | United Nations Security Council |
| UR | United (One) Russia, the Putin-Medvedev party |
| USSR | Union of Soviet Socialist Republics |
| US | United States |
| *Vospitanie* | 'Upbringing', refers to a system of political and behaviour education in schools |
| VTsIOM | All-Russian Centre for the Study of Public Opinion |
| *Vziatka* | Bribe |
| WHO | World Health Organization |
| WNC | World News Connection, online only |
| WTO | World Trade Organization |
| Xinhua | Chinese English-language News service |

# Introduction

Preparations for Putin's first retirement as president started early, as aspiring replacements began popping up everywhere. The only real mystery in the race, however, was Putin's preference among the competitors for his position, and that would not be known until mid-December 2007. His choice would reveal the candidate whom Putin thought most loyal and also provide some clues as to the course he expected Russia to follow during the next four years.

At any rate, it was clear as early as February that year that Putin was going to make sure that the new man would be surrounded by his people. In that month, he promoted Sergei Ivanov to first deputy prime minister and named Sergei Naryshkin deputy prime minister with a mandate for external economic activities. Naryshkin also kept his previous task as chief of Russia's government staff. Ivanov came to the forefront with particularly impressive credentials. Relieved of his previous post as minister of defence, he was now charged with oversight of the industrial-military complex and parts of the civilian economy.

Ivanov's promotion to the same governmental level as young Dmitry Medvedev, already at that rank for well over a year, prompted most pundits to see them as competing front-runners for Putin's favour in the next presidential campaign. Bearing in mind that poll taking is an inexact science, it is worth noting that Medvedev always came out slightly ahead in questionnaires asking citizens for whom they would vote.[1] This may have been one of the factors in Putin's ultimate choice. Another Putin-appointed possibility caught the public's attention in September, when the government was dissolved and Viktor Zubkov was named the new prime minister to replace Mikhail Fradkov.

A relative unknown, Zubkov was director of the Federal Financial Monitoring Service (FFMS) since its inception in November 2001 as a subcommittee of the Ministry of Finance. The original mandate of the FFMS was to monitor money laundering and the financing of terrorism, and it enjoyed considerable success at least in establishing a legislative and administrative framework for tackling such issues. Over the next few years FFMS lifted the licenses of nearly 30 banks for money laundering. The agency worked closely with the Council of Europe and other international bodies on these matters, so Zubkov, aged 66, was known in international anti-corruption circles. In terms of politics, the choice suggested that Putin was seeking a successor who would move the fight to curb corruption up on the national agenda. Zubkov's age made him an unlikely candidate for this task, but an able ally to someone who could take it on.

Six days after the Zubkov appointment, recently-named Minister of Defence Anatoly Serdyukov resigned, explaining that he was Zubkov's son-in-law and that he wanted to prevent the appearance of a conflict of interest. An excited notion that this act heralded a new attitude against nepotism within governing circles was squashed before the end of September, as Putin re-appointed Serdyukov. In early October, Zubkov joined the security council. President Medvedev was later saddled, or blessed, with both men for the duration of his presidency, with Zubkov as deputy prime minister.

There was some of the usual flutter in September when a member of the Valdai discussion group said that Putin told him he might run again for president in 2012, though there was no clear commitment to do so. This was an old story and, in fact, good news to most Russians. Such hints prompted a burst of silly editorials in the West. A further outburst of headlines came when Putin announced later in September that he would allow his name to stand at the top of United Russia's list of deputies for the December election to the State Duma. He pointed out then that it was possible that he could be selected prime minister in 2008. Whereas the outcry from Western pundits and politicos was deafening, most Russians heaved a sigh of relief.

The election for a new president to succeed Putin was due on 2 March 2008, but contender lineups began to take on substance only in the fall of 2007, late by Western standards. Liberal Democrat leader Vladimir Zhirinovsky had long since informed journalists that he would be a candidate.[2] In November former Prime Minister and Defence Minister, Mikhail Kasyanov, said he would run. This prompted Boris Nemtsov (SPS), Grigory Yavlinsky (Yabloko), and Garri Kasparov (United Civil Front), to assert that they would throw their names in the ring, thereby guaranteeing splits in potential 'liberal' votes. Head of the Communist Party Gennady Zyuganov committed to the campaign in October, and Sergei Mironov, leader of A Just Russia and speaker of the Federation Council, announced on 3 December that he too would join the list of nominees.

On the last day of September, Kasparov was chosen by Other Russia to represent a coalition of oppositionists in the presidential race. Because Other Russia was denied registration by the electoral commission on 10 October, Kasparov's candidacy remained in doubt. Another 'liberal', Vladimir Bukovsky, returned to Moscow from London and talked to tiny audiences about running. The fact that Bukovsky's dual citizenship and lack of a ten-year recent residency made him ineligible did not deter him, for he mostly wanted to have his Kasparov-like message presented. His arrival caused a greater stir in the Western press than it did in Russia.

The final two months of the year saw a flurry of demonstrations around the country rallying behind the slogan 'Za Putina!' (For Putin!) and much talk that he would still be in charge after his term as president was up. There was little doubt that the general population wanted that to happen. While Western pundits harped that the pro-Putin rallies were orchestrated by the United Russia party, and therefore somehow not legitimate, most Russians continued to see in Putin the only guarantee that their long hard journey would eventually lead to a 'normal life'. Theories and propositions about change at the top abounded in the press. Among them was a proposal from a group called Women of Vladivostok who suggested that Putin's wife Lyudmila put her name on the ballot.[3] No one doubted that Putin's choice would determine the final outcome and that everyone else was jockeying for position in the post-Putin world.

In the meantime, nearly lost in the shadow of the presidential contest, political parties competed for seats in the election to the State Duma, scheduled for 2 December 2007. Conducted under very stringent rules, many of them introduced since the previous election in 2003, the earlier election was very important to the subsequent presidential campaign, for Medvedev's candidacy would be billed by mid-December as a continuation of Putinism. As it happened, several of the regulations that shaped the 2007 Duma election would survive the Medvedev presidency by only a few months.

There were 44 parties and 23 blocs registered for election in 2003; 34 were still registered by October 2006, and 11 of these were eligible to run in the 2007 vote. Prior to that election, half of the 450 seats in the State Duma were held by delegates elected from single-mandate constituencies, the other half was distributed to parties on the basis of proportional representation. Party lists were the sole basis for the allocation of seats in the new Duma, i.e., exclusively proportional representation by party, and electoral blocs were banned. Parties had to win seven per cent of votes cast to earn a portion of the 450 seats; previously the floor was set at five per cent. Parties without seats had to gain a minimum three per cent of the votes to be eligible for federal funding during the next election period.

As of 1 January 2007, to be officially registered with the Ministry of Justice all parties had to have 50,000 signed-on members, as opposed to the previous 10,000, if they did not already have party seats in the Duma. The party also had to be registered in at least 50 of the 83 components of the Russian Federation. 'Against All' was no longer a choice on the ballot, and no early voting was allowed. Amendments to the Law on Electoral Rights signed by Putin on 6 December 2006 abolished the minimum threshold for voter turnout, prohibited free TV airtime for negative campaigns against other candidates or parties, and expanded the criteria for voter ineligibility to include people who were previously imprisoned for a serious crime, for extremism, or for using Nazi symbols. Official campaigning time was limited to one month. Since 2004, media had not been allowed to take positions on platforms or on particular contenders during official campaign periods; and candidates were not allowed to 'defame' each other in print or during debates.

There were other features of the 2007 election; for example, a law against 'extremism' passed in 2006 was aimed technically at skinheads, but could be

*Table 0.1* State Duma election results, 2 December 2007

| Party | % of votes | No. of votes | Seats |
|---|---|---|---|
| United (One) Russia | 64.3 | 44,714,241 | 315 |
| Communist Party of Russia | 11.57 | 8,046,886 | 57 |
| Liberal Democratic Party of Russia | 8.14 | 5,660,823 | 40 |
| A Just (Fair) Russia | 7.74 | 5,383,639 | 38 |
| Agrarian Party | 2.30 | 1,600,234 | 0 |
| Yabloko | 1.59 | 1,108,985 | 0 |
| Civil Force | 1.05 | 733,604 | 0 |
| Union of Right Forces (SPS) | 0.96 | 699,444 | 0 |
| Patriots of Russia | 0.89 | 615,417 | 0 |
| Social Justice Party | 0.22 | 154,083 | 0 |
| Democratic Party of Russia | 0.13 | 89,780 | 0 |

Note: These figures were published in Russia on 10 December 2007; later official government website figures have all the percentages higher because only the four parties with 7% or over shared in the distribution of seats. A Just Russia included Rodina, the Pensioners Party, and Russia's Revival. Eligible voters numbered 109,145,517, and the turnout was 63.78%. Two parties, the Greens and Peace and Unity were declared ineligible at the last moment because their lists contained too many false names.

used against political parties, making small liberal and right wing organizations vulnerable to the whim of zealous or partisan authorities. The Central Electoral Commission (CEC) had the authority to bar candidates for 'false' signatures, but the evaluation process was murky.

These were the conditions under which the so-called Putin party, United Russia, handily won the election to the State Duma. The results are worth posting here because they provide a picture of the political forum with which Medvedev later had to work.

Shortly after the final State Duma election results were announced, several political entities jointly nominated Dmitry Medvedev as their candidate for president. Putin said he 'fully supported this proposal', thereby pretty well guaranteeing Medvedev's success. One mainstream editorialist spoke for most when he wrote that the nomination 'signals simultaneously the beginning and end of the presidential election campaign. The election of Medvedev as president of Russia for the next four years is inevitable'.[4]

The fact that Medvedev was not from the KGB or FSB and not usually regarded as one of the *siloviki*, i.e., the politically influential clique made up primarily of former members of the Russian military and security agencies, provided the nominee with the aura of being something different. As part of the carefully orchestrated job swap, Medvedev said that he would like Putin to be his prime minister. In a speech delivered to a United Russia Party gathering on 17 December, Putin agreed to serve in that post. That same meeting officially named Medvedev as the party's candidate for president, on a vote of 478–1. Thus, the Putin-Medvedev 'tandem' was conceived, if not yet fully incubated.

As the month wound down, initiative groups began formally designating presidency seekers: Zyuganov and Zhirinovsky were nominated by their respective parties. Kasparov took his name out of the ring, claiming that he could not find a conference hall in Moscow to hold an initiative group meeting. All such locations were closed to him, he whined. On 9 December, Kasyanov was the first self-nominated candidate to register, and Vladimir Bukovsky's initiative group followed suit on the 17th, still ignoring the fact that he did not meet the eligibility criteria. The battle was on, for whatever it was worth.

## Who was Dmitry Medvedev in 2008?

A few days after Putin picked Medvedev as his preferred successor, a Russian journalist rather mean-spiritedly described the candidate to foreign readers as a 'small man and faceless bureaucrat with zero public charisma'.[5] In March 2008, the English-language, government-funded Russian TV channel RT (Russia Today) was considerably more charitable, explaining that the just-elected president 'may be relatively new to some foreigners, but his name is well known to Russians and world business leaders'. The news broadcaster then went on to provide a sketchy summary of Dmitry Medvedev's 'meteoric rise' to the Kremlin.[6]

Born in September 1965 in St. Petersburg (then Leningrad), to a family of staunch communist party members,[7] Dmitry Anatolevich Medvedev was 42 when he was inaugurated President of Russia on 7 May 2008. Much was made of his youth at the time, though Putin was only five years older when he was named Acting President by Boris Yeltsin on the last day of 1999.[8] Many Russians who remembered the stifling gerontocracy of the Brezhnev and post-Brezhnev years[9] relished the youth and vigor of their new leaders, and Medvedev already had a record of accomplishment.

The fact that he had never been elected to a political office before the 2008 presidential run was certainly no handicap, for he had served with the government as Putin's chief-of-staff and had been First Deputy Prime Minister since November 2005. As a lead manager on Anatoly Sobchak's campaign for the Soviet Congress of People's Deputies in 1998 and campaign manager for Putin during the 2000 presidential elections, Medvedev knew as much about politicking as any Russian. But that wasn't much of a challenge. After nearly 70 years of the Soviet leadership's efforts to de-politicize its population, politics as Westerners know it still represented unfamiliar ground to almost every citizen of Russia.

The future president studied law at Leningrad State University, where Sobchak was his professor of economic history. He earned post graduate degrees and became a professor himself, teaching civil law. His dissertation on the civil juridical personality of state enterprises was completed in 1990. In this connection, one needs to recall that M.S. Gorbachev's seminal law that forced state enterprises to be self-financing (*khozraschyot*), i.e., make a profit to survive, came into force only in 1988. So, Medvedev's course of study and research was inescapably a mixture of old Soviet and new perestroikite. He even wrote a widely-used textbook on civil law, the first edition of which appeared in 1991.

His links to Sobchak were important formative ones for Medvedev. In addition to serving in the Congress of Deputies, Sobchak was co-chair of the Inter-Regional Group of deputies with Boris Yeltsin, and chair of the Constituent Assembly that created the Russian Constitution of 1993. Sobchak resigned from the CPSU in 1990 along with other members of a group called Democratic Platform, an informal bloc of deputies that advocated internal party reform and supported Boris Yeltsin in his disputes with Gorbachev.[10] Sobchak was named Chair of the Leningrad City Council later that year and invited Medvedev to serve as an adviser. When he was elected Mayor of St. Petersburg in June 1991, he brought Medvedev in as expert consultant to the City Council's committee for international relations, where he dealt with and tried to attract foreign investments. Medvedev's immediate boss on that committee was Vladimir Putin, another former Sobchak student.

Medvedev worked the other side, too. In 1994 he and two young colleagues, Anton Ivanov and Ilya Yeliseev, formed a small legal consulting firm, relying mostly on word-of-mouth to find clientele. In the same year Medvedev was named a legal adviser to Ilim, Russia's largest pulp and paper concern.[11] A few years later he served as a member of the board of directors for the Bratsky Forestry Complex, and was retained by Rus Insurance Company, a Bratsky subsidiary. There were stories that he was involved in a gambling-casino agency, which may or may not explain his attempts to ban gambling casinos after he became president.[12] Those were the days when officials and business tycoons were each others' best partners, forming mutually-protective associations falling under the rubric of *krysha* (protection; literally, 'roof'). Later the target of sporadic attacks by Putin and Medvedev, arrangements such as these were both tolerated and common in post-Soviet Russia's first decade.[13] Doubtless, Medvedev witnessed first-hand the seamier side of Russia's business community as it worked in the robber-baron days of the 1990s.

Personal connections such as these were central to Medvedev's subsequent career. Russians were already the ultimate professionals when it came to patronage, acculturated as they were by decades of CPSU *nomenklatura* career mobility practices. But Sobchak, who died of a heart attack in 2000, was more than a mere patron, he was one of Russia's leading open advocates of democracy, a proponent of the rule of law, and a courageous leader of anti-coup protesters in August 1991. Sobchak's views and willingness to practice what he advocated in his speeches could not help but shape Medvedev's vision for Russia's future. It is true as well that Sobchak's (and Yeltsin's) advocacy of democracy and rule of law were still much closer to Gorbachev's interpretation of them as vehicles for making the existing system work than they were to most Western assumptions about them. Still, they were far advanced over the old Soviet theory and practice of law and politics.

Working with Putin was, obviously, a more direct boost to Medvedev's career, and good reason for Daniel Treisman to refer to him as the 'understudy'.[14] After Boris Yeltsin named Putin prime minister in August 1999, Medvedev followed him to Moscow. He arrived in November to work as deputy head of the prime ministerial staff under Chief of Staff Dmitry Kozak, with whom he had already served on the St. Petersburg City Council's international relations committee. When Putin was picked as Acting President by Yeltsin on 31 December 1999, Medvedev tagged along again, this time as deputy head of the Presidential Executive Office tasked with Putin's election campaign. His immediate boss was Aleksandr Voloshin, whom Putin inherited from Yeltsin's administration, and one of the powerful insiders in Moscow.

Medvedev was promoted to First Deputy Head of the Presidential Executive Office in early June 2000 and a few weeks later was named chairman of the board of directors of Gazprom, the largest extractor of natural gas in the world. In this latter capacity he replaced former Prime Minister and founder of Gazprom, Viktor Chernomyrdin, who was by that time Russian ambassador to Ukraine. Medvedev was a proactive chair, presiding over Gazprom's first IPO in April 2001, among other things. He was re-elected chair of Gazprom's board every year until 2006, when he resigned to take up multiple other duties.

In October 2002, Putin chose Medvedev as the president's representative to the National Bank Council. A year later, after Voloshin ran afoul of Putin over the arrest of Mikhail Khodorkovsky, Russia's wealthiest oligarch, Medvedev replaced him as chief of the administrative staff, with an expanded role re-defined as overseer of the 'Main Constitutional and Legal Affairs Directorate, the Secretariat of the Chief of the President's Administration, the Economic Directorate, the president's press secretary, the president's consultants and advisers'.[15] Some analysts saw this appointment and Voloshin's dismissal as an early step in the anti-corruption battle that Putin initiated but failed to sustain – eventually leaving the heavy lifting on that dossier to Medvedev. The change also, of course, bolstered Putin's own St. Petersburg clique in the power corridors of the capital city.

By April 2004, Medvedev was also sitting on the Security Council. In short, he popped up everywhere long before he stood for president. As First Deputy Prime Minister he found himself with specific assignments: chair of the Committee on Intellectual Property, deputy chair of a government committee on the fuel and energy complex, and (in 2006) chair of another government committee on religious communities. In May that year, he headed up the committee on radio and television and, in 2007, a council titled Support for Russia's Olympic Athletes Fund. Also in that year, he joined Putin's Commission on Military-Technical Cooperation with Foreign States. When Sergei Ivanov was promoted to First Deputy Prime Minister, there was an assumption among pundits that he and Medvedev were nose-to-nose competitors to be Putin's choice for president. At the risk of appearing to rely on 20/

20 hindsight, Ivanov never really had a chance. Appearances to the contrary, there was no competition – Medvedev served as Putin's front man in too many sectors for him to be passed over.

In terms of experience outside the backrooms of political infighting, the most important of Medvedev's chores came during Putin's second term. He was put in charge of the so-called National Priority Projects, that is, large-scale, long-term priorities for the transition of Russia from the repressive Soviet era and leaderless Yeltsin years to a developed, modern country capable of functioning as an equal among the major states of the world. To this end, Medvedev chaired a Council for the Implementation of the National Projects that met first on 29 November 2005. Working with an initial budget allocation of 180 billion rubles ($5.2 billion) drawn from government and private funds, the Council set out to address issues of education, housing, agriculture, public health, and demography.[16]

The key goal of the Projects was to invest in Russia's human capital to raise the quality of life for Russians in the sectors noted above. The success, or failure, of the Putin/Medvedev initiatives in these vital sectors will serve as one of the yardsticks to measure the consequences of Medvedev's presidency. For now, the Council is worthy of mention as a reminder of Medvedev's intimate involvement in programs to stabilize and modernize Russia long before Putin favoured him publicly as his successor.

Without doubt, the Russian people wanted Putin to stay on. A public opinion survey conducted in the spring of 2006 by the Public Opinion Fund (*Fond 'Obshchestvennoe mnenie'* – FOM) showed that 59 per cent wanted him to take a third consecutive term, no matter that it would have been unconstitutional. Nevertheless, the public was by then already taking greater notice of Medvedev. The same survey ranked him as clear second choice, with Sergei Ivanov trailing in third. 43 percent of the people surveyed said they would vote for any candidate preferred by Putin, if he did not run himself.[17] In November of the same year, a poll run by the All-Russian Center for the Study of Public Opinion (VTsIOM) produced almost exactly the same results.

The middle years of Putin's second term were significant ones for Russia's post-Soviet transition. There were clear signs of emerging order and security in both the domestic and foreign sectors. The potential for a leap forward was outlined by seasoned statesman Yevgeny Primakov as early as mid-January 2006, in a long looking-back essay titled 'We Need Stability and Security. Will 2005 Enter History as a Turning Point?' Former head of the FSB, foreign minister and, briefly, prime minister, the widely-respected Primakov saw the only real 'threats' to Russia in its demographic situation: an aging and diminishing population, a general labor shortage, and a 'vacuum' of under-populated space in Siberia and the Far East. The domestic situation is stable, he said, and democracy is slowly emerging. He voiced concerns about foreign meddling in Russian (and Ukrainian and Georgian) politics and warned that several oligarchs were spending money on anti-Putin propaganda, some doing so from abroad.[18] He urged readers and listeners (it was also a public speech) to ignore Western preaching, adding that it was time for Russians to create real political parties with real platforms of their own.

Medvedev's presidency provides us with a four-year stretch from which to judge whether Putin's eight years of consolidation made possible a breakthrough of the type recommended by Primakov.

\* \* \*

The term 'tandem' was first used to describe the Putin-Medvedev combination within days of Dmitry Medvedev's election victory on 2 March 2008.[19] How else to define a system in which the new president, Medvedev, while holding extraordinarily powerful constitutional authority, agreed to govern as an equal with the former President, soon-to-be Prime Minister Vladimir Putin?

Although he had to win an election to get there, Medvedev had the enormous advantage of standing as Putin's handpicked candidate just as Putin had been Boris Yeltsin's anointed successor. There was an important difference, however: Russians wanted Putin to be very much unlike Yeltsin, and for Medvedev to be very much like Putin. Almost from inauguration day, political analysts in Russia and abroad scrambled to discover the level of 'likeness', i.e., the degree to which Putin was the puppet-master and Medvedev the puppet.

Writing six months after Medvedev's single term as president was over, Marxist writer and labour activist Boris Kagarlitsky referred to him as 'dreamer-in-chief', much in the way Nikita Khrushchev's former colleagues labelled him 'hare-brained' as they drove him from office in 1964. Kagarlitsky's complaint was that Medvedev, now prime minister as Putin reclaimed the presidency, was adamantly sticking to his large-scale schemes even though they had failed to materialize during his presidential tenure.[20] By that time, Kagarlitsky's opinion mirrored sentiments held widely by observers of all political stripes in Russia.

Most Western and some Russian specialists have been more sympathetic to Medvedev. While noting weaknesses and his failure to accomplish very much of what his rhetoric promised, they credit him for raising expectations among both the professional and middle classes above a line below which the state cannot easily return. By unleashing previously quiescent urges for reform among these strata, they say, he opened a Pandora's Box that in the long run Putin and the powerful insiders, the *siloviki*, may not be able to shut.[21]

Who was right?

## Notes

1 See, e.g., Interfax, 16 May 2007, in which 58 per cent of 1,600 respondents said they trusted Medvedev and 57 per cent trusted Ivanov. Putin's confidence rating was 80 per cent.
2 *Moskovskiy komsomolets*, 26 January 2007.
3 *Kommersant*, 16 November 2007.
4 'Konets intrigi. Prezidentom budet Medvedev', *Nezavisimaia gazeta*, 11 December 2007.

5  Pavel Felgenhauer, 'Medvedev – A Faceless Future Russian President', *Eurasia Daily Monitor*, 12 December 2007. Medvedev is five feet, four inches tall. One Russian speaking to this author over the telephone from Moscow joked that Putin chose Medvedev because he was the only person in government shorter than he is.

6  'Who is Dmitry Medvedev?' *Russia Today*, 4 March 2008.

7  Nikolai Svanidze, Marina Svanidze, *Medvedev*, Moscow: Amfora, 2008, p. 113. This book is based on a series of interviews conducted with Medvedev between February and April 2008 and appeared only after he was elected president.

8  Yeltsin, the only other post-Soviet Russian president, was 59 when in June 1990 he was elected president of the Russian Soviet Federal Socialist Republic (RSFSR), the Russian republic within the USSR.

9  Leonid Brezhnev (1906–82) was General Secretary of the CPSU from 1966 to 1982. Yuri Andropov (1914–84) served from 1982 to 1984, and Konstantin Chernenko (1911–85), held the office to March 1985. All three died in office. M.S. Gorbachev was 53 when he succeeded Chernenko.

10 On the Democratic Platform and context, see Richard Sakwa, *Gorbachev and His Reforms, 1985–1990*, New York: Prentice Hall, 1990, pp. 181–82, 186–87. For a translation of the Democratic Platform's agenda, see *USSR Documents Annual, 1990*. Vol. 1: *Restructuring Perestroika*, Gulf Breeze, FL: Academic International Press, 1991, pp. 72–74.

11 RISI, Information Provider for the Global Forest Products Industry, No. 24. See also Daniel Treisman, *The Return: Russia's Journey from Gorbachev to Medvedev*. New York: Free Press, 2011, pp. 132–33.

12 *Pravda.ru*, 14 May 2009.

13 On *krysha*, see Chapter Six, below.

14 Treisman, Chapter 4, *passim*.

15 ITAR-TASS, 30 October 2003.

16 The National Priority Projects were outlined in a speech delivered by Putin on 5 September 2005 to members of the government and invited guests. See, 'Eto kurs na investitsii v cheloveka, a znachit, i v budushchee Rossii', *Rossiiskaia gazeta*, 8 September 2005. A translation as 'This Path is an Investment in People, which Also Means in the Future of Russia', is available in *Russia and Eurasia Documents Annual, 2005*. Vol. 1: *The Russian Federation*, Gulf Breeze, FL: Academic International Press, 2006, pp. 310–14.

17 Summary of *Fond 'Obshchestvennoe mnenie'* (Hereafter – FOM) poll, ITAR-TASS, 8 June 2006.

18 Primakov, 'Nam nuzhny stabil'nosti i bezopasnosti'. Voidet li v istorii 2005 god kak perelomnyi', *Rossiiskaia gazeta*, 19 January 2006. The reference to oligarchs paying for anti-Putin propaganda from abroad was to Boris Berezovsky, then living in luxurious political asylum in Britain.

19 See, e.g. Vladimir Volkov in the World Socialist Web Site (wsws.org), 4 March 2008.

20 Boris Kagarlitsky, 'Medvedev Taking Russia Down a Road to Hell', *The Moscow Times*, 27 February 2013. In explaining where Khrushchev had gone wrong, the CPSU accused him of 'hare-brained schemes, premature and hasty conclusions', in 'Nezyblennaia Leninskaia general'naia liniia KPSS', *Pravda*, 17 October 1964.

21 For example, see Brian Whitmore, 'The Medvedev Legacy', RFE/RL, 26 January 2012; general essays in 'Change and Continuity in Russia's Political Environment', *Russian Analytical Digest*, No. 115, 20 June 2012, 'Russia's Evolving Political System', *Russian Analytical Digest*, No. 118, 2 October 2012, and thematic essays in *Russia after 2012. From Putin to Medvedev to Putin. Continuity, Change, or Revolution?* eds. J.L. Black & Michael Johns, London: Routledge, 2013.

# 1 The Tandem

When the Constitution of the Russian Federation was confirmed by referendum on 12 December 1993, commentators referred to it as a 'presidential constitution' because it conferred upon the head of state the right to veto legislation, appoint the prime minister and ministers, chair government sessions, head a strengthened security council, and determine 'the basic guidelines of the state's domestic and foreign policy'.[1]

The format of that document was not decided lightly. Until it was adopted, Russia was still stuck with a Soviet-era Constitution, and Soviet political institutions filled with representatives who were elected while the USSR still existed. Determined to define the newly transformed Russian Federation in law, various groups produced draft constitutions for public discussion in 1993. The first of these came from President Yeltsin's office on 30 April and was amended somewhat over the next few months by a Constitutional Commission set up by him. The Congress of People's Deputies created a Constitutional Commission of its own that produced a version in May, and *Pravda* printed a Communist Party rendition in June.

The differing visions of Russia's future mirrored in these drafts were central to events that led to a Yeltsin decree on 21 September dissolving parliament, a bloody showdown in Moscow that saw tanks deployed against deputies occupying the parliament building, and the arrest of opposition leaders, among them the speaker of parliament and the vice president of Russia. The draft Constitution then put forward to the Russian people was the Yeltsin one, with further amendments that included the removal of the upper age limit for presidents, previously set at 65, and the elimination of the office of vice president.[2] Articles facilitating the impeachment of the president were mostly removed and the presidential office was greatly strengthened against possible encroachments by legislative bodies, such as the newly devised State Duma.

The president of Russia, therefore, has greater constitutional authority to shape the policy and practice of his government than do the heads of state in almost any other country, especially those in Western democratic states. With the support of a recently elected and strongly pro-government State Duma, it would seem that Putin's successor held all the constitutional cards necessary to drag Russia forcefully forward to the next stage of its post-Soviet development. Our task in this chapter is to see what happened from the perspective of the presidential office.

* * *

### The presidency and its power base

Foregone conclusion or not, the most talked about event for the Russia government in early 2008 was the campaign for the presidency.

After a year of doubt, much of it manufactured, President Putin designated Medvedev as his favoured candidate, and on 10 December 2007 five parties nominated him officially. These were United Russia, the Agrarians, A Just Russia, the Russian Ecological Party (Greens), and Civil Power. The mainstream Russian media attributed the choice to Medvedev's willingness to undertake any task asked of him. He is 'our main everything' one editorial noted, prepared to 'preserve the Putin course'. Another called his selection a triumph for liberals within governing circles.[3] That remained to be seen.

Election rules were published on 6 December 2007, with only a few new requirements: a political party could no longer nominate someone from another party, and the election fund limit was raised from 250 to 400 million rubles. Another change was the appearance earlier in the spring of Vladimir Churov as chair of the Central Electoral Commission (CEC), replacing Aleksandr Veshnyakov who held that post for the previous eight years. Apparently, Veshnyakov objected to the removal of the minimum 20 per cent turnout requirement, which rendered an election invalid if the numbers were not reached. He also opposed stricter candidate registration criteria, suggesting that tougher regulations could be used to force political 'undesirables' out of the election.[4] His name was not even included on a list of five candidates for the CEC position.

Churov, on the other hand, was a deputy in the Duma on the right-wing Liberal Democratic Party's list and was considered an 'ultra nationalist' in some circles. More to the point, in the early 1990s he served on the international relations committee in Mayor's Sobchak's office in St. Petersburg, i.e., the committee chaired by Putin and to which Medvedev was a consultant.[5]

Only the parties they headed nominated the other final candidates: Gennady Zyuganov by the Communist party, Vladimir Zhirinovsky by the Liberal Democratic Party, and Andrei Bogdanov by the Democratic Party of Russia. Candidates who were declared ineligible by the CEC were: Kasyanov; Bukovsky; Nikolai Kurianovich, ultra nationalist admirer of Hitler and Stalin; and Oleg Shenin, head of the small hard-line Communist Party of the Soviet Union. Kasyanov's disqualification was the result, the CEC claimed, of too many forged signatures.[6]

Medvedev's campaign ran on what an official called 'the so-called four I's – Institutions, Infrastructure, Innovation and Investment', which the candidate

*Table 1.1* Presidential election results, 2 March 2008

|  | % | Votes |
|---|---|---|
| *Dmitry Medvedev* | 70.28 | 52,530,712 |
| *Gennady Zyuganov* | 17.72 | 13,243,550 |
| *Vladimir Zhirinovsky* | 9.35 | 6,988,510 |
| *Andrei Bogdanov* | 1.30 | 968,344 |
| *Invalidated votes* | 1.36 | 1,015,533 |

Note: Eligible voters = 107,222,016; Turnout = 69.71%

called 'a set of work principles for the next four years'.[7] The gist of his platform was laid out at a 22 January address to the Civic Forum, a group of NGOs brought together by the Public Chamber.[8] His emphasis on the on-going importance of the National Priority Projects, open civil dialogue, an independent media, and the need for a national effort to fight corruption helped earn him the label as a liberal – and left him with 'great expectations' to fulfil.[9]

The Parliamentary Assembly of the Council of Europe (PACE) acknowledged that the landslide victory represented the 'will of the electorate', and criticized the election itself for Medvedev's 'unfair' access to the media and the 'limited choice' of candidates. There were reports of ballot stuffing and pressure on voters by employers, but few denied that Medvedev was the popular choice. Observers from European NGOs and the Commonwealth of Independent States (CIS) mission called the election free and democratic.[10]

In terms of the means to succeed, Medvedev enjoyed clear advantages over both of his post-Soviet precursors. His own Constitution notwithstanding, Yeltsin was never able to establish authority over Russia's legislative bodies, leaving Putin to spend two full terms making the presidential office repre-sentative of the powers granted it by law. To accomplish this task, Putin created a vertical power structure (the *Vertikal*) comprised of various une-lected men and women who collectively formed a management team that brought Russia out of its 1990s doldrums. That power structure membership included former FSB officers, power cabinet ministers, board members with Russia's huge industrial-energy complexes, and, of course, Medvedev, all carefully selected by Putin for specific functions. With few exceptions, the entire team remained in place throughout Medvedev's term in office.[11] In the opinion of some analysts, the *Vertikal* represented a diminution of Russia's fledgling democracy, because of its hierarchical character, i.e., governing from the top; for others, it represented a saviour mechanism that prevented the huge and diverse territory of Russia from slipping into chaos. Both assessments have large grains of truth in them. Whatever outside critics thought, the majority of Russians believed strongly that the system worked and that the forthcoming partnership was a natural 'next step' in Russia's slow transition from the Soviet system to a modern and progressive state participating in the world's concert of nations as a respected player.

Like his predecessor, Medvedev benefited from a State Duma, the lower house of Russia's Federal Assembly (Parliament), that supported his policies. This fortunate circumstance had not been reached without considerable friction. The crisis of 1993 did not end the bitter struggle for power between the executive and legislative branches of Russia's government. An object of vilification, obstruction, and other forms of hostility on the part of the Communists and Nationalists who dominated the State Duma until 1999, Yeltsin governed more or less by decree and favouritism, allowing a large part of the presidential authority to leach away to the so-called 'oligarchs', i.e., holders of great wealth used to wield influence over the country's political arena, the media, and the economy.[12]

One of Putin's important accomplishments had been to tame these oligarchs – ultimately to Medvedev's advantage. During the 1990s, entrepreneurs had profited enormously from Yeltsin's economic reforms, which for the most part involved deregulating financial institutions and privatizing the state's vast assets. Insiders tendered the assets to themselves, created huge financial empires, and controlled Russia's media, natural resources, industry, and the political scene; and they also often failed to remit their fair share of taxes. As early as 2001, Putin initiated long-term legal procedures against media and industry barons Vladimir Gusinsky and Boris Berezovsky, the latter of whom once boasted that he and six other 'bankers' controlled about fifty per cent of Russia's GDP.[13] Eventually Gusinsky and Berezovsky lost much of their Russian empires and were driven into exile. The struggle against the power and influence acquired by the oligarchs culminated in 2003 with the arrest and imprisonment of Russia's richest man, Mikhail Khodorkovsky – who received an amnesty only in 2013.

Putin made a tacit deal with the remaining oligarchs – simplified as 'pay your taxes, keep out of politics – at least publicly – and your ill-gotten gains will not be nationalized'. He agreed to consult with them regularly as a group, and called on them to be 'more Russian'. This policy worked, and Medvedev, or at least his office, was free from direct competition with the oligarchs – though their wealth still earned them considerable influence. They now tended to be supportive of the state, whose favours they coveted, and competed mostly against each other for gains in business.

Few interested onlookers doubted that, in the cases noted above, the prosecution was rooted in political expediency and the trial process was badly flawed. Whether the end justified the means in such matters depends on who asks and who answers the question. At that very difficult time, Russians saw the process (or lack thereof) as one in which Putin fulfilled an election promise to eliminate the 'class of oligarchs' and were pleased with the results of his government's and judiciary's actions against them.[14] This was the 'Russian way'. That attitude had not shifted very much as Medvedev stepped in to the presidency in 2008, but was to serve as an obvious contradiction that wore away at his image as the years passed.

**The agenda**

Criticism from the West and some internal sound and fury over Kasyanov's disqualification did not dent the optimism among Russian analysts who thought that Medvedev might provide new perspectives to leadership in their country, though no one believed that his decision to run for office was made without some very clear accommodations for the future reached beforehand between him and Putin.[15]

Significantly, as the election unfolded, a group of academicians, all economists, urged Medvedev to campaign for 'modernization from the top' and 'modernization of institutions', so as to counter traditional 'social degradation and primitivism' in the Russian economy. Whether that plea was intended as criticism of Putin or not wasn't clear, but the group was open about the internal obstacles the new president would have to face if he choose their recommended path.[16] Still, modernization was the approach Medvedev took, at least rhetorically.

Medvedev opened his inaugural address with the statement, 'I consider it my greatest duty to continue to develop civil and economic freedom', and went on to emphasize a commitment 'to innovation in all areas of life, to developing cutting-edge production, modernizing our industry and agriculture, creating big incentives for private investment and generally making every effort to help Russia firmly establish itself as a leader in technological and intellectual development'. He added 'a mature and effective legal system is an essential condition for economic and social development, supporting entrepreneurship and fighting corruption'.[17] Translating these hopes into practical results would not prove easy.

**The Tandem in action**

Very early in his presidency, Medvedev made it clear which projects would become keynotes of his term in office: modernizing the economic, political, and social life of the country, and curbing corruption. These themes will each be central to subsequent chapters and, with the exception of the modernization dimension of Medvedev's presidential platform, will be touched on in this chapter only in passing. Attention here will be paid primarily to the office of the president and its close coordination with the office of the prime minister; that is, how the Tandem worked in practice, and how the president managed the Russian Federation's affairs.

Coordination between constitutional unequals is what made the system unique. The Tandem was projected as a duo, president and prime minister, with equal authority based on a personal, not constitutional, covenant. Since power wielding in Russia seemed always to have been more personal than institutional anyway, the arrangement was by no means a shock to the system. One Russian analyst picked up on this early on, writing in November 2008 that 'the best term to describe the evolving relationship between President

Dmitry Medvedev and Prime Minister Vladimir Putin is tandemocracy', precisely because the relationship is based on personal and not constitutional agreement.[18] Among other returns derived from this arrangement was that Putin, whose popularity and influential contacts far outweighed Medvedev's, could retain authority without having to amend the Constitution to allow him to run for a third consecutive term. The stability craved by almost everyone in Russia in 2008 was guaranteed, or so it seemed at the time.

Unsung links in the Tandem were the post of Presidential Press Attaché and the Presidential Press and Information Office. In May 2008, Medvedev appointed Natalia Timakova his Press Attaché. Timakova had served in the same capacity and as Head of the Presidential Press and Information Office under Putin since 2002. Medvedev was helped as well by Yeva Vasilevskaia, who had been working with him as speechwriter since 2006. The ties between personnel in these offices and both government and private media were extensive, and guaranteed consistency in the Tandem's dealings with the public and media. With her connections, Timakova joined government ministers Tatiana Golikova and Elvira Nabiullina as one the most influential female insiders in Russian politics.

The Putin–Medvedev team had not accomplished all their goals before 2008; for instance, the National Priority Projects that were under Medvedev's management for many years appeared to have come up short. Their failure to achieve well-defined successes in these infrastructure and societal programs came in for harsh criticism in 2008 from Russian oppositionists Boris Nemtsov and Vladimir Milov, co-authors of a long, detailed, and very critical report in which the Putin regime was labelled 'authoritarian-criminal'.[19] On the other hand, polls continued to rate Putin easily the most popular leader in Russia, with Medvedev gaining but always slightly behind.

We will, in fact, turn to Russian polls regularly while telling this tale, knowing full well that opinion polling is an inexact science. Yet, the leading Russian surveying agencies are widely accepted as thorough and professional. Given that accounts about Russia are often rooted more on assumption than on fact, and the political air is filled with charges of cheating from all sides, polls at least provide acceptable versions of patterns and preferences.

On 15 April, Putin officially took on the leadership of United Russia and announced that he would agree to serve as prime minister, if he were asked, when his term as president ended some three weeks hence. When Medvedev was inaugurated on 7 May, he immediately nominated Putin prime minister, making the practice of *dvoevlastie* (dual power), to use an old Leninist term, official.[20] According to Medvedev, the choice was made 'in the interests of the continuity of Putin's internal and foreign policies', and emphasized that he was a member of 'Putin's team' himself.[21] The Tandem was officially born.[22]

A week later, Putin named his 24-person Cabinet – approved by Medvedev – and also created an inner Cabinet, or Presidium, of 15 people – his people. The Presidium was expected to meet once per week, whereas the entire Cabinet would meet on a monthly basis. The new government included a new ministry, the Ministry of Sports, Tourism and Youth Policy, and an important new sub-ministry: the Federal Agency for Commonwealth of Independent States (CIS) Affairs. Attached to the Ministry of Foreign Affairs, this latter body was intended to ease the load of the MFA and also ensure the primacy of the CIS in Russian foreign policy.

The presidency itself came in for some constitutional changes towards the end of the year. In a previously postponed address to the Federal Assembly, Medvedev proposed extending the presidential term of office from four to six years, and the term of parliament from four to five years. Whereas Western and Russian critics bayed that this proposition was intended to provide a means for Putin to come back and govern longer, Medvedev contended that its purpose was to provide greater constancy and stronger institutions in transitional times. Proponents, such as Deputy Director of Russia's Center for Political Conditions Vitaly Ivanov, vigorously defended the term extensions, saying that they would help Russia form a 'developed, strong and stable power organization', which may have been precisely why others objected to the change.[23] Bills to extend the terms were sent to the State Duma almost immediately. Only the Communist Party and Yabloko opposed them in the lower House.

During the first week of December, Putin conducted his annual call-in show over Russian TV before an audience of about 400 invited guests. It seemed odd to some observers that Medvedev, who was mentioned only in passing during the three-hour performance, did not take on this task. But these were a Putin thing that Medvedev probably would have would avoided even if asked. Responding to a question from the BBC a short time later about his own future plans for running for office, Putin said that he and Medvedev worked well as a 'very effective tandem', and that he would not consider running for president again until 2012. The term 'Tandem' stuck, and debate over what was going to happen at the end of Medvedev's term of office was already underway.

Surveys conducted at this time showed a majority of Russians fully in support of the Tandem. As an editorial in the mainstream *Nezavisimaia gazeta* put it, 'a tandem rules in Russia. It seems that the people favour this term more than *dvoevlastie*. For now both leaders are, to all appearances, satisfied with the interaction'.[24] It did not go unnoticed that by legitimizing the Tandem, the president relinquished authority and the prime minister gained authority, both unofficially. Moreover, to remain effective the Tandem had no choice but to refrain from criticizing each other – in short, they had to be each other's cheerleader.

The Tandem had its first real test as the global financial crisis deepened in the spring of 2009. As it happened, Medvedev's level of popularity remained constant and Putin's declined somewhat. A year after his election, trust in the President stood at 75 per cent and the Prime Minister at 83 per cent. Their popularity was unusually high compared to other Russian political figures and, for that matter, any Western leader. The government itself had a confidence rating of only 58 per cent. According to a poll conducted in May, nearly half the population believed that Medvedev and Putin governed as equals.[25]

On the other hand, there were signs that Medvedev wanted to shed a number of Putin appointees. He announced in February that he planned to cut the presidential administrative staff by 100 people and freeze its budget until 2011. This may have been merely an austerity measure, as he said it was, but the result would be fewer of Putin's protégés around him. When it came to leadership positions in government, the first big change came in February, when long time Minister of Agriculture Aleksei Gordeev was dismissed and sent into political exile as governor of Voronezh. Yelena Skrynnik was named his replacement in March. Skrynnik thus became the third woman in Cabinet.

With these changes came a sense that important adjustments might be in the offing. One mainstream writer claimed that Medvedev was planning a detailed program 'for the further development of the institutes of Russian democracy', though no specifics were provided.[26] He would not go so far as to suggest that proposals for political reform, if they actually existed, would come exclusively from Medvedev; rather they would be put forward as a project offered by the Tandem: 'The tandem of "president-premier" works, the decision-making process is not broken, and the quality of administration is not falling'.[27]

Enthusiasm such as that was by no means universally endorsed, and the power structure was not perceived so benignly as the recession began hitting pocketbooks. An editorial in the same mainstream newspaper pronounced only ten days later that, whereas Putin and Medvedev were still popular, the citizenry believed that the *vertikal* was not capable of 'coping with the crisis'. The editorialist went on to explain that 'Russians are sceptical about the power vertical, which was and is one of the foundations of the political project of the ruling elite' because the successes of the mid-2000s shaped the thinking of a population that now has a relative prosperity to lose – but finds itself helpless in the face of federal, regional, and municipal governance wary of change.[28] The Tandem knew this, it would seem from subsequent Medvedev statements, but could not or would not push the senior bureaucracy to more precipitous action.

Overall presidential policy was outlined in Medvedev's annual address for 2009 – delivered on 12 November.[29] After a year and a half in the job, he now felt free to set out a vision of his own for Russia's development. He pulled no punches, referring there and elsewhere to Russia's economy as 'backward'. He summarized the problems faced by Russia internally with candour and laid out a blueprint for a new kind of *perestroika*. Above all, the president emphasized the need for full modernization – economic, political, and social– which he said must be developed on the basis of democratic values and traditions.

Conceding that Russia was hit harder, if later, than many other countries by the global financial crisis, he highlighted problems caused by too many single-industry towns (*monogorody*), energy inefficiency, and antiquated industrial plants and infrastructure. These were among the economic obstacles to the modernization projects he had been harping on for over a year. His immediate priorities, however, were ending the chaos in the North Caucasus and curbing corruption. Hints were dropped again about future changes in the political system, and a greatly upgraded and focused budget for education. Pundits across the country strained to see these ambitions as oblique criticisms of Putin's record, albeit both members of the Tandem insisted otherwise.

As for the presidency, it is noteworthy that as early as September 2009, Medvedev confirmed in an interview with CNN that Medvedev and Putin would decide between them who would run for the highest office in 2012. The incumbent head of state did not rule out that he would try for a second term, and journalists began writing of a 'covert duel' between them.[30] It should not have come as such a surprise in 2011 when that early and open agreement came to light.

The modernization goal might well have been the president's most difficult ambition, for it was also indefinable. Public opinion survey results published in December 2009 suggest that a clear majority of Russians were sceptical about the likelihood of success in any attempt to modernize the country. They had no uniform ideas as to what groups in society were capable of innovation, or what approaches had to be taken if the government was to be the engine of change. One-third of the 1,600 respondents to one poll said that corruption must be curbed first, 30 per cent thought that developing small and middle business should be the starting point, and 17 per cent answered that progress must be made first in the scientific-technical sector.[31] All three opinions were of course important gateways to the modernization goal, and their existence as convictions suggested that much had to be done.

While the Tandem remained outwardly and probably internally cohesive, the ground began to shift towards the end of 2009 within the operational level of government, prompting rumours of a power shift among the *siloviki*, those political insiders who had consolidated and strengthened their positions during the first post-Soviet decade when, Constitution of 1993 notwithstanding, no one was truly in charge.[32] As Putin broke the power of the oligarchs, factions within the executive branch fought each other for access to the wealth and power generated by the rapidly increasing government stake in the economy. The potential for factions was large: Russia usually had two first deputy prime ministers and anywhere between three and seven deputy prime ministers during the 2000s. Just as they had during Putin's first two presidencies, pundits watched closely as some of these deputies stayed in place, others left for 'big business' posts, and still others became ministers in the Cabinet or joined the presidential staff, and made much of what they assumed were gains or losses in status. Few Russian and only some foreign analysts believed that the president could accomplish very much without the support of one or more of these *siloviki* cliques.

On 24 December 2009, the existing anti-crisis committee and six commissions related to the economy were abolished. One of the First Deputy Prime Ministers, Igor Shuvalov, previously headed five of the abolished commissions, including the commission on Russia joining the World Trade Organization (WTO) and the Organization for Economic Cooperation and Development (OECD), the commission on technical regulation, the commission on economic integration, and the commission for the protection of intellectual property. The commission on customs-tariff regulation was until then headed by the other First Deputy Prime Minister, Viktor Zubkov. The functions of the abolished commissions were transferred to a new single body called the Economic Development and Integration Commission. Named its chairman, Shuvalov's status was raised among the insiders; Zubkov's was lowered.

These moves may have been driven by the fact that, while the Teflon Tandem's ratings were still very high, a growing cross-section of the population was losing confidence in the government itself. The same respondents who trusted the Tandem worried about the government's handling of the financial crisis. Much of the unease was related to rising prices, unemployment, an apparent collapse of the social safety network, and increased levels of corruption and crime.[33]

In fact, government statistics showed a sharp rise in registered unemployed, up to a little over two million by November 2009. Clearly there were many more unregistered unemployed and a great majority of the citizens assumed that it was the government's obligation to resolve that and other social issues. Belief in government as the healer of all ills and engine of all change remained dominant in Russia, though the Tandem, like the tsars of old, remained above the fray, untainted by the people's economic woes – as of yet.

Chatter that the cohesion of the Medvedev–Putin tandem was starting to fray began to heat up in 2010. Predictions for the presidential elections of 2012 appeared everywhere and, by the Fall, many Russians now believed that there would be a competition between Medvedev and Putin for the position – though maybe not a public one. Some commentators suggested that head of the presidential staff Sergei Naryshkin's name would be thrown into the hat to complicate the matter.[34] The important point is that, as he became more comfortable in the presidential chair, Medvedev also seemed to be gaining stature in the public eye.

Just about every policy initiative by either man was cast as part of a contest between them for public or insider support. In the summer, political surveys had them running neck-and-neck in popularity and both, according to all the main pollsters, were well down in the ratings compared to where they had been in January; but they were still higher than anyone else. As the economy began to recover, a poll conducted in October put Medvedev and Putin back up in popularity ratings, i.e., 76 and 77 per cent, respectively.[35] Using any form of measurement, these were remarkable numbers. In late November, Putin told reporters again that he and Medvedev would decide between them whether one, neither, or both of them would run for the presidency in 2012. No one seemed to worry about the implications of that remark at the time.

In the meantime, Medvedev tried to tighten up mechanisms for implementing presidential instructions. Without naming names, he accused senior officials at all levels of submitting reports merely to meet deadlines saying, 'they have done so and so', but 'in effect they haven't done a thing'.[36] Perhaps unwittingly, he sounded much like Gorbachev who had railed against the long-standing Soviet practice of submitting report after report to accommodate the central government's expressed requirements without ever having done the work required. Strengthening managerial discipline was Medvedev's goal, but it is not clear that he achieved very much in this regard. He also ordered the government to reduce the size of the bureaucracy, which had nearly doubled during Putin's first two terms. That growth was abetted by the dramatic increase in federal authority around the Federation. The cutback task was handed over to Deputy Prime Minister Aleksei Kudrin, who was told to aim for a 20 per cent reduction.[37] As later research demonstrated, barely any of these personnel targets were met, mainly because of inertia, or perhaps intransigence, within the bureaucracy itself.[38]

The President also set in motion a series of consultations on ways and means to modernize Russia, along the lines promoted in both his famous 'Go, Russia!' article and his State of the Nation address in 2009.

In the article, Medvedev was harshly critical of Russia's 'raw materials-based' economy, its 'chronic corruption', its 'lack of freedom' – and its continued 'injustices'.[39] This was an extraordinary treatise. Medvedev opened it by asking: 'Should a primitive economy based on raw materials and endemic corruption accompany us into the future?' He went on to explain that Russia's democratic institutions were low in quality, its 'civil society weak', and self-reliance almost absent. Political modernization was necessary and important, but must not be rushed, he said, referring specifically to the calamities of the 'democratic nineties'. In Yeltsin's era Russia was a 'paralyzed country' and a victim of far-too-hasty proponents of 'permanent revolution'. Here he used a term many Russians would recognize as Trotskyite.

In this case, Medvedev avoided placing himself on a collision course with the United Russia (UR) party, which a few months before had collectively criticized a long essay titled '21st Century Russia: Reflections on an Attractive Tomorrow'. Published in early February on the website of the Institute of Contemporary Development (INSOR), it called for political modernization as the first vehicle for economic modernization. It was no coincidence that Medvedev chaired INSOR's Board of Trustees. The UR accused INSOR with trying to drag Russia back into the mess of the 1990s, but carefully refrained from levelling the same charges against the new president. The allegation itself resonated in Russia, where the 1990s was still seen as a modern Time of Troubles.[40]

At the time, an analyst described the drive toward modernization sponsored by Medvedev as merely 'rhetoric of contemporizing the country and modernizing it'.[41] Critics did not go so far, yet, as to say that the modernizing campaign was wishful thinking, and they recognized that Medvedev's plans were held back by the financial crisis. They noted, though, that the president had already staked his reputation on modernization and that he had better get the citizenry behind him if he wished to succeed. Here, ultimately, is where Medvedev's term would be judged.

Medvedev had, in fact, already turned to the public, telling a meeting of UR federal and regional leaders in May that there was simply no feasible alternative to modernization. He made the appeal universal. Only modernization could ensure that the Russian people would receive the benefits, such as pensions and employment, and long-term accoutrements of civilized society he presumed they wanted; and only a satisfied people would keep the UR in power.[42] An influential UR 'liberal', Olga Kryshtanovskaia, took Medvedev's lecture to the party as a sign that he hoped to gain enough support from members who wanted change to make it possible for him to run for a second term. In a supportive paper titled 'Modernization as Liberalization' she lauded his performance to that date: ' ... his self-confidence is growing. He is becoming a more mature politician, and he speaks fluently and confidently. He is a young man, and his presidency is pretty successful, despite all difficulties'.[43] Two years later, she admitted her mistake, explaining that the original division of powers with the Tandem was too one-sided: 'the *siloviki*, the economy, parliament, the regions and the party have been left to Putin, while Medvedev is responsible for the formal performance of constitutional obligations, the courts, the fight against corruption, and the training of a personnel reserve'. Failing to create his own team by 2010, she said, Medvedev remained dependent on Putin, thereby undermining any chance he might have at a second term.[44]

The '21st Century Russia' essay endorsed radical reforms in the law enforcement agencies, among them the dissolution of the Ministry of the Interior to be replaced by a Federal Criminal Police Service. The FSB should also be replaced by a new agency based on models found in Germany, INSOR insisted. These and other recommendations, such as reverting to popularly elected Governors and joining NATO and the EU gained little traction with the *siloviki*. Although the paper's proposals generated considerable public discussion, only the economic propositions were taken seriously. The fact that the think tank was directed by Igor Yurgens, a close associate of the president, placed the '21st Century Russia' tract smack in the middle of whatever insider debates there were about the next stage in Russia's transition.

The spurt of discussion about modernization in the political arena saw a wider use of the term 'variable-speed democracy', a model proposed by Vladislav Surkov in 2009. His reference was specifically to a project to establish a Russian version of Silicon Valley at Skolkovo, near Moscow (see Chapter Four), where unique political allowances were introduced. Some years earlier, Surkov formulated, vaguely, an unofficial state ideology termed 'sovereign democracy'. The doctrine was above all a 'doing it our own way' approach to transition, and was intended in the mid-2000s to distinguish Russia's evolving political system both from the chaos of the 1990s and the idealism preached from the West. It became a rallying cry for United Russia and also for *Nashi*, a pro-government, anti-fascist youth group.[45]

Sometimes referred to as the Kremlin's enforcer, in December 2010 Surkov urged members of *Rossiia Molodaia* (Young Russia), the *Molodaia Gvardiia* (Young Guard), *Nashi*, and other such groups 'to train [their] brains and muscles' in preparation for the upcoming Duma and presidential elections. 'You can always count on my support', he added. In an impassioned speech, Surkov called on Russia's youth to back Medvedev, Putin, and United Russia against threats from outside influences. Cooperation with the West is essential, he continued, adding none too subtly that youth must oppose any country's global hegemony.[46] Nowhere did Medvedev ever try to counter this call to arms.

There was also talk of a split within the Tandem between radical transformers and moderate conservatives. Surkov was seen as a leader of the latter camp. Medvedev's people, Yurgens and Presidential Aide Arkady Dvorkovich, fronted the other. Moderate conservatives worried about going too far, too fast, and used the crises of the 1990s as their red flag; the radical reformers insisted on sweeping political reform, absolute freedom of the press, and the end of monopolies. References to a new *perestroika* and a 'Third Way' were common.[47] Dmitri Trenin, a specialist with the Carnegie Endowment in Moscow, insisted early in 2010 that, while the Tandem was a more cohesive team than usually assumed, a showdown between modernizers and conservatives was imminent. The results of that clash, he said, might well determine the future of Russia.[48]

The important thing, however, is that political, economic, and social discourse over Russia's future rose to a new and potentially productive level. It was also apparent that Medvedev's expressed hope to shape the country's development eventually would collide with his prime minister's support for the National Champions, i.e., the huge state-dominated corporations, and the entrenched vertically-controlled political system. In short, if Medvedev was to have his way, he was going to have to be president – take charge – even as he urged his administration, the government and the governors to 'maintain unity in governing the state'.[49] Few observers expected Medvedev to move to the forefront, especially as it was increasingly obvious that orders from the top still faced the eternal handicap voiced by then-Prime Minister Sergei Stepashin when he told the Federation Council in May 1999 that, no matter how much progress there was, 'crime and corruption reduce the best ventures to nothing'.[50] One could add bureaucratic inefficiency and indifference to this list of obstacles.

When Medvedev dismissed Moscow Mayor Yury Luzhkov by presidential decree in September 2010, gurus seized upon the act as a means to strengthen his position in a potential campaign against Putin for the presidency. Luzhkov was an open supporter of Putin in the ruling Tandem, and had been at odds with Medvedev for some time. He was also co-founder and still prominent figure in the United Russia party, of which Putin was nominal leader, and head of a political machine built up in Moscow during his 18 years as mayor. The perception that Luzhkov and his city officials were notoriously corrupt, and that Medvedev was in the midst of an anti-corruption campaign that would fail if Moscow's reputation remained tainted, passed nearly unnoticed by frenzied political writers.

Although there had been rumours circulating for some time that Luzhkov was under pressure to 'retire', the actual event came as a surprise. He was fired outright, on the grounds that he 'lost the trust of the president'. All of Luzhkov's staff stayed in place as acting officials until the new mayor was selected.[51] Within a month, Medvedev named Sergei Sobyanin to the post. Former Governor of the Tyumen Oblast, Deputy Prime Minister, and head of the presidential administration from 2005 to 2010, Sobyanin had a wealth of experience. He was a member of the UR. A long time close Putin associate, he also sat on Medvedev's Modernization Commission and helped conduct the president's election campaign in 2008. Thus, his loyalties appeared to be to the Tandem itself, and not necessarily to one of its two members. From Medvedev's point of view, Sobyanin's disdain for corruption was a key consideration. Fortunately, the stench of corruption around Luzhkov and his real-estate mogul wife, Yelena Baturina, had grown to the extent that the former mayor had few cliques willing to risk taking up his cause.

Having opened the door to a clean-up of Moscow's bureaucracy and impatient with Kudrin's efforts to cut personnel, in January 2011 Medvedev signed a decree that would reduce the number of federal employees by some 20 per cent by 2013 and shed the public service of about 160,000 jobs. According to Medvedev, half of the saved funds would go to bonuses and the other half to increased wages for remaining officials. Medvedev claimed that these numbers would be attained mainly by eliminating redundancies and save the government 43 billion rubles, or approximately $1.5 billion, although the provision of bonuses and wage rises made this projection a little hazy. Numbers presented later by various ministries revealed that the number of federal government employees had grown by some 80 per cent during the years since Putin first became president – to nearly 870,000 individuals. These made up about half the total number of bureaucrats at all levels in Russia. Though the cuts were intended to save the government huge sums, and ease the obstacles the huge, unwieldy bureaucracy puts in the way of business initiatives, the spectre of unemployment froze the activities of many sectors of officialdom. Existing inefficiencies caused by sheer numbers and layers of red tape were exacerbated by internal tensions and job-loss anxiety.[52]

## The Tandem – frayed

Dismissing, or threatening to dismiss, bureaucrats did not worry the public. Results of polls conducted from 17 to 21 December 2010 and published in January 2011 showed Putin and Medvedev still running nearly equal in confidence ratings and easy victors if either of them ran for president the next year, far ahead of anyone else.[53] Twenty per cent of respondents wanted them to run against each other. Three months later, however, the Tandem's ratings were the lowest they had been in two years, though still high by any standard, i.e., well over 60 per cent, and they continued to drop.[54] Economic conditions and the usual winter hardships had caused the halo around the executive branch to fade, though not yet to the level of the generally disdained legislative branch.

Tensions within the government itself were worsened by fallout from the terrorist bombings at the Domodedovo airport, as Putin took the lead in issuing harsh retaliatory messages and Medvedev calling for calm. While President Medvedev criticized the work of senior law enforcement agencies, Putin claimed that they were getting the job done. When the president was asked by a journalist in late January if he would appoint Putin prime minister again if he were elected president in 2012, Medvedev dodged by saying that this could be discussed only if he ran and was elected. Minor jabs such as these did not mean that the Tandem was coming apart, rather that difficult times generated outbursts that were soon smoothed over.

That didn't stop 'experts' from spending much of the year trying desperately to spot differences between Putin and Medvedev, focusing on minutiae and ignoring the many more views for Russia's future they held in common. Slight differences between them encouraged scribblers in print and blogs to portray the two men as leaders of opposing visions. For example, when the president tentatively supported NATO policies on the Libyan issue and Putin called the UNSC Resolution 1273, on which Russia abstained, a type of 'mediaeval crusade' against yet another Muslim country, their approaches were treated as opposing ones. Medvedev did say that the use of the term 'crusade' was inappropriate, yet both Russian leaders called for a diplomatic resolution of the crisis.[55] The use of force was the last choice for Medvedev and Putin, though the tone of their objections differed.

Meanwhile, former Soviet President Gorbachev, who had supported Putin early on, criticized them both for implying that they would decide between them who would be Russia's next president. Calling Russia's version of democracy a mere 'imitation', he termed their stance as an 'incredible conceit'. Rumours about Sergei Sobyanin as a likely candidate for the presidency circulated in the winter of 2010, especially after Putin invited him to head the Moscow branch of United Russia. Others saw Kudrin as a possible compromise between Medvedev and Putin.[56] But neither of these suggestions followed logically from public opinion surveys. Popularity ratings for the Tandem, whether high or low, always placed Putin and Medvedev far ahead of any potential rival, and typically had Putin in the lead. This would suggest two things: the public neither saw nor cared much about punditry's search for differences between them; and that Putin remained unshakably the most respected politician in Russia.

Polls conducted by FOM on 27 March revealed that 58 per cent of the population trusted Putin and 50 per cent trusted Medvedev. In both cases, they lacked the confidence of only 17 per cent, and 23 and 30 per cent offered partial trust, respectively.[57] Later polls indicated that the majority of Russians preferred that the Putin–Medvedev Tandem continue in place, and very few expected them to run against each other. Paradoxically, surveys also revealed that trust in both members of the Tandem had fallen again, and that regard for the ruling United Russia lapsed even more dramatically.[58] This latter finding struck a cautionary note as the party began to plan election campaigns for the Duma, prompting it to reinforce its efforts.

By April 2011, commentators began referring to Medvedev as 'liberal' and Putin as 'conservative'.[59] Generally, these terms were used in reference to the Tandem's approach to economic and not political development. Both members of the Tandem advocated innovation in the economy, support for enterprise, and the integration of Russia into the world economic arena. But when differences were described as one between reliance on state capitalism (Putin) and reliance on a more open and comprehensive market (Medvedev), the spillover into the question of political modernization was inevitable. Predictions about a challenge to the status quo offered by Dmitri Trenin more than a year prior to this new rumbling now had some resonance, though not in quite the format he had foreseen.

Confirming a split in the Tandem, at least in the minds of some, was a step taken by Medvedev in March of that year to remove all government ministers from their posts on the boards of major companies. Russian economic specialists saw this as revolutionary in its consequences for foreign investment. Political analysts treated it as a bid to undermine some of the influence held by Putin supporters among the *siloviki*, because Deputy Prime Minister Igor Sechin was therefore slated to lose the chairmanship of Rosneft and two other board positions.

As it happened, Sechin announced his resignation from the chairmanship of Rosneft at the board's next meeting. Finance Minister Kudrin, Economics Minister Elvira Nabiullina, Science, Education and Culture Minister Andrei Fursenko, and Dvorkovich quickly left other boards. Reports published in July hinted that Putin had lost control over the *siloviki* anyway and that neither he nor Medvedev were in any position to alter their behaviour. In short, the tail may now have been wagging the dog.[60] By the end of September, nearly all of the senior officials named by Medvedev had, indeed, given up various directorships. Among the exceptions were Naryshkin, still presidential Chief-of-Staff and chair of Sovkomflot, and Zubkov, deputy prime minister who had been serving as Chairman of Gazprom's board of directors since June 2008. A number of lower level officials remained on boards as well.

## Presidential ambitions

Presidential aspirants began showing up in the Spring. The Communist Party nominated Zyuganov as its candidate on 14 April, and United Russia members made it clear the next day that Putin would be its presidential nominee if he chose to run.[61] The leader of A Just Russia, Sergei Mironov, responded with an announcement that his party would not support any candidate nominated by United Russia. Mironov proposed that his party and the Communists name a candidate for the presidency jointly. The Communists rejected the proposition. Vladimir Zhirinovsky said on 25 April that he would represent the Liberal Democratic Party in the race to the top.

In late November, Yabloko tested the waters by announcing that it might support its former leader Grigory Yavlinsky's repeat quest for the highest office, and on 19 December it did choose him. Party leader Mitrokhin denied persistent rumours that anti-corruption blogger Aleksei Navalny wanted to represent Yabloko.

Fringe candidates came out in December as well. For example, a meeting of the banned National Bolshevik Party (NBP) gathered some 800 signatures in support of their leader, Eduard Limonov.[62] Shortly after the explosive December 2011 Duma election, which will be discussed in detail in Chapter Three, retired Army General Leonid Ivashov revealed that he too planned to enter the competition. Former head of the Defence Ministry's International Cooperation Department and strongly nationalist, he probably was encouraged by the rise in nationalism generally and the chaotic parliamentary election in particular. The CEC eventually rejected his application as it did applications from other self-nominated candidates Limonov and Boris Mironov, the latter because of extremist literature attributed to him in 2010.

Tentatively serious candidates declared too. On 11 December, A Just Russia finally selected Sergei Mironov and oligarch Mikhail Prokhorov told a hurriedly arranged press conference that he would throw his name into the hat as a self-nominated candidate. Prokhorov's assertion that one of his first acts would be to pardon Khodorkovsky was not likely to win him many votes.

As the deadline for application papers passed, five self-nominated candidates were still in the race. On the other hand, Mikhail Kasyanov said this time that neither he, nor other members of his unregistered People's Freedom Party (PARNAS), would compete for the presidency until Russia was capable of conducting 'real elections'.[63] Apparently Kasyanov's delusions of grandeur still prevailed in some lesser political circles. As before, each self-nominated candidate faced the daunting task of providing two million signatures in their support, from 40 different regions with no more than 50,000 from each region – before 18 January. So an enormous amount of work had to be done by non-Duma candidates, some of whom could count on a mere fraction of that number of followers.

The run for the presidency consumed Russian politics in 2011, drawing attention away from the State Duma election even though it came first – just as it had in 2007. Prime Minister Putin jumped in by creating the Agency for Strategic Initiatives (Agenstvo strategicheskikh initsiativ, ASI), to serve as a new business model.[64] When he announced this Agency in May, a number of Russian analysts treated it as competition for Medvedev's innovation model, i.e., the high-tech Skolkovo version of Silicon Valley that will be discussed in the Chapter Four. Shortly thereafter, Putin introduced the All-Russia

People's Front (Obshcherossiiskii narodnyi front), a movement to attract non-party people and youth to United Russia's campaign for parliamentary seats and, of course, his own as-yet-unannounced presidential ambitions. These initiatives were taken by many as further evidence of a 'covert debate' within the Tandem, but since the President technically was above the fray when it came to the Duma election, Putin was able to work simultaneously to strengthen both the UR and his own electoral base unchallenged by Medvedev.[65]

Doubtless, United Russia's apparent weaknesses and inefficiencies was the main incentive behind the People's Front. Putin envisioned it as a broad-based coalition of political groups and associations from the left and the right, patriotic movements, trade unions and NGOs that shared the same values. Members did not need to be part of United Russia, but they were expected to breathe new life and ideas into the party. Doubtless the Front would also build up support for Putin's presidential candidacy, and also undermine the increasingly oppositionist A Just Russia. Prominent journalist Yuliia Latynina risked calling it a front of 'swindlers, thieves, and non-party members' gathered to provide backing for Putin.[66]

Seeming to take the presidential question in hand, Medvedev told reporters on 17 May that he would decide if he would let his name stand for president again shortly. He repeated this promise in June, adding in an interview for the *Financial Times* that 'I believe that any leader, who holds a presidential office, is simply obliged to want to run'.[67] He continued to hedge about any actual decision to do so, but it seemed plain to observers that he wanted to go for it again. Putin refused to commit himself as well, telling reporters in Paris that the Tandem had common programs and that, no matter who became president, the agenda would not change.

In the interim, Medvedev's political initiatives found at least some fertile soil. In July 2011, the Public Chamber allocated a large sum of money in support of roundtables, conferences, and other 'events to activate civil society and involve citizens in the process of modernization'. Up to 200 such events were proposed at a cost of about 55 million rubles (about $1.95 million). Almost simultaneously, twenty intellectuals signed an open letter favouring him over Putin precisely because of his two crusades and apparent belief in more democratic institutions.[68] By that time, Putin and Medvedev's stands seemed reversed when the Prime Minister told a worker in Magnitogorsk that 'we need new instruments, new people and deep modernization and an innovation process to secure a speedier growth of the economic and social sectors and to reinforce the political basis of our society'.[69] These were almost exactly Medvedev's words.

As the guessing games gathered steam, rumours circulated that Medvedev and Putin would run against each other; or that they would run together as a Tandem. Youth movements, 'Putin's Army' and 'Medvedev's Girls' organized joint demonstrations as late as August calling for their favourites to run as a team.[70]

## A momentous decision

All the speculation about presidential candidates came to naught when Medvedev cut the chatter off abruptly on 24 September 2011. Proposing to the United Russia Congress that it nominate Putin for the presidency of Russia, he offered a straightforward explanation:

> I was always asked when we would decide, when we could tell people, and sometimes Vladimir Vladimirovich [Putin] and I were asked: 'Have you two fought?' I want to fully confirm what I just said. What we are proposing to the Congress is a deeply thought-through decision. And even more we already discussed this scenario back when we first formed a friendly alliance. And I very much hope that the passage of years have shown us, and the majority of our citizens, the correctness of our strategy and the effectiveness of the existing governance model.[71]

Putin then strode to the podium to accept the party's acclaim, and noted that his top priorities would be to modernize the economy and curb corruption, both long-time missions shepherded by the incumbent president. To take his place as prime minister, Putin said, no one would be better suited than Dmitry Medvedev. The news was greeted with a flurry of talking heads on Russian and foreign television, and practical indifference on Russia's streets, where the idea that the Tandem would not continue in one form or the other had never been taken seriously. If it was real, that indifference was not going to last.[72]

The perceived casualness of the job swap indicated that the Tandem did not realize that their apparent sense of entitlement was, in fact, a launching pad for troubles to come. Mikhail Dmitriev, former Deputy Defence Minister and by this time President of the Centre for Strategic Research, rightly called the act 'a political detonator' and predicted that the Tandem's failure even to grant lip service to popular representation would lead to 'more radical opinions and widespread unconstructive opposition to the government'. He was to be proven absolutely correct. Other think tank heads, such as Gleb Pavlovsky of the Foundation for Effective Politics, predicted that the ruling political team would begin to fall apart as Medvedev's supporters among the insiders were left vulnerable and suffering a sense of betrayal.[73]

Although the correctness of that latter judgment is difficult to tabulate, problems among the elite arose immediately, beginning with Kudrin's public assertion that he would not stay on if Medvedev became prime minister. Kudrin cited fundamental differences on economic policies as his reason, above all on the extravagance of Medvedev's approval of a $65 billion increase in military spending over the next three years. Medvedev promptly dismissed Kudrin. A new saga of relative uncertainty replaced the old one, as the *vertikal* appeared to be disintegrating.

A mere two days before the announcement, an essay in *Moskovskiy Komsomolets* under Gorbachev's by-line again severely criticized the power vertical for allotting power disproportionately to the executive level. Gorbachev complained that Russia was sliding back into Brezhnev-like stagnation, made worse by a widening gap between the rich 'fattening glamorous crowd' and the poor. He added that a real *perestroika* should be re-introduced.[74] When Putin reminded journalists that the decision announced on 24 September was planned years earlier, and added that it was predicated on which member of the Tandem was more likely to win the election, he inadvertently confirmed much of what Gorbachev cautioned against.[75] Even though the Tandem itself had hinted at collusion about the presidency from the beginning, a sense of disquiet – even embarrassment – began slowly to emerge in Russia, above all in the world of blogging and social networking.

Hotly defending his decision to support Putin for the presidency, Medvedev told a TV interviewer a week after the momentous UR Congress that any suggestion that the election outcome was predetermined was irresponsible. Worries in some circles about what was to happen to Medvedev's modernization projects were not allayed very much, even though Putin told the Valdai International Discussion Club in November that he would maintain the emphasis on modernization. Putin added that, as prime minister, Medvedev would have carte blanche to continue his reform activities. Although some commentators still offered strong support for the Tandem as a source of strength and equilibrium at the top, not much credence was given to Putin's pronouncement about Medvedev's new role, and doubts were expressed that Medvedev would even be named prime minister.[76]

At any rate, the official stance was that the Tandem would still be in play. It was in November as well that polls showed that 43 per cent of Russians trusted Medvedev – 23 per cent did not – and 51 per cent trusted Putin – 21 per cent did not.[77] These numbers were to change dramatically for the worse after the State Duma election in December.

In late November, the Federal Assembly announced that the next presidential election would be held on 4 March 2012, which meant that the official campaigning could begin – overshadowing completely the final run-up to the Duma election. The presidential campaign intensified after the Duma election and widespread assumptions that agents of the UR employed vote rigging and intimidation techniques to win their bare majority pushed smouldering unrest into open protest. Many thousands of Russians showed that they were tired of Putin and Medvedev and the Tandem's apparent presumption about its right to govern.[78]

Putin had his say on 15 December during his annual 'Conversation with Vladimir Putin' call-in radio show. The program lasted four-and-a-half hours. He did not complain about the protests, rather he claimed that this new direct speaking of one's mind was the result of his own regime's good work. He rejected out of hand demands for a substitute parliamentary election.

The year's final ten days may well have been the deciding ones of Medvedev's entire four-year term, at least in the political sphere. Following up on promises made after the outbursts of protest in December 2011, Churov proposed and the Tandem agreed that for the upcoming presidential election and subsequent parliamentary elections see-through ballot boxes and webcams would be placed in as many of the 95,000 polling stations as possible. Some 60,000 of these boxes were ordered before the end of the month.[79] Putin allocated a budget of some $470 million to this endeavour. On that same day, data released by VTsIOM on a survey conducted on 10–11 December gave Putin a 51 per cent approval rating, and a projection of 42 per cent of votes cast for the presidency, i.e., a run-off situation. That did not mean that he actually had a rival, for the second most favoured, Zyuganov, garnered only 11 per cent.[80]

The new Duma sat on 21 December amid great uproar on the streets. Medvedev delivered his final annual presidential address to the Federal Assembly the next day, and another giant rally gathered in Moscow two days later. Medvedev and Putin rushed into compromises, rather a rarity for them, and, although no one doubted that Putin would win the presidential seat, it was clear that Russian expectations of him would be far different than they were in 2000 and 2004. Gorbachev surfaced again, harking back to the final days of the USSR and telling interviewers on 24 December (anniversary of his 1991 resignation) that Putin should not run for the presidency in 2012.

As President Medvedev began his final half-year in office, he found himself in an odd position. Chief-of-Staff Naryshkin had moved recently to the legislature as a sitting member of the ruling party and speaker of the Duma. Surkov also moved to the legislature as deputy prime minister in charge of modernization and innovation, with very few decision-making powers. Naryshkin and Surkov had been the main Putinite props behind Medvedev's presidency, Naryshkin as one of Putin's St. Petersburg bloc and former deputy prime minister; Surkov as long time deputy chief-of-staff. In late December 2011, former Minister of Defence and Deputy Prime Minister Sergei Ivanov – Medvedev's former 'rival' for the presidency nomination—replaced Naryshkin, and Deputy Prime Minister Vyacheslav Volodin took over Surkov's post. Neither man had the insider connections of the people whom they replaced. Medvedev himself was caught in lame duck limbo in which whatever leadership credibility he might have earned over the last three years was shattered by his humiliating September acquiescence.

Although he may have been confident that Putin would keep his promise to name him prime minister, doubt grew in Russia that that would happen – or even that Medvedev would accept the job when it was offered to him. Pundits spoke of the demise of the Tandem because Medvedev as prime minister would not be nearly as strong a partner to Putin as Putin had been to him. The sudden politicization of Russia's middle class, where whatever support Medvedev could muster might have been found, was thought to be a temporary phenomenon of the December eruption. Yet there was also doubt in the resilience of the current crop of activist leaders. Expert observers both inside and outside Russia predicted their slow political descent into marginal and unpopular loud voices. The potential for consistent and reasoning opposition to ensure that change would be achieved was not obvious either, given that there was so little precedent in Russia for such a postulation

## Presidential election campaign, 2012

When Putin's election platform was released in the second week of January 2012, the opposition derided it, and political bloggers called it weak and not much more than a carbon copy of the United Russia's campaign agenda.[81] Praising Russia's recovery from the global recession after 2009, he called for an 'innovation-based economy' without mentioning Medvedev – even once. The dilemma of corruption also went very nearly unremarked. The need for order, patriotism, and gradualism was the dominant theme, though he took a little time out to cast slurs on American exceptionalism. It was plain for all to see that Putin expected to win without having to work very hard for it himself.

His opponents all tried desperately to find hooks to draw voters to their causes. Zyuganov, Yavlinsky, and Prokhorov proclaimed that they would free Khodorkovsky if elected president. The fact that a December poll showed that 31 per cent of Russians now felt he should be released from prison may have evoked these promises. Prokhorov went so far as to say that he might select either Khodorkovsky or Kudrin as his prime minister. Zyuganov made a pitch to the protesters by arranging to meet with Parliamentary Assembly of the Council of Europe (PACE) election observers who visited Russia on 20–21 January 2012, and his party lodged an official complaint against the legitimacy of Putin running for the presidency while holding the post as prime minister. Few Russians appeared to care.

When the deadline for full application papers passed on 18 January, only seven candidates remained standing: Putin, Zyuganov, Zhirinovsky, and Mironov were automatically eligible because parties in the Duma nominated them. Yavlinsky and independent self-nominees Prokhorov and Irkutsk Governor Dmitry Mezentsev were confirmed but awaited a count of their signature list. Three claimants were denied registration: Vladivostok Mayor Viktor Cherepkin and prominent Orenburg citizen Rinet Khamiev failed to submit, and activist Svetlana Peunova could raise only a fraction of the necessary two million signatures. On 23 January, the CEC announced that Mezentsev had too many rejected signatures (five per cent is the ceiling) and Yavlinsky was undergoing a recount. Each candidate was allowed to add an extra 100,000 signatures as fall back, but rumours suggested that one-quarter of the names on Yavlinsky's list were rejected. When he was declared disqualified the opposition screamed in protest, paradoxically insisting that Yavlinsky should be allowed to run no matter the rules.[82] There was never any indication in any survey that he would earn very many votes.

The anger and frustration let loose after the controversial Duma election carried over into the presidential campaign with renewed energy. Some 50,000 anti-Putin demonstrators gathered in Moscow's Bolotnaia Ploshchad on 4 February. At least three other Moscow locations were sites for demonstrations led by Konstantin Borovoi (Sakharov Ave), Zhirinovsky's fraction[83] (Pushkin Square), and a pro-Putin group at Poklonnaia Gora. All four rallies were authorized and went on with no interference from the police. Large banners demanding that 'Putin Must Go!' (*Putin dolzhen uiti!*) appeared on buildings, and Putin continued offering concessions, one of which included inviting Yabloko to provide electioneering monitors though the party held no seats in the Duma.[84] Oppositionist journalists and bloggers claimed that as many as 120,000 braved the below-freezing weather in Moscow for the various marches. In its turn, the MVD claimed that up to 139,000 pro-government 'Anti-Orange' citizens gathered in defence of Putin. Independent observers said that both sides greatly exaggerated their turnouts, and aerial photographs of the rallies showed that the pro-Putin gathering was every bit as large as the anti-Putin one, and perhaps larger. One of the pro-Putin group's prominent posters asked the key question, 'If not Putin – Who?'

Activists announced that they would support any candidate who would promise to abide by a social contract with the Russian people; i.e., agree to free political prisoners, reform election laws, dissolve the sitting Duma and hold new elections, and limit the president's time in office to two four-year terms. Whoever won the 2012 election would serve merely as a transitional president until the promised reforms were implemented. Whereas Zyuganov, Prokhorov, and Mironov agreed to many of these criteria, only Mironov accepted the proposed transitional term.

Putin did conduct a campaign of sorts, publishing long essays on select issues in the Russian press during January and early February, and regularly pledging fair elections. In one of the essays titled 'Democracy and the Quality of Government' he promised to modernize Russia's political system and allow citizens the right to propose legislation with 100,000 online signatures.[85] Medvedev's ideas for moderate and legal political changes permeated the paper unacknowledged. Other essays carried Putin's perspectives on Russia's social policies, the economy, nationalities, military reform, and foreign policy. In late February, he broke his pattern of no personal public campaigning and addressed a large pro-Putin rally in Moscow.

Neither Putin's essays nor his growing approval rating, up to 58 per cent of votes cast if an election was held in mid-February,[86] muted protest. Activists were arrested in Moscow during an unauthorized demonstration in front of the federal electoral headquarters on 7 February and released shortly afterwards just as shrieks of condemnation were being prepared. Putin even hinted that a coalition government might be considered, to much scepticism; and the Finnish-owned *Moscow Times* published an opinion piece challenging Putin's claim that the elections would be fair and not manipulated.[87] How could it be, the paper argued, when the elections were to be conducted under the same old rules, by the same CEC, and the same courts that punished almost no one for fraud in the earlier Duma election.

It was at this time that Patriarch Kirill pronounced that the accomplishments of Putin's first terms in office were a 'miracle of God', a bizarre endorsement for a country that only twenty years earlier had been officially atheist, but not likely seen as odd in the new Russia.[88] As the winter months progressed, President Medvedev gradually faded from the TV screens and other media, and Putin's presence grew ever brighter.

Members of Other Russia were arrested for throwing flares and threatening violence outside the CEC headquarters on 21 February, and were released after 24 hours detention. Western critics, of course, raged at this event as well, failing to consider the fact that similar behaviour certainly would have led to detentions in their own countries. Protesters also tried to form a human chain on Moscow's 15 km Ring Road. Reports of turnout for the 'White Circle' ranged from 11,000 to 40,000, depending largely on the political stance of the reporter.[89] Garri Kasparov had his photo distributed widely in the Western press – yet again, as did Navalny, Nemtsov, left-radical Sergei Udaltsov, and liberal politician Vladimir Ryzhkov. Minor scuffles occurred between opponents and supporters of Putin, mostly *Nashi* members who accused demonstrators of taking foreign money. Police broke up these fights, sometimes with considerable exuberance.

By late February, 667 foreign individuals and organizations had been approved to serve as election monitors. Among these were 231 delegates from the CIS and 219 from the OSCE's Office for Democratic Institutions and Human Rights (ODIHR). PACE sent 37 and the Shanghai Cooperation Organization (SCO) sent 21. The OSCE/PACE added 7 more. 56 representatives came from electoral commissions in nearly 20 other countries. They had their work cut out for them. In addition to widespread pre-election expectations of vote rigging, touted as gospel by oppositionists and Western media well before the election, videos were posted on the Internet claiming to show ballot box stuffing on Election Day. Given that the videos were circulated three days before the election actually took place, stupidly or purposely, the filmed incident was a hoax.[90] That didn't stop some of the Western press and Russian activists from showing them anyway.

At any rate, the CEC expected such illegal activities to be greatly diminished, for by Election Day many of the 95,000 polling stations had two web cameras in play and over 30,000 see-through ballot boxes were distributed; 440,000 police were deployed to maintain security. The webcams were connected online so that, theoretically, anyone could watch the action at select polling stations, and Putin's headquarters promised that it would declare void the results at any station where ballot stuffing was found out.

The election itself was anti-climactic: A turnout of a little over 65 per cent of eligible voters, less than in 2008, provided a decisive victory for Putin, who earned over 60 per cent of the votes cast; Zyuganov came second with less than 20 per cent. Even in the face of subsequent charges of rigging from Zyuganov and Prokhanov, and not a small dash of sour grapes, few people doubted the validity of Putin's first round victory.

*Table 1.2*  Presidential election results, 4 March 2012

|  | % | Votes |
|---|---|---|
| *Vladimir Putin* | 63.60 | 45,602,075 |
| *Gennady Zyuganov* | 17.18 | 12,318,353 |
| *Mikhail Prokhorov* | 07.98 | 5,722,798 |
| *Vladimir Zhirinovsky* | 06.22 | 4,458,102 |
| *Sergei Mironov* | 03.85 | 2,763,935 |

Note: Eligible voters = 108 million; Turnout = 65.34% (71,701,665)

## The aftermath

As the country awaited Putin's inauguration in May, Medvedev continued to govern. In April, he announced the expansion of the city of Moscow, saying that its territory would increase by 2.5 times when a Capital Federal District was created. This latter event coincided with the appointment of long-time Minister for Emergency Situations Sergei Shoigu as governor of the Moscow region, replacing the unpopular Boris Gromov.[91] Medvedev's pet project, the Innogorod at Skolkovo, became part of the huge new jurisdiction.

The outgoing president won a few victories during his last months in office, as nearly all of his bills reforming the political process were adopted – these will be delineated in Chapter Three. In his final major interview as president, he acknowledged that the anti-corruption campaign had failed and made it plain that the long-promised overhaul of the Ministry of the Interior was only just getting underway.

Dmitry Medvedev formally accepted the position of head of United Russia after a 27 April meeting with leaders of the party, and the next day he repeated to an audience at Skolkovo that modernizing the economy would still rank high on his agenda as prime minister. Thus, as Putin's inauguration approached, the Tandem was rising shakily to its feet. Medvedev and Putin participated side-by-side in the May Day parade, even stopping for a beer together. Still, no one believed that Medvedev was anything other than a bench warmer on the new team.

On the day of his gala inauguration, and the next day, Putin signed a flurry of decrees, appearing to leave Medvedev in his dust.[92] He ordered officials to prepare for an increase in real wages by 40–50 per cent by 2018, and a reduction in mortgage rates to a 2.2 per cent level by the same year. One decree demanded that the military be 70 per cent equipped with modern weaponry by 2020. He also allocated 5,000 rubles each to WWII veterans, and various sums to former inmates of concentration camps, widows and widowers of service personnel who died in wars. Other decrees called for the implementation of measures to realize Russia's demographic policies, education and science initiatives, improve health care and housing, and sustain the government's existing social policies. There was a certain déjà vu here, for these last named were the very tasks set out for Medvedev and the National

Priority Projects in 2005. Putin nominated Medvedev for the prime minister's office.

Later developments suggest that Putin should have heeded the old adage about never making promises you know you can't keep, because within a year he found himself scolding the government for inaction on precisely these decrees.

Even though the Tandem remained in place in name when Medvedev moved into the prime minister's office, not many people in Russia or abroad had confidence in its resilience. Four years earlier, Putin's lesser constitutional authority was greatly augmented by the immense political and popular capital he had acquired over the previous eight years. Only Putin could maintain a consensus among the behind-the-scenes elites, and so justified his role as an equal within the Tandem in 2008. All Medvedev had to offer President Putin in 2012 was a certain, if fading, respect within the growing middle class, a reputation in the West as a democrat – and loyalty. In short, the Tandem continued to exist in name only.

Putin's first post-Medvedev annual address to the Federal Assembly, on 12 December 2012, provided a clue to the Tandem's new reality. Economic innovation, one of Medvedev's priorities, was passed over altogether, and Medvedev himself was overlooked. Lip service was given to democracy as the 'only political choice for Russia', but it was clear that 'laws, rules and regulations' would temper Putin's version of democracy. Any perceived interference from abroad was absolutely proscribed and the evolution of democracy in Russia would be allowed to proceed only after the country's 'unity, integrity and sovereignty' were guaranteed. The tone certainly had changed.[93]

As Medvedev slipped quietly into the background, Gorbachev began showing up everywhere. Warning again that Russia could be slipping back into a period of Brezhnev-like stagnation, he urged Putin and Medvedev to launch a new *perestroika*. In March 2013, a year into Putin's new term, Gorbachev chastised the president in a long interview with the BBC for new stringent laws against unsanctioned demonstrations and cautioned him not to be 'afraid of his own people'. Gorbachev charged that Putin's 'inner circle' was ineffective in maintaining stability because 'there are so many thieves and corrupt officials there'. That being the case, he concluded with some encouraging words: 'I have a feeling that the young generation today, which is cultured and educated, is changing the whole picture'. There was a sense of inevitability in that prognosis offered by the man who started it all by introducing *glasnost* and *perestroika* in the 1980s against far greater odds than those faced by Medvedev and Putin.[94]

On 24 April Medvedev delivered one of his last speeches as president to a gathering of business and political leaders at the Kremlin. He promised to continue to expand political and economic freedoms in Russia, fight corruption and modernize the economy. At the same time, Putin stepped down as chairman of the United Russia Party and recommended Medvedev for that post. Although he accepted the nomination, it was not apparent that

Medvedev would have the authority even as party leader and prime minister to restructure the party and carry his reforms out.

If Gorbachev was right, then the four-year term of Medvedev's presidency had come full circle. On the surface, the Tandem promised much and accomplished little, and resolved very few of the problems that beset Russia in 2008, for example, the dilemma of corruption. Yet in the face of global financial recession, domestic political turmoil, and a number of pressing international crises, the leadership in Russia remained stable and strong. That stability may have been a thin veneer covering forces stirred up by Medvedev with his rhetoric, or it may represent the eternal intuitive preference for Russians when faced with alternatives to the status quo. Subsequent chapters will explore these two possibilities.

\* \* \*

A year after Putin's re-election, a nationwide survey revealed that up to 56 per cent of the population did not want him to run for another term in 2018; 22 per cent wanted him to stay in office. While he still had the confidence of roughly the same percentage of respondents to the questionnaire as before, they overwhelmingly believed that he represented mainly the interest of oligarchs, the *siloviki*, and state officials. Over 90 per cent believed that corruption and financial crimes were worse than the president claimed.[95] Only eight per cent wanted Medvedev back. Clearly, Russians had had enough of the Tandem at the top.

## Notes

1 Articles 80–93, 'Konstitutsiia Rossiiskoi Federatsii', *Rossiiskaia gazeta*, 25 December 1993.
2 Gorbachev's Vice President Gennady Yanaev joined a coup attempt against him in 1991; Yeltsin's Vice President Aleksandr Rutskoi was co-leader of the coup attempt in 1993.
3 See the editorial 'Konets intrigi. Prezidentom budet Medvedev', *Nezavisimaia gazeta*, 11 December 2007, and in the same issue a much longer piece by Natalia Melikova, 'Triumf liberalov'.
4 RIA Novosti, 15 August 2007; 8 March 2008.
5 'Interv'iu s glavoi TsIKa Vladimirom Churovym', *Kommersant*, 9 April 2007.
6 On Kasyanov, see 'Background People: Kasyanov, Mikhail Mikhailovich', *Russia Profile*, 25 May 2010. Whether the charge was true or not, it did turn out that Kasyanov hired a number of people who failed to canvas properly, submitted false names, and then took funds from Kasyanov's team. Public support for him from Boris Berezovsky, disgraced anti-Putin oligarch-in-exile, didn't help his cause either.
7 RIA Novosti, 3 March 2008. Medvedev made this remark in a speech to an economic forum meeting in Krasnoyarsk.
8 The Public Chamber is an unelected body with no legislative powers created by Putin in 2005. Its task is to provide learned and analytical advise to government on both draft legislation and larger policy issues. Putin named the original 42 members, presumably based on merit and ability, who then named 42 others.

These 84 then named 42 more to make 126 members. It has a number of committees, and there is regular turnover of membership.

9 The speech is summarized clearly in 'Kandidat v prezidenty Dmitrii Medvedev oglasil svoi predvybornye tezisy', NEWSru.com, 22 January 2008. On the question of 'expectations' see Bobo Lo, 'Dmitry Medvedev—Putin Clone or the New Man?' *Centre for European Reform*, 13 March 2008.

10 RIA Novosti, 3 March 2008.

11 On the *Vertikal*, see papers by Andrew Monaghan, 'The Russian *Vertikal*: the Tandem, Power and the Elections', Chatham House, REP Paper 2011/01 (June 2011), and 'The *Vertikal*: Power and Authority in Russia', *International Affairs*, 88:1 (2012), pp. 10–16. For a description of this team, see Yelena Lashkina, 'U apparata, v Kremle', *Rossiiskaia gazeta*, 13 May 2008. For the best study to date of the politics of Medvedev's accession to office, see Richard Sakwa, *The Crisis of Russian Democracy: The Dual State, Factionalism, and the Medvedev Succession*, Cambridge: Cambridge UP, 2011.

12 On Oligarchies generally, see Jeffrey A. Winter, *Oligarchy*, New York: Cambridge UP, 2011.

13 The statement was made during an interview with the *Financial Times* in July 1996. On Berezovsky, see Paul Klebnikov, *Godfather of the Kremlin. The Life and Times of Boris Berezovsky*, New York: Houghton-Miflin, 2000.

14 Putin made the promise about oligarchs while campaigning in March 2000. See Treisman, p. 95. See also Philip Hanson and Elizabeth Teague, 'Big Business and the State in Russia', *Europe-Asia Studies*, 57:5 (2005), pp. 657–80.

15 See, e.g. Vyacheslav Nikonov in *Izvestiia*, 1 January 2008, and Serge Shargunov in *Nezavisimaia gazeta*, 19 January 2008. For Medvedev's pre-and immediate post-election statements on his priorities, see Medvedev, *Natsional'nye prioritety: stat' i vystupleniia*, Moscow: Evropa, 2008. For many of the same speeches and statements, I used the more readily accessible Russian presidential website, *Kremlin.ru*.

16 For a summary of the report, Maksim Yegorov, et al, 'Akademik razveial' mify ob uspekhakh. Prezident i ego preemnik popal pod ogon' nauchnoi kritiki za proshiye budushchie provaly', *Nezavisimaia gazeta*, 28 February 2008.

17 *Kremlin.ru*, 7 May 2008.

18 See Andrei Ryabov, 'Tandemocracy in Today's Russia', *Russian Analytical Digest*, No. 49, 5 November 2008, pp. 1–6.

19 Nemtsov and Milov, *Putin. Itogi. Nezavisimyi Ekspertnyi Doklad (Putin: The Results: An Independent Expert Report)*, Moscow: Novaya Gazeta, 2008; available in translation by Dave Essel as *Putin: The Bottom Line: An Independent Expert Report*, posted at www.russophobe.blogspot.com/search/label/essel.

20 *Dvoevlastie* was a term used by Lenin to describe the relationship between the provisional Government and the Soviets in 1917. In his famous April Theses (The Tasks of the Proletariat in the Present Revolution, 7 April 1917), Lenin called for an end to 'Dual Power' and for the Soviets to take power. For an interpretation of the Putin–Medvedev partnership from a psycho-historical perspective, see Juhani Ihanus, 'Putin and Medvedev: Double Leadership in Russia', *Journal of Psychohistory*, Vol. 38, No. 3 (Winter 2011), pp. 251–84.

21 RIA Novosti, 12 December 2008.

22 Western and Russian analysts made much of this new governing phenomenon. Typical were, 'Russian Leadership. A Double-Headed Eagle', *The Economist*, 19 April 2008, Pavel K. Baev, 'Putin Packs His Bag But Medvedev Still Bides His Time', *Eurasia Daily Monitor*, 28 April 2008; 'Russia. A Strange Kremlin Wedding', *The Economist*, 10 May 2008.

23 See Ivanov in *Izvestiia*, 21 November 2008.

24 'Tandem. Novoe v zhizni strany to, chto prezident ne mozhet kritikovat' prem'era, pravitel'stvo, ministrov', *Nezavisimaia gazeta*, 30 December 2008.

25  See, e.g. *Fond 'Obshchestvennoe mnenie'* (Hereafter FOM), 23 April 2009; Interfax, 22 October 2009; FOM, 19 November 2009.
26  Leonid Polyakov, 'V Rossii Medvedeva – vse pytem', *Nezavisimaia gazeta*, 3 March 2009.
27  *Ibid.*
28  *Nezavisimaia gazeta*, 13 July 2009.
29  For the full address in Russian and English, see *Kremlin.ru*, 12 November 2009.
30  See e.g. 'Evoliutsiia tandemnykh otnoshenii. Oba lidera demonstriruiut bespretsedentnuiu vnutripoliticheskuiu aktivnost', *Nezavisimaia gazeta*, 16 September 2009, and Interfax, 20 September 2009.
31  Anastasiia Bashkatova, 'Prizyvy k modernizatsii ne ubedili Rossiian', *Nezavisimaia gazeta,* 9 December 2009. The survey was conducted by the Levada Centre.
32  For a detailed explication, Ian Bremmer, Samuel Charap, 'The *Siloviki* in Putin's Russia: Who They Are and What They Want', *The Washington Quarterly*, 2006–7, Vol. 30, No. 1, pp. 83–92, and Vladimir Pribylovsky, *Vlast'-2010: 60 biografii*, Moskva: Tsentr Panorama, 2010.
33  'Reiting Medvedeva po-prezhnemu vysok', FOM, 19 November 2009; Interfax, 30 November 2009.
34  See, e.g., *Nezavisimaia gazeta*, 7 August 2010.
35  ITAR-TASS, 29 October 2010; *The Moscow Times*, 10 August 2010.
36  *Kremlin.ru*, 17 March 2010.
37  RIA Novosti, 8 June 2010. On the growth of the bureaucracy, see Darell Slider, 'Russian Federation. Can it be Rebuilt from the Ruins?' *Russian Analytical Digest*, No. 43 (2008).
38  On this generally, see Andrew Monaghan, 'The Russian *Vertikal*: the Tandem, Power and the Elections', Chatham House, REP 2011/01 (June 2011).
39  Medvedev's 'Rossiia, vpered!' (Russia, Forward!), often translated and available as 'Go, Russia!' appeared on the website *Gazeta.ru* on 10 September 2009 and was published the next day.
40  See Nikolau von Twickel, 'Medvedev's Institute Proposes Radical Reforms', *The Moscow Times*, 4 February 2010.
41  See, e.g., Yevgeny Gontmakher, 'Kurazh, dlia modernizatsii', *Rossiiskaia gazeta*, 7 May 2010. Gontmakher was one of the authors of '21st Century Russia.'
42  Rossiya 24 (formerly Vesti TV), 28 May 2010; *Kremlin.ru*, 28 May 2010.
43  *Kreml.org*, 4 June 2010.
44  Olga V. Kryshtanovskaia, 'Formats of Russian State Power', *Russian Politics and Law*, Vol. 50, No. 3 (May/June 2012), pp. 7–17.
45  On this generally, see Aleksandr Belousov, 'Political Propaganda in Contemporary Russia', *Russian Politics and Law*, Vol. 50, No. 3 (May/June 2012), pp. 56–69; for an early analysis, Masha Lipman, 'Putin's "Sovereign Democracy"', *The Washington Post*, 15 July 2006, and more recently Michael Bohm, 'Limiting Russia's Sovereign Democracy', *The Moscow Times*, 8 April 2011.
46  'Surkov – molodezhnym organizatsiiam: "Treniruite mozgi i muskuly"', *Nashi Novosti*, 11 December 2010.
47  See, e.g., Adrian Pabst, '"Tretii put" Dmitriia Medvedeva', *Rossiia v global'noi politike*, 23 October 2010; an OP-ED in *Nezavisimaia gazeta*, 5 June 2010; Gleb Cherkasov (*Kommersant*) in *Gazeta.ru*, 4 May 2010; Stanislav Belkovsky in *Moskovskiy Komsomolets* online, 27 July 2010; and Vladislav Inozemtsev interviewed for *Kreml.org*, 18 August 2010.
48  Dmitri Trenin, 'M or M (Modernization or Marginalization): Which Future for Russia?' *Carnegie.ru*, 28 January 2010.
49  *Kremlin.ru*, 24 December 2010.

50  See Stepashin's speech to the Federation Council, ITAR-TASS, 17 May 1999.
51  See *Kommersant*, 27 September 2010; Interfax, 28 September 2010; and for an overview, Elena Chinaeva, 'The Mayor is Gone, Long Live the Mayor!', *Eurasia Daily Monitor*, 28 September 2010.
52  On this generally, see Tai Adelaja, 'Deflating Bloated Bureaucracy', *Russia Profile*, 4 January 2011.
53  Interfax, 14 January 2011.
54  Interfax, 24 March 2011; *Vedomosti*, 22 April 2011.
55  Interfax, 21 & 23 March 2011.
56  *New York Times*, 22 February 2011; see also 'Foreboding Kudrin's Comeback', *Foreign Policy Journal* on line, 6 October 2011.
57  IA Regnum, 3 April 2011; FOM, 1 April 2011.
58  'Reitingi osypalis'. Do rekordno nizkogo urovnia upali reitingi Dmitriia Medvedeva, Vladimira Putina, i 'Yedinoi Rossii', otmechaiut srazu dve sotsiologicheskie sluzhby', *Vedomosti*, 22 April 2011.
59  See, e.g., Igor Naumov, 'Mezhdu liberalom Medvedevym i konservatorom Putinym. Prezident i prem'er vedut ekonomiku v raznye desiatiletiia,' *Nezavisimaia gazeta*, 25 April 2011.
60  *Nezavisimaia gazeta*, 7 July 2011. For a general description, see Pavel K. Baev, 'Medvedev and Putin Try in Vain to Shake the Siloviki Into Order', *Eurasia Daily Monitor*, 11 July 2011.
61  *Kommersant*, 15 April 2011.
62  *Nashbol.ru*, 11 December 2011.
63  Interfax, 12 December 2011.
64  Tai Adelaja, 'One Nation, Two Visions', *Eurasia Daily Monitor*, 11 May 2011.
65  For further sometimes gleeful, sometimes overwrought presumptions about major splits in the Tandem, see Nikolay Petrov, 'Medvedev Up, Putin Down', *The Moscow Times*, 12 April 2011, Pavel Felgenhauer, 'The Putin-Medvedev Ruling Tandem Disintegrates', *Eurasia Daily Monitor*, 14 April 2011, and Pavel K. Baev, 'Competition Between Medvedev and Putin: Light Entertainment', *Eurasia Daily Monitor*, 18 April 2011.
66  *Novaia gazeta*, 13 May 2011; *Kommersant*, 13 May 2011.
67  Interfax, 19 & 20 June 2011.
68  'Vybor est'. Obrashchenie k grazhdanam Rossii', *Novaia gazeta*, 25 July 2011; *Gazeta.ru*, 13 July 2011.
69  Interfax, 15 July 2011.
70  See, e.g., Aleksei Gorbachev and Aleksandra Samarina, 'Tiani-tolkai-tandem. Prezident i prem'er-ministr mogut priniat uchastie v kampanii-2012', *Nezavisimaia gazeta*, 9 August 2011.
71  *Kremlin.ru*, 24 September 2011.
72  This author was in Moscow on 24 September 2011 and noticed the indifference and cynicism first hand.
73  Both quoted in *Democratic Digest*, 26 September 2011; Dmitriev from a piece he wrote in *Vedomosti*, and Pavlovsky from an interview for Ekho Moskvy. For a particularly pessimistic opinion on what the decision meant for Medvedev's reforms, see Nikolaus von Twickel, 'Party is Over for Medvedev the Modernizer', *Moscow Times*, 28 September 2011.
74  *Moskovskiy komsomolets*, 22 September 2011.
75  For Putin's claim, see Interfax, 2 March 2012.
76  On this generally, see Dan Peleschuk, '(Lame) Duck Hunting. Medvedev to Take Backseat as Putin Moves Ahead to the Presidency', *Russia Profile*, 27 September 2011. For the plea on behalf of the Tandem, see Yury Kondratev, 'Revenstvo v tandeme', *Nezavisimaia gazeta*, 29 July 2010.
77  IA Regnum, 14 November 2011.

78 See, e.g., Maxim Filimonov, 'Vote Protest as "Watershed" Russian Leaders Cannot Ignore', RIA Novosti, 12 December 2011.
79 RIA Novosti, 28 December 2011 and 6 January 2012. The webcams were problematic because some of the polling stations had no electrical supply.
80 RIA Novosti, 19 December 2011.
81 Putin, 'Election Manifesto', Russian Federation Prime Minister, Information and Press Office, 16 January 2012; 'Rossiia sosredotochivaetsia – vyzovy, na kotorye my dolzhny otvetit', *Izvestiia,* 16 January 2012.
82 See, e.g., *Izvestiia*, 24 January 2012.
83 In Russia, elected political parties or blocs traditionally are referred to as *fraktsiia* or 'fractions', but meaning factions or blocs.
84 For descriptions of both pro- and anti-Putin rallies, Andrew Roth, 'Going the Distance', *Russia Profile*, 4 February 2012; Dan Peleschuk, 'Bowing to the Hill', *Russia Profile*, 6 February 2012; Alexander Bratersky, 'Opposition Joins Hands in Anti-Putin Protest', *The Moscow Times*, 27 February 2012.
85 Putin, 'Demokratiia i kachestvo gosudarstva', *Kommersant,* 6 February 2012.
86 Interfax, 31 January, 20 February 2012.
87 'Putin's Empty Promise of Honest Elections', *The Moscow Times*, 7 February 2012.
88 Interfax, 8 February 2012.
89 Alexander Bratersky, 'Opposition Joined Hands in Anti-Putin Protest', *The Moscow Times*, 27 February 2012.
90 'Fake Videos of Ballot Stuffing Investigated', RIA Novosti, 1 March 2012. Nikolaus von Twickel, Alexandra Odynova, 'Western Observers Call Vote Flawed', *The Moscow Times*, 6 March 2012.
91 Shoigu didn't hold the post for long. He was named minister of defence in November.
92 For a complete list of these decrees, 14 in all, see 'Bank dokumentov, 7 Maia 2012, ponedel'nik', *Kremlin.ru*, 7 May 2012.
93 For Putin's speech, 'Poslanie Federalnomu Sobraniiu', *Kremlin.ru*, 12 December 2012 (English and Russian versions).
94 Steve Rosenberg, BBC News, Moscow, 7 March 2013; and 'Gorbachev: V Rossii neobkhodimo vozobnovit' perestroiku', *Nezavisimaia gazeta*, 1 April 2013.
95 'Vladimir Putin: god posle izbraniia prezidentom', Levada-tsentr, 11 April 2013. The survey was run on 22–25 March, with 1,601 respondents in 130 population centres in 45 regions of Russia.

# 2 The Russian Federation
## Source of strength and weakness

Even as the centralization process was a dominant theme in Putin's first two terms, Medvedev still had to deal with the fact that his office represented far more than Moscow and Russians.

The Constitution of 1993 defined the state structure of the Russian Federation very carefully, guaranteeing its 'state integrity' and 'unity of economic space'. Russian is the official language of the Federation, and the ruble is its basic currency. Though each component of the Federation was allowed to maintain its own constitution and local laws, these had still to conform to the Constitution of the Russian Federation.

At its inception, the Russian Federation included 89 separate components. As a result of mergers over the years, by the end of 2008 their numbers decreased to the current 83. Although a little over 80 per cent of the country's some 142 million people are ethnic Russian, the country still includes 160 national groups. The second largest language bloc is Tatar and the third is Ukrainian. There are 26 languages other than Russian that have official standing in various parts of the Federation.

Russia is by law a secular state. About 20 per cent of the population are active believers in the largest single religion, Christian Orthodoxy, followed by 12 per cent who adhere to Islam. Thus, while clearly a Russian state, the Federation has concentrated communities of non-Russian, non-Orthodox, and non-secular populations – especially in the North Caucasus. These pose particular policy and practice issues with which the federal state must cope.

Separate units of the Federation are represented in Russia's bicameral political structure in the Federation Council, or upper house of the Federal Assembly. The Federation itself consisted of a mixture of republics, oblasts, krais, autonomous regions and two federal cities, Moscow and St. Petersburg. Many of the components (called federal subjects) of the Federation are the nominal homelands of a particular ethnic group. In spite of their wide differences in makeup, the Constitution makes all members of the Federation equal by law in their relationship with federal agencies of power, and federal authority over them is near absolute, thereby negating a series of special arrangements reached between some of the regions and Moscow during the previous three years. Many years went by, however, before some semblance of uniformity in the laws, codes, and practices defined in the Constitution was achieved. The last of the special arrangements, a 10-year power sharing treaty between Moscow and Tatarstan was actually signed as late as July 2007.

Technically equal in political access, members of the Federation vary enormously in territory, population, and resources. The regions are especially different in their access to income and employment. For example, the average income in the Moscow region in 2011 was more than five times the average income in Kalmykia; unemployment in the Moscow, St. Petersburg, and Novgorod areas was less than 10 per cent, and in Chechnya, Ingushetia, and Tuva, somewhere between 22 and 49 per cent. Inequalities such as these meant that some components of the Federation are losing population while others are filling up.[1] These trends had been in play since the collapse of the USSR, when all previous attempts from the centre to maintain some balance between the social and income condition of the country's many territorial administrations fell by the wayside.

The Russian Federation inherited by Medvedev was differently structured than the one handed to Putin in 2000. Within weeks of winning the office, Putin had created seven new federal districts in Russia each headed by a Plenipotentiary Representative named by the president. Their purpose was to 'ensure the exercise by the President of the Russian Federation of his constitutional powers, to make the work of federal bodies of state power more effective and to improve control over compliance with their decisions'. Each district encompassed a number of the republics, territories and regions of the Federation. They were named the Central, Northwest, North Caucasian (soon changed to Southern), Volga, Ural, Siberian, and Far Eastern Federal Districts.[2]

Among the regulations guiding these federal envoys was a requirement to act as a 'conduit' for the president's personnel policy in the district and to submit regular reports on national security issues and the political, social, and economic conditions in their respective district. They were also expected to coordinate the activities of all federal agencies in the district and act as liaisons between the central agencies and various levels of government within the constituent members of the Federation.[3] In effect, this office emasculated the local authority of the 'governors', especially when it came to their use of funds from Moscow. Since all the original envoys were ex-military or KGB senior officers, keeping tabs on the governors was not a difficult assignment for them.

The role of governors themselves as economic managers and flag bearers for the centre in the regions made support from the governors essential if the top heavy Federation was to run smoothly. That meant that the Federation Council, which had quickly become a forum in which regional delegates, i.e., two representatives from each of the components of the Federation, lobbied and intrigued for shares of federal largesse – and perquisites that included housing in Moscow – needed restructuring. The two representatives were chosen entirely by the territory itself, one from its legislature, and the other from the executive branch. Because no guidelines were set as to how they should be selected the common practice was for the governors to pick themselves.

In the summer of 2000, shortly after he created the presidential envoy system, Putin forced regional governors out of the Federation Council.[4] The same lack of guidelines enabled him to do this without amending the Constitution. The new rules called for a representative elected by the regional legislature, and required the governor or president to designate a representative other than himself. The absence of territorial leaders from Russia's Upper House and the new administrative tier of presidential envoys undermined the influence of the regions on the centre, and greatly strengthened the influence of the centre on the regions. In short, Putin replaced a floundering centrifugal structure with a centralized power structure, importantly breaking the control regional authorities had over federal funds and policy in what had previously resembled in many cases private family fiefdoms.[5]

Financial control was especially important. Far too many of the territorial entities relied almost exclusively on the federal purse, having no natural resources or industry on which to build a local economy. Some of them were losing population rapidly, as young people and families moved to areas where employment was more likely, so they were short of labour and had no tax base; others, such as the Moscow district, were filling up with those same people and also with foreign unregistered migrants looking for work. There were also issues with the ghettoization of ethnic groups. Mixed populations in some of the subject territories found themselves governed exclusively by the dominant nominal population, or by ethnic Russians, who inevitably elected one of their own to administrative office. High levels of corruption among officials and local ruling 'families' made the situation worse.

The 'governorships' had changed again in 2004 when, in response to September's terrorist crisis in Beslan, North Ossetia, the president recommended the abolition of local elections of regional heads. The proposal became law the following Spring, and at the same time the president's office took on the right to appoint governors directly. Even though the regional legislatures did not need to accept the named governor at first offer, they could do little more than delay the process. The vertical power structure was therefore greatly enhanced.

In contrast to Putin's early years, Medvedev was in a position to dismiss governors for incompetence or criminal activity, and his courts did not have to worry about the immunity regional leaders might have had as members of the Federation Council. The president could now also dissolve regional legislatures if they did not adjust local laws to fit with the Federation's legal and constitutional codes. Any remnant of bilateral treaties signed by Moscow and various republics of the Federation could be ignored. New tax collecting regulations, along with strengthened federal oversight, also worked very much to the advantage of the centre. So too did political reforms that forced all deputies elected to the Duma to belong to political parties and made the parties themselves more cross-national in make-up.

There were more changes to come. A flurry of activity in the last week of 2008 altered the mechanisms of the centre-regional structure again in several ways. On 25 December, Medvedev introduced draft legislation allowing a party with a majority in a regional government to recommend candidates for governor. The head of state would still make the final nomination, but now had to do so in consultation with leaders of the party in question that will offer the names of three candidates. If the president wanted none of them, another three names would be put forward. In a further change, the president's official representatives in the regions no longer had the right to make nominations.

In adopting new rules for naming governors, changes in regulations for election to the Federation Council were passed on 28 January 2009. These allowed only deputies in regional legislative assemblies or representatives of municipal authorities to stand for membership in the Federation Council. The residential requirement – previously 10 years in the region – was abolished. The changes came into effect on 1 January 2011. In-house opposition came from the usual sources. Communists insisted that election to the Federation Council should be direct, and Zhirinovsky's LDPR demanded that the Council be abolished altogether. Both argued in vain.[6]

The Federation Council was streamlined again in December 2009 by the addition of a Presidium to coordinate its positions with the government in advance. Comprised of the Federation Council chairman, the vice speakers, and the heads of eight out of 20 of the upper chamber's committees, namely the committees for constitutional legislation, legal and judicial issues, defence, economic policy, CIS affairs, Federation Affairs, Social Policy, and International Affairs, the Presidium's main function was to make recommendations regarding the Council's agenda.

An important step safeguarding the Tandem's influence over the Federation Council was taken in September 2011, when Medvedev supported the appointment of Valentina Matviyenko for the position as speaker of the upper house. She replaced Sergei Mironov, leader of the A Just Russia Party, who had held the speaker's chair for nearly a decade. Mironov ran into trouble in May after he harshly criticized Matviyenko's handling of a flood crisis in her region. He was recalled by the United Russia party, of which Matviyenko was an active member, and ousted from office. Because Matviyenko recently had resigned her post as governor of Saint Petersburg, she had to win a municipal election to be eligible for the Federation Council, which she did in August by taking some 95 per cent of the votes. Her election to the chairmanship of the Federation Council was nearly unanimous, with 140 votes for and one abstention. On taking up the position she promised to streamline the various committees, commissions, and working groups in the Council, and also to make the work of the upper house more open to the media.[7] In short, she echoed the Medvedev line.

Although there were periodic changes in governorships during Medvedev's first two years in office, a rush of new names in these positions showed up between 2010 and 2012. The first dramatic move came when Tatarstan's President Mintimer Shaymiev decided in January 2010 not to accept re-appointment if it was offered. Laws passed since 2000 called for the standardization of titles used by executive heads of republics, yet the changes were voluntary and Shaymiev had been a 'president' since he worked out his first power-sharing agreement with Yeltsin in the early 1990s. The question of title was ignored until August 2010 when President Ramzan Kadyrov of Chechnya raised it again by announcing that he would be termed 'Head of the Chechen Republic', and added that there should be only one president in the Russian Federation.

As we shall see later in this chapter, the North Caucasus posed special problems for Moscow, as political and religious extremism, economic breakdown, and all conceivable forms of social distress became the order of the day in the region. In one of his many attempts to resolve such chaos, Medvedev added another tool to the federal government's oversight machinery. In January 2010 he created a new Federal District, the North Caucasus, and appointed Governor of Krasnoyarsk Aleksandr Khloponin to the new Plenipotentiary post. Khloponin held the authority of deputy prime minister as well, making this a particularly high-level posting. The new district includes seven of the republics and territories of the region – Dagestan, Ingushetia, Kabardino-Balkaria, Karachaevo-Cherkessia, North Ossetia-Alania, Chechnya, and Stavropol Territory.[8] Khloponin's experience as a businessman and economist and lack of connection with any of the local clans made it possible for him to fight corruption – or so it was hoped – and to improve the employment and business situation in the area. Technically, he held the federal purse strings, but since the jurisdictional relationship between presidential envoys and local governments was still not fully defined, there was some uncertainty about how much leeway he had. The new district's headquarters was located in Pyatigorsk, in the Stavropol region.

Within a week of the appointment, a conference in Pyatigorsk chaired by Prime Minister Putin announced that the district would be granted a North Caucasus University, and that the number of FSB forces in the region would be increased. The official government policy was to improve social and economic conditions as the best means to ease the level of frustration and violence. Within the following month Medvedev paid surprise visits to Nalchik in Kabardino-Balkaria, and Cherkesk in Karachaevo-Cherkessia, promising help and urging officials to fight extremists and improve the economy. To assist in the social and economic reconstruction of the North Caucasus, Russia drew a $200 million credit from the World Bank to help fund a job creation program put in place in 2009. The credit agreement with the IMF was titled 'Support of Local Initiative in the North Caucasian Federal District'.

Elsewhere in the Federation, legislation sent to the Duma in late December 2009 took some influence away from the presidential envoys, all of them Putin appointees. The new rules were tested almost immediately, when Medvedev voiced concern for the way in which some of the regions were managed. He dismissed four governors and replaced them either with his own people or with Cabinet-level personnel he wanted to move out of Moscow. Former minister of agriculture, Aleksei Gordeev, was one of the latter cases. He was sent to Voronezh as governor, and his deputy Aleksandr Kozlov went to Orel Oblast to take up the governorship there. In November, Medvedev revealed that Eduard Rossel, the independent-minded, long-time governor of Sverdlovsk, would not be re-appointed.

Federal oversight seemed not to go much beyond keeping an eye on the governors, so political chicanery still ran rampant in the regions. Elections in 75 constituent territories of the Russian Federation in October 2009 saw sweeping victories almost everywhere for United Russia, providing the centre with yet another tool with which to monitor every corner of the Federation. But not without objections. Charges of manipulation of television time by local authorities, rigged votes, and other signs of corrupt practices strained Russian democracy and once again provided examples of tendencies towards political overkill, since United Russia was likely to have been victorious without the deceit. The grumbling provided a foretaste of things to come in federal elections, and should have been heeded more closely.

In fact, United Russia wasn't much concerned about such accusations. The party worked both openly and behind the scenes to have its choices nominated for governorships in regions where the old guard was gradually being replaced, such as Bashkortostan, Karelia, and Chuvashia. The UR was especially active in Kaliningrad, where it decided not to re-nominate Georgy Boos, in part because he was unpopular and in part because he failed to follow the party line. The 17-year regime of multi-millionaire Kirsan Ilyumzhinov in Kalmykia also ended without re-nomination in 2010. Ilyumzhinov's weirdness was likely a factor in Medvedev's decision to accept his resignation: he once claimed to have been abducted by extra-terrestrial beings, and he offered to have Lenin's body moved to his territory. United Russia nominee Aleksei Orlov replaced him.

Putin's political party remained strong in the provinces, but its popularity waned by the time of the next series of regional elections in March 2010, when there was competition for some 6,000 positions at various levels in 76 areas of Russia. This time United Russia's monopoly was broken in several constituencies, with both the Communist Party and A Just Russia claiming minor victories. Several commentators blamed Putin's leadership of United Russia for that party's slight decline in the regions.

Medvedev continued to dismiss and replace regional governors. By the end of 2011, he had changed over one-third of them. Of all the sackings, the most significant was the hasty dismissal of Luzhkov in September 2010. In addition to the issues related to this matter noted in Chapter One, the decision demonstrated beyond any doubt who was in charge – no regional leader, no matter how powerful, was immune from removal. The only exception may have been Ramzan Kadyrov in Chechnya and, as we shall see, that was clearly for reasons of national expediency.[9]

The purpose in changing leaderships in the regions seemed to be rooted in Medvedev's urge towards efficiency and competence, and also to show that he was doing 'something' before the December elections. In late February and early March, governors of Kamchatka, Ulyanovsk, and Karachaevo-Cherkessia were relieved of their posts. In these cases, commentators almost unanimously suggested that none of them had performed successfully, failing to handle such basic needs in their areas as housing, employment, and healthcare. On the other hand, the dangerously more efficient Kadyrov was re-nominated for the top position in Chechnya.

Changes at the top in the regions may have helped United Russia make a bit of a comeback in March, earning nearly 70 per cent of the seats offered in the 2011 regional elections, though its popular vote was down again. The ruling party did even better in the regions during the controversial State Duma elections of December that year. In too many cases, however, the electoral commission claimed an over 90 per cent voter turnout. Needless to say, much suspicion was cast upon these results. In at least one riding in the North Caucasus, for example, more votes were counted than there were eligible voters. Complaints that the 'Putin Party' was going the way of Brezhnev's CPSU, in both its stagnation mode and its desperate compulsion to hold onto power, began to creep into the media and blogger sphere. Growing sentiments such as these, tinged with futility, seriously undermined the impact of President Medvedev's rhetoric about political change and economic modernization.

The president's ambitions for the regions were outlined first in August 2009 during a speech delivered to the Federal District Economic and Social Planning Commission in Ulan Ude, Buryatia. There, Medvedev delineated issues that could apply to most regions of Russia. Using the disaster at the Sayano-Shushenskaia Hydro Electric Station (see Chapter Six) as an example, he stressed the need for infrastructure and safety control upgrades everywhere, but especially in the regions. He noted that several of the big investment projects for Siberia were frozen because of the economic crisis, adding that the entire plan had to be revisited and final deadlines set for those projects that were to continue. In the meantime, the electrical grid required a complete overhaul and prices for electricity needed to be constrained. Such issues as a demand for foreign labour, regional budgets, environment protection and workplace discipline in Siberian development were all under careful scrutiny – or so Medvedev proclaimed.[10]

The optimistic approach was in part a response to projections offered previously that year by media commentators of economic disintegration everywhere in Russia, but especially in the Maritime Krai and the Far East. The earlier cautionary notes appeared prescient as accidents and natural disasters contributed to a feeling that Russia's eastern regions were being sacrificed to a focus on the centre, as did such actions as prohibitive duties on imported motor vehicles and the cancellation of several large-scale projects. Among the ripple effects of economic decline in Siberia and the Far East was a shrinking population base as people moved away to find employment. The drop in population then sparked explosive rumours about Chinese takeovers of Siberian lands. One mainstream paper openly charged the government with discriminating against the region.[11] Defence and security analysts worried about the implications of an under-populated and under-developed Siberia and Russian Far East. Quickly spreading whispers of a 'silent' expansion by China raised concerns about Russian sovereignty along the Amur River. These concerns echoed issues raised by Primakov in 2006. There were questions as well about whatever had become of the big 2007 project to attract Russian-speaking settlers to the eastern areas of Russia – the answer to which was 'nothing'.[12]

The ever-increasing attention paid to Siberia and the Far East was both economically and politically motivated, as we shall see in later chapters, yet it was also an important cog in strengthening the Federation to the extent that talk of a future Eurasian Union could make sense.

It would not be until the spring of 2012 that Siberia returned seriously to the rejuvenation discourse in Moscow, and that was after Putin took over the file. In May, he created the Far Eastern Development Agency, a giant state corporation headed by presidential envoy to the Far Eastern Federal District Viktor Ishaev. The Agency's expressed purpose was to manage the development of Siberia. Critics saw it as a scheme for the government to govern and exploit Russia's huge resource sector without private industry competition; others saw it as a necessary tool for the development of Siberia's natural resources; and still others believed it a means to keep China at bay in Russia's Far East. Common to most analyses, however, was the assumption that the Siberian consortium would provide vast opportunity for more corruption when the construction industry and centralized political mandarins took it over. Improved transportation was expected to be the key to development. Investment funds from China were welcomed.

Ishaev was also named head of a newly created Ministry for the Development of the Russian Far East, and on 9 August 2012 the cabinet allocated 236 million rubles ($7 million) to finance the ministry's expenses.[13] One could say that Medvedev had hesitated to introduce such major infusions for Siberia and the Russia's Far East because of the need to recover from the recession. It is possible too that his passion for innovation and Skolkovo and his leanings to the West blinded him to the importance of Siberia.

Putin, after all, had cancelled a number of large-scale energy-related Siberian projects himself because of expense; and Medvedev was well aware of the importance of Chinese investment and political association with Russia. But it was Putin who led the new charge to Siberia, clearly as a part of his Eurasian Union campaign, explained further in Chapter Five.

One of the concessions promised by Medvedev after the disorder ensuing from the Duma elections in December 2011 was the return of direct elections for governors of the Russian Federation's components. This became a rallying cry for political activists throughout 2012. As a first step in that direction, Medvedev accelerated the 'resignations' of governors who clearly could not win an election to their posts.

There were other reasons for the dismissals, revealed in April 2012 when Medvedev told a televised interviewer that since becoming president he had dismissed half of the governors of Russia's regions over suspicions of corruption. 'I was forced to fire 50 per cent of the governors', he said, noting that even when there had been a lack of conclusive proof of their guilt, he had told them 'resign, or it will be worse'.[14]

## The North Caucasus quicksand

Nowhere was the link between governors and the Russian presidency so important as in the North Caucasus.[15] Putin's easy victory in the election for his second term in office was due in part to a perception that he had resolved Moscow's relationship with Chechnya. After two bitter civil wars, much bloodshed, atrocities on both sides, and horrendous acts of terrorism in Moscow, Beslan (North Ossetia), and elsewhere in Russia, relative order had been established. Shortly before Medvedev became president strongman Ramzan Kadyrov, President of Chechnya since February 2007, proclaimed that his administration would work closely with moderate Islam to counter extremism in that republic.

This apparent calm may have been the reason why, in that same month, the EU allocated 20 million euros for the rehabilitation and development of the North Caucasus in general and both Chechnya and Ingushetia in particular. In the latter two cases, about two-thirds of the funds were designated for healthcare and education. UNICEF and the World Health Organization (WHO), agencies that launched some of these programs in late 2006, assigned managers to help Russian and regional authorities disperse the funds productively. Advanced training for local doctors, ambulances, and medical equipment, were part of the enterprise. Though these programs must have helped somewhat, then Deputy Prime Minister Medvedev took it upon himself to urge regional leaders to untie the 'corruption knot' that was stifling local developments. He was speaking here mostly about corrupt land auctions by regional governments and military, yet the reference was general.[16]

To be sure, the violence was by no means over in Chechnya; rather, responsibility was shifted away from the Kremlin, leaving Medvedev to focus on other matters. Kadyrov called for and won a general amnesty from Moscow, an act that released many young men from prisons and gave them reason to shift their loyalties away from the militants to Kadyrov – but not necessarily to Moscow. Kadyrov used his paramilitary supporters, called popularly the *Kadyrovtsy*, to hunt down insurgents on behalf of Moscow and also to kill or capture his own current and former opponents in Chechnya. When the Ministry of Defence in Moscow announced in November 2008 that the Chechen-Russian units of the Russian army would be disbanded by January 2009, the field was left open to the *Kadyrovtsy* to act solely on the Chechen president's orders. For the next three years, Medvedev and the Russian public were quite willing to turn a blind eye to almost anything Kadyrov did as long

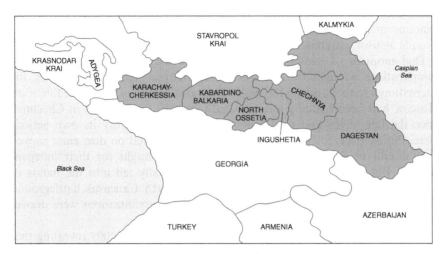

*Map 2.1* The North Caucasus (adapted from original created by Peter Fitzgerald)

as it did not affect them directly. In so doing, Moscow allowed Kadyrov to eliminate all his real and perceived enemies, raise loyal allies to positions of power, and eventually wield greater control over the small republic than Putin ever had, or has, over Russia.[17]

Kadyrov also announced that a long-discussed treaty between Russia and his republic was no longer necessary, and his officials began leaking information tying the murder of former KGB agent Aleksandr Litvinenko case to Berezovsky and even the possibility that the exiled Russian oligarch may have been financing terrorist Shamil Basaev. Nothing could have pleased Putin more, since the world's media tended to pin the Litvinenko assassination on him. Kadyrov joined United Russia, and then asked for his pound of flesh by issuing a formal demand that Moscow pay compensation for the forced deportation of Chechens by Stalin in 1944, asking for the equivalent of $300 million.

Chechnya's sudden turnabout could not hide other serious complications, the most important of these was revealed when the Russian Health and Social Development Ministry announced in 2007 that over 300,000 people were registered as unemployed in Chechnya, i.e., about 20 per cent of the officially unemployed in all of Russia. Wage arrears, damaged housing and infrastructure, and a dearth of private investment were matters that needed resolution.[18]

Medvedev eventually had to deal with all these issues, but the question of violence remained paramount. Newly appointed Secretary of the Security Council and former head of the FSB, Nikolai Patrushev, reported in October that his officers had 'neutralized' some 170 militants in the North Caucasus in 2008 to that time. They also recorded 350 arrests, and processed a dozen or so insurgents who had turned themselves in. A large number of arms caches were located, and some 2,000 homemade bombs were uncovered. This announcement was delivered with some fanfare, leaving the impression that inroads against extremists was possible in the North Caucasus.[19]

That moment of tentative optimism didn't last long. In addition to the complications wrought by Russia's war in Georgia (see Chapter Five), the international terrorist role in the North Caucasus came quickly to the forefront. Moscow had been blaming international terrorism for the wars in Chechnya since the late 1990s and used that alleged threat to justify its own actions there. Putin's pleas for understanding in this regard fell on deaf ears; as well they should in the early stages when Chechens fought for their independence.[20] But while the Chechen leadership gradually fell into the hands of radical Islamicists in the late 1990s and the North Caucasus battleground became a vortex into which international terrorist organizations were drawn, scoffing from the West dimmed only slowly.

Indeed, even when the MVD published data in March 2009 revealing that nearly 1,000 acts of terrorism, either attempted or aborted, were committed in Russia during 2008, Western pundits were either unconvinced or indifferent. The greatest number of these, by far, occurred in Ingushetia (300), with Chechnya (118) and Dagestan (87) trailing in that dubious honour.[21] The greater number of the terrorist acts were clearly home-grown and driven by Caucasus circumstances, yet both logic and the militant leadership itself made international links equally obvious. It was during Medvedev's four years that Russia grew increasingly vulnerable to organized terrorist activity as the foreign occupation in Iraq wound down, the anti-Taliban war in Afghanistan bogged down and, from 2010, the so-called Arab Spring went awry – at least in so far as Western hopes for the region were concerned.

Ripple effects from these skewed affairs exacerbated situations faced by Russia already. A separatist Chechen government-in-exile, or Ichkeria, remained a constant thorn in Medvedev's side. Ichkeria's titular head Akhmed Zakaev, lives in Britain, whence Russia has been trying unsuccessfully to extradite him, and operates a regular propaganda campaign and other anti-Russian activities from there. On the ground in Chechnya, Doku Umarov, former president of the Ichkerian government-in-exile with which he broke in 2007, conducted a campaign of terror under the aegis of a self-styled Caucasus Emirate. Umarov regularly calls on Muslims in Russia to 'activate jihad, eliminate the enemies of Allah', that is, target Russians everywhere.[22] Messages such as this one were carried in five languages by the Internet mouthpiece of the Chechen Republic of Ichkeria and the Caucasus Emirate, the Kavkaz-Centre (*Kavkaz-tsentr*), which openly advocates an Islamic state for the Caucasus. Founded in 1999 by the former Minister of Information in Chechnya, Movladi Udugov, the website's server moved around before finding its current home in Sweden.[23]

Because he is in hiding, Umarov accomplished this via videos in the Bin Laden style, usually conducted in the Russian language. Every time Umarov's Caucasus Emirate or other militant groups took credit for horrendous acts of terrorism, such as the explosions at the Domodedovo International Airport in Moscow in January 2011, Kadyrov's regime became more palatable to Moscow, and to the Russian public at large. After Moscow proclaimed the second civil war in Chechnya officially over in April 2009 and began removing Russian troops from the republic, Kadyrov initiated stricter Islamic regulation. The Kremlin ignored these breaches of the Constitution.

Russia's harsh anti-separatist, anti-terrorist policy in Chechnya was a serious sore point in Moscow's relations with Europe and the United States throughout the 1990s and early 2000s, and prompted several states to grant asylum to Chechens whom Russia labelled as terrorists. In addition to Britain, the United States (Ilyas Akhmadov, Ichkerian foreign minister) and Sweden (Aslan Adaev, head of *Kavkaz-tsentr*) refused to extradite persons charged with terrorism in Russia. The rationale for providing safe havens for a few such individuals was usually that the acts of violence and destruction were political and therefore not subject to extradition or, where extradition agreements were in place, that the process must be left solely to the judicial system and not to the government. This explanation rang pretty hollow to the victims of the acts in Russia, and demonstrated an unfortunate disconnect between Russian and Western countries in the fight against international terrorism. The disconnect was illustrated further when it took the UNSC until March 2011 before it agreed to include Umarov on its list of international terrorists associated with Al-Qaeda, and until May that year before Washington agreed to the same designation – and offered a five-million-dollar reward for information leading to his apprehension.[24]

More violence spread when tales circulated that Chechnya and Ingushetia might unite, as they had been in the Soviet Union. Ingushetia had separated formally from the Chechen-Ingush Autonomous Republic in 1992, a time of widespread civil conflict throughout the Caucasus – leaving several important territorial and resource issues unsettled, at least as far as the neighbouring republics were concerned. Although these rumours were denied vehemently, especially on the smaller Ingush side, territorial tension between the two republics caused Medvedev concern throughout his term of office. Cross-border raids by Kadyrov's forces claiming to be in search of rebels exacerbated the tensions.

Other territorial disputes and inter-ethnic hatreds compounded the troubles in the North Caucasus. For example, credit for orchestrating a September 2010 suicide bombing in Vladikavkaz, capital city of North Ossetia, in which more than 50 people were killed or wounded, was claimed by an Ingush militant leader who said that he was fighting to regain areas of North Ossetia that once had been Ingush. Because the Ossets are mostly Christian, the Ingush leader called these areas 'occupied Muslim land'. In their turn, large gangs of young Ossets attacked Ingush villages in North Ossetia. The memory of Ingush involvement in the atrocity at Beslan in September 2004, where 380 people were killed, 186 of them children, was still bitterly felt in North Ossetia.

Militant leader Shamil Basaev, terrorist campaigner and battle commander during the first two Chechen wars, once remarked that committing terrorist acts in Russia was easy, because they were 'cheap', i.e., local officials were very susceptible to bribes. Atrocities such as the one at Beslan compelled Putin in 2004 to eliminate the right of local populations to elect their governors. He believed with considerable justification that local loyalties, corruption and collusion had smoothed the way for the terrorist band to travel by truck through multiple military and law enforcement checkpoints into Beslan and take over the school where the children were excitedly attending opening day. It was in connection with Beslan that Basaev claimed that low-level Russian officials were easily bought. He also took credit for the assassination of then-President of Chechnya, Akhmad Kadyrov, Ramzan's father.[25]

The North Caucasus turned out to be far more than Chechnya in terms of violence. As Chechnya grew relatively pacified, Ingushetia and Dagestan became centres of unceasing violent acts. As the years went by, militants and ethnic nationalists in Kabardino-Balkaria also contributed to the overall pattern of belligerence. Officials and law enforcement officers were targets in Nalchik, the latter republic's capital; arms caches were found almost everywhere, traffic police were objects of drive-by shootings, and railway lines were subjected to bombs. Attacks on police facilities and personnel, and military retaliation to these assaults were the most common specific acts. The situation was so grave by the winter of 2011 that the head of the republic since 2005, and UR member, Arsen Kanokov, requested Moscow's support for a local anti-militant armed unit of the type formed in Dagestan in 2009. He also asked Medvedev to provide armed protection for officials in the republic.[26]

Publically, Moscow blamed international Islamicists for these egregious acts, but the causes were broader than that. In fact, the urge to independence and even the militant Islamic force that drove events in Chechnya were often less the engines of aggression than ethnic nationalism, tribal conflict, vendetta, old and new territorial disputes, and competition between organized crime gangs in the other areas. Extraordinarily high unemployment rates compounded the situation. That is not to say that religion-driven suicide bombers were not active outside Chechnya in the North Caucasus – they were.

Political stability, of sorts, made Chechnya a catchment for huge amounts of reconstruction aid from Moscow and infrastructure building. A perceived 'black hole' for Russian money generated anger among Russians as the years went by, especially after reports suggested that Kadyrov was living a life of luxury on the backs of Russian taxpayers.[27]

One of Medvedev's solutions to the anarchy in the North Caucasus was to change governors in Ingushetia, nominating a former Colonel in the Soviet airborne forces, Yunus-Bek Yevkurov, as governor in the fall of 2008. Yevkurov's predecessor Murat Ziazikov and the regional parliament had insisted for years that everything was under control and that outsiders were responsible for all the violence, in spite of considerable evidence to the contrary. More than 2,000 MVD troops deployed to Ingushetia in late 2007 were unable to contain the anti-government attacks. The use of 'preventive measures', short for brutality on the part of the law enforcement, had an unintended consequence as relatives of victims swelled the militant ranks.[28] The change in governors did not help ease the violence very much, but did provide Moscow with a far more accurate accounting of what was going on. In 2008, Medvedev paid surprise visits to Dagestan and Ingushetia to discuss the situation with officials on the ground. Promising assistance in fighting crime and terrorism on the one hand, and to kickstart the economy and expand educational opportunities on the other, he urged authorities in both republics to fight corruption and help build the economy themselves. Much assistance was forthcoming over the years in the form of personnel and money, but signs of real progress were not obvious as his term wound down.

It was not until 2009 that the FSB named the Taliban and its links to international terrorism the 'main threat to Russia's security', though individual officials had been saying that for some time. In this case, Col-Gen. Aleksei Sedov, director of the FSB's anti-terrorist service told delegates to a Shanghai Cooperation Organization session in Moscow that the Taliban, Al-Qaeda, Islamic Jihad, Mujahedin Jamaat, and the Islamic Movement of Uzbekistan (and Pakistan) were all operating in Afghanistan and represented great peril to Central Asia and Russia. Given the threat already posed to Russians by the Caucasus Emirate and the regular warnings since 1999 that Al-Qaeda was active in the North Caucasus this statement revealed several things, even though they remained unspoken: Russia's fear of international terrorism was well-founded and its attempts to defeat it were increasingly hapless; Moscow needed NATO and the International Security Assistance Force (ISAF) to win in Afghanistan.

An exclamation mark was added to this dilemma in November 2009, when an explosion on the Nevsky Express killed 27 passengers and wounded many others. A second bomb was found on a neighbouring track and the MVD concluded that these were the tools of experienced terrorists. The high-speed train links Moscow and St. Petersburg and often carries prominent business and political people. Several groups claimed credit for the deed, including Doku Umarov on behalf of his Caucasus Emirate. Eventually more than a dozen people were charged with the crime, most of them Ingush members of a terrorist cell led by an Islamic preacher connected to Umarov's organization. The event sent a chilling message to Russians who saw the explosion as a continuation of the terrible acts of terror epitomized by the tragedy at Beslan. Moreover, it led to a further tightening of security in urban centres and transportation hubs, such as airports and railway facilities.

In the cities, more locations, such as Metro stations, busy squares, or important government buildings, were designated as places where no demonstrations or rallies could be held without very special permission.

In an attempt to trap terrorists before they could act, the Russian Ministry of Communications issued an order in July 2009 that the postal services make all private mail or shipments, and data on both senders and receivers, available to the FSB for inspection on request. Special rooms were allocated in major post office institutions for that purpose. The order sparked protest inside and outside Russia about privacy rights and civil rights, but to no avail. In their defence, proponents of the action cited similar legislation in Germany, France, and especially the US.[29]

In April 2010, Medvedev established a separate permanently active counterterrorism operations group in the North Caucasus Federal District. The Shanghai Cooperation Organization's regional anti-terrorist structure in Tashkent was also upgraded, with Kazakhstan's Jenisbek Jumanbekov in charge. Yet the violence did not abate in the North Caucasus. Shootouts were daily fare in Chechnya, railways were attacked in Dagestan – tracks blown up, grenade launchers fired at trains, and stations raided. In the winter of 2010, Moscow deployed two armoured trains, relics of Soviet days, to the rail systems in Dagestan, Ingushetia, and Chechnya. These carried railway troops and also special devices for removing land mines, and heavy artillery for counter-attack operations.[30] This was war.

Kadyrov's activities in Chechnya may have been ignored in Moscow, but not by PACE. In the summer of 2010 a PACE report on the North Caucasus harshly criticized Kadyrov for abuses of human rights, and at the same time lauded Moscow for its efforts in providing funding for reconstruction in Chechnya. For the first time, the Russian delegation to PACE approved that body's report on the North Caucasus, calling it less biased than earlier ones.

Federal forces also had some notable successes in 2010, capturing the military emir of the Caucasus Emirate and emir of the Ingush Jamaat (Assembly) Magas and, later in the year, killing the rebel emir of Kabardino-Balkaria, Amzor Astemirov. Emir Magas (Ali Taziyev) was probably one of the organizers of the Beslan atrocity. Astemirov had chaired the Caucasus Emirate's Sharia court. Several middle-level rebel leaders also were 'neutralized', giving Moscow cause to proclaim the approach of victory in the war against terror in the North Caucasus – very prematurely.

It was in 2010 as well that Zakaev resigned his unofficial post as Ichkerian leader-in-exile and named Khuseyn Gakaev his successor. Because he was leader of a radical group on the ground in Chechnya, recently split from Doku Umarov's Caucasus Emirate, observers anticipated that Gakaev would be more effective than Zakaev, who had been living in London since 2002. Moscow was pleased to see the Islamicist militants divided, but worried that the intensity of terrorist activities was about to be upgraded.

Almost immediately the Kremlin's concerns were proven well founded. Chechnya was rocked by a suicide assault on parliament buildings in Grozny. Four radical Islamicists exploded bombs at the gates and tried to rush several building, including the office of the speaker. All of the attackers were killed, as were at least three policemen. There were about 20 other people injured (reported numbers varied), most of them civilians. Gakaev took credit for orchestrating the attack, timing it to take place while the Russian Minister of the Interior Rashid Nurgaliev was in the building.[31] Nurgaliev was not injured and rumours circulated that the attack was arranged by Gakaev solely to make his mark, knowing that it would fail.

The list of such acts in the North Caucasus is too long to account for here, yet one should note that they spread to Kabardino-Balkaria, North Ossetia, and the Stavropol Krai. Making it plain that they believed terrorism in the North Caucasus was a threat to national security, Putin encouraged special measures in retaliation, and Medvedev broadened the target by insisting that corruption was part of the problem and linked separatism, Islamicism, and organized crime (domestic and international) to the wave of violent acts.[32] Arrests of individuals connected to the Ichkerian Republic and the more virulent Caucasus Emirate in Poland (Zakaev), Belgium, Holland, and Germany over a period of several months in the fall of 2010 lent credence to the Tandem's claims that the North Caucasus was a wellspring for far more than an anti-Russia jihad. Russia's call for extradition went unheeded and Zakaev was freed in Poland, but others were kept in custody in Europe on various charges.

Terrorism was by no means confined to the North Caucasus. Muscovites were the victims on 1 March 2010, when two female suicide bombers blew up themselves and as many as 40 others in two separate Moscow metro stations. Over 100 people were hurt in addition to the violent deaths, and Umarov warned that more was coming. Nearly a year later, on 24 January 2011, the huge explosion set off by a suicide bomber in Moscow's busiest airport, Domodedovo, marked the apogee of violence during Medvedev's presidency. The blast killed 35 people and wounded at least 180 others. Foreign leaders immediately condemned the attack and many foreign pundits seized the moment to blame it on Putin's 'iron fist' tactics in the Caucasus. Russian commentators took the opposite view and called for even tougher measures, though some conceded that widespread unemployment, poverty, gangsterism, corruption, inter-ethnic, inter-religious, and some anti-Russian animosities in the North Caucasus must also be redressed. Polls conducted a few weeks later showed that up to 80 per cent of Russians feared terrorism, even as Medvedev urged security forces to make a 'maximum effort' in their fight against the scourge. He was especially anxious that they work to dissuade youth groups who are 'trapped by criminals' and duped into various forms of xenophobia. In this approach, he looked beyond Putin's simpler call for more direct police and military action to stem the tide by seeking root causes.[33]

On the practical side, President Medvedev demanded a thorough investigation and called for an increase in security for all major events in Russia and in all major exit and entry points. Airport officials and security personnel were held accountable for breaches in security and at least six were fired. Apparently there was another blast in Moscow at the same time, but it was set off prematurely. Corruption was blamed once again for facilitating such acts.

Two weeks after the Domodedovo attack, a taped message from Doku Umarov vowed that Russia would face a 'year of tears' in 2011 and that he had 50 to 60 suicide bombers prepared to strike anywhere in the country.[34] Few observers, and neither North Caucasus presidential envoy Khloponin nor

Kadyrov, believed Umarov capable of managing the Domodedovo bombing and assumed that he was taking advantage of the incident to gain support for his leadership ambitions in the North Caucasus against Gakaev.[35] Presumably it was Domodedovo that finally persuaded the UNSC to include Umarov on its list of international terrorists. Towards the end of March, forces directed by the Russian Anti-Terrorist Commission launched an air attack on a terrorist training camp in southern Ingushetia, killing 17 suspects and capturing two brothers who were believed to have participated in the airport bombing. There was some uncertainty that these were the guilty parties, but the retaliation was extensive and cheered on by frustrated and frightened Russians, some of whom were retaliating against Caucasus-looking citizens in Moscow and elsewhere in Russia.

In the meantime, Islamic extremists, nationalists, crime gangs, and vendetta-driven families slaughtered each other with impunity in Kabardino-Balkaria. The primary targets of violent acts, however, were still law enforcement personnel and government officials. In that republic, new targets included tourist hotels and minivans carrying tourists. In February, for example, a minivan was fired on and three Russian tourists were killed, and a huge car bomb was found close to a hotel in Terskol. The fact that Medvedev had ordered the construction of five resorts in the region, plus a new ski resort at Krasnaya Polyana made the area an especially ripe target as Russia began preparing for the Winter Olympics scheduled for Sochi in 2014.

There was an apparent shift in targets in Russia itself, as an explosion took place close to the FSB Academy in Moscow on 9 March and two further explosions, minutes apart, came in an apartment block owned by the FSB in northern Moscow two days later. A Chechen militant group claimed responsibility for the blast near the Academy. There were other major acts of terrorism in Eurasia, including a bomb blast at the busiest Metro station in Minsk, capital city of Belarus. The explosion on 11 April killed 12 and wounded more than 150 others, breaking the pattern of relative stability and safety in that city.

Although most Russian officials and media expressed gratification over the death on 1 May 2011 of Osama bin Laden in an operation by US Special Forces in Pakistan, no one assumed that the situation in the North Caucasus and elsewhere in Russia would be ameliorated. Indeed, FSB Director Aleksandr Bortnikov informed the government in June that special services and law enforcement had prevented over 30 terrorist or subversive acts in the year since June 2010, and a month after that the MVD announced that there were 170 recorded terrorist acts in Russia during the first half of 2011. About 200 militants and 95 law enforcement personnel were killed during that period. Most of these were in Dagestan.[36]

More significant, perhaps, was documentation from international organizations that confirmed elements of global Jihadism in the North Caucasus. Links to Al-Qaeda and other Islamicist groups were discovered in the person of Chechens, Dagestanis and others who went abroad for 'study', and returned to lead jihadist movements. Many of these were educated in jihadist institutions, often in Pakistan and Saudi Arabia. Expanding Caucasus Emirate cells were discovered in Europe in 2011 and 2012, e.g., in Belgium and the Czech Republic. These are the same 'trainees' who later began to trickle into Syria to participate in the civil conflict there. By the end of Medvedev's mandate Russia's earlier tendency to 'cry wolf' when it came to claims that international terrorists were to blame for the crises in the North Caucasus suddenly became a reality.

* * *

Strengthening the centre at the expense of the regions was a necessary step if the new Russian Federation was to achieve a balanced transition into modern statehood. In this regard the Tandem achieved considerable success.

On the other hand, parts of the periphery remained extremely volatile. The preceding litany of bombs and assassination may seem over the top to some readers, but be assured that events and people named here represent but a tip of the iceberg. The purpose of this last section was both to accentuate the scale of terrorist activity in Russia generally and in the North Caucasus particularly, and to explain the Tandem's emphasis on security as something tangible, rather than the oft-posed charges that Putin especially is simply lusting after power and authority. The political crosscurrents described in the next chapter should be seen both for what proponents say they are and also judged within the context presented here. As Medvedev stepped down, the on-going cancer of terrorism, no matter its multiple causes, carried a doomsday force with it that no amount of centralization seemed capable of withstanding.

Medvedev's record in 'ending' conflict and depression in the North Caucasus and terrorism elsewhere in the country was proven every bit as dismal as Putin's. Here, at least, there were no arguments about splits within the Tandem.

## Notes

1 On this, see David Lane, 'Dynamics of Regional Inequality in the Russian Federation: Circular and Cumulative Causality', *Russian Analytical Digest*, No. 139, 18 November 2013.
2 'Perechen' federal'nykh okrugov', *Rossiiskaia gazeta*, 16 May 2000. See also articles in 'The Political Situation in Russia's Regimes', *Russian Analytical Digest*, No. 67, 9 November 2009.
3 'Polozhenie o polnomochnom predstavitele Prezidenta Rossiiskoi Federatsii v federal'nom okruge', *Rossiiskaia gazeta*, 16 May 2000.
4 On the law on procedures for forming the Federation Council, passed after considerable threats and counter-threats, see *Rossiiskaia gazeta*, 8 August 2000. It can be found in translation in *Russia and Eurasia Documents Annual, 2000*, Vol. I (2001), pp. 33–35.
5 For this subject generally, see John Young, 'What Putin has Wrought. Centralization and the State in Contemporary Russia', in *From Putin to Medvedev. Continuity or Change?* eds. J.L. Black & Michael Johns, Ottawa: Penumbra, 2009, pp. 38–52.

6  For general background, see 'The Political Situation in Russia's Regions', *Russian Analytical Digest*, No. 67, 9 November 2009, and 'Regional Developments', *Russian Analytical Digest*, No. 86, 16 November 2010.

7  RIA Novosti, 21 September 2011.

8  *MID.ru*, 19 January 2010.

9  See Darrell Slider, 'Medvedev and the Governors', *Russian Analytical Digest*, No. 86, 16 November 2010, pp. 2–4.

10  *Kremlin.ru*, 24 August 2009.

11  See, e.g. 'Povernulis' k tsentru peredom, a k Primor'iu zadom. Neprodumannye deistviia vlastei vedut k ekonomicheskoi dezintegratsii Rossii', *Nezavisimaia gazeta*, 12 January 2009. This was an editorial.

12  See, e.g., report by Deputy Minister of Foreign Affairs Aleksei Borodavkin, *MID.ru*, 18 March 2010; V.I. Gotvansky, 'Tikhaia ekspansiia Kitaia', *Nezavisimaia gazeta*, 23 September 2010.

13  *Kremlin.ru*, 9 August 2012. See also Sergei Blagov, 'Russia Creates Far Eastern Development Agency', *Eurasia Daily Monitor*, 1 June 2012.

14  RIA Novosti, 26 April 2012.

15  For general background and analysis, see Glen E. Howard, ed. *Volatile Borderland: Russia and the North Caucasus*, Washington: Jamestown Foundation, 2011, and for the situation within a year of Medvedev's accession to office, 'The North Caucasus Crisis', *Russian Analytical Digest*, No. 70, 21 October 2009.

16  ITAR-TASS, 11 July 2007; Interfax, 13 February 2007.

17  See Patrick Sewell, 'Khan of the Chechens', *Russia Profile*, 2 January 2012, who analyses the meaning of Kadyrov's recent hints that he might soon retire.

18  See a rather frank interview with Kadyrov in *Rossiiskaia gazeta*, 10 July 2007. See also, 'Chechnya and the North Caucasus', *Russian Analytical Digest*, No. 51, 4 December 2008.

19  On Patrushev, see *Russia Profile*, 28 July 2008.

20  On this, see especially Vladimir Putin's Op-Ed, 'Why We Must Act,' *New York Times*, 14 November 1999, and the Russian version, 'Pochemu my dolzhny deistvovat', *Rossiiskaia gazeta*, 16 November 1999. The same issue of *RG* carried a piece titled, 'Dvoinoi standart. Bin Laden gotovit voinu SShA' (Double Standard. Bin Laden Prepares for War Against the USA). This too was ignored by the Western media.

21  Interfax, 2 March 2009. For more detail, see 'A Violent Summer in the North Caucasus', AEI *CriticalThreats.com*, 26 August 2009, and 'Terrorism and the North Caucasus: An Overview', *START*. National Consortium for the Study of Terrorism and Responses to Terrorism, April 2013.

22  See, e.g. *KavkazCenter.com*, 26 January 2010; *KyivPost*, 3 March 2011. See also 'Umarat' vyselili iz Rossii', *Vzgliad. Delovaia gazeta*, 8 February 2010. For background, Mairbek Vatchagaev, 'Umarov Calls on Russian Muslims to Join Jihad', *Eurasia Daily Monitor*, 25 May 2012.

23  For the English-language version, see *KavkazCenter.com*.

24  'U.S. Offers $5M for Umarov', *The Moscow Times*, 27 May 2011.

25  See interview with Basaev posted on *Chechenpress.com* on 14 October 2004, in response to questions posed by the Toronto *Globe and Mail* via e-mail. Basaev was killed in 2006.

26  See *Kommersant*, 22 February 2011; *Kremlin.ru*, 22 February 2011. For general background Valery Dzutsev, 'Russian Leadership Prepares for a Protracted War with the North Caucasus Insurgency', *Eurasia Daily Monitor*, 23 February 2011, and Tom Balmforth, 'Mt. Elbrus' Slippery Slopes', *Russia Profile*, 21 February 2011.

27  On this see the piece by Michael Schwirtz, 'Russian Anger Grows Over Aid to Chechnya', *New York Times*, 30 October 2011.

28 See the detailed piece by Marina Bondarenko, et alia, 'Slaboe zveno vertikal. Murat Ziazikov poteriat kontrol' nad situatsiei v Ingushetii', *Nezavisimaia gazeta*, 10 September 2007.

29 On this, see 'Ot redaktsii: Chuzhie pis'ma', *Vedomosti*, 21 July 2009. In the US, the 'Patriot Act' gives authorities far more leeway than the Russian law related to postal searches.

30 Andrew McGregor, 'Armored Trains Return to the North Caucasus', *Eurasia Daily Monitor*, 23 February 2010.

31 See, e.g. *Moskovskiy komsomolets*, 22 October 2010.

32 Interfax, 19 May 2010,

33 See, e.g. Interfax-AVN, 25 January 2011, Interfax, 14 February 2011. Tom Balmforth, 'Airport Terror', *Russia Profile*, 25 January 2011; Valery Dzutsev, 'Terrorism Cycle Repeats Itself With Another Moscow Bombing', *Eurasia Daily Monitor*, 25 January 2011.

34 On this see Alexandra Odynova, 'Doku Umarov Vows "Year of Terror"', *Moscow Times*, 7 February 2011. For Umarov's claim, *KavkazCenter.com*, 8 February 2011.

35 See long piece in *Svobodnaya pressa*, 15 February 2011.

36 Interfax, 15, 16 June 2011. For numbers, see also *Kavkazskii Uzel, www.kavkaz-uzel.ru*, 12 June 2011.

# 3　The political cockpit

When Dmitry Medvedev took over the reins of the presidency, he enjoyed the luxury of a Federal Assembly that was essentially impotent in so far as challenging him was concerned. The Federation Council was by then dominated by presidential appointees; the State Duma was overwhelmingly United Russia.[1] Other vehicles for political messages, such as the media, had been tamed, though not entirely. Government or compliant interests owned most of Russia's television networking, so TV both spread and complemented the government message; print media remained reasonably free and diverse, no matter that government agencies, interest groups and organized crime harried critical and investigative journalists – sometimes to the extent that journalists were beaten or even murdered. Most political parties and movements issued their own newspapers or broadsheets, and had their own websites. Internet use was beginning to spread widely, bloggers especially. Everyone's voice could be heard, if not so easily as the government's.

One of the odd paradoxes of post-Soviet Russia-watching is that a clear majority of Russians approved the very same adjustments to their political process that the West tended to condemn. It seemed that, from 1999 onward, every time the Russian president acted to bring order and stability to a near anarchic political and economic system, Western critics cried foul, charging him with authoritarianism or even totalitarianism, while Russians heaved sighs of relief. Surveys regularly demonstrated that Russian citizens much preferred stability and personal wellbeing to progress on democratic and civil rights (see Appendix, Table A.1). Those who remembered personally, or knew of, the 'liberal' days of Yeltsin, when the communist- and nationalist-dominated Duma obstructed the executive at every turn, the economy and media were controlled by uncontrollable oligarchs, and the Federation was riven by civil strife, corrupt and recalcitrant leadership in the small republics, and myriad acts of terrorism, had no problem with centralization and authoritarianism – at least in 2008. Many Russians also remembered the complete lack of political and civil freedoms under the Soviet regime, so they started their historical explanations, if often only intuitively, from a larger and longer context than did many Western and some Russian critics of the regime. This would change somewhat over the next four years, especially as Russia's growing middle class gained more political confidence.

We have seen that the political structure of Russia went through some dramatic adjustments in the four years preceding Medvedev's ascent to office. The introduction of Federal Districts, the abolition of popular election for governors, and reform of the Federation Council were always explained as means to strengthen the state. Thinking, presumably, that centre-periphery relations had stabilized, Medvedev amended the practice of presidential gubernatorial appointments by allowing the largest party in the region to nominate a candidate for the president to consider, and ensuring that the successful candidate would have to answer to local legislatures to a greater degree than they had previously. Among other things, this adjustment broadened the agendas of political parties, forcing them to become more national in approach and organization if they wished to achieve office.

The election of 2007 demonstrated that there were ample political parties in the field, though some of them were emasculated by changes instituted by Putin. Since the election was Russia's first to be based exclusively on party lists and because of the high ceiling of seven per cent of the votes to win seats Medvedev's legislature was made up of a mere four parties. Only the communists, with 57 seats, could be seen as an anti-government fraction in the House (see Table 0.1).

The new rules that shaped the election were themselves experimental, and it was clear early on that further changes could be in the works. It is fair to add that Medvedev worked hard in his four years to move the political landscape towards a more democratic system, sometimes in spite of, and sometimes together with, Putin. His small steps towards liberalization of the political scene will be featured here, all of which should be defined in contrast to earlier Soviet and Yeltsinite practices, and not in relation to standards espoused (if not always practiced) by critics from abroad.

The emergence of the Tandem made it obvious that, whereas the Constitution of 1993 demarcated the distribution of powers between Russia's executive and legislative branches, the line remained blurred in practice. The fact that elections to the Duma and to the Presidency both took place every four years, and very nearly coincided in terms of campaign schedules was a further complication. Some would say that the absence of a vice-presidency, which made the prime minister the next in line to the president was another barrier to smooth governance – though it provided the Tandem with some logic.

The important thing for Medvedev was that the political arena was relatively calm in 2008. His easy victory in the election and Putin's switch to the office of Prime Minister ensured that the Tandem would never have to deal with openly hostile splits between the executive and legislative branches of government of the type that existed during the entire first decade of post-Soviet Russia. The traditional official opposition, the Communist Party and the LDPR, and the strange mix of 'liberal' politicians outside the Duma provided no real challenge to the government.

*Table 3.1*  Results of the election to the State Duma, 4 December 2011

| Party | % of votes | No. of votes | Seats |
|---|---|---|---|
| United (One) Russia | 49.32 | 32,379,135 | 238 |
| Communist Party of Russia | 19.19 | 12,599,507 | 92 |
| A Just (Fair) Russia | 13.24 | 8,695,522 | 64 |
| Liberal Democratic Party of Russia | 11.67 | 7,664,570 | 56 |
| Yabloko | 3.43 | 2,252,403 | 0 |
| Patriots of Russia | 0.97 | 639,617 | 0 |
| Right Cause | 0.60 | 392,806 | 0 |

Over the next few years, meaningful opposition came from individuals, political and social movements, bloggers, and, in spite of claims to the contrary, a relatively activist print media. Generally, however, the critics so often lionized by Western punditry commanded little support among Russians, at least until close to the end of Medvedev's term. As a group they seemed permanently fragmented and incoherent; as individuals they were perceived as self-aggrandising and counter-productive. In a milieu where poll after poll confirmed that Russians distrusted liberal democracy of the 1990s type, and preferred to get on with their lives, the liberal opposition had little chance of success (see Table 3.1).

As Medvedev's first term got underway there were still allegations of mass violations during the 2007 Duma election circulating angrily about, and some curiosity about how the Duma would function with Putin as head of government. To achieve his objectives, Putin would have to monitor his cabinet ministers closely and shake the 315-deputy United Russia party out of its self-satisfied lethargy. The UR had already shuffled down to three informal political clubs among its deputies, one to deal with economics, the others to handle social issues and patriotism. These clubs tended to work hand-in-hand with the Tandem and usually had little reason to pay attention to proposals offered by other parties in the House.

A bone was thrown to the smaller registered parties in July in the form of a bill to increase financing for political parties supported by more than three per cent of voters in the 2007 election, i.e., from five to 20 rubles per vote – an expensive proposition for the federal budget. The amount of money an individual might donate to a political party was also raised in the bill, from 1 million rubles to a little over 4 million. The law was scheduled to come into effect as of 1 January 2009, well before the 2011 election.[2] The law passed easily, perhaps because the UR would benefit from it the most.

A week after that bill whisked through the Duma, Medvedev met with the leaders of parliamentary parties: Speaker of the State Duma Boris Gryzlov (UR), Zyuganov, Zhirinovsky, and Speaker of the Federation Council Sergei Mironov (A Just Russia). Here he laid out what he wanted from them – with anti-corruption legislation on the top of his list. They all came with prepared statements on what they wanted in return. The meeting was held *in camera* and comments made by attendees later suggest that the session went very well for everyone except Zhirinovsky who complained that his concerns – likely on foreign policy – were not addressed. The group even went fishing together afterwards.[3]

As we have seen, political propositions in the president's first annual address to the Federal Assembly towards the end of the year included extending the State Duma term to five years, and that of the president to six years. He also proposed that the government report annually to the State Duma on matters set by the parliament. After the Communist Party and Yabloko opposed bills extending the presidential term, the latter party (with no deputies in the House) set up a rotating one-deputy picket protest line outside the Duma. This was a sign of things to come: politicians turning more and more directly to the public to have their dissenting voices heard.

## The legislature

### *The ruling party*

United Russia's 11th Party Congress, which met in St. Petersburg in November 2009, accentuated the different approaches used by President Medvedev and Prime Minister Putin. Putin spoke at great length about the UR's need to lead economic reform, and Medvedev urged the party to modernize and halt its all-too-obvious practice of manipulating election results. Both men chastised the audience (600 delegates and some 2,000 guests) for seeking power without obligation: Putin warned against members using the party as an 'elite, prestige club'; Medvedev complained that 'United Russia will be able to make changes only to the extent that it can change itself'.[4] He noted that some regional authorities show signs of 'retrograde mentality and reduce political activity to intrigue and games', and called on the party to get rid of such people. Medvedev supported proposed amendments to the UR's Charter to make it compulsory for party candidates to participate in political debate during elections 'at all levels'. The Tandem lectured as a team at the Congress, yet they clearly differed in the degree to which they trusted members of the UR to use their political strength wisely and to lead Russia out of its current difficulties.

A potentially important political event for Russia came on 22 January 2010, the day for which President Medvedev scheduled a State Council session with one subject on the agenda – Russia's political system. His hope for the meeting was that it would produce some guidelines for a major overhaul of the system to help in the modernization project. In his opening address to the Council, which for the first time included leaders of all seven major political parties, Medvedev congratulated them all equally for their assistance in building Russia's political system. He went on to urge them to strengthen party organizations in the regions and implied that United Russia's overwhelming presence at the regional and municipal levels was not a good thing, because it tended to obscure natural and important regional differences. In this connection, Medvedev cautioned that Russia could never go back to a system like the one prevalent during the Soviet period; instead, in the 'foreseeable future, quite soon, we will have a modern political system of which we can all be proud'.[5] No specifics were forthcoming.

With the advantage of hindsight, one could say that this pep talk was before its time. Other than the minor tweaks to the system noted above, little of substance was accomplished on the political front before the Tandem was forced into action by the events of December 2011.

As it happened, the Russian population began to take politics into its own hands already in mid-2009, and this practice accelerated in 2010. Demonstrators in Moscow and elsewhere in Russia called for Putin's resignation in protest of the new laws restricting demonstrations and rallies. Because Article 31 of the Constitution grants all Russian citizens 'the right to assemble peacefully, without weapons, and to hold mass meetings, rallies, demonstrations, marches and pickets' the first such demonstration took place on Triumfalnaia Ploshchad (Triumphal Square) on 31 July 2009 and continued on the 31st of every month that had one. These rallies in support of the right to assemble were called Strategy-31. Up to 100 activists present were arrested at the event on 31 January 2010, among them the NBP's Limonov, Solidarnost's Nemtsov, Other Russia's Kasparov, and Memorial's Oleg Orlov. In Kaliningrad, where up to 12,000 people took to the streets, the demonstrations were licensed and there were no arrests. The people there protested higher export duties and transportation taxes, and were organized mainly by an unusual mixture of Communists and Liberal Democratic Party members, along with a few Solidarnost figures.[6]

At least one American analyst interpreted the Strategy-31 as analogous to the US civil rights movement in its early stages, but given the wide disparity of purpose among the political names involved in the Russian movement the analogy seems weak.[7] At any rate, these and other demonstrations tested Medvedev, not because his government was the target of harsh words from Russian citizens, but rather because he recognized that they had the right to complain in that manner. Both he and his aide Surkov had already noted that the political system had to change. A prominent editor picked up on this quandary: the system must be protected from fascists, organized crime, or terrorists, to be sure, he wrote, but Russia's protesters are marching under slogans in defence of the Constitution.[8] Medvedev's call for his governors to encourage multi-party systems in the regions was a good start, the writer concluded, for the existing opposition must earn legitimacy by winning seats across the country at lower levels first.

In his turn, Medvedev vetoed a law passed by the State Duma that would have placed stiffer restrictions on the right of Russians to protest, and on 7 May 2010 he signed into law an amendment guaranteeing equal access to regional media for all parties in the State Duma. He may have been buoyed by yet another survey that reported fully 72 per cent of respondents preferring order to democracy – only 16 per cent opted for the reverse. 'Order' was defined as political and economic stability (41%), social guarantees for the poor (29%), followed by peace, rule of law, and the means to exercise one's rights. Young, well educated, and relatively well-off people, i.e., the growing middle class, favoured the concept of 'democracy' narrowly interpreted.[9]

So did Medvedev. On 9 September he told a large audience of academics, politicians and economists at a Global Policy Forum in Yaroslavl that parliamentary democracy would prove a 'catastrophe' for Russia. He referred to the chaos in Kyrgyzstan, where, Medvedev believed, parliamentary democracy was the source of two major upheavals in recent years.[10] The message was that centralization and presidential democracy were safer in times of transition.

Reminding his audience of the turmoil and poverty that accompanied parliamentary democracy in Russia during the Yeltsin years (when 'democracy became a swear word'), Medvedev concluded that political change leading to more democracy would come sooner, rather than later, but still only gradually. This was classic Putin-speak. Interestingly, another poll conducted in late August showed a clear rise in Medvedev's 'trust' factor from the same time in 2009, up two points to 71 per cent, and a drop in the 'do not trust' results, to 21 per cent from 24. Only 8 per cent believed that he could not 'cope with the tasks set' (see Appendix, Tables A.2 and A.3).[11]

While all this apparent popular support boded well for Medvedev and Putin, they and the ruling party hierarchy failed to notice that, whereas the quietly emerging middle class was generally averse to extremes and wanted calmness, it was equally opposed to obviously corrupt and oppressive governance.[12] The election of 2011 would trigger those latter sensibilities.

Members of the opposition were not impressed with the president's squishy stance on political change. They took the opportunity of Luzhkov's dismissal to charge United Russia with electoral fraud in the Moscow City Duma election of October 2009. The LDPR launched five lawsuits with the Moscow City Court on 30 September, and A Just Russia followed with litigation the next day. They claimed to have new documents proving that the election was fixed. Soon afterwards Luzhkov, one of the co-founders of United Russia, announced that he would now start up his own political movement. He didn't.

With Luzhkov gone, Moscow city officials allowed demonstrators to use Triumfalnaia Ploshchad for protest rallies. As a result, over 1,000 persons gathered in the square on 31 October 2010 with authorization and the rally proceeded without major incident. A fringe group led by Limonov rallied there as well without permission, and some 28 of them were detained overnight. Similar protests were conducted in several other cities.

### The Communists

In contrast to the LDPR and A Just Russia, parties that usually supported the Tandem on major issues, the Communists consistently opposed the government in the Duma. The party with by far by the longest tradition of political organization, its members worked hard to maintain their status as the lead opposition. Long time CPRF leader Zyuganov continued to march at the head of demonstrations in protest of the 2007 elections and lead public rallies against rising prices, at which demonstrators carried posters in praise of his leadership.[13] Zyuganov's perseverance seems to have paid off, for the 17 per cent cast in his favour during the March presidential elections was generally considered a triumph for the Party. Buoyed by its 'success', the Communists continued to challenge the legitimacy of the parliamentary election in courts, in vain. The CPRF was the only party in the Duma to vote against Putin as Medvedev's nominee for prime minister.

In April Zyuganov introduced a revised Party Program, the first since 1995. It called for socialist-based development for Russia, 'popular resistance to the forcible restoration of capitalism in the country', and nationalization of the country's natural resources and means of production. The CPRF's links to the past were not forgotten, as Zyuganov told reporters that his party's founding document was still the Marx-Engels *Communist Manifesto* of 1848. On the party's agenda were plans to restore the Soviet of People's Deputies and 'crack down on russophobia, americanization, historical vandalism, and the cult of profiteering, violence, pervasive egoism and individualism'.[14] Quite an ambition!

The 13th Party Congress, at which Zyuganov went so far as to hint that a revolution was possible, adopted the Program in November. The Program may well have provided a consistency and unity to the party that no other political organization could claim, but it did not help very much as far as the electorate was concerned. The Communist Party fared poorly in the regions in October, earning no representation in any of the five components of the Federation where elections were held. Although Zyuganov had re-established a Komsomol (Communist Youth League)[15] organization a few years previously and a youth faction was slowly growing, the party still seemed to be preaching mostly to the converted and so posed no threat to either the UR or Medvedev.

Trying to take advantage of the various forms of social discontent, the Communist Party organized big events on Red Square and elsewhere to commemorate the 130th anniversary of Stalin's birthday, and won a victory of sorts when a new General School textbook on Russian history proclaimed Stalin a great manager, the victor over Nazism, and an organizer of Russian greatness, with no mention of his crimes. The text was an indirect by-product of a project set in place by Medvedev in May when he created a presidential commission 'to counteract attempts to falsify history that undermine the interests of Russia'.[16]

The apparent cleansing of Stalin's brutal regime failed to provide any obvious advantages for the CPRF at the ballot box, perhaps because Prime Minister Putin had already co-opted Soviet history for his rhetorical forays. The CPRF was embarrassed further in May 2009 when Komsomol head

Konstantin Zhukov was elected chair of the newly formed Communists of Russia, an organization that hoped to consolidate all left-wing groups in Russia, and labelled Zyuganov's party 'revisionist' and 'conciliatory' – fighting words for Marxist-Leninists. But Zhukov wasn't done. Expressing respect for rank-and-file communist party members he called their leaders 'morally mutated pseudo-chieftains'.[17] Zhukov's disenchantment was shaped by the fact that the CPRF tried to remove him in favour of one Yuri Afonin. Zyuganov's earlier success with Komsomol, which had claimed 40,000 members in 2009, was not going well.

In the face of an increasing rehabilitation of Stalin as a great national leader, a project driven by both the far right and far left, President Medvedev's speech on Russia's day of Remembrance for the Victims of Political Repression (30 October 2009) was refreshing, and a break from Putin's ambivalent depiction of the role of Stalin in Soviet history. Medvedev was unequivocal, calling Stalin's crimes 'one of the greatest tragedies in the history of Russia'. When he spoke of the enormous achievement of defeating Nazism, Medvedev credited the Russian people for the victory, not Stalin.[18]

## Voices outside the legislature

### The liberal opposition

Traditional parties without seats in the Duma found themselves striving to find a raison-d'être that would eventually get them back in. The once prominent proponent of Western style capitalism, the Union of Right Forces (SPS), seemed always to be mired in divisive struggles. Founded as an electoral bloc to oppose the communists and nationalists for the 1999 Duma election, it was shaped by reformers from the 1990s, Anatoly Chubais, Yegor Gaidar, and Boris Nemtsov. The last of these to be active in politics, Nemtsov, left the party in 2008 after criticism from within the ranks and joined Garri Kasparov and the Solidarnost movement. The rumour was that he intended, again, to focus on creating a new liberal party as Kasparov's following faltered. The SPS went through further changes in June when its next-to-be-ousted leader, Nikita Belykh, defected to Kasparov's newly-formed United Democratic movement. Four months later the SPS disbanded altogether, its remnants merging with the smaller Democratic Party (Andrei Bogdanov) and Civil Force (Mikhail Barshchevsky) to form a pro-government business party. In November, the new group adopted the name Right Cause, with indirect blessing from Kremlin officials, who hoped that the new political bloc would splinter the liberal opposition even further. It appeared that disarray in the liberal/left camp had become institutionalized.

In June Grigory Yavlinsky finally gave up leadership of Yabloko, of which he was co-founder in 1993.[19] Sergei Mitrokhin replaced him. In October, the leftist Agrarian Party merged with United Russia, while more or less at the same time the Party of Social Justice joined A Just Russia, already an amalgam of seven or eight small parties, including Motherland (*Rodina*). It seemed, therefore, that the policy of raising to seven per cent the minimum number of votes needed for parties to earn seats in the State Duma was working, if its purpose was to force fringe and even some established parties to merge to form larger and potentially more stable political entities.

On the less traditional side, even before Medvedev was elected, a split among followers of the All-Russian Civic Congress saw internationally-known Garri Kasparov lose even more of what little support he had in Russia. Co-chairs Lyudmila Alekseeva (Helsinki Group) and Georgy Satarov (INDEM Foundation) left their posts at the Congress over disagreements with Kasparov.[20] Whereas his status as a star of the Western media – which invariably refers to him as 'former world chess champion' as if that were some kind of political legitimization – changed very little, the Russian public and other liberal groups remained much less impressed with Kasparov. They saw his publicity-seeking antics as mere showboating. For example, in December 2008 Kasparov's Other Russia once again applied to hold a protest in Triumfalnaia Ploshchad, one of Moscow busiest intersections. The request was turned down and other sites were offered as alternatives. With the usual full turnout of media, Kasparov led a small demonstration into Triumfalnaia Ploshchad anyway and was detained by police, which is precisely what he had hoped for. Although few Russians cared, the incident was reported widely in the West, but with less than the usual feigned outrage.[21]

Belykh was another co-founder in 2008 of the 'liberal' movement called Solidarnost, reminiscent of the successful Polish association of the 1980s. Meetings were conducted in more than 40 locations in Russia to nominate delegates to a founding congress set for 13 December in Moscow. In addition to Belykh, Kasparov, and Nemtsov, Vladimir Milov, Lev Ponomarev (Human Rights Movement), and Ilya Yashin (Yabloko youth wing) were among the organizers of Solidarnost. In December, Medvedev named Belykh governor of the Kirov Region, prompting some cynics to suggest that was merely a way of getting an opponent of the regime out of town. In July, the Party of Social Justice (Aleksei Podberyozkin) merged with A Just Russia. It is no wonder that the majority of Russians evinced little interest in the country's extra-Duma political activity – they would have needed a scorecard to follow the same people moving to and fro from old parties to new parties and organizations to coalitions to newer parties and movements.

### The radical right

The organized political right fared even more poorly than the liberals during the run up to Medvedev's presidency. The darling of right-wing nationalism in the 1990s, Zhirinovsky, went mainstream and supportive of Putin's brand of national consciousness based on Orthodoxy and history, without the aggressively exclusionary approach taken by the radical right. The same could be said of Motherland (*Rodina*), a party that won over nine per cent of the votes cast in the 2003 Duma elections, but then splintered into various factions. One of its leading personalities, Dmitry Rogozin, went on to take up important posts with the government.[22] The radical right opposition field was then left to the leader of the National Bolshevik Party (NBP), Limonov, whose party is banned as extremist.

Even after a particularly radical clique of the NBP broke away to form the National Bolshevik Front in 2006, Limonov was not able to have his party registered. He responded by urging a union of both left and right in opposition to the government, but there weren't many takers. Undeterred, the NBP continued to act as if it were an officially authorized political party, taking part in street demonstrations and joining with both fringe and mainstream activist groups whenever it suited its agenda.[23]

Another such group, the Movement Against Illegal Immigration (DPNI), was challenged by the judicial system in the summer of 2008 when its leader, Aleksandr Potkin (aka Aleksandr Belov), was charged with inciting ethnic hatred. The charges against Limonov and Potkin represented the first faltering attempts in Medvedev's term to stem a growing xenophobia in Russia. Reports from the MVD revealed increased numbers of racist murders and beatings, especially in St. Petersburg. In the summer of 2008, Moscow's Human Rights Bureau claimed that there were about 70,000 skinheads and members of radical nationalist organization in Russia.[24] The extent to which this circumstance was due to the existence of nationalist political parties, youth unemployment, organized crime and drug syndicates, or even the patriotic tone employed regularly by the prime minister's office is not clear, but it is important that Medvedev just as regularly spoke against nationalistic extremes.

Later in Medvedev's term, radical nationalists formed a Committee for National Salvation. Though they maintained that their purpose was to challenge Putin's All-Russia People's Front and ensure democracy in the elections, the fact that co-founders included Limonov, Mikhail Delyagin (*Rodina*), and Sergei Udaltsov (Left Front), all radicals in their own right, made their claims a little suspect. Russian ethnic nationalism reached a peak of sorts on Russia's official National Unity Day, 4 November 2011, when nationalists rallied in a number of cities for the *Russky marsh* (Russian March). Thousands of teenagers, mostly young men, used the Nazi salute and yelled such slogans as 'Russia for Russian!' and 'Migrants today, occupiers tomorrow!'

In Moscow Dmitry Demushkin, head of the Slavic Union, an ultranationalist organization banned in 2010, led a group called *Russkiye* (The Russians) whose members shouted anti-Caucasus slogans and called for unity among 'football fans, skinheads, and national socialists'.[25] Police lined the streets and for the most part kept the peace. Another radical right wing Moscow gang styling itself the Shield of Moscow (*Shchit Moskvy*) conducted raids on market stalls and dormitories where migrants resided, checked their papers and turned illegals over to the police. Often enough these raids saw violence abetted by police acquiescence. Leader of the Shield of Moscow,

Aleksei Khudyakov, was associated with the Young Russia (*Rossiia Molodaia*) movement and with certain football (soccer) hooligan events.

Outbursts such as these had been building up for some time. Political rallies and demonstrations became the order of the day during the winter of 2009, as United Russia organized demonstrations in favour of the government, while the CPRF and others organized demonstrations against the government. Calls for Putin's resignation were heard for the first time since 2004, when rallies protesting the social benefits legislation were widespread.[26] Young people on both sides caused some violence, and the police were ruthless in rounding up agitators.

## The government

Facing vocal opposition outside the Duma, the government's first inclination was to blame civil rights groups, extremists, and even foreign agents who, the MVD proclaimed in January 2009, were preparing to disrupt and gain control of forthcoming municipal elections. As the years went on the *siloviki* and Putin grew more adamant in their belief that foreign agents were behind the protesters and hinted at a 'colour' revolution conspiracy in the making. This was a hard notion for Medvedev to dispel.

Later in Medvedev's second year, as the consequences of global recession began to show up in Russia, the notion of 'managed democracy' came under attack even in the mainstream press. An editorial in *Nezavisimaia gazeta*, for example, accused the UR-dominated Duma of covering up ministry inefficiencies because they were afraid of the Tandem's 'reaction to criticism'. A parliamentary report analysing the consequences of the government's anticrisis program was so careful not to offend the country's 'two tsars' that no changes were contemplated. Because the Duma failed in its part of the management, the editorialist continued, the entire value of managed democracy was undermined and a 'nagging suspicion that soon there will be no one left to manage the democracy' was growing.[27] Not surprisingly, the CPRF took up this theme more aggressively later in the year and accused the 'ruling team' of being 'no less a threat to the security of Russia than NATO'.[28] None of the opposition groups offered reasonable solutions to the crises at which they constantly pointed their fingers.

Nevertheless, in contrast to Putin, Medvedev made an effort early on to provide opponents with opportunities to express their opinions directly to him. He granted interviews to opposition newspapers, such as *Novaia gazeta*, met with INSOR representatives, and presided over meetings of various civil and human rights councils. Although the political arena calmed down somewhat over the next year and a half, unrest always simmered close to the surface. Towards the end of Medvedev's presidency the pot would finally bubble over, abetted by dissatisfaction on the part of the middle class who, persuaded by Medvedev that the political climate had changed, discovered that it hadn't.

Before that, however, the unrest passed almost unnoticed by the Tandem and their advisers. Perhaps they were lulled into a political stupor by surveys conducted in the winter of 2009 that disclosed that over half (52%) of Russians still trusted their political system. These somewhat surprising results flew in the face of Yabloko's claim that the government was using 'Bolshevik' and 'Stalinist' methods to retain power. The pattern of general confidence continued, though the percentage of believers was smaller in the large urban centres.[29]

Yabloko wasn't the only party to charge the UR with Bolshevik tendencies. The one-time Putin advocate Gorbachev now accused the ruling party of being worse than the communists in the way they held on to power. Gorbachev announced in May that the founding congress of his Independent Democratic Party of Russia would convene in September. An initiative committee was in place already, he said, adding that the new 'independent social-democratic party' would create a program designed to combat the current economic crisis. A group of economists supported Gorbachev. Although he is not generally categorized as a 'liberal,' many of Gorbachev's (few) supporters were, so this initiative splintered liberal support in Russia still further.

United Russia's overwhelming victory in local elections conducted across the country in October 2009 also evoked concerns for the nature of Russia's democracy. Every opposition party accused local authorities of intervention directly in some regions and of manipulating TV in support of the ruling party. Lawsuits were threatened, but few observers believed that any reverses would be made in United Russia's victories, among them 32 of the 35 seats in Moscow's duma. Opposition parties in the Duma showed their resentment at the federal level by walking out. With Medvedev's mediation, most of the parties were back in the House within a few days, but the poisonous political atmosphere persisted.

In the meantime, Medvedev continued to speak the reform game. In March, he submitted a bill to the Duma that would grant all parties with seats in the House equal access to state-owned media, and in April he signed another law allowing at least some representation in the Duma for parties that receive between five and seven per cent of the vote. At a pre-Women's Day (8 March) speech, he urged women to get more involved in politics, especially at the 'higher levels' of government.[30] In the fall the president offered more minor concessions, including a State Duma commission with equal representation from all Duma fractions for the purpose of compiling a dossier on reported violations of the elections law.[31]

In the final week of 2009, Medvedev told an audience at a ceremony where he handed out state awards that the country's political system definitely needed change.[32] It wasn't clear what changes he had in mind, though he spoke at the same time in favour of greater democracy for the regions. Prime Minister Putin was more direct in his approach to unrest, and improved his popularity in labour circles by stepping in to resolve several looming strikes to the advantage of workers and harshly criticizing certain oligarchs by name;

for example, Oleg Deripaska. This was a blame-shifting tactic that worked for a while.

Most of the 'liberal' leaders took part in demonstrations, but for the most part it was the Communists who were energized by the social discontent brought on by economic crises. The communists even found a new ally in November 2009 when a Congress of the Federation of Russian Car Owners (FAR) met in Novosibirsk and decided to form a public political movement in association with the local CPRF branch. With broad support in the Far East, FAR had been lobbying against vehicle road taxes since 2006. The organization was successful in forcing the UR to retract a bill raising the base rate for a tax paid annually by car owners. It was that grassroots victory in November 2009 that persuaded the lobby group to register as a political movement. By that time FAR had branches in 28 regions and confronted the UR in cities ranging from St. Petersburg to Vladivostok, though not again very effectively.[33]

None of this proved particularly menacing to the government and, in fact, United Russia won almost everywhere in regional elections conducted in October 2010, placing their people in regional parliaments and city councils in 77 of the components of the Federation. Zhirinovsky, Mironov, and Zyuganov again lodged allegations of massive electoral violations favouring the ruling party, and again failed to win more than few recounts.

## Preparing for the State Duma election

The question of coalitions tended to consume opposition groups when they were not rallying for various causes. Yabloko lost one of its key activists early in the year when Andrei Buzin quit in protest of the decision taken by the party late in 2009 to forbid coalition forming. Party leader Mitrokhin acknowledged that a few other long-time members objected to the policy and might also leave, but he insisted that it had already attracted more members and would allow the party to once again become a serious political player.

Mikhail Kasyanov, now leader of a party named the Russian National Democratic Union (RNDS), took this opportunity to call on other 'democratic' parties to merge, naming specifically Yabloko, Solidarnost, and the United Civil Front as potential co-members.[34] He wanted them to create a joint list of candidates for the Duma election and nominate a common candidate for the presidential election. Mitrokhin declined for Yabloko, accusing Kasyanov of wanting to 'go back to the 1990s'. Other liberal figures, such as Nemtsov, thought the idea sensible enough, but knew very well that when it came to choosing actual candidates and leaders the outward accord would slip away quickly.

In spite of reservations, representatives of four democratic organizations gathered in September to try yet again to form an effective coalition. These included Kasyanov's RNDS and Solidarnost led by Nemtsov and Ilya Yashin. Other groups were represented by Duma Deputy Vladimir Ryzhkov and Sergei Aleksashenko, former managing director of Merrill Lynch's branch in Moscow and of Interros, a Russian private investment firm. Yabloko boycotted the meeting.[35] Organizers called their project the People's Freedom Party for a Russia Without Tyranny and Corruption. Liberal opposition coalition-forming had failed consistently and quickly in the past, so this new attempt to bring disparate groups together was treated with more bemusement than seriousness in Russia's print media and websites. Aside from the normal differences in political opinion, the liberal genre in Russia continued to be plagued by too many generals and too few soldiers.

While the Communists kept to their niche, i.e., emphasis on economic and employment issues, at least one other left-leaning party held a founding congress in February, and selected Sergei Udaltsov leader. Under Udaltsov, the new United Labour Front immediately began to participate in the Strategy-31 rallies. Left wing and patriotic associations combined in this case, thereby adding to the growing cacophony of new social movements and leader-focused political groups.[36]

There were struggling associations on the other side of the political spectrum as well. As the strange mixture of liberals and nationalists that made up the Other Russia movement disintegrated, Limonov fashioned a new opposition party keeping the name Other Russia. With Limonov as leader, the new cluster moved further to the right on the political spectrum than its original amalgam of activists. The tactic enjoyed a brief success, for the official newspaper of the Russian government, *Rossiiskaia gazeta*, was compelled by law to publish the political platform of the re-modelled party, and did so.[37] Limonov's banned National Bolshevik Party also still operated as a private organization.[38]

A less rabid nationalist grouping took shape in September, when the founding congress of a renewed *Rodina* party was held. Academician and Chairman of the Globalization Problems Institute, Mikhail Delyagin, was again its leader. Formerly called 'Motherland: National-Patriotic Union', the party took on the name 'Motherland: Common Sense'. Another resurgent nationalist party was not a new one; rather it was the long-standing Eurasian Movement headed by Aleksandr Dugin, Director of the Centre for Conservative Studies in the Sociology Department, University of Moscow. The Eurasianists grew more vocal in the political arena in 2010, accusing Medvedev among other things of treason by catering too much to the Americans. Dugin, for example, went so far as write that the President relied on Russia's 'ultra-liberals' who advocated a 'pro-American treacherous course, oriented on the surrender of position and helping the Americans hold on to a unipolar world'. Dugin concluded that the only people who actually supported Medvedev were 'enemies of Russia'.[39] Ideologist of a Eurasian Empire dominated by Russia and sometimes accused of fascism, Dugin's philosophy was well over the heads of many of his followers, who nonetheless simplified and deployed his talking points as slogans for action.

The political bickering and jockeying for position escalated during 2011 in anticipation of the December election to the State Duma. During the first week of January, the Ministry of Justice rejected the application for registration submitted by the movement, Russia, Forward!, presumably because its name echoed too closely the title of Medvedev's famous 2009 article. But the most talked-about political event early in the year was the detention of former Deputy Prime Minister Nemtsov at an officially authorized New Year's Eve rally in Moscow. He was detained for 15 days and charged with 'disobeying police instructions' and for leading a demonstration that included double the number of people sanctioned by the city. After a Russian court rejected an appeal lodged by his supporters, his lawyer took it to the European Court of Human Rights in Strasbourg and it became an international sensation. The detention helped him earn vocal support from the West, but not much empathy in Russia. Limonov and Ilya Yashin were arrested during the same event, a Strategy-31 rally, but their cases were overshadowed by the interest in the fluent English-speaking Nemtsov.

In their turn, government supporters began to question the source of Nemtsov's financing, just as they had earlier over funding for Kasparov. In the latter case, remunerations for speeches and other events during visits to the USA were well known. Nemtsov's financial backing was murkier, but his speaking tours in the US and Canada (Columbia University, Institute of Modern Russia, the Economic Club of Canada, and so on) and verbal backing from a number of prominent American politicians, provided him with important opportunities. At least one of his talks to the US-based Institute of Modern Russia was titled 'Putinism is Corruption'.[40] Nemtsov was back in action on 31 January 2011, when he joined about 500 demonstrators in Moscow and shouted for the removal of Putin. This Moscow rally was conducted with permission from the authorities and so went on without major incident, while an unauthorized rally in St. Petersburg saw some 60 people detained. Russian civil rights groups continued to protest in public places and on the Internet. Permits for demonstrations and rallies, which were readily granted in the Fall, were limited again after nationalist gangs sparked violence at several such gatherings.

Everyone knew the demonstration protocols.[41] Pro-Kremlin youth groups and pro-opposition individuals – single protesters do not need a permit – picketed almost daily in January. Since two or more people with pickets may be treated as illegal without a permit, a pro-government demonstrator often immediately paired with an opposition solo to place him or her in jeopardy. Another oft-used tactic: apply for a permit to rally at a site for which the permit is very unlikely to be granted; ignore offered alternative site; rally anyway in unpermitted location; be detained by police; garner publicity. This practice is hardly unique to Russia, but Russia is a country where oppositionists seek international support especially vigorously, and one where foreigners, especially in the West, look upon such opposition most favourably. Kasparov, Nemtsov, and Kasyanov acknowledged this openly. In June 2011, Kasparov was even invited to speak before the US House Committee on Foreign Affairs, where he told US congressmen that Russia was a totalitarian state run by the 'KGB', and that Medvedev was merely 'bait for a trap' set by Putin to dupe people into thinking that he would lead a liberalization movement.[42] Complicating the situation in Russia, of course, are fresh memories of real terrorist acts in the cities, which makes any demonstration potentially dangerous as an exploitable smokescreen.

The use of tactics such as those noted above by no means negates the importance of the causes for which protesters rally, yet they may well have been counter-productive. Russians of all political stripes get their hackles up whenever it appears that foreigners are trying to shape their political – or economic and social – affairs. This is the chance the most vocal extra-Duma political activists took. The point is, public protests against government action, or inaction, were building up well before the controversial end-of-year election in 2011, so the only really surprising development during the post-election outpouring of anger was that it came as a surprise to the apparently out-of-touch authorities.

It was clear by 2011 as well that corruption was going to be an issue for politicians to grapple with or exploit. Articles began appearing in the mainstream press about nepotism on party lists, as current deputies found places for relatives and friends.[43] New movements, such as the pro-Kremlin *Nashi* and the oppositionist People's Freedom Party, made anti-corruption their pet theme, thereby forcing other parties to take up that challenge. Other election-related issues cropped up as well: calls to re-introduce 'Against All' on the ballot and a VTsIOM poll that showed 50 per cent support for quotas to guarantee political positions for women.[44]

The CEC readied itself by re-electing Churov its chairman in March, but not much in the way of overt campaigning began until the Fall. As the electioneering heated up, still sluggishly, in September, PACE agreed to send 40 observers, and the OSCE agreed to send monitors for the elections as well. The OSCE participation was not particularly welcomed, as even Medvedev told journalists that its Office for Democratic Institutions and Human Rights (ODIHR) all too often politicized its reports and applied what he termed 'double standards' in its assessment. The OSCE had refused to monitor the Russian presidential elections of 2008.

At least one hoped-for political change was achieved. In October, the Federation Council adopted a bill lowering to five per cent the minimum percentage of votes to earn seats in the Duma. The bill had been working its way through the system since Medvedev introduced it in June. The five per cent minimum will be in effect for the 2016 Duma election. Leaders of various opposition groups approved, but they complained that the bill came too late, noting that Medvedev already admitted in 2009 that the threshold was too high.

Prime Minister Putin promised further political changes at the Valdai Discussion Club, a gathering of a hundred or so experts from Russia and foreign countries. When the Club met in Kaluga, 7–11 November 2011, Putin was confronted with wide-ranging criticism of the Russian political system, and calmly shrugged it all off. He disagreed with the charge that Russia's current model of governance had run its course, and the expressed assumption that most of Medvedev's decrees were ignored. Putin reminded his audience that no political system was perfect, insisted that the Tandem was in good working order, and that change would come – only gradually and in an evolutionary way. His goal, he insisted, was to strengthen political institutions so as to limit the personalized system that appeared to exist at that time.[45] All in all, his promises of change were very vague.

As interested Russians prepared for the December elections to the Duma, a new women's movement emerged. Called the *Otlichnitsy* (Top Students), it was headed by Olga Kryshtanovskaia, established sociologist and leader of the liberal fraction within the United Russia party, and regular attendee at the Valdai Club. Her expressed intent was to support Putin's people's fronts, get more women elected to the Duma (at the time only about six per cent), and eventually provide a female candidate for the presidency in 2018.

## The election campaign

On 30 August, Medvedev declared the campaign for seats in the State Duma officially open by signing a decree that the election would be held on 4 December. One day prior to that pronouncement he called for a fair election with no nationalist or extremist rhetoric. Simultaneously, the Justice Department announced the names of the eligible parties: United Russia, the CPRF, the LDPR, A Just Russia, Yabloko, Right Cause, and Patriots of Russia. Only these seven parties were authorized to participate in the election campaign.

Smaller parties hoping to earn seats in the Duma rushed to link up with one of the seven contenders; favourite United Russia candidates grabbed onto Putin's coattails by insisting that a vote for them was the same as a vote for Putin as president. Medvedev climbed on that bandwagon himself after the fateful 24 September decision.

Campaign ads and state-sponsored debates filled TV screens in November as the election drew closer. The Communist and other parties complained loudly that they were discriminated against in terms of government-funded publicity, in spite of which Zyuganov, Mironov, Zhirinovsky, and even Yavlinsky appeared regularly on state television in two-or-more-person debates.[46] Neither Putin nor Medvedev took part in any of the debates.

In Sochi, after announcing the election, Medvedev again acknowledged to journalists that Russia's political system needed to be reformed 'gradually but steadily' and that there should be 'adjustments in all political institutions'.[47] His cautionary tone echoed the approach taken by Putin some months earlier when it appeared that Medvedev might be prepared to speed up political change, and then later again at the Valdai gathering. The political scene was defined more clearly thereafter; that is, on 24 September, when Medvedev nominated Putin as the UR's presidential candidate and agreed to allow his own name stand on top of the UR slate of deputies for the Duma.

As the campaign grew in intensity, accusations of cheating flew back and forth from and about all parties, and hundreds of people and groups were charged with violations, resulting in fines and in some cases a few days in jail. Two developments drew wide domestic and foreign media attention. The first came when the CEC banned televised commercials produced by several opposition parties, claiming that they promoted extremism, but no such action was taken against any UR commercial. Russian election laws make it illegal to attack another party on TV, or to promote extremism and hatred for any candidate, party, or bloc.[48] A week before the election, Commissioner Churov banned more video ads from Yabloko, A Just Russia, and the Liberal Democrats, even though the law makes it clear that only the police and prosecutors can ban videos. A second issue to gain attention was an accusation from Golos, the only independent election watchdog in Russia, that NTV reporters were smearing it by accusing it of drawing financial support from the CIA.

During the 24-hour pre-election day period, when by law no campaigning is allowed, the government deployed some 330,000 police and soldiers to maintain security on Election Day. Nearly 700 foreign observers were distributed to serve as monitors, half of them from PACE and the OSCE. Numerous abuses were recorded, and the Golos list of violations was forced off the Internet.

When the dust settled, the UR found itself with 238 seats and the Communist Party with 92. A Just Russia (64) and the Liberal Democratic Party (56) fell far behind. Yabloko earned well over two million votes, but had too low a percentage of votes to win seats. Patriots of Russia and Right Cause both had less than one per cent of the votes cast. Polls conducted by VTsIOM and FOM in the months before the election expected the UR to capture fewer votes than it did, though the party's numbers strengthened as election day grew nigh, and most exit polls mirrored the final results fairly accurately.

## The aftermath

The post-election, as expected, saw complaints and praise from all the usual suspects. Unexpected, however, was the level of public condemnation of the process. About 1,000 people were arrested as thousands hit the streets in Moscow and St. Petersburg during the first two days after the election, some of them sporting pins that called the UR a 'party of crooks and thieves'. They faced off with members of *Nashi* and the police. A few noted activists, such as Solidarnost Youth Coordinator Ilya Yashin and anti-corruption blogger Aleksei Navalny, were detained and handed 15-day administrative sentences. Facebook pages and websites (e.g., the social networking site Vkontakte), had tens of thousands sign on in support of clean election campaigns. Medvedev, whose prestige probably was hurt the most, at first insisted to journalists that the results were 'good', that the electoral process was fair and went off according to Russian law. He doubted the authenticity of widely circulated videos alleging election violations, and told international monitors that the nature of the Russian political system was not their business, rather they were there solely to judge the elections practices on the ground.[49] Medvedev backtracked a few days later and promised that the charges of fraud would be investigated.[50]

Demonstrations attended by tens of thousands calling for fair elections were held in many Russian cities on Saturday, 10 December. In Moscow's Bolotnaia Ploshchad, the turnout ranged anywhere from 25,000 to 85,000, depending on whether one believed reports by the police, the media, or the protesters themselves. In contrast to earlier rallies led mostly by vocal but fringe politicians, senior figures from all mainstream parties other than the UR attended the protest rallies. More importantly, citizens from all levels of society gathered spontaneously to demand an end to electoral fraud. In general these later events passed without incidents of violence or interference from the police, who were present in abundance. In an unusual turnabout, the events – anti-Putin banners and all – were covered extensively in the Russian print media and, after a week of hesitation, by state-controlled television.[51] Schedules for more all-national protest rallies and marches were circulated widely.

Gorbachev's description of the election as one featuring 'falsification and rigging' was indicative of a new political reality in Russia.[52] Medvedev and Putin's auras of invincibility were now sullied, due both to their 24 September announcement and to their initial unwillingness in December to admit the obvious, i.e., the attempts at intimidation, bribery, falsification, and ballot box stuffing by representatives of their own party. Medvedev and Putin may not have been directly responsible for any of these activities, and probably wanted them not to happen, but they happened on their watch and in their names.

The tendency of Western leaders and politicians to judge and lecture did not help. In response to complaints about the election from US Secretary of State Hillary Clinton, Russian officials suggested she look to the election process in her own country before complaining about Russia's. The fact that Clinton offered the opinion that Russia's elections were neither free nor fair at an OSCE ministerial meeting in Vilnius made her charges particularly unpalatable to Moscow. The Russian Ministry of Foreign Affairs called Clinton's remarks 'unacceptable' and advised the US to refrain from 'unfriendly invectives' and 'out-dated stereotypes'.[53]

Looking both for a way out and a way to appeal to Russia's nationalists, Putin blamed Clinton for some of the unrest, charging that she 'set the tone for oppositionist activists'.[54] In this, he was partially correct; there is no doubt that many of the most vocal opponents of the government relied on the foreign media to give them an international and even a domestic audience. In that regard, Garri Kasperov's statement to the US House Committee on Foreign Affairs in June 2011 that America distributed up to $70 million in 2010 to NGOs in Russia, a few of which were closely involved in Russian politics, came back to haunt Russian self-proclaimed democrats.[55] True or not, the assumption that this assertion was fact would have political and social consequences during the next presidency.

Of the 700 or so foreign monitors, it was no surprise that the CIS delegates said that there was nothing wrong with the elections, but so did monitors from the Czech Republic, Bulgaria, Britain, and Israel. In the latter case, Israeli Foreign Minister Avigdor Lieberman told Putin on 7 December that his country's monitors judged the elections fair and democratic. So too did international observers from the European Parliament.[56]

On the other hand, Director of the OSCE's ODIHR Janez Lenarcic called the election 'unfair' and replete with 'serious flaws'.[57] Therefore, much of the subsequent praise and condemnation depended at least somewhat on whose anecdotes were taken most seriously. Comments from foreign monitors, however, had little to do with the deep-rooted dissatisfaction shown by thousands of (mostly) urban citizens in Russia.

A report delivered by the Investigative Committee to the government on 21 December 2011 said that there were 2091 administrative violations recorded during the election campaign, the largest number of them in Moscow (462). Further complaints were under investigation in nine of Russia's regions.[58] Oppositionists believed that there were many more abuses than the ones the CEC and the MVD were willing to expose.[59]

Lost in the uproar, temporarily, was the fact that the elections revealed that there was now strident dissent in Russia from a previously mute middle class. This rudderless stratum of society clearly was in need of constructive leadership. But opinion polls conducted outside the scope of the parliamentary election showed that most political activists were still mistrusted by the majority of Russians. Constantly visible protesters such as Kasparov, Limonov, Yashin, and Udaltsov all could expect one per cent or less from voters if they were candidates for president. Better-known regular demonstrators, Kasyanov, Nemtsov, and Ryzhkov might get as high as two per cent of voter support.[60] In short, none of them are likely sources for constructive grassroots leadership.

Even while their leaders demonstrated along with other groups in the post-election furor and loudly alleged violations of electoral law, the Duma's official opposition parties stood together to condemn a European Parliament resolution demanding that Russia hold new 'free and fair' elections.[61] Seeking someone to blame, Zyuganov and Zhirinovsky echoed Putin in suggesting that the demonstrations in Bolotnaia Ploshchad were abetted by US special services trying to encourage a 'colour' revolution in Russia.[62] Cold War rhetoric came easily to the surface from the old guard – so did the habit of circling the wagons when external forces were perceived as threatening.

Interestingly, Putin remained the target of loud demonstrations both for and against him, while Medvedev was left almost untouched by public demonstrations. This simple fact revealed where the population believed power resided and exposed Medvedev's growing invisibility. Yabloko conducted a large and violence-free rally on Bolotnaia Ploshchad on 17 December; the

Communists led another one the next day, both in preparation for a big rally set for the following week. One of two separate rallies 'For Fair Elections' in St. Petersburg was led by A Just Russia, Yabloko and the Liberal-Democrats, the other by Kasparov's United Civil Front, part of the umbrella coalition Other Russia. In Moscow an authorized demonstration attracted between 29,000 (police estimate) and 120,000 (Ryzhkov estimate), with all the usual faces appearing in interviews for the domestic and foreign press, including: Yavlinsky, Prokhorov, Nemtsov, Yevgenia Chirikova, Kasyanov, and even recently dismissed finance minister, Aleksei Kudrin.

Clearly, political promises were in order. In his address to the Federal Assembly on 22 December, Medvedev introduced the subject cautiously, as follows:

> People have a guaranteed right to express their opinions using all legit-
> imate means but attempts to manipulate Russian citizens, to mislead
> them and incite social discord are unacceptable. We will not let instigators
> and extremists involve society in their reckless activities, and we will not
> allow foreign interference in our internal affairs.
>
> Russia needs democracy, not chaos; it needs faith in the future and
> justice. The fact that society is changing and people are increasingly
> expressing their views and making legitimate demands on the authorities
> are a positive sign, a sign of a maturing democracy. In my view, this is a
> positive trend that will benefit our country, just as increased political
> competition, which forces us to work more efficiently and to respond
> more promptly to the problems of millions of Russian families.[63]

He then pledged the package of potential reforms that included the promised restoration of direct elections for regional governors; restoring single-member district elections for Parliament; reducing the minimum membership require-ment for registering new political parties from 40,000 to 500 people; and reducing the number of nominating signatures required for a presidential candidacy from 2 million to 300,000. Prime Minister Putin had already hinted at changes such as these in an earlier post-election interview.

The spontaneous demonstrations in December galvanized organizations created earlier into action, as their faint hopes suddenly seemed attainable. One of these was the People's Freedom Party (PFP – PARNAS) formed in December 2010 by Nemtsov, Kasyanov, Ryzhkov and Vladimir Milov. This body helped with anti-corruption demonstrations in April 2011 and began positioning itself for the parliamentary elections.

The PFP's bid to register for the election was rejected in June by the Ministry of Justice, which said that there were too many 'dead souls', i.e., false names,[64] on the party's registration list and that its documentation was incomplete. Although its leadership began to unravel as so many liberal coali-tions had done in the past, Ryzhkov, Kasyanov, and Nemtsov were re-elected co-chairs on 24 September, the day of Medvedev's fateful decision about the presidency. These self-styled liberal democrats were thus able to bring their organization to bear on the explosive political events of December 2011. But their disparate personal agendas and tendency to flaunt connections abroad were handicaps when it came to making real political gains at home.

On another old political front, an extraordinary congress of the Right Cause, a pro-West party, elected tycoon Mikhail Prokhorov chairman in June 2011. Two days later in a televised meeting with the president, Medvedev assured him that 'centralized power, even in a federal state as complex as Russia, cannot continue forever'.[65] A week after that, Prokhorov told *Kommersant* that he too opposed the centralization of the political system in Russia and that he would someday like to serve as prime minister of the country. At a news conference later in the year, the new leader of Right Cause repeated that he would like to be prime minister, but only if he approved the agenda of whoever was president.

This open ambition sealed Prokhorov's political fate, for his promise fell very short. In mid-September he resigned as leader of Right Cause, leaving the party in shambles. Although he blamed Medvedev's Deputy Chief of Staff Surkov for causing splits in the party because Prokhorov would not follow the Kremlin's instructions, he was himself accused by colleagues of trying to take absolute control of the organization. In the end, it appeared that it was the party that rid itself of Prokhorov, rather than the other way around. The importance of developments such as these is, perhaps, a matter only for political buffs: in discussing Prokhorov's resignation with a small group of law and music students in Moscow a few hours after the event was noted on Russian TV, this author was startled to learn that few of them had ever even heard of him.

As a consequence of the Prokhorov affair, at least partly, several senior members of Right Cause left the party and proclaimed the revival of the Union of Right Forces (SPS), a party that won nearly nine per cent of the votes in 1999, and four per cent in 2003 when Nemtsov was its leader. Because it was too late to run in the 2011 election, the group registered as an NGO with Leonid Gozman as its president.

As the smoke cleared from the politically chaotic post-Duma election in December 2011, pundits began pontificating on the ramifications of what they assumed would be Putin's third presidency with a less supportive Duma than the ones he dealt with previously. Many of the commentators echoed Gorbachev's worries about a 'Brezhnevization' of Russian politics, i.e., stagnation, and predicted the end of reforms initiated in Dmitry Medvedev's name.

Still, 2012 opened with a flurry of political concessions. Medvedev had already warned members of the UR that change was coming whether they liked it or not. 'It didn't begin as a result of some rallies, these are just on the surface, foam if you like. It's a sign of human dissatisfaction', he said. 'It started because the old model which has served our state faithfully, truly and well in the last few years, and we all defended it, has largely been exhausted'.[66] What a change from 2008!

New bills sent to the Duma fulfilled the promises Medvedev made during the post election crisis in December 2011. One bill restored direct elections for regional governors, which Medvedev had insisted in 2009 would not return 'in a hundred years'. He reminded journalists of that remark a year later and added, 'I guess a hundred years was an overstatement'.[67] The bill was submitted to the Duma on 16 January and adopted after its third reading in May. By that time, an amendment was added to the effect that each candidate had to have signed support of 5–10 per cent of elected municipal legislators from at least three-quarters of municipalities in the region. Analysts referred to this criterion as a 'municipal filter', and oppositionists complained that it would give local United Russia an easy means to filter out unwanted candidates. The law also limits the governor's time in office to two consecutive terms.

Other bills included the previously pledged amendments to the Law on Political Parties, noted above, and the restoration of direct single-member district elections for the Duma. Requirements for a minimum number of members in a party's regional branches in at least half of the country's region were abolished as well.[68]

There was some quiet and unacknowledged relief when the ODIHR released its final report, usually the most critical of observer commentaries on Russian elections. The ODIHR report charged Russia with not providing proper conditions for fair elections and claimed that officials interfered with the process at all levels. But the criticism was considerably more muted than expected in some circles; for example, the authorities responsible for the election were given high marks for their professionalism and for following procedures. Blame for unfairness was levelled at local officials, over which central authorities may have had little control. Central Electoral Chief Churov claimed to appreciate the report.

The old guard extra-Duma opponents of the government were just as unprepared for the events of December 2011 as the country's leadership. With the exception perhaps of Navalny and Udaltsov, most of the big-name activists found their comfortable niches in the protest movement becoming irrelevant. They now had to seek new forums to survive politically. A group of 16 cultural leaders – writers, scientists, and rock stars – established a League of Voters in January 2012 with the support of oppositionist politicians. The Internet-based League proposed to get the vote out and sustain the campaign for fair elections.[69] Three days after the presidential election, a League memorandum circulated at a news conference held at the Interfax head office complained 'against the backdrop of large-scale violations, the League considers it impossible for itself to recognize the results of the 2012 Russian presidential election.' It termed the election an 'insult to civil society'. Putin's response was typical: 'at first they acknowledged that your humble servant had got more than 50 per cent, but now they've had a think, picked their noses and decided that no, for them that's too high'.[70]

Earlier, as parties in the Duma gathered support for their presidential candidates, non-parliamentary political movements adjusted in expectation of political reforms. Mikhail Gorbachev joined the League of Voters in February, just as Medvedev introduced another bill to the Duma that would maintain the proportional representation system while guaranteeing representation for each of 225 newly formed electoral districts, of approximate equal population numbers. Medvedev's own future remained in doubt for many observers.[71] An object of scorn as a result of his sudden acquiescence in the campaign for the presidency and an obvious lame duck in his final months as president, Medvedev's record of dedication in office during the previous four years was quickly forgotten by the public at large.

As the prime minister, Medvedev will be handicapped because he never created a strong political team; rather he tended to rely on Putin's people and was not able to build up a popularity base separate from his status as part of the Tandem. A sign of things to come appeared in late February when previously consistent Medvedev supporter Igor Yurgens, Chairman of the Institute for Contemporary Development, member of the Russian Public Chamber, and critic of the *siloviki*, told journalists that former finance minister Kudrin would make a better prime minister. Ironically, the volume of outcries against Putin and the elites may have saved Medvedev's political career, even if only as the moderating 'good cop' part of the team.

Activists of all stripes continued to rally and demonstrate, demanding a new Duma election even as the presidential election took place. For example, the day before that event, individuals from Yabloko, the Voyna Art Group, and three members of an all-female punk group, Pussy Riot, were detained in Moscow and charged with hooliganism for throwing items at the CEC office. Members of the latter group later sang anti-Putin songs at Christ the Saviour Church in Moscow, consciously challenging Orthodoxy with their clothing, language, and choice of a particularly sacred part of the Church. They earned little support from Muscovites, were bitterly condemned by the Orthodox Church, and eventually were charged with 'hooliganism motivated by religious hatred'.

Even though their trial and sentencing were soon to be a phenomenon of Putin's new presidency, the Pussy Riot case warrants some attention here because it reflects on emerging new divisions in Russian society – many of them driven by Medvedev's lip-service to, and likely sincere advocacy of, democratic rights. When the courts sentenced three of the women to two years in prison, outrage spread quickly through democratic and feminist organizations around the world. Russian opinions were mixed: the majority wanted them punished, but thought the sentences were too harsh.[72] Putin and Medvedev both spoke out for leniency, but the Church hierarchy and the courts were adamant. The faithful urged even stiffer penalties against such sacrilege. Nationalist 'defenders of the faith' patrols began cruising the streets to protect various religious sites from vandals. It is true that the Pussy Riot trial served as an incentive for wide ranging acts of desecration of Orthodox Churches, but the vigilante approach against such acts worried many citizens. The *Svyataia Rus* (Holy Rus) movement was the main organizer of the patrols.

For many critics of the government, the Pussy Riot incident served as one of increasing signals that the Orthodox Church was prepared to serve as Putin's right arm in bringing order to the country.

On 10 March 2012, PFP-PARNAS rallied with other groups and demanded a new Duma election, and television celebrity Kseniia Sobchak – second daughter of Putin and Medvedev's mentor Anatoly Sobchak – showed herself to be a serious political activist in her own right. A week later 10–20 people were detained in at least two locations in Moscow for demonstrating illegally. They were soon released. The Communists, and also Nemtsov and Udaltsov, called for a rally 'of millions' for 6 May, regularly reminding the media, Russian and foreign, of that date – that is, the anniversary of mass arrests on Bolotnaia Ploshchad in 2011. They and Ryzhkov appeared often on talk shows, even for state-run TV channels, as did footage of anti-government rallies and demonstrations, thereby undermining some of the accusations of sweeping censorship with which they repeatedly charged the government and Putin.

With lower numbers needed for party registration, new political blocs began to take shape in March. Prokhorov mulled the creation of a 'right-wing liberal' party, and Udaltsov talked of merging his Radical Left Front with the communists. In March as well, after successful appeals to the European Court of Human Rights and the Russian Supreme Court, the Republican Party of Russia regained the registration status taken away from it by the Ministry of Justice in 2007. Party leader Ryzhkov said that the party would compete in the next election.[73]

Another source of competition to the government emerged in April when Kudrin announced the formation of a 37-member Committee of Initiatives, made up of political analysts, journalists, academicians, and politicians. Their stated purpose was to offer unsolicited advice to the government, the State Duma, and parties outside the Duma. Among the Committee members was the Governor of the Kirov Oblast, Nikita Belykh, TV personality Vladimir Pozner, and Medvedev's former colleague Yurgens.

In 2012, the political arena was shaping up far differently than it had four years earlier. The stability guaranteed by the Tandem in 2008 was no longer seen by everyone as more important than change. The next political term was going to feel much more tension between the Putinites and their opponents than Medvedev faced four years earlier. The protagonists outside the Duma seemed still unprepared to resolve their greatest handicap, however. Broad divisions between communists, nationalists, and liberals remained intact, and each of these was sub-divided further. Personality politics, i.e., emphasis on particular leaders rather than ideas, also continued to bedevil opposition politics.

Changes made to Russia's laws on political parties greatly abetted this tension. Among other things, new political entities began springing up like mushrooms after a rainstorm when the regulation on the number of members needed for registration was dropped dramatically. By June 2012, for example, with the registration of an organizing committee for a party called Civil Platform – Prokhorov's re-entry into the political arena – the Minister of Justice said it was the 173rd party officially registered.[74] The political scorecard was growing exponentially.

Since Putin had set the membership bar very high precisely to compel parties to merge and form larger, longer-lasting political parties and eliminate most of the dozens of small, single-issue, and personality-focused parties, it is ironic that in this matter the political system had come full circle. But perhaps that was now the point – the more small parties there are, the more divided the opponents of United Russia will be.

\* \* \*

About a year after his term of office was completed Medvedev, by then prime minister, answered a question from European journalists about the state of democracy and civil rights in Russia: 'we are taking the first strides to developing our political system and democratic institutions in this country. We cannot be judged by the highest standards or from the top positions. I suggest this test: if, 100 years from now, there are still problems left, then something must have gone wrong during these years. But I have always said and I am saying now: our democratic institutions are only 20 years old. And one has to bear in mind that many traditions did not exist at all. This is what makes the Russian state different and that must be taken into account'.[75] In this instance he chastised Western commentators and leaders for their constant preaching to Russians and apparent inability or unwillingness to recognize that 'Rome wasn't built in a day'.

## Notes

1  The only full study to date of United Russia is Sean P. Roberts, *Putin's United Russia Party*, London: Routledge, 2013, who sees the UR as a 'virtual hegemony' because of the way in which the Russian electoral system has evolved – so far.
2  Interfax, 5 July 2008. At that time, one million rubles equalled about $31,000.
3  See Elina Bilevskaia, 'Prezidentskaia forel'. Dmitrii Medvedev provel neformal'-nuiu vstrechy s liderami parlamentskikh partii', *Nezavisimaia gazeta*, 14 July 2008.
4  *Kremlin.ru*, 21 November 2009; *premier.ru*, 20 November 2009.
5  *Kremlin.ru*, 22 January 2010.
6  For commentary on the implications of Strategy 31, see Tom Balmforth, 'Fractured Opposition', *Russia Profile*, 1 April 2010.
7  For the comparison with the US civil rights movement, see Leon Aron, 'Putin is Already Dead', *Foreign Policy*, 7 February 2012. For a Russia labour perspective, see 'Protest ne udalsia', *Trud*, 31 January 2010, and, of course, the websites of various Russian political movements.
8  'Test dlia pobeditelia', *Nezavisimaia gazeta*, 16 February 2010.
9  RIA Novosti, 12 April 2010. VTsIOM conducted the poll on 9–11 January, though it was not published until April, with 1,600 respondents in 41 regions of Russia.
10  *Kremlin.ru*, 10 September 2010.

11 Interfax, 20 September 2010. The survey was conducted over 20–23 August by the Levada Center, among 1,600 Russian citizens in 130 population centers.

12 For general observations on Russia's emerging middle class overlapping the period of Medvedev's presidency, see Jason Bush, 'Russia: How Long Can the Fun Last?' *Business Week*, 7 December 2006, and Donald N. Jensen, 'In Search of Russia's Middle Class', Institute of Modern Russia (imrussia.org), 29 May 2013.

13 Press-sluzhba TsK KPRF, 26 January 2008.

14 'Programma partii,' *kprf.ru*.

15 Originally All-Union Leninist Communist League of Youth, for aspiring party members aged 14–28, the Komsomol had some 19 million members in its Soviet heyday, but faded in the late 1980s and was disbanded in 1991.

16 *Kremlin.ru*, 19 May 2009. Medvedev signed the edict on 15 May. On this generally, see the somewhat cynical approach by Pavel Felgenhauer, 'Medvedev Forms a Commission to Protect Russian History', *Eurasia Daily Monitor*, 21 May 2009.

17 ITAR-TASS, 23 May 2009. For an analysis of the two Komsomols, Zhukov's and the CPRF's, see 'The Komsomol(s)', SRAS (School of Russian and Asian Studies, California) *Newsletter*, 30 September 2012. Danye Spencer translated the competing Komsomol platforms for this SRAS piece.

18 On Medvedev's stance relative to Stalin, see Tom Balmforth, 'Repudiated Personality', *Russia Profile*, 3 November 2009.

19 Yabloko is a make-up from the names Yavlinksy, Yuri Boldyrev, and Vladimir Lukin, who founded the party for the purpose of the 1993 election. As a word it means 'apple' in Russian.

20 *Nezavisimaia gazeta*, 17 January 2008.

21 Kasparov left Russia in June 2013 for Geneva and said he would not return because he was afraid that Putin's government would set up an 'investigation' against him. His departure did not evoke much sympathy in Russia (see *Nezavisimaia gazeta*, 6 June 2013), but the precedent of a somewhat hazy investigation of Aleksei Navalny then underway would have given him pause.

22 For Rogozin's career profile, see Christopher Laug, compiler, 'Prominent Right-Wing Figures in Russia', *Russian Analytical Digest*, No.135, 5 August 2013, p. 8.

23 On this generally, see Maria Nozhenko, *Right-Wing Nationalism in Russia. A By-Product of Electoral Competition or a Political Agenda for the Future?* The Finnish Institute of International Affairs (FIIA), Briefing Paper No. 135, September 2013.

24 Interfax, 23 August 2008.

25 For details see *SOVA-Center.ru*, *passim*. The SOVA Center is a Moscow-based NGO that provides regular updates on racism, extremism, and xenophobia in Russia. See also Pavel Felgenhauer, 'The Kremlin Struggles to Control Ethnic Hatred', *Eurasia Daily Monitor*, 27 October 2011. 'The Russians' refer to a large group with regional branches, 'Etnopoliticheskoe obed'edinenie – Russkiye', with a number of activist leaders besides Demushkin, e.g., Vladimir Yermolaev.

26 On the social benefits crisis, see Elena Maltseva, 'Reforming Russia's Social Benefits System: Challenges, Dynamics, and Implications', in *From Putin to Medvedev. Continuity or Change?* (2009), pp. 53–73.

27 'Eshche raz o predelakh poleznosti upravliaemi democratii', *Nezavisimaia gazeta*, 23 February 2009. See also *Nezavisimaia gazeta*, 21 January 2009.

28 See Pavel Ivanov, 'Kommunisty pokusilis' na tandem', *Nezavisimaia gazeta*, 2 November 2009.

29 Interfax, 28 February 2009; ITAR-TASS, 2 February 2009. See also Table A.3.

30 *Kremlin.ru*, 6 March 2009.

31 ITAR-TASS, 6 October 2009.

32  *Kremin.ru*, 28 December 2009.
33  See Alexander Bratsky, 'Triumphant Car Owners Push for Greater Political Influence', *The St. Petersburg Times*, 27 November 2009.
34  *Kommersant*, 10 February 2010.
35  *Moscow News*, 15 September 2010. Aleksashenko had been a deputy minister of finance in Yeltsin's government.
36  On this founding congress and others, see *Novaia gazeta*, 27 October 2010.
37  *Rossiiskaia gazeta*, 20 July 2010.
38  'Eduard Limonov reshi sozdat' partii 'Drugaia Rossiia', *Nezavisimaia gazeta*, 30 June 2010; Rosa Tsvetkova, 'Limonov gotov stat' glamurnym politikom', *Nezavisimaia gazeta*, 12 July 2010.
39  Dugin's article was cited and summarized in *Novaia gazeta* (online), 27 October 2010. See also 'Russia and Right-Wing Extremism', *Russian Analytical Digest*, No. 135, 5 August 2013.
40  For the Institute's list of speakers and panels, see *imrussia.org*.
41  For a detailed overview, see Graeme B. Robertson, *The Politics of Protest in Hybrid Regimes. Managing Dissent in Russia,* Cambridge UP, UK, 2011.
42  'Kasparov to Congress: Take a Courageous Stand', *theotherrussia.org*, 19 June 2011.
43  See, e.g., *Nezavisimaia gazeta*, 22 February 2011.
44  Interfax, 21 July 2011; RIA Novosti, 13 July 2011; *Nezavisimaia gazeta*, 30 September 2011; RIA Novosti, 16 April 2011.
45  Valdai mezhdunarodnyi diskussionnyi klub (valdaiclub.com), 12 November 2011; RIA Novosti, 11 & 12 November 2011. The Valdai Club, in its 8th year in 2011, is sponsored by RIA Novosti.
46  Russian electoral laws provide equal time on state-run TV for registered political parties, candidates and blocs, in slots allocated by drawing lots. Russian Federation Law, 'On the Election of Deputies of the State Duma of the Federal Assembly of the Russian Federation' (December 2002), Article 60 (1) 'Free air time … on equal terms.'
47  Interfax, 1 September 2011, 31 August 2011.
48  Russian Federation Law, 'On the Election … ' Article 56 (6); Article 60 (16, 64).
49  Interfax, 6 December 2011.
50  For an overall view of the election, see Joan DeBardeleben, 'The 2011–12 Russian Elections. The Next Chapter in Russia's Post-Communist Transition?' in *Russia After 2012*, pp. 3–18.
51  See, e.g. 'Further Examples of Election Law Violations in Russia's Regions Reported', Interfax, 4 December 2011; Rosemary Griffin, et al, 'Revolution in White', *Russia Profile*, 11 December 2011; Andrei Zolotov, Jr., 'Protest Movement Looks Set to Continue, while Becoming Increasingly Anti-Putin', *Russia Profile*, 25 December 2011; Pavel K. Baev, 'Russia Reluctantly Enters into a New Revolution', *Eurasia Daily Monitor*, 3 January 2012.
52  Interfax, 7 December 2011.
53  *MID.ru*, 8 December 2011.
54  Interfax, 7 December 2011.
55  See Kasparov's speech to the US House Committee on Foreign Affairs in June 2011, *theotherrussia.org*, 19 June 2011. The official amount was $9 million.
56  Interfax, 5 December 2011; *ynetnews.com*, 8 December 2011; *Haaretz.com*, 7 December 2011.
57  Interfax, 6 December 2011.
58  *Kremlin.ru*, 21 December 2011.
59  *Kommersant*, 25 December 2011.
60  VTsIOM surveys, Interfax, 7 December 2011.
61  Interfax, 14 December 2011.

62  *Kommersant,* 14 December 2011.
63  'Poslanie Prezidenta Federal'nomy Sobraniiu', *Rossiiskaia gazeta,* 23 December 2011.
64  'Dead Souls' (*Mertvyie dushi*), from a novel with that title by famous Russian author Nikolai Gogol, published in 1842.
65  *Kremlin.ru,* 27 June 2011.
66  *Kremlin.ru,* 16 December 2011.
67  *Kremlin.ru,* 24 December 2010. For the earlier statement, NEWSru.com, 15 September 2009.
68  Interfax, 23 December 2011.
69  *Moscow Times,* 19 January 2012.
70  Interfax, 7 March 2012; *Russia Today* (TD), 7 March 2012; RFE/RL, 7 March 2012. For a study that challenges the Western conception of Russia as a country without a 'civil society', see Elena Chebankova, *Civil Society in Putin's Russia,* London: Routledge, 2013.
71  *Sobesednik* online, 1 February 2012; *Argumenty nedeli,* No 3, 26 January 2012. See also Ivan Rodin, 'Medvedev ostaetsia reformatorom. No ego otgovarivaiut i ot prem'erstva, i ot vitse-prezidentstva', *Nezavisimaia gazeta,* 7 February 2012.
72  Editorial. 'Pussy Riot: Crime and Unfair Punishment. Opinion', *The Moscow Times,* 19 August 2012. After the final two members of Pussy Riot were amnestied from prison in December 2013 and became overnight folk heroines in the West—winning awards, appearing on TV with Stephen Colbert and on stage with Madonna, and lauded by politicians – the never high level of sympathy for them among Russians dropped precipitously.
73  RIA-Novosti, 16 March 2012.
74  Interfax, 5 June 2012. See also Grigorii Golosov, 'Dmitry Medvedev's Party Reform', *Russian Analytical Digest,* No. 115, 20 June 2012, pp. 5–10.
75  'Interv'iu Dmitriia Medvedeva evropeiskim SMI', *Premier.gov.ru,* 21 March 2013. See also 'Medvedev Says Russia's Democracy Needs 100 Years to Develop', *The Moscow Times,* 21 March 2013.

# 4    Economic considerations

1 Ruble = US$.040 in 2008

1 Ruble = US$.032 in 2013

Because the years 2005 and 2006 were ones of economic resurgence in Russia, due primarily to the acceleration upwards of oil and gas price after 1999, the economic situation inherited by Medvedev was relatively rosy.[1] Russia's foreign debts were paid up, or on schedule, and the 'catastrophe of 2003' long foreseen by Russian and other economists never materialized. Income from the energy sector enabled the government to greatly expand the Stabilization Fund created in 2004 and allowed it to earn revenue from investment operations set in place in 2006. Subsidized by the equivalent of $9 billion annually, agriculture was flourishing and Russia was again an exporter of grains.

Putin had broken the hold oligarchs had on the economy. Warned by the fates of Gusinsky, Berezovsky, and Khodorkovsky, Russia's billionaires were much more amenable to the government than they had been in the 1990s. In addition to protection promised for cooperation, they realized that their industrial and natural resource complexes would benefit enormously from the government as an ally and stakeholder, and lead to seats on the boards of the so-called National Champions in the economic sector. No longer in control, they still held large pieces of the action. A flat tax of 13 per cent on personal income introduced early in 2001, plus substantial reductions in both corporate profit taxes and payroll taxes, enabled the government to bring in enough revenue to cover expenditures and introduce order to the previously chaotic taxation system. Business and individuals were now both able and more willing to pay up the lesser amounts.[2]

The official beginning on New Year's Day 2008 of the long-awaited Customs Union between Russia, Belarus, and Kazakhstan was promising as well. Finance Ministers signed a final package of documents at the end of the month after a meeting of the Eurasian Economic Community (EurAsEC) Interstate Council. Delegations from Tajikistan, Kyrgyzstan, and Uzbekistan attended and showed interest in joining the Customs Union sometime in the future. In fact, as early as January 2009, the Moscow Carnegie Centre organized a seminar on 'The Eurasian Economic Community: Prospects for Development', at which all participants, unofficially, spoke in support of some future association with the Customs Union. This good start to Medvedev's economic regime was soon to be held up as the global economic crisis brought slowdowns everywhere, but mechanisms were in place to stand Russia well in the future.

## Recession

Even as the global economic recession began creeping from North America to Europe in 2008, Russia's economy continued to flourish. The country had enjoyed an unprecedented run of balanced budgets and revenue surpluses. Its international gold and hard currency reserves stood at about $477.7 billion and by July foreign reserve holdings had grown to $588.3 billion.[3] Amendments adopted in the budget code in 2007 facilitated the transformation of the Stabilization Fund in February 2008 into two separate funds: a Reserve Fund of $125 billion to be invested abroad in low-yield securities with revenue set aside for economic emergencies; and a National Prosperity Fund of $32 billion to invest in riskier higher yield projects, including federal budget expenditures.[4] The two funds were still growing as the global financial crisis set in, and the fate of the fund is a useful signpost for assessing the success or failure of the Tandem's economic policies, for which Medvedev was ultimately responsible.

The energy sector remained the busiest and most volatile of Medvedev's active economic files, sometimes leaving him to complain that his country remained a 'hewer of wood and drawer of water', but he was never able to avoid the fact that the energy sector paid the piper. The energy sector also linked Russia's foreign affairs interests to former Soviet republics in Central Asia, and also to China and the EU via a network of gas and oil pipelines.

It was on this practical side of the Russian economic scene that the Tandem worked most obviously in tandem. Medvedev and Putin bounced around European and Asian capitals pushing the Russian economic agenda. Their negotiations with the other BRICS countries (Brazil, Russia, India, China, South Africa), the Shanghai Cooperation Organization (SCO), the G-8 and G-20, the International Monetary Fund (IMF), and the World Bank were all carefully orchestrated. The activities of the Ministry of Foreign Affairs and Rosoboronexport (weapons sales monopoly) had also to be coordinated closely with the various trade and development ministries. This kind of synchronization is, of course, not unique to Russia, though it is worth noting here that, in the long run, the Tandem and its team were notably successful in their economic endeavours.

Putin and later the new President Medvedev at first insisted that Russia could withstand the global crisis because of its accumulated petro-dollars. It seemed that the Tandem could be right, and that Russia had the resources to repel the onslaught of global economic breakdown. Analysts in Moscow gloated, bizarrely, that since less than two per cent of Russians held mortgages or shares and only 32 per cent of them had bank accounts, the moneylender implosion would not hurt them. The huge Stabilization Fund and hard currency reserves, and the fact that the government had a low foreign debt, were satisfactory cushions, or so the story went. Moreover, Russia's GDP grew 8.3 per cent in the first quarter of 2008, an encouraging fact mitigated by an inflation rate that fluctuated from 7.5 per cent in the first quarter to 11–12 per cent at the end of the year.

This latter complication signalled that Russia would be affected by the global economic crisis after all. The tone changed, and Western financial policymakers were chastised for Russia's problems. During a question and answer session with journalists from G-8 countries in July, Medvedev said that the G-8 needed both reforming and additional members, such as Brazil, India and China – Russia's associates in the BRIC. He complained too about the tendency to use one country and one currency as measuring sticks, and accused the US of 'economic egoism'. This remark set a tone for the rest of the year, and was repeated more subtly in his Annual Address to the Federal Assembly.[5]

The optimists had failed to mention several key drawbacks. Most of Russia's largest employers outside the government had huge corporate debts to Western creditors, about $500 billion in fact. Reliance on commodity export for revenues and employment was easy when energy prices were high, but left the government helpless when prices fell. For example, when the price of a barrel of oil dropped from $147 in July to $86 in October 2008, Russian producers lost about $10 billion monthly. Given that oil accounted for a full third of the government's revenue and up to 60 per cent of its export income, the seriousness of the situation could not be overestimated. By the autumn of Medvedev's first year, foreign investors were fleeing Russia, selling off their Russian shares to pay their own debts elsewhere. Capitalization of large companies fell dramatically (e.g., Gazprom by two-thirds value), oil stock fell by about 60 per cent, several banks went bankrupt, and big projects everywhere in Russia were delayed or shelved altogether.[6]

Huge bailouts were the only answer the administration could come up with. A federal government rescue package of $130 billion took the form of Central Bank (*Bank Rossii*) purchases of shares in Russian companies. Loans were offered by the Central Bank to other banks at 7–10 per cent interest so some private banks lost their accounts to state banks. Although in the end these bailouts saved Russia from further disaster, they also skewed the scorecard of success or failure. The well-connected corporations, above all the National Champions, received most of the help and rumours of corruption and bribery abounded. In addition to the greatly increased unemployment and concomitant social unrest, and the near disappearance of recently launched small businesses, necessary and wide-ranging infrastructure upgrades such as military equipment, roads, rail lines, port and air facilities, and social programs were put on hold for at least the first two years of Medvedev's presidency.

In the late summer of 2008, the Central Bank pumped $14 billion into the market to help save the collapsing ruble. At the time Russian stocks were already spiralling down and the major state-controlled energy companies were losing even more value, some as high as 70 per cent. On 16 September, regulators suspended stock trading on Russia's two main exchanges, and reports suggested that up to $35 billion in foreign currency had fled the country. The Central Bank put the sum at $5 billion, but most analysts inside and outside Russia thought that number much too low.

In response, Medvedev signed a package of laws designed to stabilize Russia's financial markets on 13 October.[7] The government also placed $50 billion in Vneshekonombank (VEB) to help cover requests for loans from various oligarchs. Chairman of the bank's board was Vladimir Putin, who ordered that the loans be granted at five percentage points above the London interbank rate. Thus, the VEB loans could be priced at about 9.5 per cent. Two of Russia's biggest oil companies (LUKoil, Rosneft), its largest food chain, X5 Retail Group, and the world's largest aluminium company, RUSAL, applied for such loans. According to a report released by RosbiznesKonsalting (RBC) in November, Russia had spent to that date some $222 billion on anti-crisis measures.[8]

Shortly after the RBC report came out, Medvedev took the bull by the horns at a G-20 Summit in Washington and called for the reorganization of the 'entire international financial architecture', insisting that the post-war world economic order no longer worked. He proposed that the G-20 form an international commission comprised of 'influential and independent financial gurus', who could recommend resolutions to the crisis. In his opinion standardized international regulations based on legal treaties were a necessary first start. Although he did not say so at that moment, it was clear to observers that he blamed his partners in the G-8 for failing to regulate themselves properly. His appeal was by no means a socialist response to the crisis, as some Western politicians immediately charged; rather it was a request for cooperation, transparency, and 'fairness' in the international economy. Sadly, these are not principles likely to find much fertile ground in international financial circles. The G-20 (not the G-8) 'should become the main coordinator of the world financial system's reform and development', Medvedev concluded.[9] That was not going to happen.

Finance Minister Kudrin announced in late November that the government would tap its huge Reserve Fund for about 1 trillion rubles ($35 billion) to support public spending; that is, infrastructure development (roads, hospitals, education) as promised by then-President Putin in a speech to the State Council in February.[10] On the last day of November, the Central Bank raised interest rates to slow the exodus of foreign capital, as the ruble declined against the euro.

In his annual call-in show, conducted that year during the first week of December, Prime Minister Putin finally acknowledged that Russia was moving towards an economic crisis but expressed confidence that his country would weather the storm. He established an anti-crisis agency on 10 December and named First Deputy Prime Minister Igor Shuvalov its head.

The gloom and doom spread by the global financial crisis notwithstanding, the Bank of Russia announced in the first week of January 2009 that Russia's gold and foreign currency reserves stood at $450.8 billion, and claimed that the country's economy would grow by two per cent during the coming year. His optimism was soon proven premature. In April, Putin announced that the government was planning a three trillion-ruble ($111.5 billion) allocation on stimulus measures that year. About half of that money was built into the budget as emergency spending; the rest came from tax breaks, central bank lending, and other sources.

Back in February 2009, Kudrin told representatives of the British business community in London that his government had already transferred $40 billion to Russia's banks, and was able to maintain a favourable balance of payments because the ruble had weakened by about 40 per cent against the world's main currencies. A large surplus of nearly two trillion rubles accumulated in 2008 also helped.[11]

In March, Kudrin warned that the economic crisis in Russia could last up to three years and that the Reserve Fund had only about two years before it was fully depleted.[12] Soon after that dire prognostication, the text of Russia's anti-crisis plan was published, generating considerable discussion and again some widespread optimism – at least on the part of the government. The plan set out seven basic priorities: fulfil social obligations to the Russian population; focus support on proven effective industries and innovative technology; concentrate on domestic post-crisis development – easing 'dependence on external factors'; accelerate the modernization process; lower bureaucratic obstacles to business; normalize the Russian financial sector (banks and stock market); and use the Central Bank to provide incentives for Russians to invest.[13] No details were offered about ways and means to achieve these goals.

Many experts worried that the plan meant strong support almost exclusively for the large state and private corporations in the energy, mining, and manufacturing sectors, with huge foreign interests and debts, leaving too little for domestic problems. Another massive stimulus package instituted in May was itself a result of reports that Russia's economy had further constricted, unemployment had surged much faster than expected, and inflation had reached double digits. To cover its first budget deficit in nearly a decade, the government planned to spend most of its reserve funds by year's end.

Projections were even bleaker in late spring 2009. Kudrin announced that the Reserve Fund was down to 3.551 trillion rubles ($106.8 billion) and the National Prosperity Fund to 2.869 trillion ($86.3 billion). The ministry also said that GDP was down by 9.5 per cent from January to the end of March.[14] The economy itself shrank by nearly 23 per cent in the first quarter and, clearly, earlier forecasts had to be radically revised. Although at the end of May no new projection was released, Kudrin acknowledged that Russia might have to borrow up to $7 billion abroad in 2010.

Official government optimism rarely flagged publicly, however. According to Deputy Minister of Economics Andrei Klepach, for example, by the end of August 'the recession is generally over, and the economy is moving towards recovery'. He pointed to a slight increase in the GDP in July and a slower rate of decline in the economy than in the previous year.[15] A few weeks later, when the President delivered a brief welcoming speech in St. Petersburg to the 11th Congress of United Russia, he had cause to urge members to help Russia move away from a 'backward commodity-based' economy. In keeping with an eye to change, on 25 November Russia's Central Bank decided to add Canadian dollars to its foreign exchange reserves, cutting its addiction to the US dollar and the euro.

Surveys conducted in the early fall revealed that the public was accepting the government line: 44 per cent said the government was doing what it could; 36 per cent said it wasn't.[16] In fact, the recession was technically over for Russia when, in the third quarter, economic activity grew 0.6 per cent from the previous three months. Still, GDP was 9.4 per cent below the level of a year earlier – a phenomenon caused by the recession, low oil prices, and low gas sales. On the other hand, information released at the end of November claimed that Russia's international reserves, made up of gold, foreign exchange, and other assets were up again to the equivalent of $443.8 billion.[17]

Russia's revenues had rebounded so well by 2011 that a report showed that Russia's holdings of US debt rose dramatically, i.e., by about 1,600 per cent since September 2006. This amounted to a value of some $110 billion, from which Russia collected interest for its Reserve Fund.[18] By that time, Prime Minister Putin was taking credit for Russia's ability to survive the global recession. In his annual report to the State Duma on the government's work the previous year, Putin congratulated himself for a great many economic triumphs, including an ambitious program of weapons modernization. Speaking for four hours, he praised his ministries for bringing Russia out of the global economic crisis and predicted that Russia would become one of the world's top five economies by 2020 – no reference was made to the Tandem.[19]

That is not to say that Medvedev was no longer busy on the economic front. After withstanding the threat of recession, he began looking for new ways to generate revenue. In October 2010, after a full year of discussion, the government released a five-year privatization plan. Among the some 900 firms in which it planned to sell stakes were OAO Rosneft, Russian Railways, Sberbank and other banks, Aeroflot and RusHydro. Moscow hoped to gain about 1.8 trillion rubles ($60 billion) from the projected sales.

In April that year, Russia raised $5.5 billion in its first international bond issue since the 1998 financial crisis. The five-year Eurobond with a volume of $2 billion and a separate ten-year bond with a volume of $3.5 billion were almost immediately oversubscribed. This issue was seen as a major change in Moscow's economic policy, as was Russia's ability to borrow up to $18 billion from international markets. Later that year, Russia initiated its first overseas sale of local-currency debt by placing some $3 billion of ruble bonds on the market in September.

The privatization project announced in 2010 was launched in 2011 with the sale of a ten per cent stake in Russia's second largest bank, VTB Bank, for approximately $3.3 billion.[20] The project called for the sale of $10 billion in state assets every year until 2015. The government issued $50 billion worth of ruble-denominated bonds as well. Reports that global fund managers endorsing Russian security and asset markets reached 88 per cent in January were very encouraging for the Kremlin. The same managers had been pulling money out of the emerging-market equity funds and investing it in developed-market equity funds. In this regard, Russia was the only BRIC country receiving new money in the winter of 2011.

## World Trade Organization and the Customs Union

There were other important economic breakthroughs during Medvedev's presidency. One of these was Russia's admission to the World Trade Organization (WTO) – 18 years after it first applied in 1993. The path to entry had been neither easy nor direct, and had always been shaped by political considerations. Shortly before both presidents left office, George W. Bush supported Russian membership during a meeting with Putin in Sochi and the Vice President of the European Commission, Gunter Verheugen, waxed enthusiastic about Russia's entry during a visit to Russia's Far East a few weeks later. Given that such promises were a regular part of the Russian–West discourse since Bill Clinton first promised to support Russia's bid in 1997, Moscow commentators were distrustful of them.[21]

The war in Georgia in August 2008 (see Chapter Five) saw Russia's chances in the WTO suddenly dim, as US and European politicians threatened to keep them out forever, and even expel Moscow from the G-8. Prime Minister Putin responded with 'who cares' comments and the anti-WTO lobby within Russia, especially in the agricultural sector, grew more strident.[22] Since every WTO member holds a veto over new admissions, Moscow was likely to be blackballed by Tbilisi and/or the Baltic States and Poland, from which threats of veto had come earlier. In the Spring of 2009, the Kremlin told WTO officials that it would consider accession only as part of the Russia-Belarus-Kazakhstan Customs Union, which it said had evolved precisely because Russia was tired of making concession after concession to the WTO only to again be rejected. Left unsaid was the fact that the recession had made the rule-bound WTO less attractive to a government reliant on commodity export anyway.[23]

In the end, self-interests prevailed and the saga of Russia's quest for admission to the WTO finally reached a successful conclusion in 2011. The Customs Union gambit was shrugged off, and Georgia was appeased. A final decision was reached in Geneva on 16 December 2011, leaving the Russian Duma to ratify by June 2012 – which it did.

Time spent sitting in the waiting room for a call from the WTO had been put to good use by Moscow, as economic integration in Eurasia proceeded apace. In the summer of 2011, the president of Kyrgyzstan announced that his country would join the Customs Union as of 1 January 2012; in October the CIS Council of Heads of Government, the EurAsEC Interstate Council, and the Supreme Body of the Customs Union met in St. Petersburg, where five more of the former Soviet republics (Ukraine, Armenia, Kyrgyzstan, Tajikistan, and Moldova) signed a free trade pact with the three members of the Customs Union. By the end of the year, the Customs Union members had created a Common Economic Commission and scheduled it to replace the Customs Union as of 1 July 2012. Nearly 200 trade functions were placed within the mandate of the Commission, the head office of which will be in Moscow for the first four years. Putin's long-hoped-for Eurasian Union loomed closer, at least on paper.

The circumstance that existing regional economic organizations and associations remained intact when Russian joined the WTO had the potential of raising Russia's profile more extensively than originally assumed. A key player in the Customs Union, the Common Economic Space, and the Eurasian Economic Community, and an important member of Asia-Pacific Economic Cooperation (APEC) and various East Asian associations, Russia's eastern profile soared and provided impetus to Moscow's renewed urge to develop its own Far East.[24]

That tale was told to a certain extent when, with Putin back in office in 2012, an APEC summit in Vladivostok in September gave Russia a chance to showcase its Far Eastern resources and play up the recent accession to the WTO. Moscow spent up to $20 billion improving facilities and transportation, including bridges, in the city to impress Russia's eastern neighbours and potential trade partners. Host Putin made it clear that he hoped that APEC would be able to transcend a trend towards new economic blocs, such as the emerging Trans-Pacific Partnership. The effort Moscow put into hosting the APEC summit persuaded many analysts that Russia was turning away from the West as its major economic partner and towards the East instead. The Kremlin immediately denied such suggestions, though a foreign ministry spokesman acknowledged that a certain intransigence had set in when it came to accommodation with the West.

## Modernization

During this entire long period of economic up- and-downswings, President Medvedev remained committed to his oft-stated, if not always well-defined, project to 'modernize' Russia.[25] In the previously mentioned 'Go, Russia!' essay, he made it plain that economic modernization was on the top of the agenda for his presidency. He contrasted his plans with a continuum of failed modernization attempts, beginning with Peter the Great and ending with the Soviet Union, both of which he said, 'unleashed ruin, [and] humiliation and resulted in the deaths of millions of our countrymen'. Medvedev's more recent predecessors, left unmentioned by him, were M.S. Gorbachev, whose *perestroika* and *glasnost* in the 1980s accidentally brought down the antiquated USSR itself, and Putin who re-introduced the need for modernization as early as December 1999 in a speech often referred to as the 'Putin Manifesto'. Putin came back to the subject in his annual address to the Federal Assembly in 2007 where he referred again to the need for modernizing – in a very muted manner. The only specific modernization need referenced in Putin's address was in relation to the armed forces.[26] Medvedev hoped to learn from the mistakes of his early forerunners and build on the first steps of his more recent predecessors to re-invent Russia.

Modernization as a general societal ambition came to the forefront in November 2009 when Medvedev expanded on his 'Go, Russia!' remarks in his annual address to the Federal Assembly. Complaining again of Russia's 'chronic backwardness, dependence on raw materials export, and corruption', the president outlined domestic problems with candour and laid out a blue-print for a new type of *perestroika*. It was there that he defined modernization as a matter of developing the four 'I's': investment, innovation, infrastructure, and institutions. In the latter case, as we saw in Chapter Three, Medvedev highlighted the values and institutions of democracy as vehicles for economic change.

Responding to a question in 2009, Medvedev said that his form of modernization would be based on 'people's internal desire for change'.[27] But persuading the population of that would prove to be a daunting task. An opinion survey on modernization conducted in November that year revealed a clear majority of Russians doubtful about prospects for its success. Nearly sixty per cent believed that a transition to an innovative economy, if it was to happen at all, depended almost entirely upon government intervention, and only about twelve per cent believed that it depended on the people themselves. Leaving it to government to act as the engine of change was, of course, one of the most ancient of Russian habits.[28]

Where to go for help was a first consideration in the modernization campaign. Yeltsin had turned to foreign advisers – for example, Harvard's Jeffrey Sachs of 'shock therapy' fame – when he tried to overhaul Russia's economy in the nineties, with well-known disastrous results. Russians suffered lots of shock, but received no therapy. In his turn, Putin made a point of ignoring foreign advice, often referring to it as unwelcome and unhelpful preaching – not entirely without reason. He protected the designated National Champions and strategic industries from foreign ownership. Obsessed with re-establishing Russia as a major player in world politics and economics, and buoyed by high-energy prices, Putin regularly lent credence to Surkov's notion of 'sovereign democracy'. His aggressive Eurasianism therefore persuaded some observers in Russia that Medvedev's appeal to international participation in his modernization campaign was an early challenge to Putinism.

The modernization campaign was institutionalized officially in May 2009 with the formation of a Commission for Modernization and Technological

Development (CMTD). The Commission's mandate was 'to promote the sustainable technological development of Russia's economy and to improve public administration by promoting modernization programs in priority economic fields'.[29] Priority sectors were broadly defined as those with existing momentum, parts of the economy that could serve as a catalyst for modernization in related industries, spheres related to defence and security, and projects with social benefits for Russia's people. Thus, they mirrored the basic objectives of the anti-crisis plan set out a few months earlier.

Over the next three years, the Commission met on sites all around the country, entertained briefs from large and powerful companies, such as Gazprom, discussed modernization partnerships with the European Union, and issued press releases on such diverse proposals as energy-saving light bulbs, the creation of Russia's own computer games industry, and multi-million dollar high tech projects. The most ambitious of the latter type was announced at the end of April 2010 when Medvedev outlined the legal framework for a major innovation project announced already in March, a Russian version of the Silicon Valley at Skolkovo, in the Moscow Region. No room was left for doubt that Skolkovo was Medvedev's mission.[30] One editorial called it the 'favourite child of Medvedev'.[31] The idea was to build a new technology innovation town (Innogorod) from scratch, in an area that was already the site of Moscow's International School of Management.

Former chief of the Russian Unified Energy System (UES) and at the time general director of the Russian Corporation of Nanotechnologies (ROSNANO), Anatoly Chubais, was placed in charge of seeding the project with money from Russia's modernization and innovation budget, and $500 million in investments. Other sources of funding were sought aggressively.

Billionaire Viktor Vekselberg, head of the Renova group of companies and major shareholder in BP's Russian subsidiary, TNK-BP, was named Coordinator of the Russian part of the Skolkovo Innovation Centre. The aim was to attract young scientists for work on priorities set earlier by the president and narrowed even further to energy efficiency, strategic information technology, telecommunications (space technology), medical technology, and nuclear technology. More prominent figures and high tech leading lights were named to Skolkovo's board of directors, steps were taken to attract top foreign scientists, and grants were established for young researchers in the defence industry. Two management bodies were put in place: a council to oversee everyday operations and an advisory board for issues related to science.

In light of Putin's relatively insular approach to economic development, Medvedev's appointments as co-chairs of the scientific advisory board and its sub-units were startling. These were two Americans and a Russian communist: Craig R. Barrett as co-chair of the supervisory board to manage the project's companies; Roger Kornberg and Zhores Alferov as co-chairs of the organization's research council. Kornberg and Alferov are both Nobel Prize winners, in Chemistry and Physics, respectively. Barrett is a former CEO of Intel Corporation. Medvedev explained his choices as follows: 'I am absolutely certain that the involvement of these two exceptional people will spur international interest towards our project. We need exactly these kinds of well-known people'.[32] Several Russian pundits remarked wryly that there was an additional reason for such choices – Russian government officials at the top might be susceptible to corruption.[33] Medvedev later approved the appointment of six prominent Russian scientists, three Germans, and two more Americans to the council.

To attract innovators to Skolkovo, Medvedev offered a ten-year privileged tax regime for Russians (no property or land taxes, exemption from VAT, and so on), special entry and exit rules for foreign scientists and entrepreneurs, state grants for research projects in priority sectors of the national economy, and substantial funding for relevant research at Russian universities. Plans to send up to 500 Russians who were part of a program titled 'Managers in the Innovation Sphere' abroad for a period of managerial internship were put forward. To qualify, candidates for the program had to be under forty years of age, prepare a specific project to work on, have completed some higher education, and speak a foreign language. The Ministry of Education concluded bilateral agreements for specific courses of study with seven countries in Europe, plus the United States and Kazakhstan.

Beside financial incentives to lure foreign scientists and business to Skolkovo, immigration laws were changed to make it easier for foreign workers to bring their skills to Russia. The Federal Migration Service was now authorized to override previously set quotas to provide work permits for highly qualified foreigners on the basis of written requests from Russian employers. Residence permits were available without preconditions and workers hired under the modernization program had to pay less than half of the taxes previously required.[34]

Skolkovo was granted a special form of local self-government and there were hints that its final shape could represent an innovation that might be emulated in other parts of Russia. Arkady Dvorkovich, presidential aide and executive secretary of the CMTD, said as much in the spring of 2010 ('the simplified [regulatory] rules for Skolkovo are a test of the ideas we have for the country as a whole … '), long before the flood of changes brought on by the election crises of December 2011 and March 2012.[35] In this approach, Dvorkovich echoed Surkov's notion of variable-speed democratic evolution.

Desperate to bring the US on board, in May 2010 Medvedev met personally in Nizhny Novgorod with visiting heads of American venture capital funds to discuss prospects for joint projects in such areas as biomedical technology, energy efficiency, space and nuclear industries, and the commercialization of new technology at Skolkovo. Special Aide to the US President on national security, Michael McFaul – named ambassador to Russia a year later – and Surkov participated in the meeting. To sustain its call for help from North America, the Russian government launched an English-language website specifically to tout the merits and progress of its modernization campaign.[36] The appeal was but a part of an outbreak of Russian diplomatic overtures to the West in which the Kremlin tied its modernization campaign to foreign policy. One of the objectives of Medvedev's Foreign Policy Concept of 2008, in fact, had been 'to create favourable external conditions for the modernization of Russia'.[37] A consequence of this objective was a EU-Russia Partnership for Modernization established in late 2009. Though long on promise and short on accomplishment, discourse in this Partnership served as a useful sounding board for Medvedev's ideas.

At home, Surkov urged Russia's largest business associations, Business Russia and the Russian Union of Industrialists and Entrepreneurs, to participate in innovation projects.[38] They responded by demanding that the government stop harassing business. Nonetheless, by mid-summer 2010, over fifty Russian companies had applied to the CMTD for funding in support of various projects.[39] Russian Railways and the Alfa Group were the first domestic companies to set up offices at Skolkovo

Two important foreign companies signed on in early June 2010: Nokia, the world's largest manufacturer of mobile phones, and General Electric. Nokia agreed to help coordinate research in software development; GE reached an agreement on a joint venture within the energy and health care sectors.[40] Medvedev drew support from other large American firms during a quick visit to the Silicon Valley in 2010. Cisco Systems, for example, announced that it would invest $1 billion over the next decade in high-tech innovation in Russia, and maintain a physical presence at Skolkovo.[41] Google decided to invest in and construct a research centre at Skolkovo. Microsoft and Siguler Guff, a huge US private equity investment firm, also came on board.

The Russian public remained sceptical and continued to assume that the state was the only agency capable of generating change in any sector of society. Most Russian authorities believed that economic modernization could be achieved without major political change, whereas the bulk of Western analysts assumed that loftier goals, such as greater transparency, supremacy of law and political democracy, were necessary prerequisites to modernization. Medvedev was stuck somewhere in the middle of these contrasting belief systems.

Apparently concerned that his motives were misunderstood or simply not known, Medvedev explained himself at the annual St. Petersburg Economic Forum in June 2010. After outlining the grave circumstances facing the Russian and global economy at the time, he proclaimed rather grandly that Russia was in a position to be a 'co-founder of the new global economic order'. The goal of his modernization over the next few decades, he said, was 'to turn Russia into a prosperous country with high living standards built not so much on raw materials as on intellectual resources, an innovative economy producing unique knowledge and exporting new technology and innovative products. We will make Russia a country attracting people from all around the world to come here to realize their dreams and take up the great opportunities for success and self-realization that Russia will offer all who are ready to accept this challenge and love Russia as their new second home'.[42] No one could deny the rightness of the vision; few, if anyone, could foresee it coming to pass.

The president himself noted the sort of things that would have to be done first: use revenues from the current raw materials-based economy, but gradually wean Russia from it; use budget policy for a structural transformation based on performance; create a comfortable environment for investors; create a good business climate for Russian and foreign entrepreneurs; prepare Russian business for international competition. To assist in these last three 'to do's', he signed an executive order that day to cut the list of protected strategic enterprises from 208 to 41.

In July 2010, surveys suggested that the number of Russians who had confidence in Russia's ability to modernize rose slightly, to 17 per cent from 12 per cent in November 2009; 32 per cent still saw the chances of his success as poor, a drop from the 38 per cent revealed in the earlier survey.[43] Not a great leap forward, to be sure, but a sign that Medvedev's campaigning might finally have found an audience – precisely the audience that was to erupt onto the streets a year and a half later.

Putin suddenly became a target in the spring of 2010 as a possible stumbling block in the modernization effort. One analyst placed him and Surkov among 'conservatives' who feared that modernization along the Medvedev model would generate renewed economic and political disorder reminiscent of the days of *perestroika* and *glasnost*.[44] Another political writer predicted that 'Putin officialdom' would stifle innovations started at Skolkovo.[45] Analogies with Gorbachev's *perestroika* grew more common, put forward at first by writers who thought Medvedev's campaigns were whimsical and probably fatal politically. References to Potemkin Villages cropped up in connection with Skolkovo.[46] Gorbachev himself chimed in, warning in July that the elites would 'talk' the idea of modernization (which he supported) into irrelevance. President of the National Strategy Institute Stanislav Belkovsky, no friend of the administration, took up the theme of a renewed *perestroika* as well, reminding readers in a series of bitterly sarcastic pieces of the 'chaotic processes' that accompanied Gorbachev's failed attempts to modernize.[47] Chubais, once a leading privatizer for Yeltsin's administration and now involved heavily in the modernization process, insisted that political transformation was necessary for the campaign to succeed. One well-know critic complained that modernization, as a new *perestroika*, was impossible because United Russia resembled the old CPSU too closely and Russia's federalism was ineffective, with 'ridiculous borders that could not be formed into economically and politically self-sufficient units'.[48] Another Russian pundit believed that modernization would be possible only if Medvedev fired Putin.[49] There was never any chance of that.

Not many Russian analysts saw the struggle for modernization as a matter of competing visions for Russia's future offered by Medvedev and Putin, but a few political people did. For instance, the UR's leading liberal Olga Kryshtanovskaia proclaimed that her own party's conservatism was a barrier to modernization.[50] Because the UR is better known as Putin's party, the charge could not help but reflect on him. If there was a serious dichotomy within the ruling Tandem over Skolkovo, however, it remained well hidden. The rationale for the Tandem all along had been that the two men were 'like-minded' and shared the same visions for their country. They merely had separate portfolios. Medvedev left no doubt of their political unity of mind at that modernization forum convened in September at Yaroslavl, where he warned that parliamentary democracy would prove catastrophic for Russia. Here was unequivocal accommodation with Putin and Russia's conservative elites on the question of political modernization.[51]

That modernization campaign was energized in October 2010 when California's Governor Arnold Schwarzenegger arrived at the head of another large team of American venture capitalists and enthusiastically touted cooperation between the Silicon Valley and Skolkovo. Executives from Google, Microsoft, and Oracle were with the delegation and were plainly interested. Microsoft pledged millions in support of Skolkovo. A few weeks later, the South Korean government joined the enterprise.

Although their success or failure depended on systemic change at home, the pro-modernization campaigns had serious international ramifications for Russia. They needed investment from abroad. Towards the end of March 2011, Medvedev outlined the so-called 'Ten Commandments of Investing' in Russia so as to attract further Russian and foreign investments. These guidelines, in which he highlighted the debilitating factor of corruption, were delivered in Magnitogorsk at a meeting of the CMTD. The president emphasized his point by insisting that the country must be made attractive to both foreign and domestic business and private investment, without which 'we will not be able to change the quality of people's lives'.[52]

The link between foreign investment and domestic corruption was exposed when Rosstat published data showing that Cyprus and the British Virgin Islands were the countries with by far the most companies investing in Russia. Germany ranked third, but was assumed to be the top genuine foreign investor because many – if perhaps not all – of the companies in Cyprus and the BVI were money laundering operations run by nameless Russians who were bringing their funds home from accounts lodged offshore, cleansed by investment in real estate, financial and service sectors. Corrupt public officials usually facilitated these 'round trip' activities.[53]

Medvedev also created a mechanism to deal with corruption complaints, launched a direct investment fund, and broadened the powers of the Ministry of Economic Development. The Ministry was vested with authority to identify provisions in current and proposed legislation that 'create unnecessary obstruction to business and investment activity'. Medvedev offered further legislation to protect the right of minority shareholders to access information on public companies, along with several other laws designed to eliminate conflicts of interest where government officials still sat on boards of joint stock companies. A list of 17 such companies ordered to remove deputy prime ministers and federal ministers responsible for state regulation in their respective sectors was published.[54]

The Skolkovo Innovation Centre grew quickly in 2011, with about 300 companies signed up as residents by the end of the year.[55] The link-ups were not all one-way; for example, in March 2011 Chubais's ROSNANO opened an office in Silicon Valley. In fact, the nanotech sector remained a central part of the Skolkovo enterprise, much of it in partnership with the Massachusetts Institute of Technology (MIT). When a nanotechnology international forum gathered in Moscow in October, it coincided with the 27th meeting of the CMTD. ROSNANO had already earned over $300 million on manufactured products using nanotechnology and the meeting's agenda gave priority to training specialists for the industry. To help in this undertaking, MIT agreed to help form a branch at the Innogorod called the Skolkovo Institute of Science and Technology. The long-term plan called for 15 research centres, 1,200 undergraduates and 400 graduate students.[56] Brilliant as that prospect appeared to be, as far as popular appeal at home was concerned, even Medvedev acknowledged in April 2011 that few Russians had any idea what Skolkovo was all about.[57] As it was one of the defining pillars of his presidency, the revelation must have been dispiriting.

Putin suddenly jumped back on the modernization bandwagon in the spring of 2011, though still in general terms only. In his prime ministerial report on the government's performance during the previous year, Putin expressed a desire for modernization in the military and Russia's economic infrastructure while avoiding any reference to Skolkovo or any change in political institutions. Russia 'requires decades of steady, uninterrupted development. Without sudden radical changes in course or ill thought through experiments based in ... unjustified economic liberalism', he intoned.[58] Bloggers and journalists seized on this remark as an oblique backhand to Medvedev's brand of modernization, though it was much more likely a reference to the misguided shock therapy of the 1990s.

Putin's call for gradualism did not deter Medvedev. In China for a BRICS summit, he added a subtext to his modernization campaign. Russia's only path to a strong future lay with the 'modernization of the economy and modernization of [Russia's] political life', he told an interviewer for Chinese television.[59] Accompanied by a delegation of 100 Russian business people, he visited Hong Kong a day after the BRICS meetings and urged the business community there to participate in Skolkovo. That was when Putin chose to announce his Agency for Strategic Development to promote business by curbing bureaucratic impediments, recruiting and training young professionals, and encouraging innovation. Putin's plan focused on training and recruiting Russians; Medvedev internationalized his scheme and relied heavily on foreign expertise.

Just a few weeks later, the financial daily *Vedomosti* dubbed Medvedev's modernization agenda 'castles in the sky' and suggested that this particular campaign had become little more than presidential electioneering rhetoric.[60]

After two years of seemingly valiant effort on his part and general sympathy from the Russian media, the sudden turn on Medvedev from almost all sides seemed mean-spirited – or perhaps contrived as Putin began staking out his campaign territory.

In fact, a lot rode on Medvedev's modernization projects and how the Russian public perceived them. He displayed a sense of urgency in a speech to a large audience of Russian and foreign business and political leaders at the annual St. Petersburg International Economic Forum for 2011. Noting yet again that the dominant role of the state in the economy was made necessary by the turmoil of the nineties, he firmly rejected the idea of state capitalism for the future. Further decentralization and privatization were now necessary, Medvedev insisted, accentuating as well that the entire blueprint for modernization would work only if 'we put a relentless stranglehold on those guilty of corruption'.[61] This link had been drawn previously, but seldom as directly: curb corruption or we may never modernize. Unrepentant officialdom and *siloviki* had heard this before and probably were not impressed.

Two days later Putin also rejected state capitalism and both members of the Tandem again insisted that there were no differences between them.[62]

The president put on a brave face after the 24 September 2011 decision as his, by then, lame-duck presidency took nearly six more months to wind down. The CMTD continued to meet and, even though Medvedev's own influence dwindled, Russian and foreign business concerns showed a readiness to take up the modernization campaign – but on their own terms. It wasn't likely that the Russian bureaucracy and the huge energy monopolies, such as Gazprom, were going to allow economic favouritism – and therefore political power – to shift to a mixture of Russian and foreign high tech companies at Skolkovo.[63]

When Putin produced his long election campaign-related article on the 'new' Russian economy in January 2012, he co-opted Medvedev's modernization approach. He urged Russians to adopt a new competitive economy based on technological leadership and innovation, move away from dependence on energy exports, accelerate the privatization of state assets, and embrace competition.[64] These were themes touted by Medvedev and practically ignored by Putin over the previous few years. Political protests against ruling authorities don't have much impact when the economy is doing well. Russia's unemployment levels and inflation rate in 2011 and 2012 were lower than in Europe and the US. Increased government spending on infrastructure, which meant jobs, and on pensions and military salaries all proved beneficial to the general population. By that time Russia's economy appeared to be considerably sounder than Europe's.

One of the decrees signed by Putin on the day of his inauguration, 7 May 2012, set guidelines for long-term economic policy. Promising to maintain the modernization and pro-business policies of his predecessor, Medvedev, he ordered his still unformed government to increase the pace of economic growth, the incomes of citizens, and the technological leadership of the economy. He even included privatization of the entire non-energy sector excepting 'natural monopolies and defence-related companies'. In these objectives he echoed Medvedev.

Two weeks later Putin created the Presidential Economic Council, the purpose of which was to serve as an advisory body to prepare proposals 'on the main guidelines for Russia's socio-economic policy' and oversee their implementation. Putin chaired the Council himself, with Economic Development Minister Andrei Belousov as deputy chair. All the important economic and development ministers were on the Council, along with 25 others; among them in a decidedly secondary role was Prime Minister Dmitry Medvedev. In mid-June, however, the president set up a Council for Economic Modernization and Development with Medvedev as chairman. Its purpose was to coordinate projects between federal and regional bodies, public and scientific organizations.[65] So Medvedev was back on the modernization trail, but with far less clout and fewer assets than he had enjoyed as president.

Ironically, when Russia's economy began to show signs of decline in the winter of 2013, Putin made a point of casting blame in Medvedev's direction even though by that time the economy's main weakness was precisely the one Medvedev had often warned Putin against – absolute dependence on commodity export.

## Agriculture

Medvedev included agriculture among the modernizing targets highlighted in his inauguration speech.[66]

To facilitate his hoped-for modernization, long-time Minister of Agriculture, Gordeev, and his deputy Kozlov were dismissed in February 2009 and sent off to serve as governors in the regions. Governor of Stavropol until 2008 and former communist who switched to the UR, Aleksandr Chernogorov, was appointed Deputy Minister of Agriculture on 19 February, and a month later Yelena Skrynnik was named Minister. Skrynnik, a cardiologist and member of the UR's Supreme Council, had been the head of an agricultural equipment leasing company Rosagroleasing and worked with Medvedev on the agriculture side of the National Projects. On the face of it this looked like an appointment based on both merit and political advantage.[67] She was to hold the portfolio throughout Medvedev's term of office until May 2012, when she was dismissed and later charged with corruption and nepotism. She would not be the only prominent cabinet minister to prove disappointing to Medvedev as his term closed out.

Medvedev made it clear early on that reliance on imported food posed a danger to Russian security. He and the new minister emphasized the need for food independence and, in December 2009, the Russian Security Council approved a proposal from the new president that guaranteed national food security. The Doctrine on Food Security signed into law in January 2010 tied national security, national sovereignty, and improvement in the quality of life for Russian citizens together.[68]

The doctrine aimed to boost domestic production of basic foodstuffs to 80 per cent by 2020, provide the means to react promptly to internal and domestic threats against food supply, and ensure that most of the basic food products in Russian stores were produced domestically. Targets were set by law, e.g., 95 per cent of Russia's grain requirement, 80 per cent of sugar, 80 per cent vegetable oil, 85 per cent meat and meat products, 80 per cent fish products, and so on. These were not easy goals to reach, for Russia still imported about 45 per cent of its food, and the cities of Moscow and St. Petersburg imported about 80 per cent of their food.

Just as he was in other sectors, Medvedev was off to a good start in agricultural matters. In 2008, Russia had its best harvest since 1992, that is, about 100 million tons, and the country was back in the grain exporting business. In the spring of 2009, the Ministry announced that Russia would enjoy its second straight large grain surplus. Preparing for an international grain forum scheduled for St. Petersburg in June, Deputy Prime Minister Viktor Zubkov announced that Russia hoped to form a co-operative group of global grain producers, with attention paid to a 'grain corridor' to increase grain exports to Asia. The purpose of the corridor for Russia would be to boost production in Siberia. He added that the international group would start in the form of a 'pool' of major Black Sea grain producers.

Russia ranked as the third largest grain exporter in the world in 2009, exporting 21.4 million tons of wheat that year, and had, and still has, the largest amount of ploughed land in the world. With large and steady markets in Egypt, Saudi Arabia, Turkey, Tunisia, and Algeria, agriculture was again one of the main drivers of Russian industry.[69] That said, Russia continued also to import an enormous amount of food, especially processed food.[70]

Agricultural production is, of course, subject to forces other than the market – above all the whims of weather and natural disaster. There were serious problems during Medvedev's tenancy related to disease, drought, fire, and flood. To name but a few disease-related incidents: prior to Medvedev's election, a million chickens had to be destroyed in the Krasnodar area because of Bird (Avian) Flu in 2006, another quarter million in 2007, and a smaller number in the Spring of 2008. Though this disease, which also killed ducks and geese (domestic and wild), was more or less checked in his later years in office, the stock had to be rebuilt, making reliance on imported chicken greater than the Kremlin wanted. A bovine disease discovered in the Irkutsk Region dairy cattle herds forced authorities to slaughter some 500 animals in 2008 and call a state of emergency in the infected districts. The disease, pasteurellosis, was then contained. Outbreaks of African swine fever in 2012 forced farmers to kill about 55,000 pigs. There were other such outbreaks to disrupt production of meat and dairy enterprises, though none of them unique to Russia.

The worst crisis, however, was a severe drought in 2010 that destroyed nine million hectares of Russia's crops in June and July, causing a state of emergency to be declared in 14 regions. Three more areas were at risk. The agriculture ministry, which in February opened Russia's largest grain terminal at Tuapse on the Black Sea, was forced to revise its optimistic forecast for cereal grain yields downwards dramatically. The ministry insisted that its reserves of grain crops would provide enough for domestic use, and for feed grains to protect livestock, but exports were expected to be way down.[71]

The Russian Grain Union claimed this was the worst drought since record keeping began some 130 years ago. Sowing plans for winter grains were threatened by August, when that program usually starts. Dry soil extended the damage to other crops: sugar beet, potatoes, and corn. Winter wheat normally accounts for about 65 per cent of Russia's annual crop. Major grass fires that decimated entire farming areas accompanied the drought and left a pall of acrid smoke over huge areas and some cities.

On 5 July, Prime Minister Putin announced that Russia would suspend its grain exports from 15 August to the end of 2010, a move that was essential to Russia but also threatened to raise world wheat prices and therefore the price of bread. The world's commodity markets were shaken and there was some fear of serious inflation in global food prices, like that of 2007–8. Some countries, such as the US and Canada, benefited from Putin's decision because they were in a position to provide short-term supplies to countries left without Russian wheat until 2011. Putin told reporters that Russia's wheat harvest would amount to only 60 million tons, down more than a third from the previous year.

The ban on grain exports was extended in September and the agriculture ministry announced that sugar beet production would fall by about two million tons in 2010, down from the 24 million tons grown in 2009. Shortages had to be made up with imports. The government set aside some 8 billion rubles to subsidize railway transport of grains to regions in need and to assist farmers who kept their cattle.[72] In October, the agriculture ministry calculated that about one-third of the harvest was lost, leaving little to export anyway. Skrynnik announced that subsidies for agriculture would be raised for the coming year. She noted also that about 50 per cent of all agriculture produce came from Russian farmers, 90 per cent of potatoes, over 80 per cent vegetables, 56 per cent of milk products, and 43 per cent of meat. That meant that food supply was still heavily dependent on imports, no matter the goals set by Medvedev's food security legislation. He told the Security Council that about 25,000 farmers received aid of some sort in 2010 and that Moscow was planning to establish a permanent subsidizing agency for agriculturists.[73]

The agriculture sector got back on track in 2011 with a bumper crop of approximately 90 tons, which led to overflowing storage facilities and also a drop in domestic prices. Russia began exporting grains once again and returned to third spot among the world's grain exporters, after dropping to eighth place in 2010. To facilitate export the government promised to lower the cost of hauling grain by rail to help farmers in the interior market their crops. Increasing rates charged by the OAO Russian Railways monopoly had made it cheaper to ship by truck than by rail for distances up to 1,000 kilometres, but it was still expensive (see Chapter Six). Much infrastructure work was needed on the rail system before this problem could be resolved. Then and now the state also provides subsidies on agricultural equipment, fuel, and seasonal credit. Irrigation and land reclamation projects also greatly benefit agriculture.

Unavoidably, Russia's agriculture sector plays an indirect role in Russian foreign policy making. The Federal Service for Veterinary and Phytosanitary Oversight (Rosselkhoznadzor) and the Federal Consumer Rights Service (Rospotrebnadzor)[74] are empowered to issue sanctions or raise tariffs against imported products, almost always in consultation with, or on orders from, their parent ministries – the Ministry of Agriculture and the Ministry of Health Care, respectively. In addition to sporadic 'chicken wars' with American exporters, chicken and meats from Poland and other eastern European countries were among the products on which Moscow imposed sanctions on several occasions, expressly because of sanitation issues, but perhaps also in retaliation for limitations imposed on Russian goods in those countries – or even in response to some political act. For the most part these battles are covered in Chapter Five on foreign policy. In this connection, it is interesting that in May 2012 Rospotrebnadzor was separated from the Ministry of Health and made directly responsible to the federal government.

Trade disputes over agricultural items threatened Russia's admission to the WTO, as did increased subsidies to agriculture, but precisely because Russia imported so much food it tended to hold the slightly stronger cards, with a little less to lose in trade balance. Moreover, the Kremlin consistently pointed to the huge subsidies offered to agriculture by the EU and the US.

Already hurting from the previous year's drought and fires, Russian producers suffered another blow early in 2011 when Ukraine placed a temporary ban on the import of pigs and other animals from Russia's Northwest Federal District because of a hog cholera outbreak.[75] On the other hand, several domestic organizations urged Russians to use Russian-grown meat only, as reports of dioxin poisoning of fodder in Germany worried Russia's Ministry of Health.[76] The Russian government announced in July that it would cut all imports of pork and poultry by about one-third in 2012. This was a result of greatly improved output at home and also a policy of breaking a pattern of dependency on imported foods. There was concern that the decision would harm Russia's on-going application to join the WTO. As it happened, however, entry into the WTO did not affect domestic subsidies for agriculture.[77]

In another bit of a reverse role, Russian forbade the import of all fresh vegetables from Europe in May 2011 to protect its citizens against the outbreak of a virulent strain of E-coli in Germany. A few weeks later, imports of beef from several plants in Brazil were banned as well, in this case because the Ministry of Health found sanitary conditions problematic after an inspection of 29 Brazilian producers. In both cases the bans were temporary. Potatoes from Egypt were proscribed for the same reason. The EU provides Russia with a full third of its imported vegetables, so making the loss up was a brief boon to Russian farmers. The blanket ban against EU vegetables was partially lifted at the end of June, starting with the Netherlands and Belgium.

On the other hand an agricultural program supported by the Russian government further strengthened Moscow's relationship with Beijing. Beginning in 2011, Chinese companies leased about 400,000 hectares of Russian farmland and 800,000 hectares of Siberian forest and began work on them in 2012. Although many Russians already felt uneasy about what they see as huge Chinese inroads into their Far East, the returns from a $1 billion investment from China into a joint Russian-Chinese agricultural fund were promising. Individual Chinese investors are also buying farmland in central and southern Russia, mostly for vegetable farming.[78]

Shortly after Skrynnik lost her job, the Ministry of Agriculture predicted a lower harvest because of continued problems with heat and drought. Though the weather turned out to be not so bad as 2010, the harvest in 2012 still reached only a little over 70 million tons, leaving far less for export than had been expected early in the year.[79] Even with those results, at the end of Medvedev's term, Russia's grain production, export capacity and agricultural machinery upgrades showed great improvement. New or expanded grain terminals on the Black Sea, Baltic Sea, and the Sea of Japan make grain export targets achievable by 2020. The situation was not so promising in the meat and dairy industries, so that up to 30 per cent of beef and pork consumed by Russians was still imported in 2012.

Putin introduced a new program for developing Russian agriculture in the summer of 2012, with the same general goals as the earlier one: food independence and competitiveness on the world market. Meat, dairy and poultry production were granted pride of place.

In December that year, Putin's address to the Federal Assembly held out promise for the agricultural sector. Boasting that 55 per cent of the world's fertile land is in Russia, he proclaimed that funds would be allocated in 2013 for infrastructure upgrades and programs that will make Russia a producer of 'food for the world.'[80] Maybe, but to many observers it would seem that Russian agriculture had merely come full circle since 2008.[81]

## Energy and the pipeline 'great game'

### The 'gas war'

Putin's hints in 2013 aside, there were major economic successes on Medvedev's watch. The most important of these was steering Russia successfully out of the recession, to be sure, but another, quite different, 'success' story played out during his term. However, this one may well have been pyrrhic in its consequence, i.e., his efforts to maintain Russia's edge in the so-called 'gas wars' between Gazprom and Ukraine's Naftohaz. Because the oil and gas industry is strategically vital to both countries, Russia as exporter, Ukraine as consumer, and the companies are state-controlled (Gazprom 51%, Naftohaz 100%) the gas disputes were inevitably state-to-state affairs.

Medvedev was no stranger to the festering quarrel between Moscow and Kyiv that he inherited in 2008. As chair of the board of Gazprom, he had presided over price disputes with Ukraine since the early 2000s.[82] In January 2006, Russia suspended all supplies to Ukraine; Ukraine siphoned off gas intended for Europe, leaving European consumers out in the cold – literally. This was especially the case in parts of Eastern Europe where some countries receive up to 100 per cent of their gas supplies from Russia and have no facility to maintain reserves. The ensuing uproar led to a quick compromise, but the issue itself would not go away. Europe and Russia both began almost frantically to look for alternate routes and alternate sources of supply.

The enduring quarrel re-surfaced during the heat of Medvedev's presidential election campaign. In March 2008, Russia interrupted the supply of gas to Ukraine by 25 per cent. Gazprom maintained that the row over a large gas debt needed resolution. Ukraine threatened to divert transit gas if another cut was made, but discussion continued. Ukrainian President Viktor Yushchenko admitted to a large gas debt, up to $1.5 billion; Gazprom claimed it was a much larger amount; Prime Minister Yuliia Tymoshenko insisted that it was a much lesser amount. She flew to Moscow and eventually a temporary settlement was reached. There was far less protest from the West this time, perhaps because many Western commentators finally concluded that Russia had the right to sell its gas at world prices – up to $500 per thousand cubic metres (tcm) in the Spring, as opposed to the $179 tcm Ukraine still paid in 2008.

The interchange on prices for gas supply to Ukraine (and also to Georgia and Belarus) became more complicated when Gazprom agreed to begin paying European prices for Central Asian gas, most of which is then exported to Ukraine and elsewhere. Bitter dialogue ensued until another compromise was reached in October 2008. Still, Kyiv paid some of the debt and the two sides confirmed their 'intention of gradual transition within three years to market, economically viable and mutually coordinated prices'. They agreed as well on the necessity of uninterrupted transit of gas through Ukraine. No prices were settled publicly, and the issue was compounded by the fact that it was tangled up in domestic Ukrainian politics.[83]

The deal had a very short life span. On 1 January 2009, Russia made a partial cut in the gas supply to Ukraine because, Gazprom claimed, Naftohaz had not paid for the previous month's supply, and Ukraine refused to accept a proposed price of $250 tcm of gas. That price was a marked increase over the amount Ukraine had been paying, but still considerably less than the cost to Europe at that time of $418.

There followed another period of name-calling, claims and counter-claims. Gazprom withdrew the $250 price offer and threatened to raise it to the European level. By the end of the first week of January, Ukraine offered to pay $235, and Gazprom upped its demand to $450. Ukraine wanted to raise transit fees charged to Russia, but these were set in a contract until the end of 2010.

Gazprom cut all supplies of gas to Ukraine on 7 January, claiming that Naftohaz was stealing gas at transit sites.[84] That meant that East and East Central European countries without reserves were cut off again. The EU, of which the Czech Republic was then chair, invited officials from both sides to a meeting set for Prague the very next day, and Russia and Ukraine agreed to allow international experts monitor the natural gas transit system across Ukrainian territory.[85] A tentative agreement was reached two days later, and a gas summit was called for 17 January in Moscow.

Little was accomplished at that summit, attended by EU and other energy ministers and not heads of state, but a long meeting the following day between Putin and Tymoshenko resulted in a 10-year deal. Ukraine agreed to pay full market price for gas starting on 1 January 2010, and take a 20 per cent discount for 2009. Russia agreed to pay full market rates for transit in 2010, but keep the lower rates through 2009. Yushchenko signed the agreement in Moscow the next day. Specific prices again were not mentioned. This deal remains a point of contention in Ukraine to this day.[86]

Although the Tymoshenko–Putin deal failed to resolve the issue for very long, Ukraine's presidential election in 2010 changed the entire atmosphere for the Russia–Ukraine energy relationship. An important breakthrough for Moscow came in April, when Medvedev and new Ukrainian President Viktor Yanukovych signed a deal that gave Russia a further 25-year extension of its lease on the Black Sea port of Sevastopol in return for a 30 per cent discount on Russian gas deliveries. There still was no long-term resolution of the issue of gas prices and supply, as negotiations continued throughout the year.

Battle lines were drawn again as early as October 2010 when, at a meeting with officials in Kyiv, Gazprom made it obvious that it wanted control of the transit pipelines in return for a further price discount, i.e., no consortium of equal partners as requested by Yanukovych. Ukraine wanted to revisit the 10-year agreement reached in 2009, which Naftohaz now said was untenable. Talk of a renewed gas war circulated, but was downplayed by both sides.

Moscow's position hardened in the spring of 2011. When Ukrainian Prime Minister Mykola Azarov tried to re-open negotiations and the Ukrainian prosecutor-general said that the existing contract was illegal according to Ukrainian law, Igor Sechin went to Kyiv and was unequivocal that no amendments to the agreement would follow. Medvedev confirmed the Russian approach in late May, insisting again that that they must stick to the signed contract and proclaiming that the price for gas to Ukraine would stay the same.[87]

In August, Medvedev sounded even more aggressive, accusing Ukraine of wanting to 'sponge' off Russia by trying to achieve a cut in the contracted gas price. He added that Kyiv would have either to join the Customs Union or sell its pipeline grid to Russia if it wanted a discount on gas prices. This time it seemed that Medvedev was the first to blink. After talks between the two presidents and senior energy officials at the end of the month, Azarov told a delegation from PACE that Russia consented to review the gas contract. Moscow also agreed to establish a consortium with Ukraine and the EU to upgrade and manage Ukraine's gas pipeline network. Details of this, perhaps mythic, arrangement were still not available by the end of Medvedev's term in office.[88]

A political glitch came in October when Ukrainian courts sentenced former Prime Minister Tymoshenko to a seven-year prison term for negotiating the 'illegal' gas price deal with Russia in 2009. Watching the events unfold closely, most members of the EU saw the trial itself as illegal and political. The Kremlin, where the gas deal was deemed proper, was cautious in its statements about the trial. Some politicians and other observers in Moscow saw it as an opportunity to persuade Ukraine to move away from the EU and associate more closely with the new Customs Union/ Common Economic Space pushed in Moscow. A meeting in Moscow in December between Putin and Azarov failed to achieve any progress on the gas puzzle.

As Medvedev's term came to a close, Moscow introduced tougher options for Kyiv to consider: concessions if Gazprom was handed control over the pipelines that transit Ukraine for Europe. By that time Ukraine was paying $416 tcm for gas, which was still lower than what Europeans paid, but wanted to pay only $250. No changes were made after a fruitless conversation between Yanukovych, Medvedev, and Putin in March 2012. Gazprom was hardly suffering. In late August 2011, it announced huge profits of over $16 billion for the first quarter, one of its largest interim profits ever, and up by 44 per cent over the same period the previous year.

So Medvedev weathered this particular storm, though the gas war clearly was not yet won. His achievement for Russia was to keep the dispute contained and its concomitant political manifestations limited to Ukraine. But victories in the battles, if not the war, may have come at too great a price. Whatever interest Ukraine might have had in the Customs Union was undermined by Moscow's aggressive stance on energy supplies. Both the EU and Ukraine cut back on their gas purchases from Russia as much as they could.[89] Liquid natural gas (LNG) and shale gas began to eat into the market, and Russia switched its energy focus to Asia generally, and to China in particular. In its turn, China initiated negotiations with Kazakhstan and Turkmenistan for direct access to their energy supplies, bypassing Russia and opening up another troubling scenario for Medvedev's successor to handle.

### The pipeline 'great game'

The gas wars laid bare certain realities that were already well known, but to that time had been set aside: namely, the vulnerability of consumers, producers, and carriers of energy supplies to political whim, and the extent to which both the EU and Russia depended on gas transported from Russia through Ukraine.[90]

In 2008, the EU drew 25 per cent of its gas supply from Russia, 80 per cent of which crossed Ukraine. The EU reacted to the transit crisis by seeking other sources and routes. For example, an angry EU Commission President Jose Manuel Barroso urged his colleagues to support the US-favoured Nabucco (name from Nebuchadnezzar) pipeline project that would bypass both Russia and Ukraine to carry gas to Europe from Central Asia via Azerbaijan, Georgia, and Turkey.[91] The EU also called for plans to make the collective use of gas more efficient. Russia reacted by stepping up projects to construct its own pipelines to Europe circumventing Ukraine, i.e., the Nord Stream and South Stream.

The Nord Stream (Map 4.1) envisioned delivering gas directly to Germany from Russia under the Baltic Sea, and was already scheduled for completion by 2011. The plan for the South Stream (Map 4.2) at that time was to carry gas from Russia under the Black Sea to Bulgaria. From there a northern branch would proceed through Serbia, Hungary, and Austria, and a southern branch would go to Greece and southern Italy.

To protect Russia's sources of gas, Medvedev spent a frantic winter in 2009 dickering with Central Asian leaders. In Tashkent he signed long-term energy agreements with the president of Uzbekistan, and then conducted long discussion with his counterparts in Kazakhstan, Tajikistan, and Kyrgyzstan. At the end of March, he hosted the president of Turkmenistan in Moscow and confirmed long term oil and gas agreements with that country as well. Gazprom's CEO Aleksei Miller accompanied him almost everywhere. All of these arrangements were supplemented by trade and investment deals that sweetened the pot for Central Asian producers. In short, Medvedev and his Gazprom team tied up Central Asian gas supplies for Russia and short-circuited

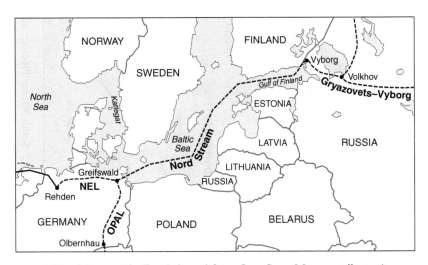

*Map 4.1* Nord Stream Pipeline (adapted from OpenStreetMap contributors)

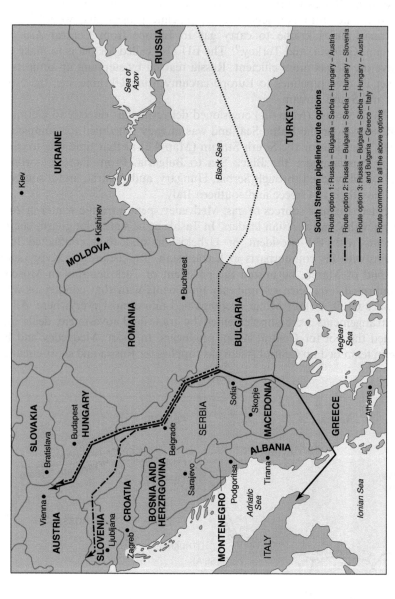

*Map 4.2* South Stream Pipeline (adapted from South Stream Transport B.V.)

Nabucco before it could find its feet. Medvedev's personal experience with the energy sector and a diplomatic style usually more muted than Putin's doubtless were advantageous in these negotiations. So was the fact that he offered European prices. Russia's status as the big energy player in the Shanghai Cooperative Organization, whose full and observer membership includes the world's major gas producers, helped considerably.

The South Stream was the most problematic of the fuel transportation projects. A few weeks before Medvedev took over the president's office, Gazprom and Italy's ENI signed a parity agreement for the further implementation of the plan, and Putin was in Sofia discussing the issue of expanding the pipeline through Bulgaria to Serbia. A tentative accord was reached, augmented by Atomstroieksport's promise to invest more in Bulgaria and construct a nuclear power plant (NPP) in Belene.

Hungary signed on the next year, creating a transit consortium of Russia, Italy, Serbia, Bulgaria, Greece, and Hungary. The Nabucco group also consolidated as Turkey, Austria, Bulgaria, Romania, and Hungary agreed to allow Nabucco pipelines to cross their territories. Not to be outflanked, Prime Minister Putin went quickly to Ankara to get Turkey's support for the South Stream's transit of Turkish territorial waters; that too was agreed. In the meantime, Medvedev rushed again to Ashgabat, twice, in the fall of 2009 and worked out special agreements with Turkmenistan, a country with huge gas deposits. A lot was at stake in these lengthy negotiations, but eventually Moscow and Gazprom prevailed.

Or so it seemed. Bulgaria backed out in 2010, so the South Stream proposal was re-routed undersea to Romania – a key member of the Nabucco group. Talk of merging the two projects grew. But then Bulgaria re-joined South Stream, and Romania wavered over Nabucco, causing the EU to cry foul over presumed under-the-table manipulation from Gazprom.

Europe's financial ordeals complicated matters and caused several long-time oil and gas pipeline projects to be scrapped in 2011. Two of these were the Burgus-Alexandropolis (Trans-Balkan) project and the Turkish Samsun-Ceyhan (Trans-Anatolian) line. Both had heavy Russian involvement. The latter project was in limbo in part because Ankara still hoped that Nabucco would make Turkey the hub for gas transit to Europe. Worried that Gazprom might be in over its head with the South Stream, especially as European financing prospectives wavered, Putin suggested that the South Stream project be aborted in favour of an LNG enterprise on the Black Sea coast.[92] In September 2011, however, a beaming Putin looked on as Germany's BASF, France's EDF, and Italy's ENI signed on with Gazprom to revitalize the South Stream. The German and French companies each took a quarter of ENI's 50 per cent, Gazprom kept its 50 per cent intact.[93]

All of these pipeline debates were complicated by the fact that Turkmenistan, a leading gas exporter, decided to construct its own pipeline to the Caspian, after several years of waiting for Russia to fulfil a promise to do so. In late 2010, Turkmenistan also joined with Afghanistan, Pakistan, and India to build a pipeline (TAPI) through those countries, bypassing Russia. American support for TAPI kept Russia on edge.

When Turkey finally agreed to allow the South Stream passage through its exclusive seabed in January 2012, Medvedev ordered Gazprom's CEO to start construction sooner than originally proposed. Completion date was tentatively set for 2015. By then Nabucco was already fading quietly from the scene.

There was further action to the east as well. Russia's oil pipeline to China was opened officially in September 2010, and oil began to flow from the East Siberia Pacific Ocean Pipeline at midnight, 31 December. If all went as planned, Rosneft, Russia's largest oil producer, expected to sell China 15 million metric tons (110 million barrels) a year for 20 years. China provided Russian companies with some $25 billion to finance construction and help develop deposits. Putin noted that this vast energy project would allow Russia to diversify its consumer base, above all to move beyond Europe,[94] a fact with implications for Russia-EU relations. At the September ceremony, Medvedev initiated negotiations on natural gas supplies and prices in Beijing.

Coinciding with these sessions was an announcement from Transneft, Russia's pipeline construction monopoly, that it would form a venture to build a $2-billion pipeline to China and other Asian sites to carry crude oil from Arctic deposits. These were huge undertakings. Already the world's leading producer of oil, Russia's crude output in 2010 set a post-Soviet record.[95]

One way to measure the bumpy evolution of the Russian oil industry is to track the saga of the Russia–British Petroleum (BP) relationship. The Tyumen Oil Company (*Tyumenskaia neftanaia kompaniia*, TNK) was founded in 1995 with the government as its major stakeholder. In 1998, the state sold its controlling shares in TNK to Alfa Group–Access Industries–Renova (AAR), a company run by Russian oligarchs. BP's involvement with the Russia energy sector goes back for some time, the key stage coming in 2003 when it joined with AAR, to form TNK–BP. BP thus became the only Western concern to own a 50-per cent share in a major Russian oil company. Putin and Britain's Tony Blair attended the signing ceremony. Already posting record profits by 2004, but wary of the government because of the Yukos/Khodorkovsky affair, TNK–BP relinquished its special tax status and reincorporated on Russian territory. British citizen Robert Dudley continued as president and CEO. The newly integrated oil company's actions disproved the flurry of doomsday prediction spawned by the Yukos case that a 'chill' would set in and that foreign investors would flee from, or not go to Russia, at least as far as energy consortia were concerned. Instead, they rushed in to pick up as many of the pieces of Yukos they could get their hands on. Inevitably, BP's success placed it on a collision course with Gazprom and also generated rifts between the two main partners and among the shareholding oligarchs themselves. In short, the history of TNK–BP also serves as an example of the quirks, caprices, and politics of doing big business in Russia.

Just as Medvedev was preparing to win the presidency, BP closed its office on Sakhalin Island where it had been involved for several years in oil, gas, and LNG exploration as a partner with Russian companies. Shell, Exxon-Mobil, and also Japanese and Indian companies were partners with Russian companies on the island. Ever-changing Russian tax regulations, pressure from local and international environmentalists, demands for greatly increased subsidies from officials (mayors) at the sites, and fears that the Russian government was trying to take control of the huge projects were all factors in BP's decision. The atmosphere was so tense already in 2006 that Foreign Minister Lavrov felt compelled to state outright that there 'were no grounds for claims of Production Sharing Agreement revisions',[96] though there probably were.

An internal feud between the BP and its Russian partners in the joint venture in Sakhalin and elsewhere drew the attention of the world's energy experts through most of 2008. BP, by then Russia's third largest oil producer, accused Russian shareholders of trying to take over the company and remove Dudley; in their turn, the syndicate of oligarchs who owned the other 50 per cent of the company sued BP after it rejected their demands for more boardroom influence on the venture. Russian state officials got into the act and warned that they would not renew work visas for Dudley and some 48 other foreign employees of the company. This threat was lifted in early July, but tensions remained.

Billionaires Mikhail Fridman, Len Blavatnik, and Viktor Vekselberg[97] led the Russian shareholders, and accused Dudley of mismanagement. On its side, BP believed that the oligarchs were responsible for a wave of regulatory pressures against the company, most of which had to do with minor labour and immigration issues. One of the Russian complaints was the number of foreign workers, mostly technicians, who the Russians said were too numerous and too costly. In July, British Prime Minister Gordon Brown raised the issue with Medvedev during the G-8 summit in Japan, but with little success. BP then launched a lawsuit against the Russian billionaires for an alleged debt to BP of $360 million. Dudley left the country in July 2008, and in early August TNK–BP's chief financial officer, James Owen, resigned. Dudley's visa was not renewed and, though he ran the company from an undisclosed location for a few months, he agreed to leave his post as of 1 December. BP gave up some of its tight control over the company, but maintained 50 per cent of the partnership. Both 'sides' claimed victory.

Disputes within TNK–BP went through another phase in May 2009 when Fridman took the position of CEO until a permanent replacement for Dudley could be found. On the other hand, as BP's influence diminished, an agreement between the Russian government and Royal Dutch Shell allowed that company to develop production and transportation mechanisms for delivering LNG from Russia, and France's Total signed on to a joint venture in northwestern Siberia. Shell had been a player in the first Sakhalin project since the late 1990s with Exxon and several Russian companies. Their first well was drilled in 2003. Gazprom took a 51 per cent control of Sakhalin-2 with Shell in 2006 after major environmental controversies. The importance of that arrangement was such that President Putin presided over the signing ceremony in Moscow.

TNK–BP continued to thrive without Dudley, even sending a representative to Kyiv in October 2010, where Prime Minister Putin presided over a joint project to construct a uranium processing plant in Ukraine by Tvel, Russia's nuclear-fuel state producer. At the same meeting TNK–BP signed a major deal on shale gas exploration. 'Rosneft was also blossoming. In August the company (later the owner of TNK–BP) won stakes in four German refineries, one of which was 50 per cent of Ruhr Oel GmbH. That latter acquisition brought them important shares in the Venezuelan state oil company, Petroleos de Venezuela. BP was part owner of Ruhr Oel, and held large stakes in other German refineries that Rosneft also purchased. In return, BP was offered a lucrative deal to explore for oil in the Arctic Ocean with Rosneft. This was a boon for BP because of its disastrous venture in the Caribbean, and potentially profitable for Rosneft. Shortly thereafter, Eduard Khudainatov was named the new president of state-owned Rosneft – on Medvedev's recommendation.[98] Head of the presidential staff Sechin chaired Rosneft's board of directors.

Russia's long-standing connection with BP stood on shaky grounds until January 2011 when a suddenly strengthened alliance between BP and Rosneft was expected to result in a greatly increased development of Russia's Arctic energy supplies. In an extraordinary turnabout, Robert Dudley showed up to sign the new agreement with Khudainatov. For general economic development, the new arrangement paved the way for the establishment of an Arctic technology centre in Russia. A lot of promise accompanied this partnership. Resembling Skolkovo's objective, the project would serve as a vehicle for Russian and international firms to develop engineering and technological practices for northern energy exploration and production. In terms of Medvedev's desire to 'modernize' the economy, the BP–Rosneft project could make Russia the leader in Northern energy exploration expertise, eclipsing the leadership held now by Norway, Finland, and Canada. Russia was already the leader in icebreaker construction. In fact, modernization in the energy sector was the only arena that really counted in the short run, at least where Russia's government budget revenues were concerned.

BP's ambitions suffered another setback when Sechin resigned as chairman of the board in April that year, much earlier than Medvedev's demand that he and other senior government officials step away from such positions. On the other hand, rising prices for crude oil because of the Arab Spring provided windfalls for Russia that prompted Finance Minister Kudrin to predict a net capital inflow by the end of the year, which would be the first since 2007.[99] But that wasn't going to happen either, Medvedev's urging at the Magnitgorsk CMTD meeting notwithstanding. A full year later, a representative of the Central Bank estimated that close to $40 billion left Russia during the fourth quarter of 2011, and the situation worsened in January 2012 due partly to perceived political instability in Russia.[100]

Momentum on the BP–Rosneft project slowed in April, when an arbitration tribunal in Stockholm issued an injunction against the shares swap worked out by Khudainatov and Dudley. The Russian billionaires with the AAR Consortium blocked the deal in court, causing Sechin's brainchild to fail. As a fall back, Rosneft opened negotiations with Japan's Agency for Natural Resources and Energy, offering that country access to eleven oil and gas licenses in eastern Siberia and three areas in the Magadan region. Japan could hold up to 49 per cent of any of these ventures, while providing all the funding. In October, former vice president of Russia's Arctic Shelf at BP, Larry Bates, was appointed adviser to the president of Rosneft at vice-president rank.[101] BP's role in Russia seemed to be disintegrating, as Putin held discussions with Royal Dutch Shell PLC, a well-known quantity in Russia, for a joint project to develop the three Kara Sea energy fields held by Rosneft. Prime Minister Putin said he felt 'comfortable' with Shell because of earlier experiences with the company, and Sechin arranged an exclusive role for Shell in parts of Russia's Arctic, the next undeveloped frontier.[102]

In March 2013, Rosneft purchased TNK–BP, making Rosneft the largest oil producing company in the world.[103]

### Other energy considerations

In August, Rosneft and Exxon Mobil teamed up for another multi-million dollar project. Exxon Mobil was granted access to Russia's Arctic and Rosneft to resources in the US's Gulf of Mexico. The two companies agreed to spend $3.2 billion in the Kara Sea. Rosneft did not have the deep-sea drilling technology that Exxon Mobil could provide. Clearly, Russia has no dearth of international oil companies as eager partners, and the Tandem just as clearly managed to persuade the world's energy giants that, risky or not, Russia's Arctic might well be the last fountainhead for huge energy profits.[104]

The agreement came just in time, for much of the expected production from the Arctic, though still well in the future, was likely to flow eastward; a fact corroborated by promises rendered at the BRICS meeting in China noted above. There Medvedev and Hu pledged to greatly expand bilateral trade ties with a focus on energy, and Gazprom Deputy CEO Aleksandr Medvedev preceded the Russian president to China by a day for discussion with the Chinese National Petroleum Corporation (CNPC). Russia had been shipping large amounts of coal to China since 2009 in exchange for loans to cover construction and development by Rosneft and Transneft, the latter to build the ESPO pipeline. Hu was in Moscow in June after an SCO summit in Kazakhstan and told the St. Petersburg Economic Forum that China hoped to prioritize energy cooperation with Russia. He visited Gazprom's head office at the time. Memoranda of understanding (MOUs) were signed, though talks still tended to stall when it came to discussing prices.

A new pipeline from the Island of Sakhalin to Vladivostok was opened in September 2011 and, after some months of talk, representatives of Russia,

North Korea, and South Korea signed an agreement for the construction of a pipeline from Russia to South Korea. The government in Pyongyang could earn up to $100 million annually in transit fees. Gazprom's claims that it would be operational by 2017 may have suffered a setback on account of the North Korean crises of 2013.

Another turning point in the pipeline business came when Russia purchased control of Beltransgaz, guaranteeing Gazprom's control over the pipeline through Belarus to Europe. More significant was the symbolic grand opening of the 1,200 km Nord Stream in September 2011 presided over by Putin and former German Chancellor Gerhard Schröder, who had signed the initial pipeline accord in 2005. A month later, it was Medvedev's turn to preside over a pipeline launch, this time an oil line from the Yamal-Nenets and North Krasnoyarsk regions also to carry oil to Germany. Chancellor Angela Merkel and the prime ministers of France and the Netherlands joined the Russian president for a ceremony held in Lubmin, Germany.[105] Obviously, the West was not forgotten in Russia's new 'Great Game'.

The old idea of a Gas OPEC was resurrected on Medvedev's watch as well. In the Fall of 2008, Russia, Iran, and Qatar revealed that they were forming a 'gas troika' and agreed that delegates would meet three times a year to discuss price-related issues. No specific organizational plans were forthcoming until the next year when a Gas Exporting Countries Forum (GECF) met in Doha and selected an organizational executive to represent the eleven participating countries (Algeria, Bolivia, Egypt, Equatorial Guinea, Iran, Libya, Nigeria, Qatar, Russia, Trinidad and Tobago, and Venezuela). Although the group was by no means a mirror of OPEC, the existence of the Forum with its headquarters in Doha was a very real step forward for Russia. A Russian, Leonid Bokhanovsky, Vice President of Stroitransgaz, was elected its first Secretary-General in December 2009. Almost two years later to the day, Medvedev opened the GECF's first summit – proclaiming that it 'marked a new stage in the development of the global energy sector'.[106] GECF members control about 70 per cent of the world's natural gas reserves.

The market for Russia's nuclear power plants (NPPs) also expanded exponentially during Medvedev's presidency. When he visited Armenia in August 2010, he signed an agreement for Russians to construct a second NPP at Metsamor. A few weeks later, Rosatom agreed to collaborate with Vietnam in building an NPP there, and later worked with Ukraine on the construction of a nuclear fuel plant. In October, Rosatom contracted to build an NPP in Venezuela, and in December India designated a third construction site for a Russian plant, which will eventually hold six power units.[107]

The next year, Medvedev opened up discussion about an NPP for Jordan during a visit to that country and confirmed another power station for Turkey in conversation with his Turkish counterpart. Putin wasn't left out of the NPP agenda: he agreed in Minsk that Russia would finance the construction of one at Ostrovets, close to the Lithuanian border. Rosatomstroieksport will build the complex with financing of some $9 billion loaned to Belarus by Moscow.

The disaster at Japan's Fukushima plant caused some re-thinking, and Bulgaria gave up on its project. Even so, Russian-built NPPs in Iran (Bushehr) and India were operational by the end of 2011, and a second in India was operational by mid-2012.

There were, of course, other economy-related developments during Medvedev's presidency, especially in the minerals sectors, but his focus on the energy and pipeline sector showed where the Tandem believed its economic lifeblood flowed.

The economics of pipeline construction is impossible without multi-state agreements and cannot be calculated accurately without considering diplomatic factors; nor can such integrative mechanisms as the Customs Union, Common Economic Space, and the anticipated Eurasian Union. The international diplomacy of Medvedev's Russian presidency will be considered in the next chapter.

\* \* \*

Huge profits from the energy and other commodity sectors enabled the state to help fund the construction of port facilities, improve railway transportation, and rebuild airports, hospitals, and schools.

Even with recession spreading in the West, European and North American companies were still investing in Russia in 2008. To cite but a few major developments in that year: the auto industry boomed, with Canada's auto parts giant Magna signing contracts in Russia along with its partner Hyundai; German manufacturers of construction and excavation equipment opened a large plant in Nizhny Novgorod; and Canada's Bombardier teamed up with Russia's Transmashholding to develop new high-tech locomotives. An Italian company bought 25 per cent of Sukhoi, and Daimler announced that it would start producing busses in Russia in 2010.

The automobile manufacturing industry clearly was doing well. General Motors announced that it would double the output at its plant in St. Petersburg to 60,000 cars annually, and in June Fiat announced that it would build two more auto plants in Nizhny Novgorod valued at about $1.1 billion.[108] It remains to be seen how Russia's accession to the WTO will influence the auto industry, as foreign cars will become less expensive for Russia buyers.

Russia's auto sector expanded again in 2010, in part because of a state-sponsored scrapping scheme that granted 50,000 rubles ($1,250) to owners trading in domestic cars over 10 years old to buy new domestic vehicles. Cheap loans also helped, but the big market remained for expensive foreign-made cars purchased by wealthy Russians. Toyota and Ford led the way early in 2011. In mid-February, Ford Motors announced plans to partner with a Russian company to make and distribute cars in that country. This disclosure made up for what appeared to be a failed expansion deal with Fiat (owner of the US company Chrysler), which had signed a memorandum of understanding with the Russian car manufacturing company Sollers in 2010 to produce up to 500,000 vehicles a year in Russia. On 18 February 2011, the Fiat deal collapsed. They and Sollers announced that they would take on independent strategies in Russia. Almost simultaneously, Ford disclosed that it had signed a MOU with Sollers. The two equal stake owners talked of enlarging plants in St. Petersburg and Kazan. Shortly before this rash of car manufacturing pronouncements, Toyota joined with Sollers and Mitsui in a project to make cars in the Russian Far East. The plan calls for the construction of a factory in Vladivostok to build about 30,000 Toyota brand vehicles annually. A personnel training program was scheduled as well.

Although the early first flush faded as the global economic crisis wounded investors everywhere, expansion began again in 2010. General Electric joined with Russian Technologies to manufacture medical equipment, IBM signed an agreement with the Russian Transportation Ministry to modernize the information technology on which the railway complex relies, and Bombardier was back, taking half-ownership of OJSC United Electrical Engineering Plants (Elteza), the signalling unit of state-owned Russian Railways. This was a prelude to an announcement from Economic Development Minister Nabiullina that Russia would spend the equivalent of $11 billion in 2011 on railway infrastructure development. Subsequently, Siemens won contracts worth over three billion euros to provide regional trains and train equipment for Russia. There were advances in the production of farm machinery too, especially after John Deere signed an agreement for joint production in Russia. In this case, the Russian government agreed to provide subsidies if the equipment was manufactured from parts made in Russia, and if tariffs on imported machinery were lowered.[109]

In addition to the emphasis on railway upgrades, the Medvedev regime saw huge amounts spent on expanding the two busiest commercial port facilities in Russia, Primorsk on the Baltic Sea and Novorossiisk on the Black Sea, and on wide-ranging highway improvements.

The potentially valuable tourist industry also began growing again in 2010, but slowly. One problem was the dearth of international standard accommodations; for example, Moscow still had less than 300 hotels regarded as suitable for tour groups, making the price for rooms the highest in Europe. New spaces are under construction, but hotel fittings and other features are usually contracted out to foreign providers, so much of the refit money leaves the country. That said, Russia generally and Moscow and St. Petersburg in particular remain popular destinations, which means the hotels stay full and prices stay high. There is a bit of a catch-22 situation in this industry.

Large service and retail industries continued to expand their franchises in Russia as well. For example, McDonald's president for Russia and Eastern Europe, Khamzat Khasbulatov, proclaimed in April 2008 that 40 new restaurants would be opened in 2008, bringing the total in Russia to 233.[110] In 2010 Dunkin Donuts returned to Russia after a 10-year absence, Starbucks expanded to some 30 locations, L'Oreal SA, the world's largest cosmetics maker, opened its first factory in Russia, and Pepsi Cola purchased a majority stake in Wimm-Bill-Dann Foods to become the biggest food and beverage company in Russia.

Another breakthrough in the service industry came in 2011 when Wendy's announced that it would open 192 outlets in Russia by 2020, involving an investment of some $132 million. Wenrus Restaurant Group Ltd. opened its first two restaurants in Russia in June 2011, both in Moscow. Most of the outlets are dual-branded, i.e., Wendy's/Arby's and offer menus from both. The beauty industry drew big stakes from the West as well, when Unilever PLC purchased 82 per cent of the Russian beauty company Concern Kalina for approximately $550 million. Unilever, which already owned the Russian ice cream company Inmark (bought in 2008), added Kalina products Pure Line and Black Pearl face and body creams and Forest Balsam toothpaste to its existing lines.[111]

These inroads from the West represent but tips of the iceberg, and does not include the large presence of Western and Chinese companies in Russia's mining and forestry, or the huge investment the Russia state and private individuals have made in the economies of Europe, Asia, Africa, and North America. These are matters for studies by others. The point here is that, under Medvedev, the Russian economy was by no means a closed one; rather it quietly joined the global economy with little fanfare. Here too lay the basis of the new middle class, potentially the human resource backbone of Russia's transition towards modernization.

In this last connection, it is worth noting that the banking system improved under closer regulation to such an extent that, by 2012, the number of Russian citizens with savings accounts reached 75 per cent, a huge leap forward from 2008 when some analysts boasted that Russians might be saved from the global financial collapse because so few of them had bank accounts.[112] True, Medvedev didn't re-invent Russia in ways that he had hoped, but his half of the Tandem laid down some important foundations for his successor to build on – if Putin is so inclined.

## Notes

1 See especially, Marshall I. Goldman, *Petrostate: Putin, Power and the New Russia*, New York: Oxford UP, 2010.
2 For a useful introduction, see Anders Aslund, 'Putin's Economic Legacy', *Russian Analytical Digest*, No. 36, 4 March 2008, pp. 5–8.
3 Interfax, 24 July 2008.
4 RIA Novosti, 31 January 2008; ITAR-TASS, 3 September 2007.
5 Medvedev, 'Poslanie Prezidenta Federal'nomu Sobraniiu', *Rossiiskaia gazeta*, 6 November 2008; *Kremlin.ru*, 15 July 2008.
6 For a summary see Peter Rutland, 'The Impact of the Global Financial Crisis on Russia', *Russian Analytical Digest*, No. 48, 17 October 2008, pp. 2–5.
7 Interfax, 13 October 2008.
8 *Kommersant*, 13 November 2008.
9 *Kremlin.ru*, 15 November 2008.
10 Putin, 'On Russia's Development Strategy Through to 2020', *Kremlin.ru*. 8 February 2008.
11 On the 2008 surplus of 1,708 trillion rubles, ITAR-TASS, 3 March 2009; Interfax, 5 February 2008.

12 Interfax, 11 March 2009. See also Sergei Blagov, 'Russia Pledges to Rescue Post-Soviet Economies', *Eurasia Daily Monitor*, 13 February 2009.
13 ITAR-TASS, 19 March 2009; Igor Naumov, 'Dorogostoiashche ambitsii', *Nezavisimaia gazeta*, 21 March 2009.
14 RIA Novosti, 21 April 2009.
15 RIA Novosti, 25 August 2009. See also Edward Hugh in 'Russia Economy Watch', 7 April 2009.
16 'Na etoi nedele', FOM, 10 September 2009.
17 RIA Novosti, 26 November 2009; see also 'Russia and the Economic Crisis', *Russian Analytical Digest*, No. 65, 6 October 2009, and Anders Aslund, Sergei Guriev, Andrew Kuchins, eds. *Russia After the Global Economic Crisis*, CSIS: Washington, 2010.
18 Bloomberg, 18 August 2011.
19 *Ekspert*, 20 April 2011; *Nezavisimaia gazeta*, 21 April 2011.
20 *Businessnewseurope*, 15 February 2011.
21 ITAR-TASS, 7 March, 17 May 2008. See also the 85-page booklet 'Russia and the WTO', Centre for European Reform, London, 2011. Putin and Bush met in early April at Bucharest for a NATO–Russia Council session, and then Bush flew to Sochi for a two-day working visit, 5–7 April 2008.
22 See, e.g. *Nezavisimaia gazeta*, 28 August 2008; *The Moscow Times*, 26 August 2008.
23 See, e.g. *Izvestiia*, 16 June 2009; and interview with the Russian Minister of Trade and Development Maksim Medvedkov on Vesti TV, 7 July 2009, translated in the WNC.
24 On the broad implications for foreign policy of Russia's membership to the WTO, see A.I. Denisov, 'Vneshnepoliticheskie aspekty y prisoedineniia Rossii VTO', *Mezhdunarodnaia zhizn'*, No. 7, 2012. Denisov was then First Deputy Foreign Minister. Translation available from the Russian Federation Ministry of Foreign Affairs, Information and Press Department.
25 For many of Medvedev's speeches on the modernization imperative, see Medvedev, *Novaia politicheskaia strategiia v Poslanii Prezidenta Dmitriia Medvedeva*, eds. G.O. Pavlovsky, K.V. Tanaev, Moscow: Evropa, 2010. Because this collection was available only briefly via inter-library loan, I have accessed Medvedev's speeches and statements as they were posted on the presidential website, *Kremlin.ru*.
26 Putin, 'Poslanie Prezidenta Federal'nomu Sobraniiu', *Kremlin.ru*, 26 April 2007; Putin, 'Rossiia na rubezhe tysiacheletiia', *Rossiiskaia gazeta*, 31 December 1999.
27 'The Results of the Year with the President of the Russian Federation Dmitry Medvedev', Embassy of the Russian Federation in Canada, Press Release, 14 December 2009.
28 Anastasiia Bashkatova, 'Prizyvy k modernizatsii ne ubedili Rossiian', *Nezavisimaia gazeta*, 9 December 2009. The Levada Centre conducted the survey.
29 *Kremlin.ru*, 15 and 21 May 2009.
30 Kremlin.ru, 30 April 2010. See also *Nezavisimaia gazeta*, 14 May 2010. The following material on Skolkovo is a summary with additional information of material contained in J.L. Black, 'Tandemology as Spectator Sport. The Course of Medvedev's Campaigns to Curb Corruption and Encourage Modernization', in *Russia After 2012*, pp.101–20.
31 'Skolkovo kak plot' i simvol', *Nezavisimaia gazeta*, 30 December 2010.
32 *Kremlin.ru*, 30 April 2010. The council's official title is the Foundation for the Development of the Centre of Research and Commercialization of New Technologies at Skolkovo.
33 See, e.g., 'Silikonovye yaitsa faberzhe', *Moskovskiy komsomolets*, 16 April 2010.

34 On this see Tal Adelaja, 'Foreigners' Paradise', *Russia Profile,* 6 May 2010.
35 *Vedomosti,* 20 June 2010.
36 The initial website was opened in July 2010 as www.modernrussia.com; a second site was created in March 2011 as *i-Russia.ru.*
37 *Foreign Policy Concept,* I. General Provisions, 'Chief Objectives', No. 2, 28 June 2008.
38 *Politkom.ru* and *Kommersant,* 30 May 2010.
39 *Vedomosti,* 20 June and 1 July 2010.
40 ITAR-TASS, 4 June 2010. General Electric (US) and Nokia (Finland) both have long histories of doing business in the USSR and Russia.
41 For a description of this tour, which was part of Medvedev's state visit to the USA, see Irina Aervitz, 'High Tech and Vekselburgers', *Russia Profile,* 29 June 2010. See also Igor Tsukanov, 'Ploshchadka dlia Cisco', *Vedomosti,* 1 July 2010.
42 *Kremlin.ru,* 18 June 2010.
43 'Vse bol'she rossiian veriat v modernizatsiiu', FOM, 10 July 2010.
44 See *Nezavisimaia gazeta,* 5 June 2010.
45 Aleksandr Golts, 'K voprosu o vyrashchivanii kukuruzy v Skolkovo', *Yezhednevnyi zhunal,* 28 June 2010.
46 See, e.g. Yulia Latynina, 'The Potemkin Village of Skolkovo', *Moscow News,* 29 December 2010. See also *Moskovskiy komsomolets,* 27 July 2010, and *Novaia gazeta,* 21 June 2010. Andrei Kulesnikov, *Gazeta.ru,* 22 June 2010, wrote that modernization would undoubtedly fail on the political side; and an editorial in *Nezavisimaia gazeta,* 28 June 2010, named Skolkovo a mere 'state of mind' on the part of Medvedev, his officials and Russian businessmen. See also E.A. Pain in *Nezavisimaia gazeta,* 3 September 2010, and Sergei Aleksashenko in *Voenno-pro myshlennyy kuryer,* 24 June 2010.
47 For the first issue of Belkovsky's series, see *Moskovskiy komsomolets,* 27 July 2010, and for Gorbachev's comments, *Ezhednevnyi zhurnal,* 14 July 2010.
48 Aleksandr Khramov in *Svobodnaia Pressa,* 4 December 2010.
49 *Svobodnaia Pressa,* 21 September 2010; Interfax, 18 September 2010. See also the Russia Profile Weekly Expert Panels 'Medvedev Halfway Into His First Term', and 'Medvedev Promises Change to Believe In?' *Russia Profile,* 12 March 2010 and 15 June 2010.
50 See Kryshtanovskaia, 'Al'ternativy modernizatsii strany ne sushchestvuet', *Kreml. org,* 31 May 2010, and 'Modernization as Liberalization', *ibid.* 4 June 2010. D. Ye. Furman, 'Posledniaia modernizatsiia', *Nezavisimaia gazeta,* 25 August 2010.
51 Interfax, 10 September 2010; see also Chapter Three, above.
52 *Kremlin.ru,* 2 April 2011, 30 March 2011.
53 For details see Svetlana Ledyaeva, et alia, 'Foreign Investment from Offshore Jurisdictions into Russia. An Analytical Overview', *Russian Analytical Digest,* No. 140, 28 November 2013, pp. 2–6.
54 Russian Federation President, Information and Press Department, Press Release, 2 April 2011. For mid-term reports on Russia's economy, see 'Russia's Economic Development', *Russian Analytical Digest,* No. 88, 29 November 2010.
55 *The Moscow Times,* 19 August 2011; Olga Razumovskaia, 'Skolkovo Innovation Hub Braving the Waters', *The Moscow Times,* 16 June 2011; *Kremlin.ru,* 24 February 2011.
56 See Justin Varilek, 'Nanotech to Play a Big Role in Modernization Plans', *The Moscow Times,* 26 October 2011. See also a full three-page spread, Paul Watson, 'Russia: Gambling on Science', *The Toronto Star,* 26 November 2011.
57 See Medvedev opening address to a joint meeting of the Modernization Commission and the Skolkovo Board, *Kremlin.ru,* 25 April 2011.
58 *Premier.gov.ru,* 20 April 2011; *Rossiiskaia gazeta,* 21 April 2011.
59 Vladimir Kuzmin, 'Moi kurs – modernizatsiia', *Rossiiskaia gazeta,* 13 April 2011.
60 'Ot redaktsii: Predvybornyi zhanr', *Vedomosti,* 20 June 2011.

61 *Kremlin.ru*, 17 June 2011.
62 Interfax, 21 June 2011. Putin was speaking at a news conference with the French prime minister in Paris.
63 'Skolkovo – chast' natsional'noi sistemy nauki', *Kommersant*, 29 February 2012; 'State-Business Relations and Modernization', *Russian Analytical Digest*, No. 105, 5 December 2011. See also 'Modernization is Becoming a Meaningless Term', *Svobodnaya pressa*, 5 October 2011, translated for WNC.
64 Vladimir Putin, 'Nam nuzhna novaia ekonomika', *Vedomosti*, 30 January 2012.
65 ITAR-TASS, 16 July 2012; RIA Novosti, 18 June 2012.
66 *Kremlin.ru*, 7 May 2008.
67 For biographical information, see 'Skrynnik, Elena Borisovna. Minister of Agriculture for the Russian Federation', *Russia Profile*, 16 March 2009.
68 For a full translation of the doctrine, see the USDA Foreign Agriculture Service, Gain Report, No. RS1008, 11 February 2010. For the quotes from Medvedev and Skrynnik on food security, see Stephen K. Wegren, 'Prospects for Russia as a Global Food Exporter', *Russian Analytical Digest*, No. 133, 18 July 2013, pp. 9–16, with graphs.
69 See Olga Liefert, et alia, *Rising Grain Exports by the Former Soviet Union Region*, United States Department of Agriculture, WHS-13A-01, February 2013; and Tai Adelaja, 'Cutting Across the Grain', *Russia Profile*, 4 March 2010.
70 See special issue of *Russia Profile*, 22 June 2009, on Russian 'Food'. Rankings among grain exporters change almost yearly, though the US tends to lead. Australia, Canada, France, Ukraine, Kazakhstan, Brazil, and the EU collectively are among the others that move in and out of the top five.
71 On this generally, see Lauren Goodrich, 'Drought, Fire and Grain in Russia', *Stratfor. Global Intelligence*, 10 August 2010.
72 ITAR-TASS, 14 September 2010.
73 *Kremlin.ru*, 24 December 2010; Interfax, 23 November 2010.
74 The agency's official title is the Federal Service for Control in the Sphere of Protection of Consumers' Rights and the Well-Being of Humans.
75 See for general background Tai Adelaja, 'Russia's Pig Deal. Russia Cuts Import Quotas on Pork and Poultry as Home Output Rises', *Russia Profile*, 1 August 2011, and 'A Grain of Discomfort', *Russia Profile*, 8 August 2011.
76 ITAR-TASS, 9 January 2011; Unian (Kyiv), 5 January 2011.
77 Anatoly Medetsky, 'WTO will be Painless for Agricultural Sector', *The Moscow Times*, 1 December 2011.
78 Andrew E. Kramer, 'Russian Farmland, Chinese Farmers', *New York Times*, 22 September 2012.
79 RIA Novosti, 13 September 2013.
80 *Kremlin.ru*, 12 December 2012.
81 On this possibility, see analysis by Wegren, *op.cit.*
82 For the early background, see Margarita M. Balmaceda, *Energy Dependency, Politics and Corruption in the Former Soviet Union: Russia's Power, Oligarchs' Profits, and Ukraine's Missing Energy Policy, 1995–2006*, London: Routledge, 2006.
83 For the 'Russian-Ukrainian Gas Memorandum', signed in Moscow by Prime Ministers Putin and Tymoshenko, see *Ukrayinska Pravda*, 4 October 2008.
84 See *Moscow News*, 8 January 2009, and 'The Russia-Ukraine Gas Conflict', *Russian Analytical Digest*, No. 56, 3 March 2009.
85 *Wall Street Journal*, 8 January 2009.
86 'Gazprom Ukraine Facts.' Gazprom website, 20 January 2009. The agreement was signed in Moscow on the 19th and gas flow was re-started the next day. Note that this is strictly Gazprom's version of the affair. For a Ukrainian perspective, see 'Ukraine and Russia Energy Relations', special issue, *National Security &*

*Defense* (Kyiv), No. 6 (2010). For subsequent commentary on the Ukraine-Russia gas arrangements in 2009 and the political bitterness it generated, Tom Balmforth, 'One Step Back, Two Steps Forward', *Russia Profile*, 24 November 2009, and Pavel Korduban, 'Putin, Tymoshenko Agree on Gas and Deride Yushchenko, Saakashvili', *Eurasia Daily Monitor*, 1 December 2009.

87  *Rossiiskaia gazeta*, 30 May 2011.
88  Interfax, 25 September 2011. Pavel Korduban, 'Ukraine and Russia Prepare New Gas Agreement', *Eurasia Daily Monitor*, 28 September 2011. On Medvedev's earlier stance, see Korduban, 'Kyiv Insists On Revision of Gas Contracts with Russia', *Eurasia Daily Monitor*, 4 May 2011, and Rudolf den Hoedt, 'Gazprom Back in the Game – and Ready to Take on Brussels', *European Energy Review*, 18 July 2011.
89  A complication for Ukraine is that the contract is a take-or-pay one, which means that Ukraine has to pay for at least 80 per cent of the contracted amount of gas whether it takes it or not.
90  On this issue, see Katinka Barysch, ed, *Pipelines, Politics and Power. The Future of EU-Russia Energy Relations*, London: Centre for European Reform, 2009; Kari Liuhto, ed. *EU-Russia Gas Connection: Pipes, Politics and Power*, Turku: Pan-European Institute, 2009 (Electronic); and J.L. Black, 'The New Geostrategy: Russia and the Competition for Control of Gas Pipelines to Europe', in *From Putin to Medvedev. Continuity or Change?* eds. Black & Michael Johns, Ottawa: Penumbra, 2009, pp. 129–135.
91  For statements from Barroso see Robert Wielaard, 'EU: Europe Must Invest in Energy Security', AP, 20 January 2009, and Barroso speech in Ankara, 13 July 2009, EU Press Release, *Europe.eu*, 13 July 2009. Speech/09/339.
92  On this generally, see Vladimir Socor, 'Russian Energy Projects in the Black Sea Reach End of an Era', *Eurasia Daily Monitor* 18 March 2011; Adnam Vatansever, 'The Risks of a Russia-Turkish Energy Bargain', *European Energy Review*, 31 March 2011. Both authors tend to take a dim view of Russia's energy activities without offering much in the way of productive alternatives.
93  Anatoly Medetsky, 'New Western Partners Mean Green Light for South Stream', *Moscow Times*, 19 September 2011.
94  Bloomberg, 31 December 2010. For the early decision, 'China, Russia Strike $25 Billion Oil Pact', *The Wall Street Journal*, 18 February 2009.
95  Bloomberg, 2 January 2011.
96  *MID.ru*, 27 September 2006. Lavrov made this statement at the Tenth International Sakhalin Oil and Gas Conference at Yuzhno-Sakhalinsk.
97  All three of these billionaires were born in the Ukrainian SSR and studied later in Moscow. Leonid Blatavnik became an American citizen in 1978 (and therefore 'Leonard', or 'Len') and founded Access Industries in 1986. Fridman founded the Alfa Group consortium in 1989, and Vekselberg co-founded the Renova Group with Blatavnik in 1990.
98  Interfax, 5 September 2010.
99  See 'Flirting with Foreign Finance', *The Moscow News*, 6 April 2011, and Tai Adelaja, 'Russia's Central Bank Figures Show that Russian and Foreign Investors Are Pulling their Money Out of the Russian Economy', *Russia Profile*, 7 April 2011. See also 'Capital Flight and Off-Shore Investment', *Russian Analytical Digest*, No. 140, 28 November 2013.
100 'Capital Flight Problem Continues', *The Moscow News*, 21 February 2012.
101 Bloomberg, 25 May 2011; Interfax, 26 October 2011; see also Guy Chazan, Gregory I. White, 'BP's Arctic Venture with Russia's Rosneft Founders', *The Wall Street Journal*, 18 May 2011.
102 *Vedomosti*, 27 May 2011.
103 *Russia Today* (RT), 21 March 2013. As part of the deal BP took a 20 per cent stake in Rosneft, giving Dudley a seat on its Board of Directors.

104   See Mathew Hulbert, 'The Rush to Russia', *European Energy Review*, 7 February 2011, and Tai Adelaja, 'Oily Interests', *Russia Profile*, 31 October 2011.
105   RIA Novosti, 25 October 2011; Mathew Hulbert, 'Nord Stream: Neue Sorgen for Europe', *European Energy Review*, 26 September 2011.
106   *Kremlin.ru*, 15 November 2011. The summit was held that day in Doha.
107   Interfax, 21 December 2010; APP, 3 September 2010.
108   AFP, 2 June 2011, RIA Novosti, 17 February 2011. See also regular reports in automobile company websites, such as *GMauthority.com* and *www.fiat.ru*.
109   Bloomberg, 18 September 2010.
110   Interfax, 22 April 2008; for a later leap forward, see Rachel Nielsen, 'McDonald's Looks to Expansion', *The Moscow Times*, 11 April 2012.
111   *Wall Street Journal*, 12 October 2011; Bloomberg, 25 June 2011.
112   On this trend, see Tai Adelaja, 'Personal Bankruptcy Redux', *Rusia Profile*, 2 April 2012, and 'In Piggy Banks We Trust', *Russia Profile*, 31 May 2012. In the latter piece, he points out that the trend towards savings was reversing as people again lost trust in the banking system.

# 5    Themes in foreign affairs

President Medvedev delivered several major statements on his foreign policy preferences during the first few months of his term. The first of these came in July when he signed a new Foreign Policy Concept into law. For the most part the document maintained existing patterns in foreign affairs, though it toned down the criticism of Russia's 'Western partners' that characterized Putin's foreign policy pronouncements. In introducing the Concept to a select audience of MID officials and ambassadors, he was critical of the ambassadorial corps for not always standing up in defence of Russia's interests, and singled out the newly established agency for the CIS (see Chapter One) as a vehicle for extending Russian influence in Eurasia. The Concept itself called for a renewed world order with the UN as the central player in it. Moscow's contribution would as much as possible be achieved through cooperation with the Troika (China, India, and Russia) and its extension, the BRIC. Reliance on, and adherence to, international law was the second major theme of the Concept, which was at the same time an implicit criticism of western behaviour. In terms of regions of the world, Russia's clear priority was the CIS.[1]

According to one diplomat in the audience, 'he called on us to be more decisive and aggressive so as not to be forced out of there by non-regional players such as the United States … In fact, that is why we are creating an agency for CIS Affairs under the Foreign Ministry'.[2]

A little more than a month later, Medvedev clarified his foreign policy doctrine further in a long interview for television arranged by *Kommersant*. He listed five basic principles for Russia to follow: 1. Adhere to the principles of international law; 2. Seek a multi-polar world; 3. Avoid confrontation and isolation; 4. Protect its citizens and business communities abroad; and 5. Focus on regions where Russia has 'privileged' interests.[3] With the exception of the fifth principle, the fundamentals outlined in the interview raised few eyebrows, even in light of the war in Georgia just a few weeks earlier.

Medvedev's stance echoed points made by foreign affairs specialist Yevgeny Primakov in the retrospective essay (see Introduction) printed in 2006. Primakov warned then that Europe and the West had grown unresponsive to Moscow's interests even though Russia presided over the G-8 that year and had already become an energy power.[4] In response to what he termed 'indifference' towards Russia on the part of the West, Primakov recommended that the Kremlin concentrate on strengthening its niche in the CIS, develop multilateral relations through the Shanghai Cooperation Organization and the Eurasian Economic Community, and reach some kind of accommodation with Ukraine – but not at Russia's expense. These priorities would appear to both reflect and help shape policies pursued by the Tandem during Medvedev's tenure, especially as concern arose that Western indifference to Russia was moving towards outright hostility.

When it came to Russia's status in international affairs, Medvedev held far stronger cards than the ones drawn by Putin in 2000. Putin was initiated into an office burdened by Yeltsin's extremes generally, and the wars in Chechnya particularly. In terms of diplomacy, Russia's status in the world had improved considerably by 2008, but its public image was still fashioned both by the Chechen conflict and by Cold Warrior suspicions on both sides of the old East-West divide. Western and above all American politicians tended to target Russia to bolster their own personas as patriotic and tough; former East bloc politicians employed the 'Russian threat' in the hope for gains within the EU and NATO. Russian politicians played the same game to stoke their own political ambitions and gave bluster pride of place ahead of diplomacy. Too many decision-makers in politics, military, and media still refused to allow facts to get in the way of their assumptions. Medvedev and, a little later, Barack Obama had these deeply rooted habits with which to cope.

After Putin's attempts to forge a new accord with Washington early in his first term, offering such concessions that US Secretary of State Colin Powell spoke of a 'seismic sea change of historic proportions' in their bilateral relations,[5] met a rather stunning lack of response, Moscow grew more openly assertive in the international sphere. Driven by continued NATO expansion eastward, and US unilateralism in the form of abrogating the ABM Treaty, the invasion of Iraq, and plans to deploy missile defence systems in Europe, Moscow decided that it had little to lose by pursuing its own national interests in Central Asia, Ukraine, and the Balkans.[6] Putin was especially fearful that the 'colour' revolutions in Georgia ('Rose' 2003), Ukraine ('Orange' 2004), and Kyrgyzstan ('Pink' 2005) were encouraged by Washington in an attempt to squeeze Russia out of its traditional areas of geopolitical interest. These and some other points of contention soon paled, however, when long-smouldering tensions with Georgia burst into flames.

## War in Georgia

All the best laid plans of his Concept notwithstanding, Medvedev's foreign policy activity over the first few years was framed primarily by events in Georgia. The August clash between Russian and Georgian armed forces provided so many signposts for Medvedev's foreign policy decisions that special attention will be granted to it here, with emphasis on the sequence of events.

Festering sores in the Moscow and Tbilisi relationship came to a head in January 2008 when, during a Georgian presidential campaign, President Mikhael Saakashvili boasted that if he were re-elected he would re-integrate Georgia 'at all costs'. This promise was very threatening to Abkhazia, South Ossetia, Ajaria and, indirectly, to Russia. The first two territories had actually functioned independently of Georgia from the early 1990s after a bloody civil war, and so developed de facto independent territorial administrations long before the events of 2008. The fact that they both border Russia and have, necessarily, received much economic, military, and political support from Moscow severely handicapped their regular requests to international agencies that they be freed from Tbilisi.

Strategists in Moscow were forewarned that their country would be isolated in any regional dispute when Saakashvili's electoral victory was deemed good enough by Western observers, even though it was tainted by myriad allegations of electoral violations, many of them reported by the OSCE. Russia's concern deepened when most Western countries supported Kosovo's unilateral declaration of independence from Serbia in February. Rightly or wrongly, Russian commentators could not help but see double standards at play.

Foreign Minister Lavrov met with Sergei Bagapsh and Eduard Kokoity, the elected presidents of Abkhazia and South Ossetia, two days before the Kosovo proclamation. In a statement issued after the meeting, Lavrov's Ministry concluded that any recognition of Kosovo 'will certainly have to be considered in terms of the situation in Abkhazia and South Ossetia' and that both Kosovo's 'plans to unilaterally proclaim independence' and the expressed intent of other states to recognize the legitimacy of such an act would devalue 'generally recognized principles and norms of international law'.[7]

When Western countries quickly acquiesced on Kosovo, the unrecognized republics within the internationally recognized borders of Georgia lobbied Russia aggressively to support their own bids for independence. They believed that their claims were more justified and certainly of longer standing than the Kosovar claim. Moscow was caught between a rock and a hard place: Most Western states and NATO were clearly on the side of Tbilisi, and Georgia held veto power over Russia's hope for accession to the WTO. Not incidental to the differing perceptions was the fact that Georgia is the transit territory for oil and gas from Azerbaijan to Europe. Moreover, Moscow and its friends in Beijing and New Delhi traditionally oppose separatism, still fearing the potential 'domino effect' of such movements.

In March 2008, governments of the Abkhazian and South Ossetian separatist territories again appealed to the international community finally to recognize their hard-won independence from Georgia. Just as Georgia separated from the USSR, leaders of these republics assumed they had the right to separate from Georgia – after all, their hated existence within Georgia was not decided by some historical evolution, rather it was determined by Stalin. An important EU concern, rightly enough, was the fate of thousands of ethnic Georgians who had been driven from their homes in South Ossetia and Abkhazia in the 1990s and later.

The requests submitted to the UN General Secretary and heads of EU countries stressed the right of self-determination for nations, and pointed to the simple fact that the two 'republics' had already been functioning independently for many years with long-time responsibility for the real 'political-legal foundations for the development' of their respective territories.[8] The 'Kosovo Effect' was again highlighted, but the appeals fell on deaf ears anyway. Russia's response was to lift standing economic sanctions against Abkhazia and to maintain an existing commercial embargo, transport blockade, and visa restrictions against the rest of Georgia. Later in March, Saakashvili again rejected a proposal to sign a non-use-of-force agreement with Abkhazia.

Business went on. In March, a Russian passenger ship arrived in a Georgian port for the first time in 18 months, and Aeroflot resumed flights to Tbilisi at about the same time. Hoping to get into NATO's Membership Action Plan (MAP), an expectation that was rejected at a NATO summit in Bucharest in April, Georgia offered Abkhazia 'unlimited autonomy', including a special cabinet seat. That offer was rejected in Sukhumi.

A more direct intervention from Moscow came on 16 April when Putin signed a decree authorizing government agencies in Russia to deal directly with Abkhazian and South Ossetian officials. This provoked an outburst of angry statements from Georgia, the EU, PACE, NATO and other organizations that worried that some kind of annexation process was underway. Tbilisi accused the Kremlin of interfering in Georgia's domestic affairs and lodged an appeal with the UN. Georgian troops were moved to the borders of the secessionist regions. Citing the fourth principle of Russian foreign policy, Putin warned that Russia would protect Russian citizens in the region if they were attacked, though the RF Ministry of Foreign Affairs also said that it would not recognize a unilateral declaration of independence from either of the territories. Thousands of South Ossetians and Abkhaz had taken up Russian citizenship after 2001.[9] The precedent of Kosovo was reiterated regularly as the situation heated up, and Russian officials reminded their European and North American counterparts that, as recently as 1998, they had all labelled the Kosovo Liberation Army (KLA) a terrorist organization.[10] Talk of war circulated in May as Georgia and Russia continued to build up forces on the north and south borders of Abkhazia and South Ossetia.

Georgia accused the Russian air force of shooting down an unmanned reconnaissance plane over Abkhazia on 20 April. Volleys of accusations and threats continued: Georgia threatened to block Russia's entry to the WTO; Russia threatened to sign a military agreement with Abkhazia. When more Georgian drones were shot down in March and May, Tbilisi blamed Russia, probably rightly, yet Abkhazians claimed credit for all of them.

On 2 May, Georgia demanded that Russia remove the 400 extra troops it had sent to join the UNSC- and OSCE-mandated peacekeeping force in Abkhazia, but the force still had not reached the numbers prescribed by the United Nations, so no withdrawal was forthcoming. A few weeks later, Russia sent in unarmed Railway Troops purportedly to fix the Abkhazian railway system, calling it 'humanitarian aid'.[11] The railroad, which goes to Tbilisi, had been unsafe for years and part of the peace process was a Russian agreement to repair it. Although the force withdrew when the task was completed, from the Georgian perspective this too was a provocation. One consequence of the sequence of misadventures on both sides was that the EU and the US finally sent delegations directly to Abkhazia in June. These initiatives were welcomed by Russia where it was thought that perhaps Western observers might finally see a somewhat different picture from the one drawn for them by Saakashvili.

In its turn, the South Ossetian government alleged that soldiers in Georgian gun posts fired into the Tskhinvali area in July, killing three and wounding others. Abkhazia announced that it would help the Ossetians if Georgia attacked. Pundits began speaking more seriously of a coming war. Tbilisi recalled its ambassador from Moscow in July, shortly after a visit to Georgia by US Secretary of State Condoleezza Rice, who alleged Russian interference in Georgian affairs. Shortly after Rice's visit, German Foreign Minister Frank-Walter Steinmeier arrived in Tbilisi and later released a plan for peace in Abkhazia, which the Abkhazians rejected. Saakashvili took the opportunity to proclaim grandly that the West now supported Georgia and that 'it is exactly in Tbilisi and around Tbilisi that currently the fate of the new European world order is being resolved'.[12]

Events of 7–9 August shook the world. Georgian forces launched an assault on South Ossetia on the opening day of the Olympics in Beijing (where Bush and Putin met twice). The invasion involved a midnight bombardment of Tskhinvali with GRAD missiles and the death of civilians in their beds. During the surprise attack, Georgian forces overran Russian peacekeeping positions, killing 10–15 of their former fellow peacekeepers. The Georgian president denied his renewed troop build-up mere hours before the attack, yet boasted on Georgian TV a few hours later that his 'heroic' forces had conquered most of Tskhinvali. A large Russian force (up to 200 tanks) moved across the border 12 hours after the Georgian assault. Saakashvili later claimed many times that he had acted only because Russian forces had come first through the Roki Tunnel. He lied. Russian troops drove Georgians out of Tskhinvali and moved on to Gori, into Georgia proper.

Both sides were accused of committing atrocities, apparently correctly. George W. Bush's oft-repeated reference in 2005 to Georgia as a 'beacon of liberty for the region and the world' rang more than a little hollow. Saakashvili's 'liberty' clearly was never intended for Ossetians or Abkhazians, who welcomed Russians with unreserved relief.

The Western outcry was deafening. Politicians and media talking heads fulminated about a return of Soviet 'imperialism'. Saakashvili was interviewed and/or quoted many times in the Western media, playing up his image as 'pro-Western' to the hilt and presenting himself as leader of a small 'democratic' country bullied by larger Russia. The Russian and Ossetian sides of the story were almost completely absent. Attitudes created by the initial onslaught of outrage were barely dented when the fact that Saakashvili 'started it', as they say on the playground, began appearing begrudgingly much later.

The politicization of the issue was immediate. An election campaign in the US ensured that President Bush and the two candidates for his position rushed to blame Russia; leaders of Poland, Ukraine, and the three Baltic countries stood beside Saakashvili on the night of 12 August when he spoke to a large crowd in Tbilisi and also blamed the Kremlin for everything.

A few niggling questions crept in. For example, several commentators wondered why the Georgian build-up was not reported by the some 130 US military advisers located in Georgia training troops for operations in Afghanistan – or was it? Why was Western intelligence unaware of Russian troops gathering on its border with South Ossetia – or was it? American Ambassador to Russia, John Beyrle, later in August told journalists in Moscow that Russia was 'fully justified' in sending troops in after its own soldiers had been killed.[13] Gradually, Western leaders backed away from blaming Russia unequivocally. NATO and President Bush instead called Moscow's response 'disproportionate' – referring mostly to weapons deployed, and the destruction of Georgian military assets outside the dissident territories. No western general voiced the obvious, i.e., for reasons of military contingency they would have done exactly the same thing. Speaking in Germany in November, Condoleezza Rice admitted that Russia had to act when its troops were overrun, adding the line that Moscow's response was disproportionate. Western media outlets and campaigning politicians ignored even these tentative retractions.

Medvedev met with the South Ossetian and Abkhazian leaders in Moscow on 14 August, and Russian forces began to draw back from Georgia to the separatist republics three days later. On 26 August, Medvedev recognized the independence of Abkhazia and South Ossetia,[14] and Ukraine suspended various scheduled cooperative meetings with Russia. Tbilisi severed diplomatic ties with Moscow on 30 August.

When it met in Dushanbe on 28 August, the Shanghai Cooperation Organization did not entirely support Moscow in this action, presumably because China is a member and is adamantly opposed to any form of separatism. The Collective Security Treaty Organization, with many of the same members but not China, gathered in Moscow a week later and fully supported Russia.[15] In accordance with their promise to French President Nicolas Sarkozy a week previously, Russian forces began formal withdrawal on 13 September. The process was completed within a month, and some 200 EU observers arrived and took over most of the former Russian posts. Rumours that Ukraine supplied Georgia with arms, perhaps even during the conflict itself, provided another of the mysteries emerging from the affair. Russian public opinion and the Union of Georgians in Russia, representing hundreds of thousands of Georgians who live in Russia and send home remittances that are very important to the Georgian economy, overwhelmingly supported Medvedev's actions.[16]

Other than the citizens themselves, there were no innocent parties to this conflict. Leaderships in Russia, Georgia, South Ossetia, and Abkhazia all contributed in their own way to the implosion in August. Russia's image abroad was badly damaged and, as more facts emerged, so was Saakashvili's. Immediate and harsh blame-casting in the West revealed a blatant Russophobia that caused a Russian public already wary of NATO and the US to distrust them still more.

Russians grew sick of seeing or hearing of Sakaashvili's repeated appearances on Western television as a victim of imperialistic Russia and talking heads constantly referring to some sort of Soviet-type plot to recapture the former empire. A burst of national pride and in some cases jingoism gave Medvedev's presidency a boost. As his 'victim' image paled even at home, Saakashvili lost the confidence of Georgians, not so much because he lost a war, but because his multiple lies were too obvious. Abkhazia and South Ossetia were left in limbo.[17]

## Ripple effects

Diplomacy eventually won through. In the first week of December, NATO agreed to re-open dialogue with Russia, and the EU resumed talks with Moscow on their Partnership and Cooperation Agreement (PCA), whose original 10-year term was allowed to lapse in 2007.

Renewed competition for sway in the South Caucasus began to take shape in early January 2009, when Georgia and the United States signed a Charter on Strategic Partnership. The Charter was filled with glowing language about shared values and mutual interests, and called for the common protection of Georgia's territorial integrity and – not to be forgotten – energy transit from Azerbaijan through Georgia to European markets. On the other hand, it was clear that the EU and PACE had begun to rethink the Georgian crisis, belatedly acknowledging that Georgia instigated the actual fighting. The change of heart was due in large part to a report prepared by an international fact-finding commission established by the EU and headed by Swiss diplomat Heidi Tagliavini. Released more than a year after the event, the report concluded that whereas all sides shared responsibility for the war, the fighting began 'with a massive Georgian artillery attack ... against the town of Tskhinvali'. The report added that Russia was justified in defending its peacekeepers who were attacked and killed in violation of international law, and also said that Russia's response was disproportionate.[18] No one ever clarified what a 'proportionate' response might have been.

The altered stance in Europe did not relieve Russia of unexpected responsibility for reconstruction in South Ossetia. Russia had little choice but to provide huge reconstruction funds when neither Tbilisi nor Western countries offered any – a further unplanned drain on Medvedev's first budget. After Georgia cut off gas supplies to South Ossetia in the winter, Russia shipped in energy sources and constructed a pipeline from the north. The Kremlin also provided financial aid to Abkhazia.

In March 2009, Moscow began again to issue entry visas to Georgians. After several false starts, talks between Russia, Georgia and the two breakaway regions opened in Geneva in May. Georgia rejected a Russian proposal that it sign a non-aggression agreement with South Ossetia and Abkhazia. The Abkhazians refused to attend anyway, claiming that the UN draft report did not adequately reflect their de-facto independence from Georgia. The Russian and South Ossetian delegations also then walked out. There was still a long way to go.

A parliamentary election conducted in South Ossetia on 31 May, just as a NATO exercise protested by Russia got underway in Georgia, revealed some minor shifts in position. Although the EU again refused to recognize the election or send observers, representatives from ten individual countries, among them EU members Germany and Italy, did serve as official observers. The voter turnout was large, about 82 per cent, and the current party in power returned with nearly half of the votes. Moscow again called the EU's refusal to recognize the election a 'predictable application of double standard', referring to the 'Kosovo Effect' once more.[19] According to a release from the US Embassy in Tbilisi, Washington 'regret[ted] the decision to hold so-called "elections" in the South Ossetian region of Georgia'.[20] Hardly any doubt here of the American position.

On 15 July 2009, the UN Observer Mission in Abkhazia officially came to an end. After 16 years in place (since August 1993), Russia vetoed its extension in the United Nations Security Council. On that same day, President Medvedev paid a quick unannounced visit to South Ossetia, one week after US President Obama left Moscow. Georgia raged about this meeting, and even in Russia there was some expressed concern about the perceived level of corruption in that small republic and the treatment there of ethnic Georgians. Although Medvedev committed some 8.5 billion rubles to the reconstruction of South Ossetia, he made a point of saying that it must not be wasted on corruption – likely in vain. In August, the Russian government promised billions more for infrastructure and social development in Abkhazia. Privately, it is safe to assume, many Russians began to see the victory in Georgia as a costly one.

Direct civilian flights between Moscow and Tbilisi started up again in early 2010, though diplomatic relations remained antagonistic and sporadic, with Switzerland continuing to represent Moscow's interests in Tbilisi. The inauguration of Abkhazia's incumbent President Sergei Bagapsh in February was called a 'farce' in Tbilisi and an important event in Moscow. Days after his installation, Bagapsh opened a three-day state visit to Moscow where he signed ten accords related to security matters.

There was some movement towards cooperation as opposition to Saakashvili grew in Georgia. Leader of the Democratic Movement-United Georgia party, Nino Burjanadze, met with Putin in Moscow on 5 March 2009. Former speaker of the Georgian Parliament, she urged her government to deal with Russia without preconditions. Another Georgian party, the Movement for Fair Georgia, led by ex-Prime Minister Zurab Nogaideli, signed a cooperative agreement with Russia's United Russia party.

In February and April, Moscow arranged with officials in Sukhumi and Tskhinvali to allow Russia to base troops in Abkhazia and South Ossetia, and the RF Ministry of Defence announced later that it would deploy S-300 RAMs to Abkhazia. This was a clear point of no return. As time went on and Russia's own North Caucasus shook with unmanageable violence in Dagestan, Ingushetia, and Chechnya, little changed in the standoff between Russia and Georgia. Saakashvili struggled to strengthen his political position in Tbilisi, and Moscow solidified its ties with the recalcitrant territories. There were added complications. The decades-old Nagorno-Karabakh issue lurked in the background, to the extent of renewed talk of war between Armenia and Azerbaijan. Medvedev chaired multiple meeting between the Presidents of Armenia and Azerbaijan, with no progress, but also no regression. Resumed war between two of the three South Caucasus countries inevitably would have drawn Russia, Georgia, and other interested parties in. Fortunately, the status quo held.

After months of negotiations and much posturing on both sides, Russia and Georgia finally came to terms in a Swiss-mediated accord allowing international monitoring of cross-border trade through Abkhazia and South Ossetia. This agreement also cleared the way for Russia's entry into the WTO. Faced with crises throughout the entire Caucasus, Medvedev was able to achieve a state of fragile stability in Moscow's links with hot spots in the South Caucasus, keeping them separated from the more direct domestic turmoil of the North Caucasus. But no observer of the region had illusions about any kind of permanent settlement – anywhere – in the near future.

Even as Medvedev's term ended, Moscow fretted about NATO's confirmation at its Chicago summit, 20 May 2012, that Georgia would eventually be a member,[21] and reacted angrily in June that year when the Obama Administration's leading Russophobe Hillary Clinton, promised Georgia help in preparing its coastal defences. Clinton's statements in Georgia to the effect that the 2008 war resulted in Russian 'occupation' of Georgian territories prompted further angry responses from Moscow, where such remarks were called 'revisionism', evidence of Washington's indifference to the death of Russian peacekeepers and South Ossetian civilians as a result of Georgia's midnight surprise assault, and of Clinton's failure to face realities.

The two sides picked away at each other's scabs, just as they had done prior to the war of 2008. For example, in August 2012, on the fourth anniversary of the war, Saakashvili visited villages near the South Ossetian border and promised that Georgia would enter NATO and the EU and then return the 'occupied' lands to Georgia.[22] Saakashvili was trying to stem the tide of his waning popularity at home.

No longer president by that time, Medvedev became a target – at home. One day after Saakashvili's foray, a documentary film shown in Russia blamed Medvedev for indecision, and even cowardice, for not acting in South Ossetia sooner. Former Chief of the Army General Staff Baluevsky intoned that Medvedev's hesitation cost 1,000 lives. Medvedev, who was in Tskhinvali when he heard of the remarks, immediately denied the accusation and said the critical officers 'are either ignorant or are distorting the real facts on purpose'. He claimed to have ordered the troops to enter South Ossetia within two and a half hours of learning of the Georgian invasion.[23]

The constant strain was lifted somewhat only as a result of a parliamentary election campaign in Georgia, which featured naturally enough the 'Russia question'. The president's party, the United National Movement, regularly characterized challenger billionaire Bidzina Ivanishvili and his Georgia Dream party as Russian proxies. When election results came in on 2 October 2012, the Georgia Dream coalition won and Saakashvili's party went into opposition. Ivanishvili's agenda included closer ties with Russia, opening embassies and re-starting almost defunct trade, yet also to maintain ties with the US and continue to apply for membership in NATO.

One of Ivanishvili's first political acts was to participate in meetings with the opposition where he blamed them for the war against Russia in 2008. He did not hold Russia blameless; rather he accused Saakashvili of giving them an excuse to attack. Change for the better was in the air, but it had taken five years, ate up Medvedev's foreign policy file, and was still by no means assured.

Probably the most damaging ripple effect from the war in Georgia was the impact it had on Russia's image in the outside world, an image that seemed about to improve as Medvedev settled in behind the presidential desk. International polls tended to portray his predecessor, Putin, as the determining factor in almost all dimensions of Russian life, and his influence was regarded as detrimental when it came to the evolution of democracy and human rights. Putin's image was particularly unfavourable in the United States and Britain, where Cold War attitudes were stoked by his centralizing and authoritarian practices.[24]

Well-publicized cases of corruption in business and bureaucracy further tainted Russia's image abroad, as did high profile assassinations such as those of journalists Anna Politkovskaia (2006) and former FSB agent Aleksandr Litvinenko (2006). In these and other such cases, the immediate reaction by Western media, some politicians, human and civil rights groups, along with some Russian oppositionists and NGOs was to blame Putin – sometimes even for the actual murder. Subsequent revelations to the contrary, both real and circumstantial, rarely changed already set minds. The almost ritualistic demonization of Putin by Western media and politicians left Medvedev confronted with assumptions about his administration and his prime minister standing in the way of discourse with foreign leaders.[25]

## Looking east – toward Beijing

In terms of international politics, one of the by-products of the crisis in the South Caucasus, Russia's so-called soft-underbelly, was an energized Russian geo-strategic push eastward, where its economic interests were already directed, towards a friendlier climate.

General associations formed in the East during the 1990s grew into full-fledged chartered organizations with permanent secretariats, headquarters, and agendas by the early 2000s. These bodies included the economic and political Shanghai Cooperation Organization (SCO) and the military Collective Security Treaty Organization (CSTO). Moscow and Beijing provided powerful bookends for the SCO, with the Central Asian countries in between, and the Commonwealth of Independent States (CIS) provided the seven-country membership of the latter organization. Beijing hosts the secretariat of the SCO, and Moscow is the site for the permanent headquarters of the CSTO.[26]

The SCO was given its formal institutional basis in June 2001, Putin's second year as president, and adopted a charter in 2002. At that time it included Russia, China, Kazakhstan, Kyrgyzstan, Tajikistan, and Uzbekistan. Mongolia, India, Pakistan, and Iran were granted official observer status between 2004 and 2007; in that latter year, Turkmenistan and Azerbaijan gained unofficial observer status. The SCO continued to expand its reach during Medvedev's tenure in office: Sri Lanka, Belarus, and Turkey became Dialogue Partners and, in 2012, habitually invited guest Afghanistan was named an official observer.

Primarily a political and economic organization, the SCO has an anti-terrorist structure (from 2002), a business council, an energy club, a research & educational centre (Yekaterinburg), a joint environmental protection agency, and a disaster management centre (Krasnoyarsk). The SCO also organizes anti-terrorist training operations. Its councils of heads of state, heads of government, and heads of foreign ministries meet on a regularly scheduled basis, as do heads of ministerial departments. The energy club remained extant while also morphing into the Gas Exporting Countries Forum (GECF) discussed in Chapter Four.

The combined population of participating countries equals about one half of the entire world's population, so its potential on the world's stage cannot be taken lightly. In addition to huge numbers of people, the SCO includes leading energy producers (Russia, Kazakhstan, Uzbekistan, Turkmenistan [by contract], and Iran), and major energy consumers (China & India). The SCO established an Afghanistan Contact Group in 2007 at the specific request of President Hamid Karzai, and keeps an anti-drug trafficking office in Kabul. During Medvedev's last year and a half in office, preparations for a role in Afghanistan after NATO withdraws its troops in 2014 were high on the agendas of both the SCO and the CSTO. These roles envisioned both the integration of Afghanistan into Central Asian economic projections and insulating their own borders from renewed Taliban militancy and the already exponentially growing drug trade.

It is hardly surprising then that the SCO featured prominently in each of Medvedev's annual addresses and, with the CSTO, gained even greater importance to Moscow after Prime Minister Putin introduced the idea of a

Eurasian Union in late 2011–12.[27] Subsequent publicity campaigns, which even included a contest to devise a logo for the still unformed Eurasian Union, kept the concept out there for Russia's neighbours to digest, yet since both the Customs Union and the Common Economic Space were themselves only in their infancy, the Eurasian Union remained little more than a theoretical objective during the final months of Medvedev's presidency.

The eastward priority was not acknowledged formally until February 2013 when Putin's new Foreign Policy Concept was approved. Article Six made it plain: 'The ability of the West to dominate the world economy and politics continues to diminish. The global power and development potential is now more dispersed and is shifting to the East, primarily to the Asia-Pacific region'.[28] Myriad frustrations experienced by Medvedev's office in its dealings with the West, including the fading reset with the US, gave Putin less to lose by confirming the eastward trend.

In 2008, the CSTO, which counts Russia, Belarus, Armenia, Kazakhstan, Kyrgyzstan, Tajikistan and (until June 2012) Uzbekistan as members, is not a NATO of the East, as several member states like to describe it. Mutual strategic, political and economic interests, especially in Central Asia, link its membership but not by binding agreements such as Article 5 in the NATO charter that commits members to mutual defence. Primarily a military organization, the CSTO formed a Peacekeeping Corps in 2007 with a mandate to be deployed anywhere on the territory of its member states, with permission of the host country. The CSTO conducts military exercises, has compiled a joint data bank on drug trafficking and, in conjunction with the SCO, operates a permanent anti-drug trafficking program. Member states train their officers in Russian Military academies and purchase weapons from Russia at domestic rates. As of December 2011, every member has the right to veto the siting of foreign military bases on each other's territories.[29]

These two bodies hold official UN status as regional organizations and over the past several years have ratified agreements with each other for cooperation on security matters, organized crime, and anti-terrorism. As early as 2006, the Russian Foreign Ministry proposed, and repeated often during Medvedev's tenure, that the CSTO and NATO cooperate in Afghanistan on matters related to security, and called on NATO to deal with the CSTO as a collective organization, rather than bilaterally with each member. NATO equally consistently rejected this idea until September 2010 when General Secretary Anders Fogh Rasmussen asked for greater cooperation with regional organizations in the Afghanistan conflict.

The US continued to express reservations about dealing with the CSTO as a collective until March 2011, when US Assistant Secretary of State for South and Central Asia Robert Blake noted the advantages of dealing with the SCO as a regional organization. He made a pronouncement to that effect in Beijing. It was generally assumed that the US's need for stability in Central Asia (in light of crises throughout the Middle East) and assistance in the conflict in Afghanistan, drove Washington's apparent volte-face.[30]

The SCO had already gained greater international legitimacy in 2010, especially after UN Secretary General Ban Ki-Moon lauded the expansion of UN–SCO cooperation in June that year.

In addition to a shared need to counter political challenges to the status quo at home, and mutual struggles against drug trafficking, terrorism, separatism, and religious extremism, CSTO members are held together by gas and oil pipelines and long-term energy-contracts; huge cross-border investments in infrastructure (roads, airports); large-scale joint manufacturing enterprises – e.g., Russia–Uzbekistan Chkalev aviation industry; education & culture (a Eurasia university system is shaping up), and widespread Russian language TV.[31] As members of the CSTO, Armenia and Belarus are drawn into Russia's eastern orbit. Yerevan relies on Russian support because its potential enemy, Azerbaijan, is tied to the West's oil markets, and Minsk has substantial political, economic, and military ties with no one else but Russia. A permanent Russian military base is located in Armenia.

It would still be a mistake to think of either the CSTO or the SCO as treaty-based alliances. Having only recently gained statehood themselves, their member-states are fiercely independent and sometimes suspicious of each other, and are connected far more by the common interests noted above than by binding legal formulas.

A phenomenon that coincided with Medvedev's presidency, though he had little to do with it, was the emergence of the BRICS as an influential force in international affairs, and one that further strengthened Russia's presence in the East. The acronym 'BRIC' was coined in 2001 to refer to Brazil, Russia, India, and China, countries all deemed to be at a similar stage of new and rapidly advancing economic development.[32] South Africa was added to the roster in 2010, making the acronym 'BRICS'. The BRICS, of course, is not an exclusively 'eastern' association; rather it serves as a valuable linchpin in Moscow's connections with its most important eastern and south-eastern partners: China and India.

There was no inkling in 2001 that the BRIC might eventually take on a political role in international affairs, yet by the time the group's first formal summit of heads of state gathered in Yekaterinburg in 2009 to discuss global economic issues, there was no doubt of its potential political clout. Although that meeting had mostly to do with the international financial crisis, the June opening was symbolic of shifting centres of influence in international affairs: Brazil, Russia, India, and China presented a common front on the world stage. They called for a revision of voting rights in the IMF and raised the possibility of replacing the dollar as the main global reserve currency. The BRIC meeting coincided with an SCO summit and resulted in a joint statement revealing a common world vision and agreements on world food issues.

We saw in Chapter Four that the BRICS summit at Sanya, China in April 2011 issued a joint Declaration stressing common economic goals.[33] The bloc jumped into international relations as well, agreeing to help raise the profiles of Brazil, India, and South Africa at the UN. The Declaration promoted 'multi-lateral diplomacy' in international conflicts, and mentioned the then-current NATO attacks on Libya specifically as something to be avoided. It supported Russia's bid to enter the WTO and issued a strongly worded condemnation of international terrorism. After the meeting, India and China announced that they would resume the military cooperation with each other that was suspended in August 2010. The summit was the third such meeting since 2009, a sign of the increasing consolidation of the BRICS as a fixture in Russian foreign policy.

By the end of Medvedev's term, Moscow and Beijing were both pushing the BRICS to take a more activist stand on economic action in the world arena. Above all, its membership hoped to alter global financial institutions to better reflect the growing participation of BRICS in the world economic order. At a March 2012 summit in Delhi, for example, reform of the IMF to take into account the importance of India and China was at the very top of the agenda. The meeting communiqué also insisted that the G-20 serve as the basic agency for world economic regulation, rather than the G-7. The latter group is made up of finance ministers from the seven wealthiest developed countries in the world. They meet regularly, and exclude Russia.[34]

From the Russian perspective, this long process culminated in February 2013, well after Medvedev stepped down into the prime ministerial office, with the creation of a full blown Concept of Russian Federation Participation in BRICS.[35] The Concept emphasized the members' common support of international law, desire to reform 'obsolete' international financial organizations, and strengthen the UNSC's role in international conflict resolution. In March that year, Putin proclaimed that the BRICS should be transformed 'from a dialogue forum, which coordinates positions on a limited number of issues into a full-fledged mechanism of strategic cooperation'.[36] It would seem that the BRICS had been a major component of Putin's file in the Tandem all along. It was clear also to all observers that Moscow and Beijing both wanted the BRICS to do for the Far East what the SCO did for Central Asia, i.e., block US influence and, in China's case, to sustain Russian support in its accelerating territorial disputes with Japan.[37]

The unity of BRICS already had been tested during the civil war in Libya in 2011. Of the five UNSC members to abstain from voting on Resolution 1973 on intervention, four were BRICS countries, excepting South Africa, and the fifth was Germany, Russia's leading trading partner in Europe. Only three days prior to the UN decision, G-8 foreign ministers all agreed that violence against civilians in Libya was unacceptable, and the Russian minister's advocacy of resolution by 'peaceful political means' was representative of the generally accepted approach – or so Lavrov thought.[38]

Thus, the rush to use force in Libya exposed splits in NATO, even as Russia's abstention, rather than veto, helped maintain recent accommodations with the US. From Moscow's perspective, application of the 'humanitarian aide' concept was too quickly turned into energetic intervention to force regime change. Russia was also concerned, but silent about losing another energy partner and weapons customer it had in Iraq.

On 24 March, the State Duma adopted a resolution (350-32-0) calling on the Western coalition to cease its 'hostilities' in Libya and urged all sides to accept a ceasefire. The statement said, in part, that the UNSC intervention was 'damaging Libyan civil infrastructure ... and [causing] new civilian casualties'. The Russian and German foreign ministries released official statements revealing shared opinions on the Libyan affair. When, a little over a month later, NATO planes bombed what they claimed was a command centre in Tripoli and instead hit the house of Gadhafi's youngest son, killing him and three of Gadhafi's grandsons, all under the age of 12, Russia sharply criticized the West for overstepping the mandate given NATO by the UNSC and labelled the action a war crime. The Russian (and much of the European) public was outraged and vented some of its anger against Medvedev for 'allowing' such a travesty to happen. Like the Kosovo example for the Caucasus, the Libyan model was to come back and haunt Russian–Western relations in other existing and subsequent Middle East hot spots.

The BRICS did not always automatically take Russia's side in international disputes. When UNSC members Russia and China vetoed the resolution to impose sanctions on Syria in February 2012, they were isolated on the Council. The remaining 13 all voted in favour. These latter included Germany and two BRICS members, India and South Africa. Members smoothed over their differences at the BRICS summit in Delhi and coordinated their stances on Syria, Iran, and in the UN. In the former case, BRICS demanded that no outside military interference be tolerated and offered humanitarian aid to both sides. In addition to the previously mentioned call for the IMF to cede more voting rights to China and India, it invited the UN to refrain from trying to depose 'unwanted' regimes. After he was back in the president's chair, Putin was able to persuade the BRICS to work even more closely together and create some of its own financial institutions, including a bailout fund and a development bank.[39] His success with the BRICS did not carry over to the IMF, which in that year returned American and other 'old guard' officials to their former places of domination in the organization.

Pushing further south in Asia, Moscow assured closer ties to Vietnam, as Rosatom agreed to cooperate with Hanoi in constructing a nuclear power station. At the fifth East Asian Summit (EAS), held in Hanoi on 30 October 2010, leaders of the 16-nation Asian bloc decided to admit both Russia and the United States in 2011. The EAS works closely with the Association of Southeast Asian Nations (ASEAN), which opened its 17th summit in Hanoi just two days earlier. It was there and then that the deal to build a nuclear power plant was signed. A further diplomatic drive southeast was blocked briefly when, in late October 2010, Medvedev confronted Japan's campaign for the Kuril Islands directly, visiting the islands and ordering a greatly expanded military upgrade for them. The visit was the first by a Russian leader since Soviet occupation at the end of World War II. The sensitivity of the issue is such that the two countries have not signed a peace treaty to formally end the war precisely because of the territorial dispute over the Kurils. In the recent instance, Tokyo went so far as to temporarily recall its ambassador from Moscow.[40] Although the outburst of fury from Japan and jingoism from Russia died down fairly quickly, Japanese-Russian relations remained unsettled – to the silent delight of China.

Russia's modern-day 'drang nach osten' always focused primarily on China either as a partner or as a competitor. Well before Moscow and Beijing were tied closely together in the multi-lateral SCO and BRICS, the two countries shared principles on several fronts: support for a multi-polar world to counter an apparent US unipolar world; opposition to UN military missions that went beyond humanitarian operations; and diplomatic resolution to international conflicts. In the 1990s, they opposed NATO intervention in Bosnia and Kosovo, and they both had hot spots that they hoped to keep isolated from Western interference, such as Chechnya and Tibet. These were fundamental matters, but common agreement on them did not in themselves make Russia and China allies. In the 1990s, then-Foreign Minister Primakov proposed a Moscow–Delhi–Beijing axis, but the notion was downplayed until 2002 when George W. Bush referred in his State of the Union address to an 'axis of evil,' that is Iran, Iraq, and North Korea. This pronouncement hit Russia like a bombshell, because it appeared to foreshadow unilateral military action. Russian Foreign Minister at the time, Primakov protégé Igor Ivanov, resurrected his mentor's idea during a visit to Delhi shortly thereafter.[41] Although the notion kept cropping up in all three capitals, it was not institutionalized until 2005, when the three heads of state, defence ministers, foreign affairs ministers, and economic ministers began to hold regular meetings and issue joint statements. This was an extraordinarily important development.[42]

Medvedev was, in fact, a bit of an old China hand. He was in charge on the Russian side of the Russia–China 'National Year' arrangements for both 2006 and 2007 and also made China the site of his first post-election state visit outside the CIS countries. After the state visit in May, he was back in China for three days in September with an agenda that included diversifying Moscow–Beijing trade relations (i.e., going beyond oil, gas and coal), and explaining his modernization vision.[43]

The first 'axis' conference between foreign ministers during Medvedev's presidency was held in Yekaterinburg in May 2008 and resulted in the release of an extensive communiqué.[44] The three ministries confirmed their support for each other's vision of international affairs, the SCO, and common efforts to stabilize Afghanistan. Cooperation in agriculture, industrial development, and intellectual activities were stressed. China and Russia supported the idea of a 'greater role' for India in the UN, implying permanent membership of the UNSC, and welcomed India's decision to upgrade its role as an observer country in the SCO. The next day officials from Brazil joined the ministers to make it a BRIC meeting.

The tone of the carefully orchestrated relationship between Russia and China was set for the rest of Medvedev's term during a meeting in Beijing in March 2010.[45] Russian Deputy Prime Minister Andrei Denisov and his Chinese counterpart worked out a detailed agenda relating to Central Asia and the SCO, and agreed on a Plan of Consultations for the year. Within weeks of this meeting, Chinese Vice President Xi Jinping (later President) was in Russia on a five-day visit (20–25 March) for wide ranging discussions with Medvedev and Putin – separately. At Barkhiva, he and Medvedev spoke of their countries as each other's strategic partners. In Moscow, Putin and Xi launched the Year of the Chinese Language in Russia with much pomp and ceremony.

Medvedev paid another state visit to China in September 2010 for his fifth meeting with President Hu that year. They talked about trade, security issues, and North Korea. Highlighting the visit was a ceremony at which the presidents celebrated the completion of the first oil pipeline connecting their countries.[46] Russian oil started flowing into China at the end of the month, adding yet another link in the mutual dependency chain.

The Kremlin also intensified its ties with the third party in the axis. Prime Minister Putin travelled to India in March and signed 15 deals worth about $10 billion. These included the agreement to construct new power units at a nuclear power station in India and several weapons purchases by that country. Altogether, Russia and India now had some 200 joint projects underway. In April, Indian officials said that their country would now like to join the SCO, changing their previously unenthusiastic position.[47] It was assumed that the Indian delegation felt that their observer status limited the influence they might have on the organization.

When it came to the question of new full memberships, India's case was complicated by the fact that Pakistan wanted full membership as well, and that was not looked upon so sympathetically by most of the members. Iran also applied for membership, and that too was problematic. Aware that the Indian request would likely not succeed, Medvedev sent Lavrov to India in November to confirm that Russia would support India as a member of the UNSC if the UN initiated any such changes, and signed preliminary agreements related to India's orders for Russian Sukhoi PAK FA-50 fighter jets. The Russian president's state visit to India a few weeks later followed trips to Delhi by the US's President Obama, China's Premier Wen, and France's President Sarkozy, all of whom promoted trade. India, of course, hoped to use such links to balance China's growing power and influence in the region, and Russia is Delhi's primary source of weaponry and nuclear energy infrastructure. So, competition within the axis always hovered close to the surface – nor should it be forgotten that India and China still have important conflicting territorial claims.

The axis foreign ministers held their 10th ministerial meeting in Wuhan, China, over two days in November 2010. The top item on their long agenda was discussion of a 'new security architecture in the Asia-Pacific region'.[48]

Coming just a week after the US president promised to support India's bid for a permanent seat on the UNSC, this meeting had an unusual precedent to moot.

An important manifestation of the Moscow–Beijing–Delhi link-up is that it provides mutual support for policies toward Iran and other countries that might be targets of Western interference. Contrary to Western hyperbole, Russia does not stand alone in these cases. One result of Medvedev's state visit to Delhi was a joint statement by India and Russia to the effect that Iran had a right to use nuclear energy for peaceful purposes, and that the issue of Iran and nuclear weaponry should be resolved by diplomatic means. A package of some 30 bilateral documents was signed too, including a memorandum of understanding (MOU) on research into the peaceful uses of nuclear energy, a fifth-generation fighter plane design contract, and easing visa restrictions on certain categories of citizens.

Bilateral Russia–China bonds also were strengthened further in 2008. Trade value had nearly doubled since 2006, and unrest in Tibet made Moscow's support more important to Beijing than previously. Much was made of the fact that China was the first non-CIS country visited by Medvedev after his inauguration. In a burst of ebullient camaraderie, the tour saw agreements reached on joint language training projects, and wide-ranging economic cooperation. The two sides issued statements against weapons in space, and voiced common positions on world affairs. Medvedev addressed a large audience at Beijing University. He and Hu Jintao signed a joint condemnation of the US plans to place missile defence systems in Eastern Europe.[49]

Russia assigned eight military transport planes to carry aid to China in the aftermath of the devastating earthquake there later in 2008. A symbolically important agreement between Russia and China was finalized on 21 July, when the border between them was fully demarcated. Russia handed over two long-time controversial islands in rivers that separate the two countries. One has only to recall the violence and nationalistic fervour sparked by disputes over such islands in 1969 and subsequently to understand that this concession was no small matter.

The relationship was given a further boost during a meeting between Prime Minister Putin and Wen Jiabao in Moscow in late October. They signed covenants on pipelines, nuclear cooperation, oil supply, and other economic matters. Moscow agreed to fund Russian language study centres for China. The defence ministers of Russia and China had their turn in early December in Beijing to plan a full-scale anti-terrorist military exercise for 2009, oppose the deployment of US missile defence systems in Eastern Europe, and again censure the US and EU opposition to their proposals to outlaw weapons in space.[50] Economic and military ties between the two countries grew exponentially.

China and Russia remained in lockstep on most international issues, but there were hiccups. A wave of hostility burst from an increasingly nationalistic China when a Russian warship fired on and sank a Chinese cargo vessel in

February 2009. Beijing lodged a formal protest; Russian authorities said that the ship was fleeing the port of Nakhodka without permission and was wanted for violating Russian border laws. Several Chinese sailors went missing. The issue blew over diplomatically, but festered in the Chinese press for some time, suggesting that the 'hail fellow, well met' public front might prove shallow if their perceived national interests cease to coincide.

Such incidents did not prevent Russia and China from signing the $25 billion oil pact mentioned in the previous chapter, which set the stage for the construction of a cross-border pipeline for crude oil. That agreement was preceded by a conference between the Russian and Chinese finance ministries in Beijing, the third of what had become an institutionalized mechanism for financial dialogue established in 2006.[51]

All the economic and political closeness aside, there was growing unease in Russia about China's military and economic strength. Although the Kremlin never expressed open concern, a long editorial in *Izvestiia* mirrored a widespread behind-the-scenes worry. The editorial writer claimed that China was second only to the US in expenditures on military build-up and that it was gradually encircling Russia's other major partner, India, by means of big projects in Pakistan, Myanmar, Bangladesh, and Nepal. Above all, the paper claimed that China represented 'an overpopulated territory threatening a huge wave of migration'. The target of that emigration, *Izvestiia* warned, was Russia's Far East, which could become little more than a raw material appendage for an imperialistic China. Russia's Eurasianists and others took observations like these seriously, and spread them widely.[52]

None of this slowed the steam engine of Moscow–Beijing mutual reliance at the top levels. President Medvedev was in China again in mid-April 2011 to attend a meeting of BRICS. He granted interviews for Chinese TV, participated in the Boao Forum for Asia, and toured Hong Kong. In return, the Chinese president flew to Moscow after the SCO summit in Astana. He and Medvedev issued a joint statement on international relations in which the BRICS, the SCO, and the APEC were highlighted as important to both of them. They reiterated earlier pronouncements on missile defence and the Iranian nuclear weapons issue, and agreed that the SCO should serve as an agency for the rehabilitation of post-war Afghanistan.[53]

The significance of the SCO emerged again in June 2011 when Afghanistan was finally granted official observer status in the organization. Afghan President Karzai visited Moscow on 20 January ostensibly to discuss drug trafficking and terrorism, but the possibility of an increase in Russian weapons sales to Afghanistan (paid for by the US) was raised as well.[54] This discourse may have facilitated the rise in Afghanistan's standing at the SCO.[55]

During the summit in Astana renewed bids for full membership from observer states, Iran, India and Pakistan, were rejected. Moscow supported India's application but Beijing vetoed that idea, perhaps seeing the change of status as a vehicle for Russia and India to dilute Beijing's growing dominance in the organization.[56] So the competitive side of Moscow and Beijing's participation in the SCO had not gone away. Iran's application was a non-starter, especially after Teheran sued Moscow for its failure to deliver on a contract to sell Iran S-300 anti-missile systems. The official reason for rejecting Iran's application was the fact that the country is under sanction from the UN and therefore not eligible. An unspoken consideration was the simple fact that Iranian membership would saddle the SCO with the weight of Tehran–Washington animosity, something it did not need or want.

On the other hand, as a neighbour of most Central Asian countries and a potential arena for competition between China, India, Pakistan, and Russia, Afghanistan's accession to the SCO was a natural for everyone concerned. Putin spoke of this after the SCO heads of state summit, noting also that the organization had set up a joint investment account, expanded its Business and Youth Council and its Energy Club, and confirmed the project to create an SCO university. In the latter case, all member states signed an Education Charter in Moscow at the November 2011 sitting.[57]

At a meeting with India's Prime Minister Singh in Moscow the following month, the Russian president made a point of saying that India should be a full member of the SCO, which suggested that this proposal was still alive and well, and that Russia did not mind challenging China over it. Medvedev confirmed his earlier commitment to back India's bid for a permanent seat on the UNSC.[58]

The premier's half of the Tandem was especially active in courting China. Putin was in Beijing earlier in the Fall accompanied by a delegation of Russian corporate executives. Russian analysts concluded that the lack of success in expanding trade and other interests with Western Europe drew Putin eastward, where he appeared to have greater opportunity to grow existing trade links. Among other things the long-lasting deadlock on pricing gas supplies to China was up for discussion. Nine agreements were signed, including arrangements for Chinese funding of the construction of an aluminium smelter in the Irkutsk region. China agreed to invest up to one billion dollars in various other Russian and CIS projects. Although the pricing mechanism for Russian gas sales to China was left unresolved, China surpassed Germany as Russia's leading single country trade partner during Medvedev's presidency.

A week after he announced that he would be a candidate for the presidency in 2012, Putin published the explosive article in *Izvestiia* touting further integration of Eurasia in the guise of a Eurasian Union based on the Common Economic Space that will emerge from the existing Russia, Kazakhstan, Belarus Customs Union. The new mechanism, if achieved, will resemble the European Union. This will be some time in the distant future, for the plan calls for the existing economic integrative associations to evolve into a Eurasian Economic Union by 2016. Each member will join voluntarily and be one of equal sovereign partners in the enterprise. Putin denied specifically that the Union represented some sort of revived USSR, even though the new project envisioned eventual political integration.[59]

As Medvedev's tenure drew to a close, Russia's dealings with Central Asia appeared less settled than previously, and Russia seemed to be slipping further behind China as the dominant player in the Far East.[60] Although Moscow continued to strengthen its interaction with each Central Asian country bilaterally, and both the SCO and the CSTO pursued integration, precarious intra-Central Asian relations posed a constant threat to their unity. Wealthy and theocratic Turkmenistan remained aloof, if not hostile to blandishments from Moscow's integrative agencies; Uzbekistan wavered in its commitment to the CSTO, and withdrew from it in the Spring of 2012; volatile territorial disputes between Uzbekistan, Tajikistan, and Kyrgyzstan in the Fergana Valley were always close to the surface; friction between Kazakhstan and Kyrgyzstan over oil supplies; political unrest in Kyrgyzstan; concern in Moscow about the huge numbers of Tajik workers, many of them illegal, in Russia; and Beijing's increased investment in Central Asia infrastructure (rail lines and energy pipelines), were but some of the disruptive hazards facing Moscow's Central Asian policy. The overarching source of potential conflict in the region, however, is water supply. Dam construction projects in Tajikistan and Kyrgyzstan could impede water flows in Uzbekistan and Kazakhstan, and force Russia to take sides – a prospect that would seriously slow any integrative movement.

In the background from the Kremlin's standpoint were the geostrategic threat of growing US influence and, paradoxically, the even greater danger of a revitalized and aggressive Taliban coming out from under NATO in 2014. These two considerations were part of the glue that brought the Russian and the Central Asian governments together in the first place, and provided the SCO and CSTO with both initial and sustaining raisons d'être.

When SCO foreign ministers met in the early Spring of 2012 to prepare for a summit later in the year, they set an agenda for combating the drug trade and bitterly criticized NATO for allowing drug trafficking from Afghanistan to grow 40-fold since the conflict began. A large percentage of these drugs passes through Russia on the way to Europe and contribute to a serious drug abuse problem in Russia itself. Delegates even considered the possibility of suing NATO because the Alliance voluntarily took over the anti-drug task from the UN in 2003, and so had judicial responsibility for it.

At the SCO heads of state summit in Beijing shortly after Putin's inauguration, multiple agreements were signed related to security matters. He and the president of China took the opportunity to issue more joint statements on various international issues. In addition to upgrading Afghanistan to Official Observer status, the summit designated Turkey as a Dialogue Partner, the status granted Sri Lanka and Belarus in 2010, and 'welcomed' the proposal that India and Pakistan join the body's security grouping – without admitting them as full members. Officials representing the UN, the CSTO, the CIS and the Eurasian Economic Community attended. It appeared as if more doors had opened almost immediately after Putin returned to office. The SCO aggressively opposed unilateral anti-missile system deployment in Europe, and called for a nuclear-free zone in Central Asia. Members resurrected the mantra used by the organization when it was created in the 1990s, i.e., its purpose was to fight 'terrorism, separatism, and extremism'. They also specifically opposed the use of force in Iran and Syria. So order was restored to Moscow's satisfaction – or so it seemed.[61]

China's intimidating presence in Asia raised further problems for Russia in Siberia and even more so in Central Asia, where Tajikistan agreed to lease some 6,000 hectares to Chinese agricultural concerns for development. Beijing's decision to order a feasibility study for a China–Kyrgyzstan–Uzbekistan rail line also caused some upset in Moscow.[62] The line would link up with existing rail in Afghanistan, Iran, and Turkey, thus connecting Central Asia generally, and Kyrgyzstan in particular, to the Pacific and Europe. Among other things, the line itself might be constructed with wider tracks than those used by old Soviet railways, making it difficult for Russia to be involved. China also significantly raised its interests in the energy and agricultural assets of Kazakhstan, with which it shares a long border. In 2010 during the recession, the Bank of China provided large credit lines to Kazakhstan's welfare fund and to its copper industry, much of which is now being repaid in resources. In short, Beijing's economic and soft power diplomacy in Central Asia may eventually be more menacing to Russia's interests than American inroads could ever be. Beijing has openly criticized Moscow's economic practices, and the Russian military has voiced concerns about China's military modernization at the presumed expense of Russia.[63]

It was also in 2010 that Kazakhstan took the chairmanship of the OSCE and pledged to suture together the East-West divide. While Nazarbaev urged the organization to give up its stereotypical presumptions about former Soviet states, Western members worried that Kazakhstan's turn at the helm would lead to a Russia-led bloc in the OSCE. Since the chairmanship is held for a calendar year and the host country's foreign minister presides, doubtless OSCE business was mooted at the foreign ministerial sessions of the SCO and CSTO. As it happened, there was little evidence either of the promised bridging of divides, or of any powerful Russian influence in the OSCE's deliberations.[64]

In the larger scheme of things, however, the strategic partnership between Moscow and Beijing was reinforced in 2012. This was clear in Putin's inclusive plans to develop Siberia and the Russian Far East, and in several joint naval exercises in the Yellow Sea. On 12 December, Moscow and Beijing agreed to a 72-hour visa-free regime for their country's nationals who travel as tourists. At a conference held in Moscow two days before that, Lavrov told a gathering of Putin's election agents that Russia and China had 'absolutely identical views on the state of affairs in the world'.[65] He could have added 'for now,' but didn't.

## Looking west – toward Washington

All talk of intensified eastern connections and Putin's oft-feigned indifference to Washington aside, Russia's relations with the United States remained very important to the Kremlin. Like all of his 'reforming' predecessors,

Gorbachev, Yeltsin, and Putin, Medvedev was to start his term in office optimistic about relations with the United States and to end it on a sour note as an early blush of comradeship descended into rancorous tenseness. Still, no matter how compelling the idea that global power is shifting eastward, Moscow's strategic concerns remained absorbed with the West. Its broad economic links still lie primarily with the European countries, and its military doctrine focuses on NATO and the US. Increasingly, Russia shares a war against international terrorism with the West. In fact, a substantial majority of Russia's population resides in the Western part of the country and regard themselves as part of West European culture. Even the Eurasianists see Russia as a bridge between east and west, and certainly not as an Asian country.

One of the quirks of history is that Russian and American presidential elections have tended to fall within the same year, and this may be where part of the problem started. After choosing their president in March, usually with little fuss, Russians watch the American campaign with interest and bemusement – often because, some Russians joke, the US presidential election is the only time that their country is part of the public discourse in America.

Russian pundits watched the US elections in 2008 to gauge how relations between their two countries might evolve after the Bush administration was replaced. Authorities and journalists in Russia were not surprised to see their country maligned for domestic purposes in the US campaign, but also hoped that a new government in Washington would look beyond their usual contacts in Moscow, that is, 'liberal reformers', for their opinions on Russia.[66] That wasn't going to happen.

As early as February 2008, the US Director of National Intelligence named Russia an external threat to America, especially in connection with its oil and gas leverage, potential for cyber space activities, and growing strength in Central Asia. Director J. Michael McConnell indirectly lumped Russia together with Al-Qaeda and Iran as a source of danger. In this instance, the Kremlin demanded an explanation and did not get one.[67] In light of statements such as that, it is hardly surprising that surveys of the general Russian population showed that the United States was regarded as the only state threatening their country and NATO the only menacing bloc. The old image prevailed in another, quite different, dimension that year and subsequent ones as Russians were again frustrated, amused, or simply puzzled by annual US State Department reports on religious freedoms around the world that invariably treated Russia as a country in which such freedom was in grave jeopardy.

Neither of the attitudes that these opinions represented meant that the RF–US association was broken, though the two sides were stuck in their traditional positions of suspicion. When Presidents Putin and George W. Bush met for bilateral talks in Sochi, 6 April 2008, it was their 28th head-to-head. As usual they issued a joint declaration promising cooperation in the future, and failed to agree on the pressing strategic issues of the moment: US missile defence sites in Eastern Europe, NATO expansion, and Russian troops in Georgia and elsewhere. Putin told the press that Russia's stand on those matters was unchanged and charged again that the anti-missile sites were part of a defensive wall against Russia, not some rogue state.

The joint declaration included generalized agreement on promoting security, reaching settlements on START, the INF Treaty, defence technology, stopping the spread of WMD, support for the Non-Proliferation Treaty, support for civilian-use nuclear energy development, and combating global terrorism. Economic and political cooperation were also listed as mutual goals, and the US promised to help Russia accede to the WTO.[68] Few specifics followed, again as usual.

Soon after he settled into his Kremlin office, Medvedev relieved Yury Ushakov of his duties as ambassador to the USA. Almost at the same time, the Bush nominee for the post of ambassador to Russia, John Beyrle, irritated his potential hosts by telling a US Senate hearing on 19 June that corruption was hampering the relationship between the two countries. Although the Russia government was itself widely-publicizing the dilemma of corruption, lectures from America were the last thing it wanted – and said so. Beyrle arrived in Moscow on 3 July, less than two months before Russian tanks entered Georgia. He surprised his Russian critics later when he told journalists in Moscow that Russia was fully justified in sending armed forces into South Ossetia after Russian soldiers killed during the Georgian midnight assault. He added that the US State Department had been urging Saakashvili not to attack, revealing both that Washington saw it coming and making a lie of Saakashvili's claim that he had prior American support.[69]

It may be that the Russian leadership understood, as they said at the time, that presidential electioneering in the US made it impossible for any candidate to suggest that even part of the blame for the August 2008 war might lie with Georgia. But the harshness of the harangues could not help but leave scars. Republican candidate John McCain spewed anti-Russian invective at every turn and his VP candidate Sarah Palin told an ABC interviewer that Georgia and Ukraine should be admitted to NATO and that NATO would be obligated to defend Georgia against Russia. She also believed that Israel should have carte blanche to attack Iran if it felt threatened by that country's alleged nuclear weapons program. The Russian media and Russian nationalists picked up on every verbal assault and passed them on to their increasingly resentful readers and listeners.[70]

Russian analysts like to say that they prefer Republican presidents in the United States, because they will always know where they stand with them. Doubtless, however, Obama's victory came as a relief to the Kremlin. Moscow insiders hoped that the new American administration would make it possible to ease the growing tensions between the two countries.[71] As the year went on, these hopes were mostly realized. When Presidents Medvedev and Obama met on 1 April 2009 in London on the eve of a G-20 meeting they spoke of compromise. Medvedev later called Obama 'my new comrade', and the American president agreed to visit Russia in July. They discussed differences openly and agreed to move 'beyond Cold War mentalities'. Soon after the G-20 meeting Lavrov praised its decision to 'create a Financial Stability Board involving Russia', because it provided a forum for Russia's proposals on reform of the world financial architecture. In an optimistic evaluation of Russia–West relations, he opined that Cold War attitudes might soon be muted, though he realized that they were far from disappearing altogether.[72]

For Moscow, issues related to the re-opening of negotiations about a replacement for the soon-to-be defunct START I, further NATO expansion, and the siting of missile bases in Poland and the Czech Republic were paramount; for Washington, Russia's perceived threat to Georgia and Ukraine, arms sales to Iran, and pressure to get US forces out of Central Asia topped the agenda. Both had long-standing lists of grievances, and both were keen to normalize relations. Prior to a meeting between Hillary Clinton and Medvedev in March 2009, Mikhail Gorbachev met with Obama in Washington and Henry Kissinger conferred with Medvedev in Moscow, though the connection between the two meetings, if any, was obscure. Obama blinked on the missile sites in Eastern Europe. Medvedev blinked on selling S-300 missiles to Iran, and ordered a reduction in the number of troops posted in Kaliningrad. The dialogue was therefore off to a very good start.

The mood for compromise carried over into the first summit between the two presidents in July, in Moscow. Although there was still no meeting of the minds on the issues noted above, they agreed to cut their numbers of deployed nuclear warheads to 1,500 each, in accordance with the START I treaty, which was up for renewal in early December. Russia agreed to allow US overflights of troops and weapons to Afghanistan, and they created a joint Presidential Commission with working groups tasked with specific mandates.[73]

The most important event in RF–US relations in 2009 was the decision by President Obama to abrogate his predecessor's plans to site air defence missiles in Poland and the Czech Republic. Almost immediately after this was announced on 16 September, major American companies initiated talks with Russian officials about investments, and the START negotiations were given a boost. Medvedev and Obama met for the second and third times in Pittsburgh, where the G-20 convened in September, and in Singapore where APEC CEO's held a summit in November. Moscow and Washington made progress on START talks, but ran into a bit of a roadblock on the still unresolved question of Iran's nuclear facilities. An editorialist in Moscow asked the key question: was this a 'reset' or merely a 'respite'?[74] Perhaps the history of the expression in connection with the US–RF relationship tells the tale. US Vice-President Biden introduced it during a conference in Munich when he said that the US needs to 'press the reset button' in its relations with Russia. Secretary of State Clinton picked up on it and later, in Moscow, presented Lavrov with a large red button that used the wrong word, 'reload' (*peregruzka*) rather than 'reset' (*perezagruzka*). Lavrov laughed it off, but the cranky Russian press made much of the linguistic error.

All these developments may have been the source for rumours that began to circulate in 2010 to the effect that a new Russian foreign policy doctrine was in the works. A Ministry of Foreign Affairs report, said to be approved by Medvedev in February, appeared suddenly in *Russkiy Newsweek*. The magazine claimed that the report, titled 'Program of Effective Application of Foreign Policy Factors on a Systematic Basis for Purposes of Long Term Development of the Russian Federation', advocated a sharp turn towards Europe and the US in Russian foreign policy, mostly to facilitate Russia's modernization. This coincided neatly with Medvedev's focus on Skolkovo. Other speculators claimed that the new doctrine, if adopted, advocated no such thing, because of sharp criticism in it alleging American culpability for the global financial crisis.[75] The Ministry report also maintained the high priority for China in Russia's international vision. It seems that the detail was in the eye of the beholder, but it was clear that Medvedev was making a point to nurture relations with the US, in contrast to policies emphasized previously (and later) by Putin.

At any rate, the modernization file was kept active as a component of foreign policy. Foreign Minister Sergei Lavrov pushed the modernization project during visits to France and Germany and in essays published in both those countries.[76] On separate trips to the United States he and Medvedev lobbied aggressively for American participation in Russia's 'modernization' and, as we have seen, modernization was an important objective built into his Foreign Policy Concept.

Halfway through Medvedev's presidency, it still was not clear that a meeting of the minds could be reached with the US and its new president. When yet another 'chicken war' materialized in the winter of 2010, the US Secretary of Agriculture Tom Vilsack went so far as to challenge Russia's entry into the WTO in connection with the issue. The trade issue was resolved in late June, only to have it resurrected again in August. That too was settled, and Russia lifted sanctions it had imposed against 68 US chicken-producing companies, but the charges and counter charges still rankled. Trade difficulties were old hat, and had not prevented the RF–US working group for political coordination from meeting in Moscow in January 2010 to discuss a broad range of regional issues such as Iran, Afghanistan, the Middle East, Latin America, and the Caucasus. Chairing the group for Russia was Deputy Foreign Minister Sergei Ryabkov, and for the US Undersecretary for Political Affairs William Burns. This working group and others conducted their business throughout the year as planned.

Just as the working group met in January, the reset was strained by a different game of chicken when the US decided to deploy Patriot missiles to Poland, about 60 miles (100 km) from Russia's border at Kaliningrad. As far as Moscow was concerned, this negated gains made earlier when Obama decided to end ballistic missile defence (BMD) deployments to Poland and the Czech Republic. A few weeks later, the US announced plans to place interceptor missiles in Romania as further defence against Iran. This meant that there would be US installations close to the Black Sea. Russian analysts thought it absurd to think that Iran might ever launch missiles against Europe.

At that time, with discussions about START apparently bogging down and disagreement on Iran moderated only somewhat, Russian-American relations appeared to have come full circle. US Secretary of State Clinton and Lavrov took the lead in accelerating the diplomatic end of the START discussions. A meeting in Moscow on 18 March provided insights into potentially incompatible approaches: Clinton criticized Russia for its expressed plan to complete the nuclear power station at Iran's Bushehr, and Lavrov equally strongly defended Russia's commitment to that project. Clinton also told Russians that the US wanted to drop the Jackson-Vanik Amendment for Russia,[77] but since this had been promised frequently since 1997, Russians were not impressed.

Even when START was finally renewed officially, with great publicity on 8 April 2010 in Prague, a Russian statement that was added to the protocol modified it to the effect that START would remain viable only so long as the US missile defence system did not grow to threaten Russia. A day later, leaders of a rebellion in Kyrgyzstan threatened to close the Manas airbase, the US's most important transit base for troops going to Afghanistan, and implicated Moscow in its successful overthrow of the Bakiev government. Thus, the reset bounced along with few of its objectives met.

Russia's relations with Washington went on the upswing only after Medvedev concluded that he needed US help with his modernization aspirations. Bringing American businessmen and technology innovators on board with Skolkovo became a priority and helped ease the chill between Moscow and Washington. Moscow's agreement to support UN sanctions against Iran also abetted the reset. Yet even this mood change was interrupted by further unilateral US and EU sanctions against Iran that were bitterly opposed by Russia. Medvedev told US journalists in Washington that such sanctions ignored Russia's concession in the affair, and noted that the US had nothing to lose because it had no economic ties with Iran, whereas Russia and China did. Medvedev brought this and other subjects up during a state visit to the US in mid-June. He held a press conference in Washington and answered wide-ranging queries frankly. Few minds were changed.

In reality, the relationship had matured enough that no diplomatic damage was done when eleven Russian spies were arrested in the United States, where they had been living as moles. These people, mostly couples, had stolen identities, four of them Canadian, and were presumed to be seeking information on top-secret nuclear warheads. Moscow and Washington both said that the event would not hinder improved mutual relations. Within a short time a swap was arranged and ten of the Russian imposters were sent back to Moscow in return for four Russians who were already in prison charged with spying for Western countries. Medvedev awarded the returned Russian spies medals. One of them, the beautiful 'Anna Chapman,' was lionized by the media on returning to Russia and was later named to the council of the *Molodaia gvardiia* (Young Guard), the youth wing of the ruling United Russia party.[78]

This spy story was treated as a bit of titillating gossip by the media on both sides of the Atlantic until November, when news that the head of Russia's deep cover US spy operations, 'Col. Shcherbakov', defected, perhaps as early as June, and may have been responsible for the exposé noted above.[79] The Duma's security committee confirmed the report. Hardly credible rumours circulated that a Russian hit squad was now out to get him. Shcherbakov, whose first name was not then given, served with the SVR as head of the American Division, that is, the 'C' Section. Shcherbakov turned out later to be Col. Aleksandr N. Poteev.

The case of Russian arms dealer Viktor Bout caused some real problems for the reset. Bout was arrested in Bangkok in 2008 and, in the face of vigorous protest from Russian officials, was secretly whisked off to the US in November 2010. Russia had been trying to extradite him to Moscow, where a concern that Bout might have had access to sensitive information was probably more pressing than his guilt or innocence.[80]

All these points of contention seemed not to interfere very much with the Medvedev–Obama dialogue.[81] It was the war of words at lower levels that kept tensions high. In the US Obama won the battle over ratifying START when Republican Senators decided to support it by year's end. At the same time, however, another group of US senators prepared a draft resolution in support of the territorial integrity of Georgia, and John McCain called on Obama to resume arms sales to Tbilisi. The Russian media played up McCain's 'unreasoning Russophobia' as one of the chief roadblocks in the way of an American-Russia rapprochement.[82] Russian politicians inside the Duma catered to the public's nationalist urges to win personal support and also to undermine oppositionists outside the Duma who were favourites of the Western media. It was not easy to get off this unconstructive merry-go-round.

Mutual need prevailed when Russia's Federal Assembly ratified START III in early 2011.[83] Shortly thereafter, Russia and the United States exchanged notes in Moscow (Lavrov and Beyrle) that entered a civilian nuclear cooperation agreement into force. George W. Bush had withdrawn the accord in 2008, but Obama re-introduced it and Congress passed it in December 2010. The agreement enabled the RF and US to work together for the safe sale of nuclear fuels to countries that want to develop civilian nuclear programs, and also called for an exchange of research reactors.

This modus vivendi did not last long either. A new missile defence system for Europe became the last weighty point of contention between the two countries after the START agreement was concluded. Russia continued to demand joint control of the system; the US and NATO continued to resist such requests, asking Russia to take on a more limited participatory role. The issue was partly one of perception, as American and some European leaders saw Iran and other 'rogue states' as threats from which Europe needed protection, while the Kremlin insisted that the defence system was intended mainly as a buffer against Russia. Even if such claims were misdirections for the benefit of both domestic audiences, the risk of a new arms race was nonetheless real.

Other tests soon emerged. For example, in November 2010 a senior US state department official repeated Washington's stance that the southern Kuril Islands belong to Japan.[84] The famous Magnitsky case also strained relations. While domestic in jurisdiction, the Magnitsky affair had far more serious ripple effects internationally than either the Bout issue or the Pussy Riot farce. Sergei Magnitsky was a Russian accountant whose death in prison in 2009 generated widespread accusations of corruption and human rights violations. A Russian human rights council determined that he was badly beaten just prior to his death. Magnitsky's 'crime' had been to expose Russian police, the court system, and senior officials to charges of corruption in connection with an audit of Hermitage Capital Management; his report claimed that Hermitage – whose co-founder William Browder was expelled from Russia – was the victim of fraud on the part of officialdom. Instead of arresting the accused, the police arrested Magnitsky in November 2008, and the rest is history. International outrage transcended the usual human and civil rights organizations and became a talking point for governments around the Western world. The issue was present through the remainder of Medvedev's presidency.

Still, when US Vice President Biden was in Moscow in March 2011 for meetings with Medvedev with an expressed aim to 'energize' the two-year old reset, he agreed to help Russia acquire the better public image in the US that it badly needed. Biden also promised that the Administration would try again to cancel the Jackson-Vanik amendment for Russia, and claimed that Russia's entry into the WTO was a top priority in Washington – yet again.[85]

In addition to START and ultimate Russian entry into the WTO, there were some minor gains in the international arena that could be credited to the reset. Moscow agreed to apply limited sanctions against Iran if there was no movement on the nuclear weapon file, and provided a northern supply route (Northern Distribution Network, NDN) for US and NATO supplies to Afghanistan. The NDN suddenly grew in importance late in 2011 when Pakistan closed its border with Afghanistan as an access route for supplies to American forces after US drones killed Pakistani soldiers on the border. Russia also supplied about one-third of the fuel used by NATO in Afghanistan.

Washington did its part by slowing the once inexorable progress of Georgia and Ukraine towards NATO membership. Russia offered tacit support for the UN-backed no-fly zone established for Libya, and US Defence Secretary Gates told an audience in St. Petersburg, during a two-day visit to Russia in March, that Russian cooperation in Afghanistan and Libya was welcomed. Yet, obvious mutual distrust remained on both sides.

Bombast on the Russian side grew more strident as Medvedev's term in office wound down, and a new presidential election campaign started to warm up. Abstention on a UNSC resolution did not mean Russia supported it, and subsequent comments by Russian officials made it clear that they were adamantly opposed to the use of force by foreign interventionists in Libya. Prime Minister Putin went so far as to accuse the US of making 'shooting first' a standard practice, and cited Belgrade, Afghanistan, and Iraq as prior examples. He noted that bombing military installations would inevitably involve the deaths of many Libyan citizens, and repeated these phrases in connection with Syria later.[86] Here too China and Russia were in full agreement, just as they had been on Bosnia and Kosovo in the 1990s, and Libya became a catch phrase for both countries in their objections to later talk of intervention in Syria and Iran.

There was a parallel rise of anti-Russian rhetoric in the US during 2011. This may have been due in part to the extraordinarily long pre-presidential election campaigning period in the US, where Russia has always been an easy target. A congressional blacklist of some 60 Russian officials deemed culpable in the Magnitsky affair, proposals from congressmen that Russian assets in the US be frozen, accusations that Russians planted a bomb close to the US embassy in Georgia, complaints among food export lobbyists in the US about Russia's expected cuts in imports, and calls for opposition to cooperation between NATO and Russia on missile defence, were all wholly or in part products of domestic political posturing. Russian observers expected this trend to get worse in 2012.

Consternation arose in some Russian circles when rumours circulated in May that Michael McFaul would be named to replace Beyrle as US ambassador in Moscow. Whereas Beyrle was by then respected in Russian diplomatic circles as both knowledgeable and generally sympathetic, the possibility of McFaul's nomination was greeted with apprehension. One mainstream paper suggested that he had for a long time been 'mired in Russian intrigue'. Others granted his expertise but warned of his inclination to preach.[87] McFaul, whose official nomination was proffered on 14 September, was then an adviser to the American president on Russian affairs.

Even though the reset seemed about to become unravelled in the eyes of some observers, on 14 October Foreign Minister Lavrov issued an invitation to President Obama to come to Russia. Although no dates were announced, the State Department said that it was considering the invitation seriously. A month later, after Obama and Medvedev held a private discussion on the sidelines of the APEC summit in Honolulu, both told reporters that all was well with the reset.[88] They must have been kidding.

As Medvedev's last full year came to a close and Russia became a more targeted object for attention in American political campaigning, a speech delivered by House Speaker John Boehner to the Heritage Foundation on 25 October 2011 lifted even the most blasé Russian eyebrows. Insisting on American exceptionalism and its right to defend the US version of 'liberty and freedom' anywhere in the world, Boehner harshly criticized Russia and labelled Obama's reset a form of appeasement. He accused Russia of 'using old tools and old thinking ... to restore Soviet-style power and influence' and called Putin, presumably the next president, 'someone to harbour intense Soviet nostalgia'. Boehner named Georgia as a country seriously wronged by Russia.[89] Other Republican candidates and politicians took up the cudgel, with John McCain again leading the way. Politicians catering in this way to

American voters who were already distrustful and, to be frank, startlingly ill informed about Russia, may well have destroyed whatever gains the reset might have managed.

Russia's parliamentary election on 4 December saw a further souring of RF–US relations. As noted earlier, a few days before the election, US Secretary of State Clinton called Russian State Duma elections neither free, nor fair, even though they had not yet taken place. Clinton's prognostication turned out to be correct, but not before Medvedev and Putin lashed back, suggesting that Clinton tend to problems in her own backyard and keep her nose out of Russia's business. Later, Putin used his annual call-in show to rail against American 'arrogant' lecturing and continued indifference to Russia's national interests.

Whether Washington was indifferent to Russia's national concerns or not, the interests of the two countries often differed greatly, most particularly in the Middle East. Russia is a neighbour to Iran on the Caspian Sea, and has valuable financial interests there, as it does in Syria and did in Iraq and Libya. Moscow generally, and Gazprom particularly, lost billions in contracts with the US-led invasion of Iraq and was badly hurt financially with the NATO-led bombing of Libya. Both those countries were customers for Russian weaponry and energy development and, until overtaken by civil conflict, so was Syria. Russia has its only naval base on the Mediterranean in Syria, the supply and maintenance facility at Tartus.

Moscow was concerned as well about the possibility of North Caucasus militants joining movements generated in the Middle East by the Arab Spring and drawing the global jihad back to the Caucasus and Central Asia when they return as seasoned combat veterans. This fear proved to be prescient when North Caucasus militants flocked to participate in the Syrian civil war. One analyst wrote in 2013 that up to 400 militants from the North Caucasus were fighting in Syria, and predicted that they would return to wreak havoc on their homeland.[90] In fact, most of the countries swept up by the Arab Spring, and Syria, have strategic and financial significance for Moscow quite different from their importance to the US, or even to Europe. The ideological affinity that so many Western politicians insist is the glue that keeps Russia from joining them in heavier-handed action against the 'rogues' is, in fact, very slight, though Moscow certainly feels that its interests are better protected with strong governments in power in the Middle East.

Tensions between Russia and America were exacerbated by three events in March 2012. The first of these came when the State Duma Ethics Committee censured several deputies from A Just Russia and the Communist Party, and also representatives from PARNAS and Yabloko, for meeting privately with recently arrived Ambassador McFaul in January. The second was marked by the opening in Washington of a US House Committee on Foreign Affairs hearing under the witness-leading title 'Russia 2012: Increased Repression, Rampant Corruption, Assisting Rogue Regimes'. Among other speakers, William Browder appeared before the Committee and told it that Russia was 'akin to a criminal enterprise'. He emphasized above all the Magnitsky case.[91] Republican speakers to the Committee waxed especially harshly against Russia.[92]

To add a postscript on perspective, in July 2013 a Russian court found Browder guilty of tax evasion and asked Interpol to assist in having him arrested. Interpol rejected the request, saying that the case was mainly 'of a political nature'. Interestingly, a mere two weeks earlier, the European Court of Human Rights (ECHR) rejected a complaint lodged by Mikhail Khodorkovsky and Platon Lebedev that their trial was politically motivated. The Strasbourg-based court judged that the original charges were legitimate, not political – though the trial itself was unfair. Critics of the tendency of Russia's authorities to exploit the judicial system for raw political ends are right to do so, but it is also true that when one sets the political hyperbole aside, there are two sides even to these stories.

The third event in March was marked by Republican presidential candidate Mitt Romney's claim that Russia was America's 'number one geopolitical foe'.[93] The bilateral relationship was so soured by that time that even as the Jackson-Vanik Amendment for Russia finally was abrogated in December 2012, in keeping with WTO regulations, the Magnitsky Act was adopted. Russia almost immediately retaliated by creating a black list of its own, naming individuals involved in what Russia called American civil and human rights abuses, including US officials who authorized the use of torture, were involved in the 'kidnapping' of Russian citizens, or served as commanders at Guantanamo prison.

The 'war of lists', as the Magnitsky Act and retaliation series was called by some journalists, was not so serious as the fact that it caused Russian lawmakers to step up the process of banning American citizens from adopting Russian orphans. In February 2012, with Medvedev in office, the Ministry of Foreign Affairs issued a statement that said, in part: 'Against the backdrop of an unending series of crimes against adopted Russian children in the United States, the Russian Foreign Ministry believes that the adoption procedures for US citizens should be suspended until the US-Russia adoption agreement, signed on 13 July 2011, comes into force'.[94]

The ban had been in the works for some time, driven by the mysterious death of several Russian children apparently at the hands of their adoptive American parents. The number of such deaths was slight in relation to the large number of adoptees – there were 962 Russian orphans adopted by American families in 2012 alone, many with various disabilities[95] – but the issue was an extraordinarily sensitive one, especially after a Russian child was packed on to a plane and sent back to Russia by adoptive parents who said they no longer wanted him. Whatever the rights or wrongs of the individual cases, they both fed and helped shape the anger against America growing in Russia.

The 'orphan debate' was divisive in Russia as well, as thousands marched in protest against the law, while others began a nation-wide demand that

Moscow redress the many flaws in its own domestic facilities for orphans and provide incentives for Russian families to commit to adoptions themselves. A clear majority of Russians supported the law, however. This was one issue where the public on both sides were aggressive in their condemnations of each other. From the international perspective, the issue highlighted – and the Russian media emphasized – the fact that, of all the countries in the entire world, only Somalia and the United States had not yet ratified the international Convention on the Rights of the Child.[96]

Although these last two actions came while Medvedev was sitting in the prime minister's chair, they started on his watch and mirror the fluctuations – perhaps even the haplessness – of his presidential regime when it came to relations with the US. An article published in *Vedomosti* at the end of the year proclaimed that, in fact, the reset was long over, its end signalled by Hillary Clinton's statement on the Duma elections.[97] If true, the rise and fall of the reset will mark both a major success and a major failure for Medvedev's presidency, and perhaps Obama's as well.

* * *

## Defence matters

It should be borne in mind that Moscow's relationship with Washington has been defined since World War II primarily by their mutual military capabilities. This has been true to a far greater extent than has Russia's dealings with any other country, although since the early 1990s the looming presence of NATO moving inexorably closer to Russia's border has always been in the mix.[98]

Medvedev's predecessors enjoyed very few successes in military-strategic interchange with Western countries. Yeltsin's defence strategies were overshadowed by NATO expansion and the fact that many important military, arms reduction, and diplomatic agreements, several of which preceded the collapse of the USSR, fell by the wayside during his and Putin's first terms of office. The Cooperation and Partnership Agreement (CPA) with the EU (1997) was suspended by 2007 mainly because of difference between the two sides on an Energy Charter. The Conventional Armed Forces in Europe (CFE), signed by the Warsaw Pact and the USSR in 1990, dissolved over Western failures to ratify necessary post-Soviet amendments agreed in 1999 and the continued presence of Russian forces in Georgia and Moldova. Putin imposed a moratorium on the CFE in 2007, leaving it to Medvedev to finally cancel it altogether – and to regularly hint at its resurrection.[99]

After the ABM Treaty was abrogated unilaterally by the US in June 2002, its replacement, the Strategic Offensive Reduction Treaty (SORT), agreed in 2002 and in force by June 2003, failed to satisfy either side fully. START II negotiations stalled and eventually were dropped; and the US failed to sign on to the Intermediate-Range Nuclear Forces Treaty (INF). Moreover, as we have seen, President Bush proposed to construct missile defence systems in Poland and the Czech Republic.

Although the NATO-Russian Council (NRC), in place since 2002, provided Moscow with a forum in which to express its opinions on carefully prescribed areas of mutual strategic concern, Russia had no influence on NATO whatsoever as the Alliance grew. Three former Warsaw Pact countries were added to its list in 1999, seven more members from Eastern Europe, including three former Soviet republics joined in 2004. After Albania and Croatia entered in 2009, NATO had a larger contingent of countries than the EU. Until 2008, Georgia and Ukraine were poised to join the Atlantic Alliance, and NATO continued to act in the international arena in whatever manner it wished after it adopted a new strategic concept in 1991, moving away from its traditional collective defence rationale to take on a conflict resolution role. The Alliance then decided to move 'out of zone' to assist the OSCE and the UN in conflict management missions. Russia, with no allies and stripped of the USSR's defensible borders, felt itself in jeopardy. That was when Primakov warned that, besides the obvious strategic dangers NATO expansion posed, it would cause a psychological storm in Russia – put Russia and Russians on the defensive, force it to re-arm when it needed revenues for other things, and out of fear and isolation give rise to nationalism and xenophobia.[100] He was mostly right.

Fifteen years later, in 2008, Russia still had no military allies in the West unless one counts Belarus and Armenia in the CSTO. Its large but weakened armed forces were stuck in the midst of a floundering rebuilding program and a half-hearted transition from a conscripted to volunteer army. For defence against any serious attack from the outside, the Ministry of Defence had little choice but to rely on nuclear deterrence. To this end, Medvedev's new military doctrine (2010) retained the principle that 'first use' of nuclear weapons in the face of overwhelming odds was possible, even if by conventional forces.[101] Western and NATO analysts and politicians railed at this change from Soviet policy when Putin first introduced it in 2000, but harped on it less when it was confirmed for the third time in 2010. Apparently the critics recalled by then that they had similar doctrines themselves.[102]

In this connection, it is worth repeating that the Minister of Defence throughout Medvedev's term was Anatoly Serdyukov, appointed by Putin in February 2007 and replaced by Putin in November 2012. Rightly or wrongly, therefore, Medvedev cannot help but be tainted by, or congratulated for, whatever achievements or failures are attributed to Serdyukov's term. In light of the sweeping scale of corruption uncovered within the ministry and Serdyukov's forced resignation because of them, it will be the failures that will linger the longest. It is also worthy of note that Russia's envoy to NATO, Dmitry Rogozin, held that post during most of Medvedev's tenure as well. Leader of the *Rodina* party until 2011 and known as a fiery Russian nationalist, Rogozin was named ambassador to NATO by Putin in January 2008, probably for the purpose of confrontation. Rogozin left the NATO posting only after he was appointed deputy prime minister in charge of anti-missile defence and negotiations with NATO, on 23 December 2011. A sub-text to the appointment was the need to clean up Serdyukov's growing mess.[103]

There was an earlier, more predictable failure. In addition to his new foreign policy Concept, Medvedev leapt into international security issues during his first few months in office. Speaking in Berlin on 5 June 2008, he launched an initiative to develop a pan-European security treaty, a legally binding document based on the principle that no Euro-Atlantic country or organization would be entitled to enhance its own security at the expense of any other country or organization in the region. To accomplish this end, after about a year of discussion, he sent a draft European Security Treaty to heads of states and leaders of organization such as NATO, the EU, the CSTO, the CIS, and the OSCE.[104]

His central point was that real European security was possible only if Europe's integral parts, including Russia, joined as an organic whole for security purposes.

Medvedev summarized what he thought was the importance of his security proposal in a speech delivered at the University of Helsinki on 20 April 2009. 'European security is still far from perfect', he noted, adding 'we need to deal seriously with the architecture of European security'. He went on to urge the EU and the US to join Russia in a 'legally binding document, based on the equality and mutual respect of all the signatories'. None of NATO, the EU, the CIS, CSTO, or the OSCE is capable of providing anything but piecemeal security to all of Europe, he insisted. Instead, a new over-arching forum should be created, and a binding treaty devised for everyone.[105]

Critics, i.e., almost everyone outside Russia, judged the proposal as little more than an attempt to undermine NATO and the OSCE. The original proposition did not even include the United States. The OSCE Ministerial Council discussed it briefly at its regular meeting in Athens in early December that year, and a few weeks later the first NATO–Russia Council to convene after the war in Georgia had the draft treaty on its agenda. Washington said it was studying it 'carefully'. After the initial burst of 'don't call us, we'll call you' platitudes, the project faded away, never taken seriously.[106] Although the CIS states supported the proposed treaty and it cropped up in bilateral discussions with Germany, Italy, and a few other countries from time to time, Medvedev's promise as European peacemaker was to all intents and purposes over within a year and a half of his accession to office, leaving Moscow to face the issue of European missile defence for the remainder of the term.[107]

Still, policy is important and the military doctrine adopted in February 2010 was revealing, for it treated both the US and NATO as the only potential threats to Russia's military security. One of Medvedev's first acts as commander-in-chief had been to fire General Yury Baluevsky and replace him as Chief of General Staff with Army General Nikolai Makarov. The move was likely an attempt to stifle internal resistance to Serdyukov's reform of the military's budget management. Makarov, who was also appointed First Deputy Minister of Defence, was therefore in place a month before the war with Georgia broke out, which prompted substantial amendments upwards to the military budget for 2009.

The war made it evident that Russia needed to reorganize its armed forces, and upgrade its on-the-ground weaponry (battle gear, ground surveillance systems, and armoured vehicles). Line of command and communications were also flawed. Almost immediate promises to speed up Georgia and Ukraine accession to NATO – proclaimed mostly by individual Western politicians – spurred much of Russia's activity in this regard, and prompted calls for a full renovation of Russia's nuclear deterrence. These considerations did not prevent Serdyukov from pursuing cuts in personnel that would bring armed forces numbers down to about a million by 2012 and reduce the officer corps by nearly half. The latter reform caused great unease and the distrust of the ministry already present in the senior ranks was exacerbated. The target was never reached.

Insofar as strategic issues were concerned, Pentagon plans to site missile defence systems in eastern Europe was the ever present challenge to Medvedev, and the one to which he was most consistently aggressive in response. He caught a break early on when President Obama re-worked the Bush plan not long after taking office in Washington. The original project for high-speed interceptors in Poland and radar in the Czech Republic was replaced with plans for lower speed missiles that were presumed to be capable of stopping anything from Iran, but not so threatening to Moscow. Although Obama's proposal provided for upgrades over the next four years, the change provided a window through which both new presidents could seek accommodation, and eventually paved the way for the important START treaty that set limits on nuclear arsenals in both countries.

Russia's perspectives on the European missile shield proposed by NATO and the US was based on the assumption that deployment of a missile defence network would undermine the effectiveness of Russia's own strategic rocket forces and propel them into an unwanted arms race.[108]

Military-strategic disputes of this sort are driven as much by ingrained distrust, easily stoked by politicians on both sides for selfish, short-term gains – so they skew diplomatic negotiations on all other issues. Since his Prime Minister, Putin, was the leading cheerleader behind an aggressive approach, Medvedev was never able to steer negotiations with Washington, though he benefitted considerably from Obama's moderating approach.

Ironically, NATO served as the primary engine of cooperation between Russia and the West generally, and Russia and the US in particular. Given that all cooperation between Russia and NATO was halted after the Georgian War for a month, and full military cooperation did not start up again until the first post-war Joint Chiefs of Staff meeting was held in January 2010, this may seem surprising. The fact is, NATO needed Russian technical and intelligence assistance in Afghanistan, and this was made clear at a NRC session in April 2009.[109] In turn, it was very important to Russia that NATO succeeded in Afghanistan prior to its planned withdrawal from that country by

2014. Lavrov attended another NRC meeting in December that year when Afghanistan was on top of the agenda. He was able then to have NATO at least address the Security Charter proposed by Medvedev in June 2008 and studiously ignored since then by the European leadership.

After Russia's new military doctrine cited NATO as the primary danger to the security of Russia, in February 2010 a Strategic Concept Experts Group advising on a new NATO strategic concept travelled to Moscow for discussions. Madeleine Albright led the NATO contingent of so-called wise elders. Given that just a few weeks earlier she told the European Parliament that Russia would have no say in NATO policy making (Moscow should not try to 'be the tail that wags the dog'), and mouthed only platitudes to an audience at the Moscow School of International Affairs, not much was gained by this tour from the Kremlin's perspective.[110] Breakthroughs came later in the year when Russia contracted for major weapons purchases from France, Italy, and Germany in spite of NATO regulations that forbade such sales to Russia, and furious objections from many of Russia's own defence and arms manufacturing officials.

Medvedev contradicted his own military doctrine by telling journalists in Paris in late February 2010 that Russia does not, in fact, consider NATO a threat.[111] Moreover, some NATO officials suggested in March that it was time for Russia to be asked to consider joining the Alliance.[112] Although this renewed notion gained no traction in either Moscow or Brussels, tensions between Russia and NATO eased further as the US, its NATO partners, and Russia agreed to cooperate in fighting piracy on the high seas. In September, Secretary General Rasmussen repeated to journalists that NATO should invite Russia to participate in a European missile defence system and called for mutual cooperation in Afghanistan. Rasmussen's remarks were made in the context of an upcoming NATO Summit, the primary purpose of which was to adopt its new strategic concept. In anticipation of the summit scheduled for November 2010 in Lisbon, he travelled to Moscow for a working visit.

The summit produced few surprises, other than a much-needed spirit of cooperation with Moscow. Help from Russia in Afghanistan included a NATO purchase of 21 Russian Mi-17 helicopters designed specifically for the mountainous and desert terrain of the region. In connection with the NDN, Moscow agreed to expanded transit staging bases and provided lists of goods that could be conveyed across Russian territory; NATO agreed to increase anti-drug trafficking cooperation. Medvedev attended the NATO Summit as a guest, met with Obama, other leaders, and Afghanistan's Karzai, whom he invited to visit Moscow.

Russia's relations with NATO improved considerably after the Lisbon Summit. At a security conference in Munich on 5 February 2011, Lavrov called for the re-negotiation of the defunct CFE with NATO, and Clinton called for cooperation on missile defence. Two weeks later, Medvedev announced that a special group had been formed in Russia with Rogozin as chair to prepare proposals for missile defence collaboration with NATO.[113] Later in the month, Lavrov told reporters that Russia would work in partnership with NATO if the Alliance would agree in writing to a pact not to target each other's defence systems. Joint exercises were renewed and even the Polish prime minister said that Europe's missile defence would be best served by cooperation with Russia.[114]

All this emerging goodwill seemed to have been wasted when NATO bombers killed Gadhafi's youngest son and three grandsons. The Kremlin, the SCO, the CSTO, and even the BRIC accused NATO of going well beyond its UN mandate by attempting to assassinate the Libyan president. The Libyan situation jerked relations between Moscow and Brussels back to its immediate post-Georgian war level. Russia also took umbrage at what it believed was NATO's continued indifference to ever increasing drug trafficking from Afghanistan through Tajikistan to Russia.

NATO's desire to establish a missile defence system for Europe separate from a Russian one was suddenly back in play and further strained the relationship. In May 2011, Medvedev cautioned NATO that failure to include Russia as a partner in the European system could result in a new Cold War and force the Kremlin to turn to a nuclear strike defence system. Rasmussen countered that he wanted to establish a 'true, strategic partnership' with the RF, and that two independent missile defence systems 'that cooperate' was the way NATO would go. Missile defence, Libya, memberships for Ukraine and Georgia, were issues that simply could not be patched over. When the Russia–NATO foreign ministers Council met in Brussels, everyone mumbled nice words about cooperation, but the real opportunity passed them by.

Surveys conducted in December 2011 demonstrated that the issue of NATO expansion eastward still rankled Russian citizens. Whereas answers to a question of whether or not NATO posed a threat to Russia was tied at 34 per cent for each of 'yes' and 'no', a full 60 per cent of the 1,600 respondents believed that eastern expansion of NATO was dangerous for their country.[115] The NATO card seemed to have been played badly by both sides, leaving them uncertain about what would happen in Central Asia, Russia's still soft underbelly, when NATO draws down in Afghanistan.

The irony of what appears to have been a futile Russia–NATO discourse is that it is highly likely that Moscow's Ministry of Defence wants NATO to stay in Afghanistan until the 'job is done'. Strategists in Moscow and the CSTO capitals are convinced that Afghan military and police forces are not capable of containing the Taliban. If they are right, and they probably are, as NATO withdraws the Taliban will again be a grave threat to Central Asia and, if it allies with Al-Qaeda and Caucasus rebels, a serious danger to Russia as well. In 2012, Russia had some 7,000 troops stationed at three bases in Tajikistan, which shares a 1,200-km (750-mile) border with Afghanistan. Kyrgyzstan hosts a Russian airbase at Kant, near Bishkek, with about 700 servicemen. The CSTO uses this base for mounting anti-drug-trafficking operations. Undoubtedly, these contingents will be strengthened as NATO leaves, but Russia does not want to bear the brunt of any future Taliban excursions. For the Kremlin this remained a serious catch-22 situation.

## Notes

1 For the Concept, *Rossiiskaia gazeta*, 16 July 2008; see also *The Moscow Times*, 16 July 2008, and Bertil Nygren, *The Rebuilding of Greater Russia: Russia's Foreign Policy Towards the CIS Countries.* London: Routledge, 2009
2 Quoted in V. Solov'ev and M. Zygar', 'Za MID vo vsem mire', *Kommersant*, 16 July 2008.
3 *Kommersant*, 31 August 2008; *Kremlin.ru*, 31 August 2008. The TV channels represented at the interview were Channel One, Rossiia, and NTV. The interview was conducted in Sochi. For a detailed clarification and summary, see Foreign Minister Sergei Lavrov, 'Mir v poiskakh novogo ravnovesiia', *NG Dipkur'er*, 15 September 2008.
4 On Russia's term as G-8 chairmanship, see Pamela A. Jordan, 'International and Domestic Dimensions of Russia's G-8 Presidency in 2006', *Canadian Slavonic Papers*, Vol. 50, No. 304 (2008), pp. 397–424.
5 On the specific concessions and their consequences, see J.L. Black, 'Russia and the USA: Sea Change or More of the Same?' *National Network News*, Fall-Winter 2001–2, pp. 13–15. Among other things Russia closed a large surveillance base in Cuba and a naval base in Vietnam.
6 See J.L. Black, *Russia Faces NATO Expansion. Bearing Gifts or Bearing Arms?* Lanham, MD: Rowman & Littlefield, 2000, and *Vladimir Putin and the New World Order*, Lanham, MD: Rowman & Littlefield, 2004.
7 *MID.ru*, 15 February 2008. After the war of 1999, UNSC Resolution 1244 guaranteed Serbian territorial integrity, which included Kosovo.
8 For a Russian perspective, see Svetlana Gamova, 'Yashchik Pandory priotkryvaetsia. Yuzhnaia Osetiia poprosila o priznanii vchera, Abkhaziia sdelaet eto segodnia', *Nezavisimaia gazeta*, 6 March 2013. South Ossetia was designated an Autonomous Oblast in the USSR, and named itself the Republic of Ossetia when it first declared independence from Georgia in 1990. Abkhazia was a full Autonomous Soviet Socialist Republic. It renamed itself the Republic of Abkhazia after a bitter civil war for independence in 1992–93.
9 In January 1992, 100 per cent of South Ossetians voted to join the Russian Federation. Moscow denied the application. In 2001, a Russian law allowed former citizens of the USSR in 'unrecognized states' to take up Russian citizenship (along with pensions and social benefits). For Medvedev's explanation of his obligation to protect Russian citizens in Georgia, see his speech, plus questions and answers, at the Valdai International Discussion Club, 12 September 2008; transcript translated in full for the SRAS (School of Russian and Asian Studies), 15 September 2008.
10 See United Nations Security Council Resolution 1160, 31 March 1998, for the official UN designation.
11 *MID.ru*, 3 June 2008.
12 Agentsvo Voennykh Novosti, 18 July 2008. (Hereafter AVN).
13 Beyrle, in answer to a question from a Russian reporter: 'It is clear to us that the Russian troops were fully justified to retaliate after the attack on Russian peacekeepers in South Ossetia. But they have now entered the territory of Georgia and the territorial integrity of Georgia is under threat', *Kommersant* (22 August 2008). Aleksandr Gabaev conducted the interview. See also C. J. Chivers, Ellen Barry, 'Georgia Claims on Russia War Called into Question', *New York Times*, 7 November 2008.

14  *MID.ru*, 26 August 2008.
15  For membership lists and functions of the SCO and CSTO, see charts in *Russia after 2012*, pp. 225–30.
16  FOM, 13 August 2008; ITAR-TASS, 15 August 2008. The organized Georgian community in Russia amounted then to about 700,000 people, though unofficial data suggests that there were about 2 million Georgians in Russia.
17  For a typical cross-section of wildly diverse opinion on the conflict, see Stephen Sestanovich, 'What Has Moscow Done?' and Charles King, 'The Five-Day War. Managing Moscow after the Georgia Crisis', *Foreign Affairs*, No. 6 (Nov-Dec 2008); Mathew Collin, 'A Conflict of Interests: The Cold War Between Russia and Georgia is Heating Up', *Russia Profile*, No. 7, August-September 2008; Edward Lucas, *The New Cold War: Putin's Russia and the Threat to the West*. London: Bloomsbury, 2008; Frederick Starr, Svante E. Cornell, eds. *The Guns of August 2008. Russia's War in Georgia*, New York: M.E. Sharpe, 2009; Ruslan Pukhov, ed. *The Tanks of August*, Moscow: Russky Mir Foundation, 2010. See also essays in special issues of *Nationalities Papers*, Vol. 40, No. 5 (2012), and *Central Asia Survey*, Vol. 28, No. 2 (2009).
18  Report by the Independent International Fact-Finding Mission on the Conflict in Georgia, September 2009.
19  Interfax-AVN, 1 June 2009; *Russia Today* (RT), 1 & 12 June 2009; RIA Novosti, 2 June 2009.
20  Embassy of the United States: Georgia, Press Release, 1 June 2009. The release was issued in the name of Robert Wood, Deputy Departmental Spokesman, Bureau of Public Affairs.
21  See NATO Declaration. Chicago Summit, 20 May 2012, Articles 29 & 30.
22  'Saakashvili: Georgia will Enter NATO and EU and Return "Occupied" Lands', *KyivPost*, 7 August 2012; Interfax-AVN, 7 August 2012.
23  See Nikolaus von Twickel, 'Medvedev Defends Role in Georgia War', *The Moscow Times*, 10 August 2012. Putin later claimed to have telephoned Medvedev twice from Beijing, on 7 and 8 August, implying that he made the decision to invade. Medvedev said that he, and he alone, made that decision. See also von Twickel, 'Putin Contradicts Medvedev on Georgia War', *The Moscow Times*, 9 August 2012.
24  See, e.g. C.J. Chivers, 'Putin's Heir Shows Hints of Less icy Style', *New York Times*, 28 February 2008. Marcel H. Van Herper, *Putinism. The Slow Rise of a Radical Right Regime in Russia*. London: Palgrave Macmillan, 2013, relates Putin to such rightwing figures in Europe as Mussolini and Berlusconi, and sets him in the fascist continuum.
25  On this see opinions of Stephen F. Cohen, 'Stop the Pointless Demonization of Putin', *The Nation*, 7 May 2012, and 'Demonizing Putin Endangers America's Security', *The Nation*, 16 September 2013. Andrei P. Tsygankov, *Russophobia: Anti-Russian Lobby and American Foreign Policy*. London: Palgrave Macmillan, 2009, presents a Russian perspective. For a more theoretical approach, Iver B. Neumann, Vincent Pouliot, 'Untimely Russia: Hysteresis in Russian-Western Relations Over the Past Millennium', *Security Studies*, Vol. 20, No. 1 (2011), pp. 105–37.
26  For a useful framework, see Alexander Cooley, *Great Games, Local Rules. The New Great Power Contest in Central Asia*, Cambridge: Oxford UP, 2012. See also 'Russia's Economic and Security Relations with Central Asia', *Russian Analytical Digest*, No 71, 25 January 2010, Alyson J.K. Bailes, et al, 'The Shanghai Cooperation Organization', SIPRI Policy Paper No. 17, 2007, and Marcel de Hass, ed. *The Shanghai Cooperation Organization. Towards a Full-Grown Security Alliance?* Clingendael: Netherlands Institute of International Relations, 2007.
27  Vladimir Putin, 'Novyi integratsionnyi proekt dlia Evrazii – budushchee, kotoroe rozhdaetsia segodnia', *Izvestiia*, 3 October 2011. A full translation can be found

on the Russian Federation Prime Minister, Information and Press office website *Premier.ru*.

28 'Kontseptsiia vneshnei politiki Rossiiskoi Federatsii', approved by Russian Federation President V.V. Putin on 12 February 2013.

29 For an overview, Yulia Nikitina, 'The Collective Security Treaty Organization Through the Looking Glass', *Problems of Post-Communism*, 59:3 (May-June 2012), pp. 41–52.

30 For the larger picture of Great Power competition for Central Asia, see Elizabeth Wishnick, *Russia, China and the United States in Central Asia*. Carlisle, PA: US Army War College, 2009.

31 See 'Russia's Economic and Security Relations with Central Asia', *Russian Analytical Digest*, No. 71, 25 January 2010; and Jeff Sahadeo, 'Russia and Central Asia. Does the Tail Wag the Dog?' in *Russia After 2012* (2013), pp. 167–83.

32 Apparently the term was coined by Jim O'Neill, chief economist for Goldman Sachs in a paper titled 'Building Better Global Economic BRICs'.

33 For the full declaration, Xinhua, 14 April 2011.

34 The G-7 includes the US, UK, France, Germany, Italy, Canada, and Japan. Their net 'wealth' is determined by the sum value of their monetary assets less liabilities. The G-7 nations represent about 63 per cent of net global wealth.

35 'Kontseptsiia uchastiia Rossiiskai Federatsii v ob'edinenii BRIKS', signed by President Putin on 9 February and published on 21 March 2013, *MID.ru*, 9 March 2013.

36 RIA Novosti, 22 March 2013.

37 On the importance of the BRICS to Russia, see N.A. Kosolapov, 'BRIKS kak mezhdunarodnoe politicheskoe prostranstvo', *Rossiia v global'noi politike*, 3 March 2013. See also 'Russia and the BRIC', *Russian Analytical Digest,* No. 91, 14 February 2011.

38 *MID.ru*, 15 March 2011. See also 'Russia Profile Weekly Experts Panel: A War With Libya?' *Russia Profile*, 25 March 2011.

39 *Kommersant*, 20 November 2012.

40 See for general background, 'Japan to Withdraw Ambassador from Moscow Over Island Dispute', RFE/RL, 2 November 2010. Medvedev visited the islands again in July 2012, as Russia's prime minister.

41 For the CPRF reaction, see Vasily Safronchuk, 'SShA vdivaiut "os" sla', *Sovetskaia Rossiia*, 5 February 2002. See also *Vladimir Putin and the New World Order,* pp. 163–66.

42 For a glimpse ahead, 'Global 2030. The View from China, Russia and India', *World Politics Review*, 24 April 2012.

43 Sergei Blagov, 'Russia, China Establish Stronger Economic Ties', *Eurasia Daily Monitor*, 30 October 2008; Vladimir Frolov, 'Medvedev's Trip to China – A Signal to the West?' *Russia Profile*, 30 May 2008.

44 *MID.ru*, 16 May 2008.

45 For general background, see 'Russia-China Relations', *Russian Analytical Digest*, No. 73, 23 February 2010.

46 For general discussion see Tom Washington, 'Medvedev in China', *The Moscow News*, 27 September 2010.

47 *The Hindu*, 4 April 2010. See also Neeta Lal, 'India, Russia and the US. Three's a Crowd?' *World Politics Review*, 6 April 2010; for an early prognosis for the Russia-India link, see Tom Balmforth, 'The Nucleus of a Beautiful Friendship', *Russia Profile*, 8 December 2009.

48 *MID.ru*, 11 November 2010.

49 For background see Bobo Lo, *Axis of Convenience: Moscow, Beijing and the New Geopolitics*, Washington: Brookings Institute, 2008.

50 Interfax, 10 December 2008.

51  The two governments signed a 'Memorandum of Understanding on Launching a China-Russia Finance Ministers' Dialogue Mechanism' during Putin's visit to China in March 2006.

52  On the leading Eurasianist, see Andreas Umland, ed. *The Nature of 'Neo-Eurasianism:' Approaches by Alexander Dugin's Post-Soviet Movement of Radical Anti-Americanism*, Armonk, NY: M.E. Sharpe, 2009; *Izvestiia*, 25 December 2010.

53  *MID.ru*, 16 June 2011; Interfax, 16 June 2011.

54  *EurasiaNet*, 20 January 2011.

55  For a series of articles on the question of security in Central Asia, especially in light of NATO's forthcoming withdrawal, see 'Security in Central Asia', *Russian Politics and Law*, Vol. 51, No. 1 (January-February, 2013). Note items on Russian and US interests in the region and the role of the SCO in protecting the area from Taliban incursion.

56  *Kommersant*, 15 June 2011.

57  *Premier.ru*, 8 November 2011.

58  For differing perspectives, see John Lee, 'Why Russia Still Matters in the Asian Century', *World Political Review*, 19 January 2010, and Stephen Blank, 'The End of Russian Power in Asia', *Orbis*, Spring 2012.

59  For greater detail and analysis, see essays in 'The Eurasian Union Project', *Russian Analytical Digest*, No. 112, 20 April 2012.

60  Stephen Blank, 'China's Central Asian Profile Continues Growing', *Eurasia Daily Monitor*, 21 March 2011; Alejandro Sueldo, 'Kremlin Fear of China Drives its Foreign Policy Opinion', *The Moscow Times*, 30 August 2011; Dan Peleschuk, 'Crouching Bear, Hidden Tiger', *Russia Profile*, 5 July 2012.

61  See, in general, Jacob W. Kipp. 'Whither Russia: Looking East and Ready to Embrace It', *Eurasia Daily Monitor*, 14 May 2012.

62  See e.g., Roman Muzalevsky, 'China-Kyrgyzstan-Uzbekistan Railway Scheme. Fears, Hopes and Prospects', *Eurasia Daily Monitor*, 30 May 2012.

63  See e.g., Wang Jisi, 'China's Search for a Grand Strategy', *Foreign Affairs*, March/April 2011; *Nezavisimaia gazeta*, 17 April 2012; Bobo Lo, 'A Partnership of Convenience', *New York Times*, 7 June 2012; and Wang Jisi, '"Marching Westwards". The Rebalancing of China's Geostrategy', *Center for International and Strategic Studies* (Beijing), 7 October 2012.

64  See *EurasiaNet.org*, 19 January 2010, and the OSCE website for that year, *www.osce.org*.

65  *MID.ru*, 9 & 12 December 2010.

66  See e.g., Natalia Roeva in *FORUM-msk.ru*, 6 January 2008.

67  Interfax, 7 February 2008. See *Annual Threat Assessment of the Director of National Intelligence for the Senate Select Committee on Intelligence*, 5 February 2008.

68  US White House, Press Release, 6 April 2008.

69  *Kommersant,* 22 August 2008.

70  On the Palin comment, see Valentina Pop, 'Palin says war with Russia could be NATO option', *www.euobserver.com*, 12 September 2008; RIA Novosti, 12 September 2008. McCain's attacks on Russia were such that he was featured regularly in the Russian press as a proponent of the Cold War's 'the Russians are coming!' scenario. See, e.g., Vladislav Vorobev, 'Operatsiia "Makkein"', *Rossiiskaia gazeta*, 15 August 2008. See also Andrei P. Tsygankov, *Russophobia ... op. cit.*, and Jack F. Matlock, *Superpower Illusions: How Myth and False Ideologies Led America Astray – and How to Return to Reality.* New Haven: Yale UP, 2010. Matlock was US Ambassador to Russia in the Gorbachev era.

71  See Pavel Felgenhauer, 'A Restart of US-Russian Relations', *Eurasia Daily Monitor*, 15 January 2009, and, for an overview at the end of 2009, 'US-Russia Relations', *Russian Analytical Digest*, No. 66, 20 October 2009.

72 Sergei Lavrov, 'Krizis v otnosheniiaki s Zapadom: Kakoi krizis?' *Itogi*, 18 May 2009. See also his, 'Face to Face with America: Between Non-Confrontation and Convergence', *Profil*, No. 38, October 2008.

73 White House, Office of the Press Secretary, Washington, 6 July 2009.

74 'Perezagruzka ili peredyshka? Moskve i Vashington putaiutsia nachat' vse snachala', *Nezavisimaia gazeta*, 30 December 2009.

75 See, e.g., *Yezhednevnyy zhurnal*, 21 May 2010; Roger McDermott, 'Kremlin Contemplates a Seismic Shift in Russian Foreign Policy', www.worldsecuritynetwork.com, 20 May 2010; 'Russia Profile Experts Weekly Panel: Russia's New Foreign Policy Doctrine', *Russia Profile*, 21 May 2010; and Walter Laqueur, 'Moscow's Modernization Dilemma. Is Russia Charting a Foreign Policy?' *Foreign Affairs*, November/December 2010.

76 For example: Lavrov, 'L'Europe-Atlantique: une sécurité égale pour tous', *Revue Défense Nationale*, No. 5 (May 2010), and jointly with German Foreign Minister Guido Westerwelle, 'Chto i nam, i nemtsam khorosho', *Rossiiskaia gazeta*, 31 May 2010.

77 The Jackson-Vanik Amendment was adopted in 1974 as a provision to the US's Trade Act to deny Most Favored Nation status to countries with non-market economies that restricted emigration. In Russia's case that meant the emigration of Jews, although that was not stated in the Amendment.

78 Anna Vasil'yevna Kushchyenko (b. 1982) married British subject Alex Chapman in 2001, thereby gaining a British passport, and moved to New York in 2009.

79 *Kommersant*, 11 November 2010.

80 For one perspective, see Howard Ames, 'Moscow Seethes as Bout Flies to the US', *The Moscow Times*, 17 November 2010.

81 On this, see Samuel Charap, 'The "Transformation" of US-Russia Relations', Chatham House. REP Roundtable Summary, 13 October 2010.

82 *Nezavisimaia gazeta*, 20 December 2010.

83 The US Senate ratified START on 22 December 2010 and the Russian Duma and Federation Council ratified on 25 and 26 January 2011. It came into effect on 5 February 2011.

84 Philip J. Crowley, US Assistant Secretary of State for Public Affairs, said this in November 2010 after Medvedev's visit to the Kuril Islands; the policy statement became a subject for Russian media attention after it was part of a survey on the Kuril question published by *Fond 'Obshchestvennoe mnenie'* on 8 February 2011.

85 Interfax-AVN, 10 March 2011.

86 Pavel Felgenhauer, 'Acute Anti-Americanism is New Official Policy in Moscow', *Eurasia Daily Monitor*, 26 Jan 2012.

87 *Rossiiskaia gazeta*, 30 May 2011; *Nezavisimaia gazeta,* 31 May 2011.

88 *Kremlin.ru*, 14 November 2011.

89 'Speaker Boehner on Reasserting American Exceptionalism in the U.S.-Russia Relationship', www.speaker.gov, 25 October 2011.

90 Vladimir Mukhin, 'Siriiskii platsdarm severokavkazskikh boevikov', *Nezavisimaia gazeta*, 4 September 2013.

91 Hermitage Fund press release, www.hermitagefund.com, 21 March 2012.

92 US House Committee On Foreign Affairs, 21 March 2012.

93 See on this Vladimir Frolov, introduction, 'Russia Profile Weekly Experts Panel: Is Russia the United States' Number One Foe?' *Russia Profile,* 6 April 2012.

94 *MID.ru*, 11 February 2012.

95 RIA Novosti, 1 January 2013.

96 The Convention was adopted by the UN General Assembly in 1989, and is the most ratified of all UN civil rights treaties, in this case for all people under the

age of 18. Among other things the Convention forbids either death sentences or life imprisonment for children, both of which are still possible in the US.

97 *Vedomosti*, 29 December 2011.
98 On this, see Vincent Pouliot, *International Security in Practice: The Politics of NATO-Russian Diplomacy.* London and New York: Cambridge UP, 2009, and J. L. Black, *Russia Faces NATO Expansion, op. cit.*
99 Russian Federation Ministry of Foreign Affairs, *Daily Press Release*, 14 July 2007; see also foreign affairs specialist Sergei Karaganov, 'Rekviem po dogovoru', *Rossiiskaia gazeta*, 7 May 2007, who expressed relief that the CFE was gone.
100 'Opravdano li rasshirenie NATO? Osoboe mnenie Sluzhby vneshnei razvedki Rossii,' *Nezavisimaia gazeta*, 26 November 1993. Primakov was then the director of the Russian Foreign Intelligence Service.
101 'O voennoi doktrina Rossiiskoi Federatsii,' *Rossiiskaia gazeta,* 10 February 2010, Art. 16: 'Russia reserves the right to use nuclear weapons in response to the use of nuclear and other types of weapons of mass destruction against it or its allies, and also in case of aggression against Russia with the use of conventional weapons when the very existence of the state is threatened'. Medvedev signed the *ukaz* making the doctrine law on 5 February 2010.
102 On this issue see Jennifer G. Mathers, 'Nuclear Weapons in Russian Foreign Policy: Patterns in Presidential Discourse 2000–2010,' *Europe-Asia Studies*, Vol. 64, No. 3 (2012), pp. 495–519.
103 In November 2013 Serdyukov was charged with criminal negligence, for which there could be a short prison term. One specific accusation was an order forcing soldiers to construct infrastructure for an elite holiday resort owned by his brother-in-law.
104 The 14 Article draft treaty was posted on *Kremlin.ru*, 29 November 2009.
105 *Kremlin.ru*, 20 April 2009.
106 See Volha Charnysh, 'Russia Drafts European Security Pact,' *Arms Control Today*, January/February 2010, 'Russia Unveils Proposal for European Security Treaty', RFE/RL, 30 November 2009, and Bobo Lo, 'Medvedev and the New European Security Architecture', Centre for European Reform, *Policy Brief*, July 2009. For a later analysis, Glenn Diessen and Steve Wood, 'Russia's Proposal for a New Security System: Confirming Diverse Perspectives', *Australian Journal of International Affairs*, Vol. 66, No. 4 (August 2012), pp. 450–67.
107 See especially Mikhail Tsypkin, 'Russian Politics, Policy-Making, and American Missile Defence', *International Affairs* (Chatham House), Vol. 85, No. 4 (2009), pp. 781–99.
108 See Luca Ratti, 'Back to the Future? International Relations Theory and NATO-Russian Relations Since the End of the Cold War,' *International Journal*, LXIV, No. 2 (2009), pp. 399–417.
109 See Richard J. Krickus, *The Afghanistan Question and the Reset in U.S.-Russia Relations.* Carlisle, PA: US Army War College, 2011.
110 *Kommersant*, 28 January 2010; 'Remarks of Madeleine K. Albright at the Moscow State Institute of International Affairs', 11 February 2010, NATO website, *www.nato.in.*
111 Olivier Royant, 'Notre rencontre avec Medvedev', *Paris Match*, 25 février 2010; see also *Paris Match*, 1 Mars 2010.
112 On this, see 'Russia Profile Weekly Experts Panel: Another Attempt to Get Russia Into NATO', *Russia Profile*, 10 September 2010; Charles A. Kupchen, 'NATO's Final Frontier', *Foreign Affairs*, May/June, 2010; Tomas Vakasek, 'Membership for Russia a Step Too Far for NATO?' Centre for European Reform, *Policy Brief*, August, 2010.

Interestingly, recently declassified NATO archival documents provide details of the Soviet application to join the Alliance in 1954, a submission sometimes

denied and sometimes acknowledged by both sides. See 'Summary Record of Meeting of the [NATO] Council ... ' in Paris, 7 April 1954. NATO Secret (unclassified) Summary Record C-R(54) 14. Copy No.367, 9 April 1954.
113 Interfax, 21 February 2011; Global Security Newswire, 22 February 2011.
114 AVN, 17 March 2011.
115 'Russians Still Fear NATO Eastward Expansion', Interfax, 1 December 2011.

# 6 Society, daily life, and the corruption conundrum

If the expression 'the buck stops here' has any application to Russian governance, part of Medvedev's job as head of state was responsibility for the social development strategy outlined by President Putin in February 2008. The strategy, planned for culmination by 2020, was tied to the National Priority Projects devised in 2005 by Putin, and then handed to Medvedev to manage. The purpose of the Projects was to stimulate substantive improvements in the fields of demography, healthcare, education, research and development, and social infrastructure.[1] As head of government and its cabinet ministers from 2008 to 2012, Putin was himself responsible for on-the-ground implementation of the strategy he formulated early in 2008, so the success or failure of this enduring enterprise could be laid firmly at the Tandem's door.

The National Welfare Fund of some $25 billion in 2007 was intended to facilitate progress in these sectors, but, as we have seen, it was used instead to bail out banks and the National Champions during the early stages of the global economic recession. Medvedev got off to a reasonable start anyway. Within weeks of his inauguration reports from the Health and Social Development Ministry claimed that poverty had been reduced dramatically over the previous two years: the number of people living below the subsistence level was cut by 23 per cent (6 million), and real incomes grew by 25 per cent. It was hoped that the poverty level would decrease further when the State Duma nearly doubled the minimum wage per month as of 1 January 2009. The increase was pegged to the rising subsistence level bar.[2] Clearly, the new targets would be hard to reach during the financial crisis.

Even still, as the impending inflation materialized in the summer of 2009, Medvedev signed into law a program to raise pensions to a level of 7,700 rubles (approx. $250) monthly by the end of 2010. First priority went to people who relied solely on pensions and those whose pension was less than the minimum cost of living in their region.[3] But this wasn't enough.

## Social unrest

At the beginning of Medvedev's presidency social unrest was driven more by economic conditions than by political interests, though political activists did their best to harness the growing number of public demonstrations to their advantage. The global financial crisis began to hit households in the winter of 2009, mostly in the form of unemployment. Reports from Rosstat in February 2009 set the number of registered unemployed at 1.7 million (unregistered numbers ranged between 5 and 6 million), and predicted that the number would rise well above 2 million by the end of the year. Although Medvedev ordered the allocation of 44 billion rubles to help ease the situation, the number of registered unemployed rose to 2.26 million by the Spring, and projections of a 10–12 per cent inflation rate raised fears of widespread public upheaval.[4]

In an attempt to blunt the public outcry and mute calls for the prime minister's resignation, United Russia organized counter rallies, replete with sport and TV stars, and people carrying posters with pro-Putin slogans, none of which eased the bitterness. The tension was heightened by a common perception that the government was handing large bailouts to wealthy oligarchs while the people suffered. The new circumstance was particularly galling to Russians who still had not made up for their loss of savings in June 1991 when the Soviet government froze bank accounts, and to still others whose savings were wiped out in the crash of 1998.

By the middle of Medvedev's term, even the political rallies organized by opposition parties took on more and more of a social hue in that placards were waved and slogans shouted against high transportation taxes, exorbitant export duties, and unemployment. As thousands gathered in Moscow, Kaliningrad, St. Petersburg, Vladivostok and other cities in March 2010 to protest the worsening employment situation and high utility costs, Putin signed an executive order to increase the budget allocation to the Federal Service for Labour and Employment by 4.19 billion rubles.[5] High housing tariffs were a particular irritant targeted by demonstrators.[6]

Other issues drew unexpected protest support. For example, rallies in Moscow opposed the construction of a high-speed toll highway from Moscow to St. Petersburg through the Khimki Forest. These and the spreading international outcry sparked wide-ranging environmental protests that turned to violence in the summer of 2010. Activists battled with loggers when trees were first taken down in the birch forest, which is part of Moscow's Green Belt and home to many species of wild animals and some endangered plants. Environmentalists organized round-the-clock vigils in the forest, government offices were trashed, journalists beaten, arrests made, and so on. Medvedev suspended the project in late August. It was during these demonstrations that Yevgenia Chirikova made her name as an activist leader. In the long run, the protests failed. The Russian Supreme Court declared the project legal, and it was back on track in December. Intervention from a French international corporation that owned 50 per cent of the concession, a complaint from Sarkozy, and threats of a major lawsuit over broken contracts assured that the project went ahead. However, the power of organized protest was clearly noted.[7]

Khimki protesters tended to target Putin, not Medvedev. Political rallies against unemployment and other social issues in September evoked an outburst from Putin who said that demonstrators marching in unauthorized locations deserved a 'whack on the head' for such effrontery.[8] He accused protesters of catering to Western media and deliberately causing provocations by their unlawful actions. Such accusations were not entirely misplaced, though they certainly could not explain away the discontent of the great majority of participants in the rallies. Doubtless, Putin hoped to shift blame from his cabinet to opposition activists. However, shortly after Medvedev fired Luzhkov, demonstrations in Moscow were authorized more readily. For instance, a rally of over 1,000 in Pushkin Square heard speeches aimed against Putin and the government by activists such as Garri Kasparov with no repercussions, and permission was granted for further demonstrations on Triumfalnaia Ploshchad.

Generally, dissatisfaction in Russia was rooted in the perceived level of quality of life. A survey conducted on 26–27 February 2011 showed that 55 per cent of respondents believed that the quality of life in their region was poor, and only 24 per cent said that life was good. Another survey revealed that the large majority of Russians in school hoped to work in state service, banks, or in the management of a large company; barely anyone looked forward to employment in agriculture, construction, the trades, factories, or the military.[9] Presumably visions of large incomes, security, and maybe access to bribes were the attractive features of the preferred career profiles.

When the number of registered unemployed in Russia reached 5.7 million at the end of February, Putin announced that 105 billion rubles would be allocated in support of Russia's unemployed before the end of the year.[10] Medvedev took up the cause of workers in the first week of April as well, when he addressed a meeting in Gorky and acknowledged the poor working conditions faced by many Russian workers, noting again that Russia suffered a serious shortage of skilled labour. By calling for higher wages in some sectors and a more productive trade union movement, he hoped to attract young people to the trades.

The explosion of political protest in December 2011 tended at first to obscure the fact that Medvedev's final budget indicated decreased expenditures on housing and municipal services for 2012. Mindful that he could be the political victim of deteriorating social conditions, Putin prepared one of his long campaign essays precisely to address social uncertainties. 'Building Justice. A Social Policy for Russia' was printed just two weeks prior to the presidential election.[11] In it Putin cautioned that the Russian population was aging and that pension savings might become a problem. Attention to personal health and a healthier lifestyle was one way to manage the problem. Raising the levels of pension contributions from the government and even the retirement ages – both still low by Western standards – were other ways to cope. The aging factor also meant that Russia needed more working immigrants, and families needed to have more children, he said, promising programs to achieve both.

Rumours and official accusations of large-scale corruption in the sectors where the public was directly involved also inflamed crowds, especially in Moscow where the community of Rechnik in the West of Moscow was the site of a bizarre affair that touched on living conditions, corruption, and political infighting. Existing housing in the area was declared illegal by Moscow city authorities, and all inhabitants were turned out of their homes in the middle of the night in January. Although pending demolition was frozen three weeks later while the Procurator General's Office investigated, suspicion of corruption ran rampant. Other communities, including a yacht club, were also said to be 'illegal' by city authorities. Much of the public's suspicion fell on Yelena Baturina, Mayor Luzhkov's wife and Russia's richest woman, who amassed a fortune in real estate and development deals while her husband was in office. Towards the end of February, Medvedev stepped into the fray and set up a Rechnik working group with instructions to resolve the matter by 1 April.[12] One of the ironies of the situation is that at about the same time the president declared that private housing was one of the main social priorities of his administration for 2010.

In one of his first acts as president in 2012, Putin decreed an increase in wages for everyone between 40–50 per cent by 2018. This decree and the opening day edicts mentioned in the first chapter ordered the implementation of measures to realize Russia's demographic policies, education and science initiatives, health care and housing programs, and sustain the government's existing social policies. All much easier said than done, and, because Putin's 'new' demands embodied precisely the directives handed to Medvedev in 2005 and again in 2008, it makes one wonder if the bureaucracy ever actually pays any attention to the myriad orders from on high – from the *Vertikal*.[13] An insider author of a recent study of the informal ways and means (*sistema*) of getting things done in Russia through connections, bribes, and trade-offs suggests that, in fact, the president and his executive can achieve very little without the support of dense networks made up of bureaucrats and power brokers who function outside the constitutional institutions and mechanisms.[14]

## Infrastructure

Infrastructure failures shook the complacency of state and local planners throughout Medvedev's term. As domestic prices for gas consumption rose in 2008, in part to meet requirements for entry into the WTO, functions of the energy complex began to break down. The semi-privatized Unified Energy System (UES) failed to deliver electricity in some areas. The number of local blackouts increased, as did gas-related explosions. Paradoxically, Gazprom continued to expand its programs for constructing pipelines to carry gas to Europe and Asia while its domestic delivery system deteriorated. The rapid fall in energy prices by October 2008 slowed revenue intake for government and the oligarchs, Russia's two largest employers. In turn, labour unrest fuelled incidents of xenophobia and acts of race hatred became a recurring problem, especially among youth groups.

Since most of Russia's public utilities infrastructure was constructed during the 1960s–1970s, and there has been no major maintenance program since the collapse of the Soviet Union, they tend to be wasteful and potentially dangerous. The terrible explosion at the Sayano-Shushenskaia hydroelectric power station in August 2009 served as a case in point – it was built in the late 1960s and last upgraded in 1987. When a turbine burst, the turbine hall was flooded, the plant itself was destroyed, and up to 75 people were killed. Medvedev referred to the tragedy as the 'Chernobyl of the 21st century'. As we have seen, at that time he urged regional governments to upgrade infrastructure and safety regulations. This and other such incidents were also tied to problems caused by graft and corruption, for which people were regularly arrested with little noticeable effect in terms of improvements. With ample justification, one Russian writer referred to 2009 as a year when 'the excessive number of catastrophes ... underscored how woefully ineffective, incompetent and corrupt the government is'.[15]

Sporadic electricity blackouts and water shortages plagued Russian citizens, especially in Siberia and the Far East, for the next four years. Train and plane accidents, methane explosions in mines, and natural disasters added to the general unease. In July and early August 2010, raging forest and peat fires in Central Russia and a heat wave in Moscow caused the government to introduce medical relief programs, including housing reconstruction, as thousands were left homeless when their wooden homes burned to the ground. Nearly a quarter of a million people were deployed to fight fires burning in 17 regions of the country. The fires killed dozens of people and forced the evacuation of many more. As they continued to spread in August, Prime Minister Putin took charge of the fire fighting and clean up operation. The fires were a by-product of the rare heat wave and a severe drought, both of which had unfortunate manifestations in the agricultural sector and for the daily lives of urban dwellers. The government, in fact, did what it could, but took the brunt of justified accusations that its policies seemed always to be reactive, rather than preventative.

In December 2010 and January 2011, still more widespread electricity outages hit closer to larger populations in Moscow, Novgorod, Tver, and other urban centres, producing further problems for thousands of Russian homes and businesses. Though some of the outages were relatively lengthy, e.g., in Tver, there were signs that Russia's capacity to handle such emergencies was improving. The electrical power shortages themselves were exacerbated by the fact that air pollution in Russia had increased by some 30–35 per cent in 2010, primarily from the raging summer forest fires and heat waves.[16]

The rapid rise of electricity costs prompted Medvedev to warn the State Council Presidium in March 2011 that the situation was 'alarming.' He noted that the system had not been overhauled for more than twenty years and ordered his government to oversee its upgrade and regulation. Eight months later, he told a government meeting that, 'according to estimates, over 60 per cent of the public utilities infrastructure has outlived its service life ... Unless we deal with it now, in five or seven years there will be a disaster'. By then, the government had already capped price increases for electricity, twice, limiting them in March to no more than a 15 per cent rise.[17] For many citizens that disaster moment was already here.

Light and heat source breakdowns have an immediate impact on people's daily lives, and a less direct but perhaps longer-term consequence on the economy. For the economy in general, however, the infrastructure weaknesses in Russia's transportation system are especially serious. The value of train transport to agricultural and industries where large quantities of products must be moved over long distances cannot be overestimated, and because roads and highways are either in an extraordinary state of disrepair, or simply do not exist, this has long been a major difficulty. A 19th-century Russian adage usually attributed to Gogol, is that Russia has two problems – fools and roads. Setting aside the 'fools' part of the saying for others to deal with, the road problem seems not to have changed very much over the last two hundred years. Soon after Medvedev was inaugurated in 2008, an analyst wrote that the 'continued deterioration of Russia's road networks' causes thousands of towns and villages to be cut off from the rest of the country for parts of each year. He calculated that transportation costs equal about 40 per cent of the cost of agriculture products.[18] Road transportation problems are not unique to the agricultural sector, of course, but it is the sector that would benefit the most from physical improvements – as it would from better storage and refrigeration facilities.

The economic losses due to roads in disrepair are one thing; a chronic culture of drunk driving is another. These factors and the exponential growth in the number of cars and trucks since the early 1990s have meant that Russia suffers from about 30,000 deaths in road accidents each year. To put that statistic in perspective, the EU has double the number of kilometres of roads that Russia has, triple the number of cars, and half the number of deaths. Though the number of road deaths is decreasing, the annual totals are still the highest in Europe, and are worsened by the ease at which traffic cops can be bribed.[19]

Programs to modernize the road and other transport systems (including the extensive canal network that is functioning reasonably well) were launched in 2010 with trillions of rubles promised for the purpose of doubling the length of the federal highway network. The grand undertaking promised job-creating expansion in the cement, asphalt, and road-construction machinery industries. Accusations that corruption eventually ate up about 70 per cent of the federal and private funds allocated to these projects may have been exaggerated, but were readily assumed by the public to be true. Certainly, road construction projects did expand highway access and road repair was a constant industrial enterprise; yet the same complaints about highway and, for that matter, inner city transportation were voiced in 2013 as they were in 2008. President Putin acknowledged the eternal dilemma in 2013 by pledging $43 billion for upgrades in Russian roads and railroads, making a point of bringing this to the attention of potential foreign investors.[20] Gogol would have cheered him on, probably with much irony.

## Natural disasters and other calamities

With perceived and real infrastructure flaws, various natural and semi-natural large-scale disasters caused greater damage than they might otherwise have done. That damage went deeper than the economic losses mentioned in Chapter Four, because they shook whatever faith the Russian people may have had in their government's ability, and in some case its willingness, to ensure the population's safety.

For instance, when the temperature reached 100°F in Moscow on 29 July 2010, the highest since such records have been kept there, many people died because the city did not have the means to protect them. Almost double the usual number of deaths per day was recorded in the capital in August, that is, 700 as opposed to 365. As the year ground on, the fire and drought threatened a major increase in food and animal feed prices, although Medvedev told a Rossiia 1 TV interviewer in August that he ordered the government to forestall any such rise. He was compelled to provide subsidies, as we have seen, but had no means to save elderly and asthmatic people from death-dealing smoke and smog that came with the fires.

Once again, the fires and heat demonstrated high levels of bureaucratic inefficiency and flaws in fire fighting infrastructure in both civilian and military organizations (thousands of soldiers were called in to help fight the conflagration). Political and social consequences followed, among them a drop in the popularity ratings of both Medvedev and Putin, and especially of Luzhkov, who went on holiday at the peak of the crisis. The fires were brought under control only by mid-August, and states of emergency in most areas were lifted. Still, danger hovered throughout the month, and new outbreaks of wildfires in six districts of the Volgograd region during the first week of September killed at least eight and injured nearly four times that many. About 1,000 people had to be evacuated before the fires were contained.

During an interview in early September, Medvedev blamed the outbreak of fires in Volgograd on 'negligent' bureaucrats. Reports showed that up to 1,000 officials were later held liable for the fires. Federal agencies filed over 600 lawsuits related to incompetence and issued hundreds of administrative procedure warnings. Such problems as failure to spot fires early enough, poor decision-making, substandard equipment and training, and a lack of proper collaboration between various levels of bureaucracy combined to make the results of the fires much worse than they might otherwise have been. Medvedev demanded more fire fighting training programs.[21]

In the winter of 2011 Russia's more traditional problem, snow, caused further electrical grid breakdowns. Heavy snowfall and rains brought unusual weight to bear on trees and power lines, causing them to snap throughout the regions of Ulyanovsk and Samara and in the Republic of Tatarstan. Over a quarter of a million people were left without power for days.

In Chapter Two, we saw that Russians were already burdened by a fear of domestic terrorists acts. For example, in April 2010 a few weeks after female suicide bombers killed 40 and injured over 100 others in the two Moscow Metro stations, surveys revealed that more than 70 per cent of the city's dwellers were afraid that they might suffer a similar fate.[22]

Other types of disasters weighed heavily on the Russian psyche as well. A general state of anxiety was fuelled by major accidents, such as a fire at an arms depot in the Udmurtia Republic that injured at least 75 people in May 2011, and a plane crash in June that killed 45. The plane, a twin-engine Tu-134, is a mainstay of Russian civil aviation, but old. Although the crash was blamed on human error, Medvedev ordered all Tu-134s withdrawn from service within a year. The most dramatic air accident came in September 2011 when a plane carrying a professional ice hockey team from Yaroslavl crashed and killed all but one person on board.[23]

Russia's worst maritime disaster occurred in early July that same year when a boat carrying hundreds of passengers on a weekend Volga River cruise sank and some 130 people perished. Lifeboats failed to launch, people drowned in their cabins, and rescue attempts were ineffective. The president declared July 12th a day of mourning for the dead and missing. More troubling for the future, however, was the sinking of the *Kolskaia*, a huge floating oilrig in the Sea of Okhotsk in December, which killed over 50 crewmembers. This terrible accident added to a feeling among some Russians that their country's safety regulations, technology, and superstructure were handled inadequately. With two days to go in the year, a blazing fire lasted for a day and a half in the nuclear submarine, *Yekaterinburg,* already in for repairs. Several fire fighters were injured. Weapons had been removed from the sub and there was no radiation leak, but the incident added to a feeling of inadequacy.

Incidents like these reminded Russians of the *Kursk* tragedy of 2000 when 118 sailors drowned in a sunken submarine while Putin's government wasted time blaming NATO and refusing to accept Western offers of assistance. The inefficiency and incompetence covered up by wild and almost childish accusations – especially from the Admiralty – sounded to many Russians like one of the carryovers from Soviet days that they had hoped had faded away over the previous decade.[24] Frantic blame casting by officialdom after disasters seemed to be an ingrained habit over which the public had no control, and contributed to the political anger voiced after the Duma election in 2011.

## Demography and health

Russia initiated its first census in eight years during the fall of 2010, and a preliminary report in November put the Russian population at 141.2 million. Although this represented a further drop in overall numbers, the government tried to look on the bright side by noting that the rate of decline was slowing.[25] Medvedev had some support here from the United Nations, whose Development Program branch released a report in October showing that male life expectancy had risen in Russia, from 58.8 years in 2005 to 61.8 years in 2008, and that there was 'considerable progress' in poverty reduction.[26]

Still, a prominent Western political economist wrote in 2011 that overall Russia's 'population has been shrinking, its mortality levels are nothing short of catastrophic, and its human resources appear to be dangerously eroding'.[27] These were precisely the trends that Medvedev had hoped to turn around. Improvements in health care, social education, less smoking and alcohol consumption, assistance to family structures, and so on were among the recommendations from experts in Russia and from around the world.

Instead, the census results prompted a report from the Federal Migration Service that Russia needed about five million immigrants a year in compensation. Yet, more immigration was not what a lot of Russians wanted. Rioting by nationalist youths and soccer hooligans in December took on a racist character. Tensions rose after a street brawl in Moscow followed a soccer match in early December. The death of an ethnic Russian in the brawl sparked demonstrations of people who shouted 'Russia for Russians' and attacked anyone who did not 'look' Russian. Although the number of illegals in Moscow, mostly from the Caucasus and Central Asia, is huge and varied, the gangs focus on physical appearance. Medvedev's public statements against the growing racism appeared to be in vain. A general disrespect for the police tended to make the situation more volatile.[28]

The on-going demographic predicament had obvious implications for the labour force, and presented Russian authorities with a bit of a predicament. An early 2011 study issued by the Institute of Demography at Moscow State University titled 'Migration in the Development of Russia' emphasized again that the population is declining and also growing older. Only migrants could make up for increasing worker shortages and the chronic problem of low labour productivity among Russians. Another issue was the number of Russian and illegal migrant workers who were employed in the black market, doing unskilled work, and paying no taxes.[29]

Medvedev tried to mute the growing angst about immigrants, repeating time and again a message he delivered to an international forum on social diversity in Yaroslavl. Social diversity can 'teach us to co-exist and interact with those who are not like us', he expounded there in September 2011. Defeating poverty and improving the quality of life for the 180 different ethnic groups who live in the Russian Federation were his main answer to the dilemma of rising ethnic tensions and hate crimes. Translating these good words into deeds, especially at a time when surveys were showing that Russian society was increasingly ghettoized, was the stumbling block.[30]

In the meantime it was obvious already in 2010 that mounting anger amongst Russia's less educated and unemployed youth was about to explode into violence against the closest and most vulnerable targets. For example, Moscow's Human Rights Bureau reported in March 2010 that over 30 xenophobic attacks were recorded in the first three months of the year; ten people had been killed and 28 injured. Moscow and Vladivostok, and the regions of Altai, Nizhny Novgorod, and Kaliningrad were the sites of most of these assaults – so they were well spread out. The main targets were Kyrgyz, Uzbeks, Koreans, and Africans, though racist gangs also attacked Russians whom they didn't like.[31]

The Federal Migration Service denied on several occasions that the level of xenophobia in Russia was dangerous, but that may have been wishful thinking. A nationalist rally on Moscow's Manezh Ploshchad on 11 December turned into a forum for physical attacks on anyone suspected of being from the Caucasus, and then on the police. Fights spread and a number of arrests were made. Radical youth, bikers, and skinheads provided the energy for the rally, which prompted moderating words from government but little real action against the root causes of racism.[32]

Adding a complication to Russia's population depletion was a revelation earlier in the year from the head of the Federal Migration Service Konstantin Romodanovsky that an average 350,000 people leave Russia each year either for temporary work or to settle abroad. In fact, about 70,000 of them stay abroad permanently. Hoping to stem this tide and also to resolve the population problem, Putin proclaimed the second stage of the Russian Demographic Development Program in February. He earmarked 876 billion rubles for the second half of 2011 with a target of stabilizing the population at 143 million by 2015. The general aim was to raise the average life expectancy from the low 60s for males to 71, which is the age reached on average by females, and improve the birth to death ratio by 25–30 per cent over the level recorded for 2006.[33] Plans to improve migration policy were also announced at Novo-Ogarevo.

Fundamental to the demographic issue, of course, was the question of the national health. Over the previous four years, Medvedev had signed a number of edicts intended to improve the health of Russians, stem the spread of addiction to drugs and alcohol, and improve the well being of the country's work force. Early in his term, he acted vigorously to slow the obvious damage caused by alcohol abuse. On 1 January 2009, for instance, he signed a decree on the formation of the Federal Service for Regulating the Alcohol Market. Its purpose was to fight the illegal marketing of alcohol, but also to bolster revenues from the industry for the government.

Multiple reports and sociological commentary drew attention to consequences beyond the rampant poor health that too much alcohol consumption caused, such as domestic violence, work place accidents, and lost work hours.

Medvedev's concerns were confirmed in July when a national survey showed that alcohol consumption patterns had changed very little since the late nineties. Some 74 per cent of respondents said that they drink alcohol, down only slightly from the 77 per cent admitting to doing so in 1996. About half of these were frequent drinkers, and the large majority were males. The president addressed this and the other troubling dependence issue directly a few weeks later saying 'alcoholism and drug addiction should be fought by comprehensive measures. The problem cannot be solved with the help of foolish bans. We have already tried that'. In commenting on alcohol consumption statistics, he called them 'monstrous figures' and warned an audience in Zvenigorod that such habits were 'degrading' the Russian gene pool.[34]

Alcohol abuse was such an obvious problem that, in late June 2009, former President Gorbachev called for a new anti-alcohol abuse campaign like the one he instituted in the 1980s. Data showed that more than half of deaths among Russians between the ages of 15 and 54 were alcohol-related. In September 2011, Medvedev proposed a series of measures that included stiff penalties for pedaling alcohol to minors under 18, tightened rules for selling to people under 21, and a ban on the sale of alcohol near schools, healthcare facilities, and sports centres. Street vendors of alcohol were abolished as of the following year, and such questions as a minimum price for retailed vodka and a government monopoly on alcohol production were opened up for discussion.[35] These 'questions' were not easy to resolve, but the government finally decided to double the price of vodka. The new minimum price of 89 rubles (about $2.95 US) for a half-litre of vodka took effect just in time for the 12-day Orthodox Christmas holiday in 2012. Later, in March, Health Minister Gennady Onishchenko recommended that no retail alcohol sales be allowed after 9:00 pm, as opposed to the 11:00 pm deadline at that time. Previous attempts to mitigate the effects of heavy alcohol use had all proven ineffective, and even dangerous because they drove Russians to rely on home brew (*samogon*).

Vodka was not the only villain. By 2010, Russia was fast becoming one of the world's biggest beer markets, and most restrictions on alcohol did not apply to beer because it was not yet officially designated an alcoholic beverage. Large foreign corporations, such as Anheuser-Busch Inbev, Carlsberg, and SABMiller controlled about 95 per cent of beer sales in Russia.

Manifestations of problems caused by alcohol abuse could be found everywhere. In addition to the damage it causes to the overall health of Russians, domestic violence and accidents in the workplace, statistics released by the Ministry of the Interior showed that drunk driving was responsible for 252 deaths and over 1,000 injuries between the first of January and the end of March 2010. More than 2,000 people were killed and 18,000 injuries caused by drunk drivers in 2009.[36] These data prompted the Duma to approve a draft law prohibiting the consumption of alcohol before driving a car. Though almost everyone was in favour of the new law, pessimists worried that it would lead to even more corruption on the part of law enforcement. Medvedev introduced further anti-alcohol abuse legislation by signing a law restricting beer sales outdoors and late at night. The new law signed on 20 July 2011 was set to take effect in 2013. It restricts sales from 11 pm to 8 am, the same hours as for vodka sales. Sidewalk kiosks and sales at train stations will be banned, and advertising alcoholic drinks will be limited.

Just as his term was ending, Medvedev brought more anti-alcohol abuse legislation forward as a preliminary to a government-sponsored

'De-alcoholization of the People Program'. Beer was reclassified as an alcoholic beverage in November 2011, and its sale was banned officially as of 1 January 2012 during the hours mentioned above, except in bars and cafés. The tax on vodka sales was raised dramatically and the government sponsored programs to educate people about alcohol consumption. Such laws have met with little success in the past, so we must wait to see what the fate of these regulations will be.[37]

Long infamous for their alcohol habits, Russians took the lead as the world's top heroin consumers in 2009. According to Viktor Ivanov, head of the Federal Drug Control Service, his country is the transit and drop-off territory for vast amounts of the drug passing through to Europe from Afghanistan. For that reason, the war against the Taliban led by the US has huge implications for Russia's drug problem, because its 2.5 million addicts almost all use Afghan heroin. A report released in September 2011 said that Russia was flooded with heroin from Afghanistan since the beginning of the NATO invasion of that country, and was ill equipped to deal with it.[38]

Information released by the UN Office on Drugs and Crime in October 2009 claimed that Russians used about one-fifth of all heroin consumed in the world, all of which comes from Afghanistan. Medvedev already had warned that drugs represented a threat to the country's national security and in 2009 introduced stiff legislation to combat it.[39] Subsequent disclosures of wide ranging corruption within Russian's drug control agencies tended to negate whatever progress he might have initiated. He remarked on this himself during a TV interview in December 2010 when he added that drugs in the schools and on the streets were one of the 'biggest dangers today', and informed the interviewers that up to 160,000 Russian children had drug problems.[40]

A report carried by the *New York Times* shortly after that interview suggested that Medvedev's concerns were greater even than he implied, in part because drugs contributed to the rise in HIV/AIDS in Russia to near epidemic level. The article claimed that over a million people in Russia abuse drugs intravenously and often share and infect each other with used needles. It went on to note that Russia had neither the infrastructure, nor the inclination to adopt needle exchange programs (though there are some) or drug substitution therapy. This was especially true in the regions. In response to more than a half million registered HIV cases, and easily the same number unregistered, the government announced programs to double its spending on HIV drugs to the equivalent in rubles of about $600 million and to expand prevention training for youth.[41]

There seemed to be no slowing of the drug intake. Another report posted by Ivanov in March 2012 acknowledged that there were five million drug addicts in Russia, mostly on opiates. There were likely many more. In fact, in both mid-June and in October the Drug Control Service raised these figures to say that up to 8.5 million Russians were addicts.[42]

Another hard-to-shake addiction came in for intense government scrutiny – smoking. Medvedev regularly cautioned against it and in 2010 initiated several bills to limit places where smoking was allowed and where cigarette advertisements could be placed. He also ordered a campaign to educate children against smoking. But it wasn't until November 2012 that the government submitted a bill to lawmakers outlawing all cigarette advertising and sponsorship immediately, with bans on kiosk sales and smoking in public places to go into effect 1 January 2015. Russian and foreign tobacco companies (e.g., Philip Morris and British American Tobacco) lobbied against the changes. In response, Putin cited the World Health Organization (WHO) data to the effect that 39 per cent of Russians are habitual smokers and that smoking-related diseases kill 23 per cent of Russian men and cause immense economic damage.[43]

Prime Minister Putin's entire Cabinet supported the anti-smoking bill, and 83 per cent of the population told pollsters they were in favour of a complete ban on tobacco advertisement. This response represented a remarkable change in attitude from previous years.[44]

Throughout Medvedev's presidency, the rampant drug addiction, alcohol abuse, and attendant HIV/AIDS epidemic placed a heavy strain on Russia's medical care budgets – as did the global financial crisis in the early years. Nevertheless, in March 2009, Medvedev ordered an addition 21 billion rubles added to the federal budget for health care institutions, primarily in the regions, and for children's care. Later that Spring he told a television interviewer that cardiovascular diseases were the biggest medical causes of death in Russia and claimed that centres specializing in the disease were under construction.[45] Cardiovascular issues are, of course, greatly aggravated by heavy smoking, drinking, and drug abuse.

Expanded health programs for children was a central theme of Medvedev's annual address to the Federal Assembly on 30 November 2010, as were a number of other benefits to families with three or more children. Tax relief, free land in the country for dachas, improved sports and childcare facilities, and also special tax benefits for businesses that support sports and other programs for young people, were some of the incentives listed. Following up on these promises, Medvedev signed laws protecting child rights and safety. These included changes in family law to remove some barriers preventing adoption by step-parents, and the enactment of other legislation designed to bar people with criminal records from employment in education, health care, sports, and other services for youth.[46]

Healthcare received another boost in February 2011, when the government designated 150 billion more rubles to upgrade medical facilities in the city of Moscow over the following two years. Prime Minister Putin announced this allocation as he, Medvedev, and Sobyanin each made short photo-op visits to health-related institutions in that city.[47]

Putin promoted a healthy life style in his annual address to the Federal Assembly in December 2012, noting that among Russians, especially males, there is an 'irresponsible attitude in society towards healthy living'.[48] His expressed support for health and fitness in 2012 was one way to address the non-political social ills with which Medvedev was still struggling, with limited success. Another approach appeared in a report released in March 2012 by a special commission made up of immigration experts from trade unions and government calling for massive funding to make Russia attractive to skilled immigrants. In March, Romodanovsky also told the Russian Human Rights Council that the country needed a large influx of foreign workers and that Russia's labour force could be short some 10 million people by 2025.[49] That said, Putin had announced in January that the Russian population had grown in 2011, bringing the total back up to 143,030,106. In May, Minister of Health Tatiana Golikova proclaimed that the population was expected to climb by 1.8 per cent by 2020.[50]

One byproduct of Medvedev and Putin's birth rate incentives was the resurrection of the old Soviet award system for large families. At a gala ceremony in June, the president handed honours (Order of Parental Glory) to select families with seven or more children, and promised further incentives for multi-child families. At the end of Putin's first year back as president, Russia was able to report its first natural population growth in over two decades. A small step, to be sure, but births were up by seven per cent and deaths down by 1.5 per cent.[51]

This optimistic trend could be explained in part by year-end VTsIOM survey results, which showed that 40 per cent of the population was now satisfied with their way of life, in contrast to 26 per cent at the start of the year and 24 per cent a year and a half earlier. Paradoxically, the percentage of Russians who said they were willing to participate in demonstrations also rose, from 21 to 29 per cent.[52]

These numbers may also reflect the emergence of a middle class relatively content with their lot in life. By international standards, 26 per cent of Russia's population still lived below the poverty line, so the old two-tier (rich and poor) division of Russian society now must account for a third, middle tier. Even before the report noted above came out, Prime Minister Putin acknowledged the poverty issue often and proposed a number of solutions to it. Already in January, he told his government that 'raising living standards and reducing the number of people living below the poverty threshold' was the main goal of government for 2012.[53] A gallant idea but, in light of the fact that his subsequent federal budgets inexplicably called for further decreases in health care spending, it raised the question as to how it could be achieved.[54]

There were undeniable improvements in the social sphere during Medvedev's tenure as president, even if mostly at the level of mechanics – that is, institutions and policies set in motion. Progress was slow and the lack of a great leap forward in the field of social services could be laid at the door of stifling layers of corruption on the part of bureaucratic providers.

## The NGO phenomenon

A feature of the new Russia that overlaps all the considerations important to the development of Russian society noted in this chapter, and also touches on the foreign policy, economic and, above all, political sectors, was the fate of Non-Government Organizations (NGOs) in Russia.

If one is looking for a theme that unwittingly provides definition to Medvedev's four years as president, the NGO question may prove apt. To trace the NGO phenomenon in Russia, one can go back as far as the late 1980s and 1990s when, during the era of *perestroika* and shortly after the dissolution of the USSR, thousands of Western NGOs rushed to assist first the changing USSR, and then the newly formed Russian Federation, learn the fundamentals of democracy and civil society. NGOs intending to help shape the new Russia sprouted up everywhere, some of them registered with the Russian government, some of them not. Earnest volunteer experts on everything from agricultural techniques to higher court practices carried their skills and knowledge to Russia; select Russian citizens travelled to university and government centres in Europe and North America to learn 'how we do it'. Doubtless, great benefits did accrue from most of these interactions, especially in the fields of medicine, social services, legal services, pedagogical practices, and so on. Equally doubtless a great many of the NGO personnel assumed they were bringing light into Russia's political darkness, and 'therein lies the rub'.[55]

Soon after he settled in to his second term, Putin submitted a law to the Duma to create a national registry of foreign organizations operating in Russia and also of Russian NGOs receiving funding from abroad. The bill was greeted with such an outcry that Putin was compelled to order amendments to take the criticisms into consideration. He signed the revised version on 10 December 2005, and the law went into effect the following April.[56] By October 2006, only 130 NGOs were fully registered with some 90 still on the waiting list. Only three were rejected at that stage. The procedures for registration were extremely slow and cumbersome, and doubtless burdened further by bureaucratic inefficiency and corruption.

Although only a fraction of NGOs (called Non-Profit Organizations in Russia) in Russia received foreign funding, the fact that estimates of their numbers ranged from 277,000 to 600,000 made the process a problematic one.[57] The law required foreign and state-funded NGOs to report on their activities in detail, notify the Federal Registration Service (FRS) of incoming funds and the manner in which they were spent; it also allowed officials such interpretive leeway that they could deny or delay registration almost at whim. Western governments and Russian rights organizations (many of them funded NGOs themselves) continued to deride the law as undemocratic. Russians who supported the action worried that foreign funding skewed Russian politics and may even have been responsible for the 'colour revolutions' in Georgia, Ukraine, and Kyrgyzstan. The Kremlin countered as well that Russia's proposals for foreign-funded NGOs were no more demanding than similar requirements in Western countries, including the US.

Delays were such that, in April 2008, the Public Chamber stepped in and demanded that the greatly expanded FRS speed up the process, and a year later Medvedev introduced a simplification of the registration rules. On 12

May 2009, he established a working group on non-profit organizations for the purpose of bringing the law governing such groups into line with international human rights obligations. Medvedev also told the Presidential Council for Civil Society Institutions and Human Rights that he was willing to review the law, which he admitted was abused often by government officials.

In spite of, or maybe because of, Medvedev's apparent support for moderating the NGO law, little headway was made before the election crisis of 2011 drove the government's NGO agenda into extremes. A law signed by Putin shortly after his return to the presidency forced foreign-funded NGOs involved in political activities in Russia to register as 'foreign agents'. Medvedev's prior attitudes were lost in the shuffle when, even with him as its titular leader, the United Russia party led the charge against NGOs, claiming that unnamed foreign governments were using them as cover for subversive efforts at regime change in Russia – and again insisted that the registration requirements were not greater than restrictions legislated in most Western countries. Critics of the new law see it as a vehicle with which to stifle dissent. So Medvedev's presidency ended with the NGO file also coming full circle – perhaps another good metaphor for the proxy presidency.

## The corruption impasse

Of all the agendas shared by the Tandem, the corruption file was the one most obviously left to Medvedev. In this portfolio, more than any other, he had history to contend with, that is, a home-grown mafia arising from Russia's rapid transition to a market economy, linked in its practices to the old Soviet shadow economy and related corruption that predominated in the USSR.

Corruption was recognized as a handicap slowing growth on all fronts well before the fall of the Soviet Union, and it was, to a certain extent, a natural consequence of the fact that members of a single public organization, the Communist Party, wielded unchallenged supremacy for so many decades. Nikita Khrushchev recognized the problem, but his tenure was short, and he was replaced by Leonid Brezhnev, whose policies could be characterized by stagnation for some 17 years. Brezhnev's failure to restrain his Party turned corruption into the national sport. One of his elderly successors, Yuri Andropov, railed against the degradations corruption caused the party, but he left the problem still uncurbed to Gorbachev, General Secretary of the CPSU from March 1985.

Gorbachev was faced with a huge and cumbersome ruling elite that neither wanted nor understood the need for change. Membership in the Communist Party was almost the sole vehicle for upward mobility, and members perceived any challenge to the system as a threat to their personal careers. The CPSU provided entrée to local and national political and social power, and unique privilege: access to dachas, special health care facilities, rare consumer goods, mutual protection, and bribes (*vziatki*) of all kind. In effect, the CPSU was the institutional framework for a giant *krysha*, a 'roof' for millions of members for whom quality of work and efficiency were of only secondary concern. The term was often used to describe links between illegal and legal enterprises and individuals, sometimes officials and organized crime, for mutual benefit, i.e., 'families'.[58] David Remnick's characterization of the CPSU *apparat* as 'the most gigantic mafia the world has ever known' was well founded.[59]

It didn't take long for Gorbachev to realize that efforts to reform the system would be wasted if the public were left out of the equation. Urging the population to work harder, with neither incentive, nor purpose, quickly proved pointless and forced him to adopt a 'democratization' program in the workplace. When that failed to bring the public onside, he had little choice but to introduce *glasnost* (openness, publicity), to demonstrate precisely why citizens should be working harder. That first small step towards transparency backfired in that the consequent shattering of the CPSU's monopoly on the dissemination of information proved fatal to the USSR itself. The public suddenly took up the cause of re-shaping Soviet society, but instead of more productive labour they put their hammers and sickles down and took up pen, politics, and strikes.

Russia's post-Soviet leaders inherited the corruption conundrum, and allowed it to mutate and become more viral during the 1990s.[60] Every prime minister in the 1990s knew the truth of Sergei Stepashin's remark in 1999 about 'crime and corruption reducing all the best government ventures to nothing'.[61] Putin faced this dilemma himself after he replaced Stepashin as prime minister in August that year and during his first four years as president. Early in 2001, he handed the Security Council a special mandate to fight corruption and, a little more than a year later, created a Council for Combating Corruption responsible directly to him. The State Duma formed a commission of its own to fight corruption in 2003. But Putin had far more pressing business with which to deal, and the Duma's enthusiasm for ending corruption was feeble to say the least. Thus, there was little pressure on these bodies to put an end to bureaucratic corruption, which in turn was complicated by the relentless growth of the bureaucracy itself.

The super-bureaucratization of present-day Russia was not Putin's invention either. It had its first spurt during the Gorbachev years, as the Brezhnev system was dismembered in the name of *perestroika*. It was under Gorbachev and Yeltsin that the *krysha* system took its current form; that is, the 'roofs' were privatized along with the national assets,[62] and the oligarchs took advantage of Russia's confusing, contradictory, and ever changing regulations to generate great wealth. As we have seen, Putin wrested political and economic power from the leading oligarchs – and at the same time provided an answer to the 'Who is in charge?' queries that dominated public conversation during the unstable Yeltsin era: officialdom and mandarins – just as they had during much of Russian history.

Clearly, shifting economic power to the state did not resolve the corruption problem. In the year before Medvedev became president, evidence suggested that corruption had spread more widely than even in the 1990s. Some analysts believed that bribery and kickbacks were so integrated into the system that the general population saw it as part of a normal way of life. It provided a perverse sort of order that they understood and with which they could live.[63]

Not surprisingly, then, everything that Medvedev attempted in the way of modernizing the economy, upgrading the military, democratizing the political system, and creating norms for greater social equality ran head on into the dilemma of corruption.

Indeed, a headline corruption case coincided with the presidential campaign. The dramatic detention of Deputy Minister of Finance Sergei Storchak in late November 2007 illustrated the problem Medvedev would soon have to face directly. The public was treated to a flood of charges and counter-charges in what appeared to be more of a struggle for power within the *siloviki* than a simple corruption scandal. Political brawls intensified as senior officials jockeyed to gain position under the new president. The in-house competition was accentuated when senior officials from the Gosnarkokontrol (Federal Narcotics Control Service) were arrested on various charges of corruption and its head, Viktor Cherkesov, called the arrests a consequence of political intrigue rather than a legitimate 'catch' of corrupt villains in the system. He and others accused the newly established and much-touted Investigative Committee, which prepared the charges against Gosnarkokontrol personnel and Storchak, of political motivation in a war between the presidential administration and the FSB on the one hand, and various other official 'services' on the other.[64] The consensus was that corruption charges themselves had become weapons in the struggle for post-Putin status.

The fact that the Procurator General's Office dropped a second charge against Storchak in early December, and the Investigative Committee immediately appealed the action taken by what was technically its own parent office, suggested that there was more going on than met the eye.[65] By mid-December 2007, offices of the Investigative Committee were themselves the subject of spot inspections all across the country. The inspection sweep was complete by the end of the year with no great disclosures.[66] At least one widely read Internet broadsheet in Russia linked the Storchak case to the Khodorkovsky trial and suggested that Finance Minister Kudrin was the real target of the investigators.[67] One can only assume that Putin would have been fully versed in these machinations and perhaps even an instigator of some of them. None of this storm in the media did Storchak any good: on 4 January 2008, his initial term of custody was extended for another four months, and that term was extended in April to 9 July.

Medvedev and Putin were well aware of the rampant corruption. Putin, for example, responding to a journalist who asked what was the most difficult issue he had to face during his first two terms as president, said tersely 'corruption'.[68] He spoke out against corruption often enough, but certainly had not emphasized it to the extent that response suggested he might have.

Medvedev's efforts to cure the disease went in a somewhat different direction. Publicity was the key to the new approach.

As First Deputy Prime Minister, Medvedev told an All-Russia Civics Forum on 22 January 2008 that 'disregard for the law manifests itself in crime, including corruption in government agencies – corruption that has an enormous scope today. The fight against it must evolve into a national program ... Russia is a country of legal nihilism. No other European country has a similar level of disrespect for the law ... a phenomenon rooted in our hoary past'.[69] A week later he delivered the same 'legal nihilism' message to the Association of Russian Lawyers. This was an astonishing admission and certainly one that Putin would not have made in public.[70]

Medvedev was the first Russian leader to grant the reduction of corruption priority in practice, as opposed to merely in speeches. In this ambition, at least, he was more than Putin's parrot, though not necessarily his competitor. He was also the first Russian leader to admit openly that corruption is a long-standing part of Russian culture itself. In contrast to Putin, who tended to blame foreign influences and oligarchs for his country's ills, Medvedev did not hesitate to place a large part of the blame on Russia's own 'people in power'.[71] And he did this in January while campaigning for the presidency.

In his insistence that corruption was ruinous for Russia, the president-to-be could turn to evidence supporting his position that was gathered by Georgy Satarov, head of the NGO Information Science for Democracy (INDEM).[72] Satarov wrote the day before Medvedev's speech to Russia's lawyers that the level of increase in corruption in granting government contracts was catastrophic. He maintained that INDEM research showed that the bribe percentage of such contracts increased precipitously during Putin's first two terms, that is, from 10 per cent in 2000 to 50–70 per cent in 2008. 'One can hardly be surprised', he went on, 'that the young people of today try to become officials, and not businessmen'. It may be that Satarov's timely break with Garri Kasparov's political coalition a few days earlier gave him greater credence with the mainstream press so that his opinions were widely reported.[73]

There was not much optimism expressed, however. Writing in the *Nezavisimaia gazeta*, Dmitry Furman called Medvedev's 'fiery' speech against legal nihilism and corruption 'interesting', and went on to imply that the almost overwhelming support for Putin's policies meant that stability would likely retain its current precedence over law. Full democracy would have to wait as long as fear of a 'colour' revolution was pervasive in the Kremlin.[74] A few weeks later Putin gave the renewed anti-corruption campaign a kick-start by warning an MVD board that law enforcement officers and agencies must cleanse themselves of corruption before anyone could expect to resolve the issue nationally.[75]

Admonition was one thing; results were another. It would be two full years into his presidency before Medvedev was able to introduce a new version of Russia's National Strategy for Countering Corruption and another National Plan for Countering Corruption in 2010–11. These two anti-corruption documents fine-tuned a similar plan and strategy signed into law early in his first year as president. At the earlier time, he made reducing corruption a personal crusade, warning then and in the 2010 edicts that corruption threatened Russian security, stalled economic development, and damaged the country's image abroad.

The 2010 Plan was a culmination of preparatory legislation and a domestic propaganda campaign. Even before he took office, measures adopted in 2008 to slow corruption were extensive. They included a set of new rules calling for an anti-corruption audit of all legal transactions in the Ministries of Justice and Trade and Development, pay raises to policemen to make them less anxious to obtain bribes, and further powers granted to the Investigative Committee, whose members were given the same immunity as Duma members.[76] Following Medvedev's lead, the Public Chamber debated steps to limit corruption and the question of 'legal nihilism' was discussed openly in the press and in legal circles.[77] In short, the issue of 'rule-by-law' was introduced to the public discourse seriously for the first time since Gorbachev raised it in the mid-1980s.

Medvedev had kept to his campaign promises, and much was accomplished on the corruption file between 2008 and 2010, at least on paper. Soon after his inauguration, he signed a new anti-corruption decree into law and the State Duma created another anti-corruption council. The new council had more teeth than its predecessor, and all parties in the Duma were represented on it. Its job description included the study of all existing legislation having to do with corruption and the right to prior examination of draft laws.

Argument over solutions suddenly filled the media. Some pundits and politicians called for much tougher penalties; others suggested that more transparent economic regulation would be enough. Sergei Mironov urged the government to make penalties for corruption equal to those for treason and demanded that the property of convicted corrupt officials and of their families be confiscated. The Kremlin website posted letters about corruption from people around the country,[78] and in late May Medvedev created a new body to handle government real estate, a sector where corruption was especially rife. The Agency for the Management of State Property was turned over to Yury Petrov, whose background, with a Ph.D. in law from St. Petersburg University and work at that institution during the decade of the 1990s, paralleled Medvedev's own.

Talk was backed up by action, emblazoned in headlines: long sentences handed down to hated traffic cops for demanding bribes, the arrest of a deputy minister in Moscow's regional government for taking bribes, the head of Moscow's police department arrested for 'abuse of office,' i.e., corruption.[79] In June that first year, he signed a decree to give prosecutors greater supervisory powers and demanded that loopholes in anti-corruption legislation be closed. This came shortly after he formed a new anti-corruption council at the highest level, with himself in the chair. Presidential Aide Naryshkin, head of an equally new inter-departmental anti-corruption committee, was given a month to prepare a report on how best to tackle the corruption crisis.

Naryshkin submitted a four-stage plan at the end of June. Draft proposals on other ways to fight corruption came later from the Duma and the Investigative Committee. Medvedev told an audience of law students at the University of St. Petersburg that a full regulatory framework for fighting corruption would be in place before the end of the year. His first National Plan to Fight Corruption was signed into law on 31 July and published in *Rossiiskaia gazeta* in August 2008,[80] and his new council on corruption met at the end of September. The law was forwarded to the State Duma for review. This was very quick work for Russia.

To draw the public's attention to the extent of the problem, documents were circulated to show that the number of corruption-related crimes increased in Russia during the first half of 2008, up six per cent over the same period in the previous year. The Prosecutor General's Office claimed that some 27,000 incidents of abuse took place during that period – 4,000 of them criminal offences.[81] The papers were filled with names of arrestees.[82] It wasn't clear if such information helped or hindered the cause by making it appear so daunting.

Sceptics were already confirmed in their doubts when, in October 2008, Storchak was released after nearly a year in custody and ordered not to leave the country. In an odd twist he returned to his post as deputy finance minister, never having lost it officially. The release was interpreted by many as the resurgence of his former boss and supporter, Kudrin. Pundits could also point to late year reports from Minister of the Interior Nurgaliev that over 70 per cent of Russia's businessmen in the regions were involved in corruption, willingly or not. News from the Military Prosecutor General's office was even less encouraging. In November, it reported that corruption crimes grew 35.43 per cent in 2008 to that date, even though general crime in the military had dropped.[83] It was almost as if Medvedev's efforts were conducted in a vacuum.

The State Duma balked at the new corruption legislation already in late November and early December, with members proposing amendments and suggesting that it may take up to a year to approve it. Medvedev angrily responded that because the legislation was written by experts in the field, no amendments should be offered by less qualified deputies – and exhorted them to get on with it.[84] The bill was signed on 24 December.

Procurator General Chaika revealed the scope of dishonesty again at the end of April 2009. Reporting to the president, he pointed out that nearly 39,000 corruption-related crimes were forwarded to the courts in 2008, an increase of 5.2 per cent over the previous year.[85] In fact, the package of anti-corruption laws passed in December of the previous year was already seen as inadequate. Supplements introducing criminal accountability for people offering bribes, widening the net of 'family' guilt to include parents and adult children, and a law against lobbying were among the new steps debated in the Duma.

When Medvedev chaired a meeting of the anti-corruption council in March 2009, he threatened to dismiss any official who did not declare all sources of income, and he admitted that there had been few successes in the battle to that date.[86] More amendments to the anti-corruption package of laws were prepared for presentation to the Duma. These included a delineation of the office-holders who had to report their financial holdings, among them the president, prime minister, federal judges, secretary of the Security Council, and other senior officials. None of this convinced the public. Surveys in April showed that the citizens did not believe corruption on the part of bureaucrats could be stopped, and Medvedev admitted again, 'there is simply no success yet' in fighting corruption.[87]

During the Summer, Medvedev signed an order making it a law that officials must report any attempt to bribe them, on pain of penalty.[88] The president continued to complain that his efforts to curb corruption had achieved only 'very modest results', and he urged officials and citizens alike to utilize the new anti-corruption laws. In addition to the new incremental laws, the MVD announced in June that, by the end of the year, police would have name badges sewn into their uniforms so that they could be identified if they asked for bribes.

Anti-corruption warriors must have felt they were banging their heads against a wall when Transparency International reported that the number of people in Russia who take bribes was actually rising.[89] The new president had to face international disapproval generated by widely cited international corruption ratings every year. In 2007, for example, the Corruption Perception Index produced annually by Transparency International placed Russia 143rd out of 180 countries.[90] There was slight improvement in 2008 (126th of 154 countries listed), but the new ranking was still horrific for Russia's international prestige and attractiveness to foreign investors. Results for each of the next three years saw little change.

Government procurement practices became the target of intensive scrutiny in the spring of 2009,[91] especially in the military where Defence Minister Serdyukov purged his entire logistics support section. In his turn, Medvedev kept pushing ahead: during his 'modernization' address to the nation on 12 November, the president claimed that 4,500 cases of corruption were reviewed in the first six months of 2009, involving 532 government officials and over 700 law enforcement officers as suspects. He proclaimed that this 'social evil' must be thwarted and warned that corrupt officials would be jailed – if caught.[92] Gathering his forces, the lengthy Strategy of 2010 called on the Public Chamber, the Chamber of Commerce and Industry, the Association of Russian Lawyers, political parties, public organizations, and other bodies to help turn popular opinion against bribe-taking and bribe-offering. 'An atmosphere of strict intolerance to corruption' must be created, the document intoned, throwing down the gauntlet to habits ingrained by history.

By April that year, few people would deny that corruption was a nationwide problem. Corruption perpetuated long-standing mistrust of government agencies and officials at all levels, served as an almost insurmountable hindrance to small business growth, rendered the judicial system impotent, and embarrassed Russia abroad. Sporadic but enthusiastic public drives against individual corrupt officials seemed not to alter the overall situation to any great degree, and Russian non-government commentary on the new Plan and Strategy was subdued, at best patronizing, at worst outright scornful.[93]

Ironically, the anti-corruption campaign had an internally negative consequence for small and medium-size business, precisely the sector Medvedev hoped to galvanize. Reports in 2010 showed that police had investigated over a quarter million 'economic crimes', a term that covered such things as fraud, embezzlement, counterfeiting, and tax evasion. Eventually over 100,000 people were incarcerated in Russia for 'economic crimes', a large number of whom were self-employed small and medium-size business operators. Thus, both an overreaction on the part of government and a self-destruct capacity among the emerging business class had long-term deleterious consequences for Russia's modernization.

Medvedev made an effort to ameliorate this situation in early December 2011 by introducing an amendment to the Criminal Procedural Code stipulating that criminal proceedings for tax-related crimes must be based on documentation authorized solely by tax officials. He was well aware of the fact that when law-enforcement agencies could initiate criminal charges for tax-related crimes, as they could prior to this amendment, they sometimes used them to extort bribes, or even to orchestrate takeovers, or raids (*raiderstvo*), against small to medium-size business.[94] At the same time, the now independent Investigative Committee was given the right to launch tax-related cases, based on documents provided by tax authorities.

The importance of this amendment to Medvedev was such that when, in November 2013, the Investigative Committee lobbied for the right to open tax cases without documentation from tax authorities, he openly challenged President Putin's support for the agency's request. Putin publicly rebuked his prime minister, and Medvedev backed off.

Inculcating 'intolerance' towards corruption remained an imposing challenge. The president knew that he had to get the Russian public on side – in the face of surveys that tended to confirm the opinion of Stanislav Belkovsky, who insisted that the 'universal acceptance of corruption' within Russia's population would prove impossible to change in the 'foreseeable future'.[95] Public criticism of the National Strategy portrayed it as a way of putting the old *apparatchiki* in charge of implementing a program purported to protect the country from – the *apparatchiki*, i.e., the foxes guarding the henhouse.

Hoping to persuade the public that something was being done to curb corruption, Chaika reported in January 2010 that over 800 senior officials were charged with crimes related to corruption in the previous year.[96] A new spate of arrests and trials of corrupt officials from all walks of bureaucratic life were again highlighted in the Russian media, implying that no one was exempt from charges. However, while in practice regional finance ministers and CEO's of large companies were among the list of culprits, the top levels of officialdom were still left almost untouched. Moreover, 'catch and release' was the norm for the upper tier of cheaters.

Particularly depressing was the news from the military. Serdyukov's widespread dismissals and forced retirements of senior officers and purge of his entire procurement section notwithstanding, Chief Military Investigator Aleksandr Sorochkin told an interviewer in March 2010 that 'the dimensions and scope of corruption of individual officials [in the military] is mind-boggling'.[97] There seemed to be no let-up in the news about corruption in the military; for example, the autumn issue of *Komsomolskaia Pravda* reported that graft in the military housing sector, the distribution of bonuses, and procurement cost the Ministry of Defence billions of rubles.[98]

Video showing troops in Vladivostok being fed dog food to cover up the theft of food by a senior MVD officer typified the rot in the military to an infuriated public. The guilty officer, who was shown distributing cans of dog food re-labelled as 'high quality beef', was prosecuted and the whistle blower, a veteran of two Chechen wars, was dismissed – angering the public further.[99]

Equally distressing was the news from the educational sector, where systemic corruption was found at both ends of the spectrum: bribes to secure places in kindergarten classes and to gain university admission. Revelations of bribes taken in Russia's higher schools (VUZs) hit the press in 2009 and 2010. In a survey conducted in the latter year by FOM, up to 40 per cent of students in state VUZs claimed to have had bribe-taking instructors. For some of the more prestigious schools, bribes could be as high as 80,000 rubles for access to examination questions. In some schools, the system of bribery was hierarchical, that is, the teacher had to pass some of his or her illegal earnings on to higher authorities at the school. As late in Medvedev's term as March 2012, corruption in the education system remained pervasive.[100] Low salaries, a long existing cultural of accepting bribes for favours, and an extremely valuable career-determining commodity to sell are easy explanations for this phenomenon.

Foreign investors have not helped. In March 2010, for instance, the US Justice Department charged German carmaker Daimler with bribing Russian officials to purchase its vehicles over the years 2000 to 2008. The Russian Ministry of the Interior was accused of taking nearly half of this amount, and six other Russian businesses or official agencies, including the military, were charged with the remainder. The hypocrisy of the country's senior bureaucrats pleading with Russians to purchase domestic vehicles while they picked up Mercedes themselves did not pass unnoticed by the media.[101] Germany's Siemens and America's Hewlett-Packard were also under investigation for allegedly handing millions under the table in return for business opportunities in Russia.

An odd consequence of the hardly shocking revelation that foreign companies provided Russian officials with bribes was a public pledge in April by some multinationals that they would offer no ('further' left unsaid) bribes in Russia. Initiated by the Russian-German Chamber of Commerce in Moscow, the pledge was taken by fifty-six companies, mostly German, including Daimler, Siemens, and Deutsche Bank. Several large Russia-based companies, such as St. Petersburg's Lenergo and TNK-BP, signed on and more followed. Russian cynics suggested that this would merely force corporate bribers to pay higher amounts and guard their secrets more closely.

The public at large remained uncertain about Medvedev's campaign to end corruption. A poll of some 2,000 Russian citizens conducted in January 2010 found that seventy-nine per cent believed that the level of corruption in Russia was high, and fifty-eight per cent believed that in a year's time it would be higher than it was when the question was asked.[102]

Even as the question of corruption hovered as a gloomy shadow over Russia's quest for effective transition to a modern state, a few signs of a public desire for change emerged in the summer of 2010. Medvedev's chances of bringing the citizenry on side in the struggle against corruption were bolstered by fury over government and business officials claiming special privilege and getting away with blatant acts of injustice, some as extreme as hit-and-run crimes and mysterious in-prison deaths. One sign of the growing outrage was a 'blue bucket' campaign against the flashing blue lights (*migalki*) used by wealthy drivers, or their chauffeurs, to ignore traffic and other rules. Another was a detailed poll conducted in June by the Academy of Sciences that showed that the public was far more interested in social fairness than they were in modernization. The respondents believed that modernization would succeed only if corruption was checked first.[103] The newly focused popular anger might have been a cause for the other telling change: opinion polls in the spring and summer of 2010 found Medvedev running nearly neck-and-neck with Putin in popularity, and *Nezavisimaia gazeta*'s quarterly ranking of the most influential people in Russia placed Medvedev slightly ahead of Putin for the first time.[104] That lead was short-lived but nonetheless significant. But these encouraging words were tempered by almost simultaneous discouraging words on the corruption front. Chaika told a meeting of the heads of law enforcement agencies that the size of average bribes had surged by a third as the government's campaign against them faltered, and complained that law enforcement agencies had slacked off in their anti-corruption efforts.

By that time, the investigators themselves were the objects of closer scrutiny. MVD Director Nurgaliev issued an order in April creating a new anti-corruption subdivision within his own ministry. Called the Office of the Organization of the Prevention of Corruption and Other Offenses, the new division was tasked with collecting and making public information on the incomes of MVD officials.[105] Shortly thereafter the Investigative Committee was elevated from an arm of the Prosecutor General's Office to a separate federal agency, with Aleksandr Bastrykin as its head. A subsequent bill made the Committee answerable directly to the President, thereby further confusing the relationship between the MVD, the PGO, and the Investigative Committee. A huge number of personnel (investigators) transferred from Chaika's office to the new structure, which had dozens of directorates and regional branches.

One Russian writer responded to Chaika's remarks with the prediction that the 'Christian crusade against corruption' will fail because corruption 'is part of the Russian mentality'.[106] That is precisely what Medvedev had complained about in the first place. Adding insult to injury, in October Transparency International ranked Russia 154th of 178 countries for 2010, on a par with Laos, Cambodia, Congo, Papua New Guinea, and Tajikistan; and WikiLeak exposés caught foreign diplomats privately referring to Russia as a 'virtual mafia state'.[107] Perhaps that is why Medvedev's crusade against corruption was almost frantic in 2011 as he dismissed dozens of generals from both law enforcement and the military, replaced governors, and ordered senior government officials to give up their seats on boards of major companies.

Anti-corruption mechanisms expanded as well. The tax service opened a hot line and e-mail address in January for citizens to report corruption offences without having to leave their name. The Public Chamber followed suit in February with its own phone hotline and website, calling on citizens to report corrupt officials. At about the same time, an announcement that more than one-third of the people who committed corruption-related crimes in 2010 were policemen confirmed a commonly held opinion.

Medvedev took accusations against law enforcement officials very seriously. Senior policemen and ministry of interior personnel were dismissed, demoted, or transferred in droves. The head of Moscow's traffic police was sacked in January 2011, and a month later the deputy head of the FSB was fired for 'ethics violations'. Between then and June, over 60 more police generals, three colonels, and two deputy ministers were dismissed from the MVD. Another one-third (119 of 335) of the senior police officers could not pass the screening test established in 2010 and lost their jobs.[108] The extent of charges leveled against former policemen, prosecutors, tax inspectors, customs agents, and even judges were such that Medvedev had to create a prison system for them alone – to protect them from other inmates. Ten such police prisons were requisitioned, using old prison colony facilities.[109] Bastrykin told a board meeting in February 2011 that over 1,000 members of their own Investigative Committee were prosecuted for corruption the year before.[110]

Among the new anti-corruption rules was a bill to increase fines for both commercial bribes and the taking and offering of illegal inducements. Following up on his earlier judgment that financial penalties were more effective than the threat of prison terms, Medvedev's amendments to the criminal code and code of administrative offences set penalties at multiples up to 100 times the bribe amount.[111] He then ordered the immediate dismissal of any state official implicated in schemes to siphon off funds allocated to regional communal and housing services. This latter decision was made shortly after the head of the Kremlin's control department, Konstantin Chuichenko, informed Medvedev in a televised meeting that the equivalent of nearly $900 million allocated to such services had been stolen over the previous two years.

The public seemed finally to take notice after Police Major-General Aleksandr Nazarov told *Rossiiskaia gazeta* that the average value of a bribe had more than doubled since 2010 and that large bribes were up by 30 per cent since 2009. Tens of thousands of violations were recorded within officialdom in both the federal and regional spheres of government.[112] In May 2011, *Moscow News* reported that property prices in Moscow were inflated by about 60 per cent as a result of widespread corruption.[113]

Corruption watchers in Moscow had their day as senior police officers, city tax officials, and the former head of the Moscow Metro system were arrested and charged with various crimes. The President and Vice President of the Bank of Moscow, Andrei Borodin and Dmitry Akulin, and Yelena Baturina, wife of ex-Moscow Mayor Luzhkov, were all caught up in corruption investigations and fled the country.[114] The condition of municipal services in Moscow was such that Luzhkov's replacement, Sobyanin, told journalists that every sphere in his municipal services was corrupt, and that he had to use lie detector tests to weed the miscreants out.[115]

Officially sanctioned separate demonstrations against corruption on the streets of Moscow led by *Nashi* and liberal activist People's Freedom Party were described by detractors as interesting, but unlikely to break the everyday opinion that corruption is not evil, rather it is part of Russia's reality.[116] Yet even this old assumption was frayed at the edges by 2011. The public was angered again over reports of wide-ranging acts of nepotism on the boards of major companies, as members of the *siloviki* handed the children of prominent officials executive positions and seats in local legislative assemblies. Reports on these and other acts of venality helped dissipate much of the old 'so what' attitude.[117] New anti-corruption websites began attracting large audiences. Among these was a website owned by Aleksei N. Navalny whose *RosPil.info* had thousands of daily visitors. The Communist Party created a website of its own specifically to expose corruption on the part of officials, indelicately naming the agency and website the Anticorruption Committee in the Name of J.V. Stalin (http://beyvora.ru).

Perhaps driven by surveys that showed that more Russians believed that the level of corruption among officials had risen over the previous year (proving the accuracy of predictions made in earlier polls), Medvedev returned to his original thesis, telling a meeting of young parliamentarians that the only way to reduce 'unbridled' corruption was to create a completely new political culture.[118] As it happened, the same surveys showed that the percentage of Russians who condemned bribe taking had increased slightly, a small step toward the healthy 'intolerance' of corruption that Medvedev called for in 2009.

The link between Medvedev's anti-corruption and modernization projects was spelled out often, but rarely as directly as they were in a speech delivered to a large audience of Russian and foreign business and political leaders at the annual St. Petersburg International Economic Forum in June 2011. Noting that the dominant role of the state in the economy was necessary after the disorder of the 1990s, Medvedev made it plain that his entire scheme for modernization would work only if 'we put a relentless stranglehold on those guilty of corruption'.[119] In this instance he may well have been preparing the epitaph for his own two pet projects.

The reality of corruption within Russia's key government ministries continued to jump up and bite him. An investigation of 35 ministries by experts close to government found that, whereas the Ministry of Defence was the most corrupt, it was followed closely by the Ministries, respectively, of Transport, Economic Development, Health and Social Development, and Finance, most of which were central to the Tandem's development strategies.[120] Nearly a year after Chaika complained about bribes growing larger, both a spokesman for the MVD's Economic Security Department and Transparency International's Russia office reported that the average bribe had risen still further.[121] Four years of anti-corruption exhortation and a wellspring of legislation seemed not to have deterred predatory bureaucrats and business tycoons, even though more big names were openly under investigation.

In late November and early December 2011, the Transparency International's bribe index again placed Russia high among the world's most corrupt countries and, with China, among the worst to offer bribes when doing business abroad.[122] With justification, Russian economists expressed concern that corruption within Russia's large companies would offset any advantages Russia might gain from that year's entry into the World Trade Organization.[123]

There followed a dismal litany of failures. An announcement a year before that more than one-third of people who committed corruption-related crimes in 2010 were policemen merely corroborated what the Russian public already assumed. Pollsters reported that law enforcement was still the leader insofar as popular perception of corrupt officialdom was concerned, followed in order by members of the armed forces, local self-government and health and social development ministry agencies. These survey results appeared at exactly the same time that the FSB reported that most such acts were committed by organized crime.[124] It would not be unreasonable to assume that both statements were true and connected.

Chaika admitted in January 2012 that more than 50 per cent of people convicted of corruption in Russia received suspended sentences, and Nurgaliev told the MVD board that 'the average size of bribe and commercial palm greasing in identified crimes almost quadrupled' since 2010 – and there were almost 10,000 instances of bribery identified in 2011.[125] The Investigative Committee reported in January 2013 that 42 cases related to senior regional officials were investigated in 2011 and another 29 in 2012. Altogether the Committee was considering more than 25,000 cases of corruption, a substantial increase over 2011. The rate of actual convictions was still low – plus ça change, c'est la même chose![126]

Director of Transparency International-Russia, Yelena Panfilova, put the apparent discrepancy between the many people caught and extraordinarily increased anti-corruption legislation on the one hand, and the equally apparent increase in corruption on the other, down to 'much is done only for appearance's sake. Therefore no real breakthroughs in the fight against corruption have taken place'.[127] Medvedev acknowledged failure a few days before he stood down. Results of his campaign against corruption were still only 'modest', he said, while blaming others for his failure: 'Let's be frank. Officials are a corporation. They don't want anyone to interfere in their business', he said in an interview, resurrecting at the same time his original plaint that centuries-old Russian 'habits and mentality' were at the root of the problem.[128]

Admitting failure was itself a very unusual matter for Russian leaderships, and it is possible that Medvedev accomplished more than he thought. Beating the anti-corruption drum over a long period may finally have inculcated the intuitive desire for change that Medvedev said he wanted in 2009.[129] Outrage over revelations in October 2011 by the Investigative Committee that OboronServis, the defence ministry's agency for privatizing and outsourcing maintenance work for the military, had defrauded the department of some 300 billion rubles ($100 million), turned the internal desire for change into an explosive external one. The defence problem was dropped into Dmitry Rogozin's lap in late December 2011. As part of his new post as deputy prime minister to oversee the military industrial-complex, he was tasked with curbing corruption in the armed forces. Rogozin replaced Sergei Ivanov, who was moved up to the post as presidential chief of staff after Naryshkin was elected speaker of the Duma. Arrests were made and the investigation continues. Public anger was palpable and added to the explosive mix on the streets.

In the business sector, a survey of small and mid-size business groups was released in January 2012 showing that pressure from government officials seeking bribes had risen sharply over the last few years. About 36 per cent of small business owners claimed to have faced 'at least one case' of pressure for a bribe from an office holder.[130] There seemed to be little more that Medvedev could do about the smaller business predicament, but he still worked at restricting corrupt opportunities for big business. Revisions were made to Russia's civil code in an attempt to curb the use of offshore sites as vehicles for siphoning money by business or state agents. The revised code compels offshore companies to reveal their beneficiaries, whether the shell site owners are Russian or foreign. This makes managers subject to the same disclosure requirements as state officials. Companies doing business with state companies and banks must now declare their beneficiaries.[131]

Later in January, new head of the presidential administration Ivanov claimed that prosecutors had forestalled over 1.5 million violations of verification procedures for small and middle-size businesses by bureaucrats. They also exposed two million violations of citizens' social rights, he said.[132] If these astounding figures were correct, they suggest that Medvedev's campaign against corruption by officials was actually working in at least some sectors.

In March 2012, Medvedev signed into law his final National Strategy for Combating Corruption, 2012–13.[133] Even though nobody pretended that there had been significant improvement, one could find some grounds for optimism in this document. The legislative framework demanded in the earlier Strategy was now in place, monitoring bodies existed, and training programs for officials were underway. Inspections had increased. To be sure, polls conducted in March show that most Russians still believed that the level of corruption remained the same or was increasing. Plainly, more 'waiting and seeing' was in store for anti-corruption advocates.[134]

When he published the essay 'Building Justice: Social Policy for Russia' at the tail end of his tepid campaign for the presidency, Putin had the ideal opportunity to position himself as an anti-corruption leader. He didn't bother. The subject of corruption passed almost unnoticed as he wrote at length about the needs of the Russian people,[135] yet soon after taking the office back, Putin took up the anti-corruption campaign with a passion. Perhaps he realized how debilitating the level of corruption was to all of his own newly sponsored projects.

With Putin's brand on the file, Medvedev's legislative and institutional work and, above all, his attempts to inculcate an anti-corruption mood among Russians may soon be forgotten. But he warrants considerable credit for doing all the necessary legwork. A poll conducted in July 2012 revealed that the percentage of Russians who were dissatisfied with corrupt authorities had reached its highest level in 13 years; that is, 29 per cent.[136] Since the same survey showed equal or greater levels of public concern over rising prices, falling incomes, the inability of the government to deal with increasingly harsh economic realities, and a perceived government indifference to the welfare of its citizens, Putin will have his hands full.

Interestingly, in September 2012, some months after Putin had taken over the anti-corruption portfolio, the Chairman of his Anti-Corruption Council, Sergei Ivanov, came back to one of Medvedev's ideas. The key to ending corruption, he said, was getting the authorities and the public working together. He went on to appeal to the public to be proactive, provide law enforcement with information, and support the notion of an Anti-Corruption Map of Russia.[137]

In what might be Putin's last term as president, he may have decided to leave his mark by fulfilling all those promises made in the name of the National Priority Projects he set in motion in 2005. One could say that the Tandem started them, because Medvedev was placed in charge then, and oversaw their progress later as president. If we use the consequences of the National Priority Projects as a yardstick with which to measure the effectiveness of Medvedev's presidency – as suggested in the Introduction – then one could conclude that 'ineffective' fits the description. Yet, on going back to the expectations of 2008, the same editorialist who predicted the inevitability of Medvedev's victory in the presidential campaign explained in December 2007 that the newly nominated candidate 'understood his responsibility for the National Projects' and had a great skill 'in creating institutions as preconditions for development'.[138] In that, he may in fact have been successful.

For those institutions to be fruitful, however, corruption must be defeated. It remains to be seen if Putin's utilization of Medvedev's institutional efforts is not merely for what Panfilova called 'appearance's sake'.

## Notes

1　Russian analysts have been using 2020 as their turning point target for some time. See, e.g., 'Russia – 2020. Part II', *Pro ET Contra*, Vol. 15, issue 1–2 (January-April 2011). Maria Lipman, Nikolay Petrov, *Russia in 2020, Scenarios for the Future*, Washington/Moscow: Carnegie Moscow Centre, 2011.
2　Interfax, 11 June 2008. For interesting detail on the lives of ordinary people in Russia as Medvedev came to the high office, see Jennifer Patico, *Consumption and Social Change in a Post-Soviet Middle Class*, Stanford: Stanford UP, 2008.
3　Interfax, 25 July 2009.
4　RIA Novosti, 21 April 2009. For a general discussion a year later, see Yuri Zagrakhtovich, 'Russian Unemployment Figures Rising Rapidly', *Eurasia Daily Monitor*, 22 April 2009.
5　*Kremlin.ru*, 2 March 2010.
6　Improved housing had been promised to Russians on a regular basis since it was placed high on the agenda of Gorbachev's *perestroika*. For an overall view, see Jane R. Zavisa, *Housing the New Russia*, Ithaca, NY: Cornell UP, 2012.
7　See, e.g. Ronald Oliphant, 'Khimki Battlefield', *Russia Profile*, 27 July 2010; Natalya Krainova, 'Khimki Forest Battle Takes Violent Turn', *The Moscow Times*, 31 July 2010; Jonathan Earle, 'Khimki Forest Activist Beaten Up', *The Moscow Times*, 17 April 2012.
8　*Kommersant,* 7 August 2010. 'Why Russia Needs Me', *The Economist*, 9 September 2010. Putin used the expression on several occasions.
9　FOM, 4 March 2011; IA Regnum, 7 March 2011.
10　RIA Novosti, 4 April 2011.
11　Putin, 'Stroitel'stvo spradvedlivosti. Sotsial'naia politika dlia Rossii', *Komsomolskaia Pravda*, 13 February 2012.
12　ITAR-TASS, 26 February 2010. See also Roland Oliphant, 'The Villain of the Villa', *Russia Profile*, 17 February 2010.
13　Monaghan, 'The Russian *Vertikal* … ', (2011), *passim*.
14　See details provided in Alena V. Ledeneva, *Can Russia Modernize? Sistema, Power Networks, and Informal Governance*, Cambridge: Cambridge UP, 2013.
15　Vladimir Ryzhkov, 'A Year of Increased Graft and Deadly Disasters', *The Moscow Times*, 22 December 2009. A prominent oppositionist, Ryzhkov was not likely to support the government, but in this case the majority of Russians undoubtedly would agree with him.
16　RIA Novosti, 25 February 2011; Andrew E. Kramer, 'Russia Breathes Easier as Moscow Skies Clear', *New York Times*, 12 August 2010.
17　For a summary of Medvedev's statement, RIA Novosti, 23 November 2010; on price capping announcements, Interfax, 7 February 2010, 11 March 2011.
18　See Maxim Krans, 'Fools and Roads', *Russia Profile*, 31 May 2008.
19　For general accounts, 'Russian Traffic: Behind the Grim Statistics', *Russia Today* (RT), 19 November 2009; Irina Titova, 'Russia Sees Six-Year Decrease in Road Deaths', *St. Petersburg Times*, 16 September 2012. See also below, under 'Demography and Health'.
20　For Putin's pledge and appeal to foreign investors, see *Canadian Business Magazine*, 21 June 2013. On the ongoing road problems, Anna Arutunyan, 'Road Rage: Reality in Russia: 10 Facts about Russian Roads that Will Make you

Weep', *The Moscow News*, 7 November 2013. For a cross-section of exposés on corruption in the transportation sector, see e.g. Andrew Osborn, 'Russian Corruption Means Foie Gras Roads Would be Cheaper', *The Telegraph* (UK), 22 July 2010, and 'Moscow Streets are Lined with Gold', *Russia Today* (RT), 2 December 2010.

21 Interfax, 4 September 2010.

22 'Rossiiane boiatsia stat' zhertvoi terakta', FOM, 8 April 2011. This survey was conducted on 3–4 April 2011.

23 The terrible plane crash that killed the President of Poland, Lech Kaczynski, and 97 other passengers at Smolensk in April 2010 caused a serious international stir and evoked great sympathy in Russia, but was not seen as a result of Russian incompetence by the Russian public. Russian air control attempted to divert the plane because of a storm, but the Polish pilot tried to land there anyway – perhaps on the orders of the very high level officials he was carrying.

24 For the politicization of the *Kursk* tragedy, see Igor Maksimychev, 'Politizatsiia tragedii', *Nezavisimaia gazeta*, 24 August 2000, and Black, *Vladimir Putin and the New World Order*, pp. 77–80, 196–99.

25 *Rossiiskaia gazeta*, 8 November 2010.

26 The UN report titled 'The National Human Development Report in Russia 2010' was summarized in *The Moscow Times*, 25 October 2010.

27 Nicholas Eberstadt, 'The Dying Bear: Russia's Demographic Disaster', *Foreign Affairs*, November/December 2011, pp. 95–108.

28 See for general background and analysis, Martin Larys, Miroslav Mares, 'Right-Wing Extremist Violence in the Russian Federation', *Europe-Asia Studies*, 63, No. 1 (2011), pp. 129–54, and K. Kumkova, 'Russia Facing a Demographic Time Bomb?' *EurasiaNet*, 25 October 2010.

29 See, e.g. Svetlana Kononova, 'Immobile, Ineffective, Illegal', *Russia Profile*, 21 March 2011; and Anya Ardayeva, 'Demographers Warn of Looming Population Crisis for Russia', *Voice of America*, 20 March 2011.

30 For the surveys, see FOM, 6 April 2011 and *Spravedlivost'*, 6 April 2011. For Medvedev's speech, *Kremlin.ru*, 8 September 2011.

31 See long Interfax report, 20 March 2010, and monthly reports from SOVA.

32 For an overview of the skinhead subculture in Russia, see Hilary Pilkington, Albina Garifzianova, Elena Omelchenko, *Russia's Skinheads. Exploring and Rethinking Subcultural Lives*, London: Routledge, 2013.

33 Some data suggested that the male life expectancy in 2010 was 60, but Health Minister Tatiana Golikova claimed that it was 64.3, and female life expectancy was 71. Whatever the numbers, the difference between male and female life expectancy is huge. See Golikova report in *Vserossiiskaia perepis' naseleniia 2010*, 2 February 2011.

34 For data and commentary see Interfax, 29 August 2009, ITAR-TASS, 5 August 2009, and Aleksandra Koshkina, 'Alkogol'noe ravnovesie', FOM, 4 September 2009.

35 See Svetlana Kononova, 'Medvedev's Sober Thought', *Russia Profile*, 23 September 2009.

36 See 'United Russia Balks at Easing Drunk-Driving Law', *The Moscow Times*, 16 October 2012. Drunk-driving laws were tightened up still further in 2013, with higher fines, and longer sentences if people were killed. See report from *Russia Today* (RT), 14 March 2013.

37 For general comment, see Svetlana Kononova, 'On the Road to Sobriety', *Russia Profile*, 31 May 2010, and K. Kumkova, 'Russia: Binge Drinking', *EurasiaNet*, 15 December 2010.

38 'Drug Scourge is the 9/11 Legacy for Russia', *The Moscow Times*, 9 September 2011

39  See Tom Balmforth, 'Lethal Injection', *Russia Profile*, 23 October 2009.
40  *Kremlin.ru*, 24 December 2010.
41  See Michael Schwirtz, 'H.I.V. Spreads in Russia As Addicts Are Ignored', *New York Times*, 23 January 2011. For political and other manifestations of the HIV/AIDS crisis in Russia, see Ulia Pape, *The Politics of HIV/AIDS in Russia*. London: Routledge, 2013.
42  Interfax, 20 June, 25 October 2012; Interfax-AVN, 2 March 2012. These figures were confirmed in a report released by the government in September 2013, see RIA Novosti, 17 September 2013.
43  Kononova, 'Farewell, Tobacco', *Russia Profile*, 11 October 2012; Bloomberg, 11 October 2012.
44  FOM, 17 October 2012.
45  *Kremlin,ru*, 16 May 2008.
46  *Kremlin.ru*, 24 December 2010.
47  On this, see Claire Bigg, 'Flurry of Hospital Tours Heralds Russian Health-Care Revamp', RFE/RL, 19 February 2011. For a dissenting opinion, see Tom Balmforth, Gregory Feifer, 'Russian Health Care Provides No Real Safety Net', RFE/RL, 14 August 2011.
48  'Poslanie Prezidenta Federal'nomu Sobraniiu', *Kremlin.ru*. 12 December 2012.
49  For a general treatment, see Tai Adelaja, 'Immigration Business', *Russia Profile*, 20 March 2012.
50  RIA Novosti, 3 May 2012; Interfax, 20 January 2012.
51  Interfax, 5 December 2012.
52  *Nezavisimaia gazeta*, 6 December 2012.
53  Interfax, 12 January 2012; RIA Novosti, 12 January 2012. See also Patico, *Consumption and Social Change*, op. cit.
54  For example, the draft federal budget for 2014 called for a full 25 per cent decrease in healthcare spending. See Interfax-AVN, 3 Jul 2013.
55  This author conducted briefing sessions for several organizations preparing to send volunteers to Russia and other former Soviet Republics in the late 1980s and early 1990s, and was taken aback by how many of the volunteers were planning to take both their needed expertise and their long festering political agendas with them – sometimes not in that order.
56  'O vnesenii izmenenii v nekotorykh zakonodatel'nykh aktakh Rossiiskoi Federatsii', *Rossiiskaia gazeta*, 17 January 2006. The law was first submitted in December 2005.
57  For widely differing views and numbers, see, e.g., Lisa McIntosh Sundstrom, 'Norms, and NGO Development: Lessons from the Russian Campaign', *International Organization* Vol. 59, Spring 2005, pp. 419–49; 'How to Deal with NGOs. Part II: Russia', Yale Center for the Study of Globalization online, August 2006; C.J. Chivers, 'Kremlin Puts Foreign NGO's on Notice', *New York Times*, 20 October 2006; Centre for European Policy Studies, CEPS Working Document No. 287, April 2008; Sara Flounders, '450,000 NGOs in Russia', *Workers World*, February 2011; and Robert Orttung, 'Kremlin Nationalism versus Russia's NGOs', *Russian Analytical Digest*, No 138, 8 November 2013, pp. 8–11.
58  For a detailed analysis of *krysha* and its consequences, see 'Russian Organized Crime', Center for Strategic & International Studies, Washington, DC, Task Force Report, 1997. See also Annelise Anderson, 'The Red Mafia: A Legacy of Communism', in Edward P. Lazear, ed. *Economic Transition in Eastern Europe and Russia: Realities of Reform*, Stanford: Hoover Institution, 1995.
59  David Remnick, *Lenin's Tomb. The Last Days of the Soviet Union*, New York: Vintage, 1994, p. 183. Parts of the following section are summaries of material contained in J. L. Black, 'Tandemology as a Spectator Sport. Medvedev's

Campaigns to Curb Corruption and Encourage Modernization', in *Russia after 2012*, pp.101–20.

60 For an interesting description of this mutation and detail on how it worked from an insider, see Alena V. Ledeneva, *How Russia Really Works. The Informal Practices that Shaped Post-Soviet Politics and Business*, Ithaca, NY: Cornell, UP, 2006.

61 See Chapter One for this reference.

62 The word *krysha* is also sometimes translated simply as 'protection racket,' though it has a broader meaning than that.

63 Sergei Kanev, 'Kak ustroeny "kryshi" v Rossii', *Novaia gazeta,* 22 October 2007; FOM, 11 November 2007.

64 See, e.g., 'Who's on First?' *Russian Intelligence*, 23 October 2007; Brian Whitmore, 'Russia: As Elections Near, Rivalries in Putin Circle Heat Up', *RFE/RL*, 15 October 2007.

65 'Investigation Committee Challenges Decision to Drop Charges Against Storchak', ITAR-TASS, 5 December 2007.

66 *Rossiiskaia gazeta*, 15 December 2007.

67 'Business Regime', *Gazeta.ru*, 16 December 2007.

68 *Kremlin. ru*, 14 February 2008.

69 See 'Dmitrii Medvedev: Glavnoe dlia nashei strany – eto prodolzhenie spokoinogo i stabil'nogo razvitiia', *Rossiiskaia gazeta,* 15 February 2008.

70 For Medvedev's speech to the Association of Russian Lawyers, see www.Medvedev08.ru, 29 January 2008; for an analysis of that speech *The Moscow Times*, 30 January 2008.

71 'Kandidat v prezidenty Dimitrii Medvedev oglasil svoi predvybornye tezisy', *NEWSru: V Rossii*, 22 January 2008; 'Dmitrii Medvedev: Rossiia budet razvivat' grazhdanskoe obshchestvo', Interfax, 22 January 2008

72 INDEM was founded by Satarov in 1990. It promotes democracy and highlights corruption issues; see *www.indem.ru*.

73 For Satarov's data and analysis, 'V Kremle. Tranzit (8),' *Yezhednevnyi zhurnal*, 28 January 2008. For a general discussion of the subject, see Jonas Bernstein, 'Will Russia's Next Anti-Corruption Campaign Succeed Where Others Failed?' *Eurasia Daily Monitor*, 30 January 2008.

74 *Nezavisimaia gazeta*, 7 February 2008. See also an analysis in the main government newspaper of Medvedev's speech to the All-Russian Civil Forum, where the 'continuation of calmness and stability' is depicted as his top priority: 'Dmitrii Medvedev: Glavnoe dlia nashei strany … ', *op. cit.*

75 *Kremlin.ru*, 6 February 2008.

76 *Kommersant*, 1 February 2008.

77 See Elizabeth Swanson, 'Getting Tough on Corruption', *Moscow News*, 21 February 2008; Ben Aris, 'Anti-Corruption Drive Takes Off', *Russia Profile*, 4 March 2008; Robert Coalson, 'Russia's Destructive Culture of Lies and Mendacity', RFE/RL, 15 March 2008; Marina Pustilnik, 'Russia Ready to Fight Corruption', *Moscow News*, 3 October 2008.

78 See Anna Malpac, 'Kremlin Publishes Letters on Corruption', *The Moscow Times*, 30 May 2008.

79 ITAR-TASS, 20 & 21 March 2008; *Rossiiskaia gazeta*, 9 April 2008, 12 May 2008. For part of the debate, Natalia Antipova, 'Morkovka korruptsiiu ne pobedit', *Izvestiia*, 6 February 2008.

80 'Natsional'nyi plan protivodeistviia korruptsii', *Rossiiskaia gazeta*, 5 August 2008.

81 Interfax, 9 April 2008; *Kremlin,ru*, 19 May 2008.

82 Interfax, 25 July 2008. See also *Izvestiia* and *Rossiiskaia gazeta*, 26 June 2008, for charges against customs officers, some of them department heads.

83   Interfax, 6 November 2008; RIA Novosti, 9 December 2008.
84   *Kremlin.ru*, 25 December 2008 (Federal Law N 273-FZ). For Medvedev's exhortation, see WNC translation of broadcast on NTV-Mir, 16 December 2008.
85   Interfax, 30 April 2009.
86   *Kremlin.ru*, 10 March 2009.
87   Interfax, 12 May 2009; RIA Novosti, 27 April 2009.
88   *Nezavisimaia gazeta*, 17 July 2009.
89   *The Moscow Times*, 4 June 2009.
90   Transparency International, *Corruption Perception Index*, Berlin, 2007.
91   *Rossiiskaia gazeta*, 24 June, 5 July 2009.
92   *Kremlin.ru*, 12 November 2009; Tom Balmforth, 'Despite the President's Proclaimed War on Corruption, Over the Past Year Russia Gained a Mere Tenth of a Point in TI's Corruption Index', *Russia Profile,* 19 November 2009.
93   See, e.g., 'Bor'bu s korruptsiei rasplanirovali na dva goda', *Kommersant,* 15 April 2010, and Aleksandra Samarina, 'Medvedev ob'iavil voinu "krysham"', *Nezavisimaia gazeta*, 15 April 2010.
94   The amendment, Federal Law No. 407-FL, was signed into law on 6 December 2011. On *raiderstva*, see *Nezavisimaia gazeta*, 29 August 2008. In 2013, President Putin introduced an amnesty for select small and medium-size business owners in prison for precisely that reason, and to get them back into the small business sector; see, e.g., Andrew E. Kramer, 'Stimulus in Russia: Amnesty', *New York Times*, 18 August 2013.
95   Interview with the *Svobodnaia pressa,* 19 April 2010, www.svpressa.ru., a well-known Moscow oppositionist website, and *Moskovskiy komsomolets*, 15 April 2010.
96   *Rossiiskaia gazeta*, 11 January 2010.
97   *Komsomolskaia Pravda,* 1 March 2010. For specific 'kickback' cases uncovered by the chief military procurator Sergei Fridinski, see *Nezavisimoe voennoe obozrenie,* 17 April 2010, and RIA Novosti, 30 April 2010. For continuing problems *Nezavisimoe voennoe obozrenie*, 30 August 2010, and 'Spring Cleaning for the Power Vertical', *Russia Profile*, 21 April 2010.
98   *Komsomolskaia Pravda,* 28 October 2010; Roger McDermott, 'Maskirovka and Russian Military Procurement: Corruption, Deception and Crisis', *Eurasia Daily Monitor*, 8 September 2010, and 'Black Holes, Vanishing Rubles and Corruption in the Russian Military', *Eurasia Daily Monitor*, 9 November 2010.
99   RIA Novosti, 23 May 2010.
100  See Anna Vasileva, Natalia Sergeeva, 'Ekzamen na korruptsiia', *Kommersant*, 15 March 2012; For an overview, Eduard Klein, 'Corruption and Informal Payments in Russia's Educational System', *Russian Analytical Digest*, 2011, No. 97, pp. 5–9. See also Anna Nemtsova, 'In Russia, Corruption Plagues the Higher-Education System', *The Chronicle of Higher Education*, 22 February 2008.
101  Maria Antonova, 'Daimler Accused of Bribing Russians', *The Moscow Times*, 25 March 2010, and Svetlana Kononova, 'Treasure Mainland', *Russia Profile*, 1 March 2010, on foreign managers and bribery.
102  'Indikator "Korruptsiia v Rossii"', FOM (n.d.). The questions were asked on 16–17 January 2010, in 100 populated areas of 44 components of the Russian Federation.
103  Daria Nikolaeva, 'Grazhdane predpochitaiut innovatsiiam bor'bu s korruptsiei', *Kommersant,* 10 June 2010. On the 'Blue Buckets', see Roland Oliphant, 'A Bucket of Fury', *Russia Profile,* 2 June 2010.
104  'Politik', *Nezavisimaia gazeta*, 30 June 2010. Kudrin, Surkov, Sechin and Sobyanin followed the Tandem in order on the list of 'very influential people.'
105  *Kommersant-Vlast'*, 2 April 2010.
106  Olga Radko, 'V Rossii prodolzhaet protsvetat' korruptsiia', *Novyi Region,* 22 October 2010.

107 RIA Novosti, 1 & 2 December 2010. Transparency International, *Corruption Perception Index, 2010*; *Vedomosti*, 27 October 2010.
108 *The Moscow Times*, 31 May 2011.
109 On this, see an interesting article with interviews by Andrew E. Kramer, 'Russian Prisons for Police Thrive, but Some See Politics', *New York Times*, 5 June 2011.
110 Interfax, 17 February 2011.
111 The bill was signed into law on 4 May 2011.
112 *Rossiiskaia gazeta*, 1 March 2011.
113 *Moscow News*, 4 May 2011.
114 Baturina sold most of her assets in Russia and moved to London after her husband was forced to resign, see 'Baturina Flies in for Questioning', *The Moscow Times*, 29 June 2012. The Russian Prosecutor General charged Borodin and Akulin with fraud in 2010. Borodin was granted asylum in the UK in 2013, the same year that the MVD opened a new money laundering case against him and Akulin, accusing them of transferring $1.5 billion to accounts in Cyprus. See *RAPSI. Russian Legal Information Service*, 11 November 2013, and Howard Amos, 'Ministry to Push for Borodin's Extradition', *St. Petersburg Times*, 6 March 2013.
115 Interfax, 22 April 2011. For a detailed account of the type of information Luzhkov could tell an investigator about the 'exorbitant level of corruption' in Moscow if he dared – or if the investigator dared ask – see Andrei Kolesnikov, 'Vse, chto vy khotel sprosit' u Luzhkova, a on ne mog otvetit', *Novaia gazeta*, 1 November 2011.
116 Denis Belikov, 'Moskvu perekroiot dlia bor'by s korruptsieu', *Moskovskiy komsomolets*, 17 April 2011.
117 See *Vedomosti*, 12 & 16 May 2011.
118 *Kremlin.ru*, 13 May 2011. This meeting was held in Kostroma. For the surveys, see 'Rossiane ubezhdeny, chto uroven' korruptsii povyshaetsia', FOM, 13 May 2011.
119 *Kremlin.ru*, 17 June 2011.
120 *Novaia gazeta*, 7 June 2011.
121 Interfax, 10 August 2011.
122 *Novaia gazeta*, 22 November 2011; Transparency International, *Bribe Payers Index*, 2 November 2011, and RIA Novosti, 1 December 2011.
123 See, e.g., Oleg Nikiforov, 'Korruptsiia kak ekonomicheskii faktor', *Nezavisimaia gazeta*, 17 January 2012.
124 Interfax, 13 January 2012.
125 Interfax, 13 February 2012.
126 *Kommersant*, 17 May 2013.
127 *Kommersant*, 2 March 2012.
128 RIA Novosti, 26 April 2012.
129 *Kremlin.ru*, 14 December 2009. See Chapter Three, above.
130 Andrew Roth, 'What the Market Will Bear. Experts Say Attempts at Reform to Eliminate Corruption From Business have Largely Been Unsuccessful', *Russia Profile*, 12 January 2012.
131 *Business New Europe*, 24 January 2012. Some exceptions were allowed, e.g., for Rosneft.
132 Interfax, 12 January 2012.
133 For the full text in English, see *CIS-Legislation.com*, Presidential Decree of the Russian Federation, 13 March 2012, No. 297.
134 'Problema korruptsii v Rossii', FOMnibus, 17–18 March 2012. For Chaika's report on the National Strategy, see *Kommersant*, 2 March 2012. See also Anna Sulimina, 'Tackling State Corruption', *Moscow News*, 6 March 2012. See also *Nezavisimaia gazeta*, 10 December 2012.

135 Putin, 'Stroitel'stvo spravedlivosti. Sotsial'naia politika dlia Rossii', *Komsomolskaia pravda*, 13 February 2012. Putin mentioned corruption only as something that new young entrepreneurs may be able to avoid.
136 'Poll Shows that Concern Over Corruption Highest Since 1999', *The Moscow Times*, 12 July 2012. The poll was conducted by the Levada Centre.
137 See Natalia Korchenkova and Sergei Goryashko, 'Bor'bu s korruptsiei delaiut obshchestvennoi nagryshkoi', *Kommersant*, 29 September 2012.
138 *Nezavisimaia gazeta*, 11 December 2007.

# Concluding remarks

There is no reason to doubt that the Tandem arose for the very reasons that Putin and Medvedev offered in the first place: mutual trust, friendship, and a common vision for Russia. Putin could have pushed Constitutional change through the Federal Assembly with relative ease and taken on a third consecutive term himself. He chose not to do so, even though a clear majority of Russians would have approved. So, what was the point of the Tandem? Was Medvedev a mere caretaker serving as president, while Putin worked out of the prime ministerial office relatively free of a rancorous and divided *siloviki*? Or was Medvedev a loyal partner tasked with setting the stage – a modernization core and curbing corruption – to facilitate Putin's ultimate goals, Russia's political and economic leadership in Eurasia, and renewed status as an important player in a multi-polar world? The answer is probably both. On the face of it, Medvedev appeared to function as a proxy president only rarely stepping outside the confines of evolutionary Putinism, to which he added a 'liberal', legalistic, and perhaps even moral scaffold. The strength of that scaffold cannot be assessed until Putin's third term unfolds more fully, but this account of what actually happened during Medvedev's four years in office will furnish clues for later assessments of the entire Putin era.

There were lots of things in Russia that still needed to be fixed by the end of 2012. Medvedev promoted political liberalization on the political, economic, and social fronts and, though his attempts to nurture change appeared to run up against the unassailable fortress of the status quo, the uproar following the Duma election in December 2011 revealed unexpected breaches in the barricades. He made important strides forward in the realm of anti-corruption legislation. To be sure, corruption persisted at all levels of society in 2012, but public resentment of it reached higher levels than ever before (see Appendix, Table A.1). Medvedev introduced changes to the criminal code and to the government's procurement practices both to make corruption more difficult and to ease the way for business start-ups and maintenance. His efforts provided steps to a set of stairs that still has a chance to lead upwards, rather than downwards.

In the global arena, Russia swung from the depths (Georgian War) to the heights (the Reset) in its relations with the West, yet by 2012 it was weighed down again with a number of pressing confrontational issues with the West. Moscow's eastern offensive was much more successful in economic and political terms, though it was hardly complication free.

In the larger scheme of things, however, who can say in good conscience that Medvedev's calls for reforms to the G-8, G-20, and IMF, and his appeal for an all-European security architecture, were not things needed? It may well be that his particular recommendations were self-serving and not entirely feasible in their first form, but the principles they represented are undeniably important ones. To shrug them off as if they were not worth a second thought, as most European and North American leaderships did, reveals far more about Western obduracy than it does about Russian scheming.

On the home front in those short four years, Russia moved further and further away from the country's circumstances of 1992 than a mere twenty years in time would suggest possible. By the end of his term, the Constitution of 1993 had survived intact, and even if government interests and expediency too often overruled democratic practices, a democratic political system and structures existed. Elections were held on a regular basis, and there was freedom of conscience, freedom of assembly, and freedom of expression, no matter how badly the government might have wished to limit them – or how aggressively critics insist they don't exist. One way or another, every voice was heard during Medvedev's tenure, which would suggest that the globalization of communications technology might in the end have greater import for Russia than global economics. By 2012, the country had a market economy, was still multi-partied and, if also centrist and authoritarian, was far more democratic than anything that could have been dreamed of in the USSR, and far more functional than it had been under Boris Yeltsin. Significantly, the Tandem withstood a few blips to remain by far the leadership team most trusted by Russians (see Appendix, Tables A.2 and A.3).

There are a few circles in Russia, and even more abroad, in which every Kremlin act is perceived as a potential 'return' to Soviet days. Closer looks suggest that this presumption is patent nonsense, and the most vociferous critics would do well to bear in mind how far Russia has come. Foreign critics should also be more wary of living in glasshouses themselves. This doesn't mean that there is nothing to criticize, but the Western tendency to preach and apply obvious double standards has been counter-productive; the Russian tendency to bluster, cast blame wildly, and simply not get the job done has been equally counter-productive. With the fortunate timing of Barack Obama's accession to the US presidency, Medvedev helped mute these tendencies. For the most part, in fact, leaderships in Russia, the EU, and the United States now recognize an innate mutual dependency that none wishes to see deteriorate altogether.

Primakov's recommendation in 2006 that Russia focus its diplomatic efforts on the CIS seemed to be bearing fruit by 2012, especially in the Customs Union, the CSTO, the SCO, and also with Moscow's 'axis' partners, Beijing and Delhi. His advice that Russia mend its relations with Ukraine, however, seemed to have gone unheeded. Drawn in opposing directions by the EU and the Customs Union, torn by internal political polarization, and confronted by an unbending Gazprom, Kyiv seemed more distant from Moscow by mid-2012 than it had been in 2008.

The great leap forward predicted by Primakov may not have happened either, yet the Medvedev presidency gave Russian and foreign observers a chance to sit back and assess options for the future after the whirlwind Yeltsin and Putin presidencies. Above all, it enabled Russian citizens to recognize that there were options.

There is, then, a legacy to consider. Granted, Medvedev was unable to make substantive inroads on his expressed goals of modernization, liberalization, and curbing corruption, yet the rhetoric of his presidency energized the political and social community. While it may be true, as his former ally Igor Yurgens put it, that there 'were more right things said than serious actions taken' over the previous four years,[1] it is also true that there was evolution. The political arena now includes an educated and activist middle class, many of them young and professional. Their ambitions for change represent genies that won't be pushed back into the bottle without a fight. Medvedev also encouraged and participated in the spread of Internet and other communication technology use in Russia, thereby muting, even indirectly countering, perceived government clampdowns on the media. No Russian government, even Putin's at its strictest, will ever again be able to control the dissemination of information in the manner of the old CPSU.

Reflecting on Vladimir Putin's first post-Medvedev address to the Federal Assembly, delivered in December 2012, Russian political analyst Maksim Glikin said that it appeared from the speech as if the previous four years 'had not existed. They must be expunged from the Russians' memory.'[2] If Glikin's musings were accurate, Putin expected to pick up where he left off in 2008, and the messages delivered over time by the Medvedev presidency on innovation and modernization will be sacrificed in the name of unity, centralization, and Great Statehood. If that is what Putin intends, it won't be easy.

## Notes

1 *Novaia gazeta*, 4 May 2012.
2 Maksim Glikin in *Vedomosti* online, 31 December 2012.

# Appendix

*Table A.1* Levada Centre polls on social issues that most concern Russian citizens, 2005–2012

Question: Which of the following problems among social issues trouble you most of all, and which do you consider the most serious? (You may select no more than 5–6 variants of the answers)

|  | 2005 | 2006 | 2007 | 2008 | 2009 | 2010 | 2011 | 2012 |
|---|---|---|---|---|---|---|---|---|
| 1 Price increases | 71 | 70 | 64 | 82 | 76 | 72 | 73 | 67 |
| 2 Poverty, the impoverishment of a large part of the population | 53 | 51 | 52 | 45 | 56 | 51 | 52 | 48 |
| 3 Corruption, bribe-taking | 24 | 25 | 27 | 27 | 28 | 33 | 27 | 35 |
| 4 Growth of unemployment | 39 | 34 | 30 | 25 | 51 | 38 | 41 | 33 |
| 5 Economic crisis, poor conditions in industry and agriculture | 33 | 29 | 28 | 29 | 38 | 36 | 32 | 32 |
| 6 Moral crisis, culture, morality | 22 | 24 | 28 | 26 | 26 | 28 | 26 | 31 |
| 7 Sharp split between rich and poor, uneven distribution of wealth | 27 | 30 | 32 | 35 | 30 | 29 | 27 | 29 |
| 8 Growth of drug addiction | 29 | 29 | 25 | 29 | 25 | 32 | 25 | 24 |
| 9 Inadequacy of many types of medical services | 29 | 31 | 32 | 31 | 27 | 26 | 24 | 24 |
| 10 Deteriorating environmental conditions | 17 | 24 | 22 | 23 | 18 | 31 | 25 | 21 |
| 11 Growth of cost, inadequate education | 27 | 28 | 26 | 26 | 16 | 29 | 18 | 20 |
| 12 Influx of newcomers, migrants | 7 | 10 | 9 | 12 | 11 | 11 | 12 | 16 |
| 13 Increase in criminal offences | 29 | 29 | 28 | 27 | 22 | 21 | 21 | 16 |
| 14 Strength, arbitrariness of officials | 9 | 10 | 9 | 10 | 13 | 18 | 14 | 13 |
| 15 Weakness of state power | 11 | 11 | 9 | 9 | 9 | 13 | 10 | 8 |
| 16 Roughness, cruelty of police | 6 | 8 | 9 | 9 | 12 | 12 | 7 | 7 |
| 17 Growth of nationalism, deterioration of inter-ethnic relations | 4 | 10 | 7 | 5 | 5 | 6 | 9 | 7 |
| 18 Threat of explosions, and other terrorist acts where you live | 15 | 10 | 6 | 4 | 5 | 10 | 12 | 6 |
| 19 Impossibility of receiving justice in the courts | 5 | 6 | 8 | 7 | 7 | 9 | 6 | 5 |

*Table A.1* (continued)

| | 2005 | 2006 | 2007 | 2008 | 2009 | 2010 | 2011 | 2012 |
|---|---|---|---|---|---|---|---|---|
| 20 Restrictions on civil rights, democratic freedoms (freedom of speech, press) | 2 | 2 | 1 | 2 | 3 | 4 | 4 | 4 |
| 21 Delays in workers' wages, pensions, benefits, etc. | 4 | 5 | 3 | 4 | 6 | 5 | 6 | 4 |
| 22 Spread of HIV/AIDS | 6 | 5 | 8 | 7 | 6 | 6 | 3 | 3 |
| 23 Terrorism in North Caucasus | 7 | 4 | 4 | 2 | 9 | 8 | 7 | 3 |
| 24 Conflicts between different branches of government, at different levels | 3 | 2 | 2 | 2 | 4 | 3 | 3 | 2 |
| Other | 1 | 1 | 3 | 3 | 2 | 2 | 2 | 2 |
| Difficult to answer | 1 | 1 | 3 | 1 | 1 | 1 | 3 | 2 |

Note: The most recent poll was conducted 10–13 July [2012], from a representative population of 1,600 people living in 130 towns and villages in 45 regions of the country. The score listed is a percentage of the respondents; the statistical margin of error is no higher than 3.4%.

Source: "Rost tsen i bednost' — glavnye trevogi rossiian," *Levada-tsentr.* 8 August 2012. Translated and summarized by J.L. Black.

*Table A.2* Trust in Russia's basic social and political institutions, October 2011

| | Fully trust | Partially trust | Distrust | N.A. |
|---|---|---|---|---|
| Prime Minister Putin | 52 | 31 | 9 | 8 |
| President Medvedev | 50 | 34 | 9 | 7 |
| Church, religious organizations | 49 | 25 | 10 | 16 |
| Army | 37 | 36 | 13 | 14 |
| Media | 30 | 47 | 16 | 7 |
| Government | 30 | 45 | 17 | 8 |
| State security, special services | 26 | 37 | 16 | 21 |
| Regional authorities | 28 | 40 | 22 | 10 |
| Russian commercial banks | 24 | 39 | 18 | 19 |
| Small and middle-sized business | 23 | 39 | 18 | 20 |
| Federation Council | 22 | 44 | 17 | 17 |
| Procurator (Prosecutor) | 22 | 37 | 21 | 20 |
| State Duma | 21 | 47 | 22 | 10 |
| Local authorities | 23 | 41 | 26 | 10 |
| Courts | 19 | 43 | 22 | 16 |
| Militia/police | 20 | 40 | 29 | 11 |
| Big business | 16 | 37 | 26 | 21 |
| Trade unions | 16 | 31 | 26 | 27 |
| Political parties | 10 | 44 | 30 | 16 |

Source: *Vestnik obshestvennogo mneniia, Dannye. Analiz. Diskussii,* 2 [112], April-June 2012, p. 12.

*Table A.3* Trust in Russia's basic social and political institutions, 2007–2013

| | Fully trust | | | Partially trust | | | Distrust | | |
|---|---|---|---|---|---|---|---|---|---|
| | 2007 | 2009 | 2013 | 2007 | 2009 | 2013 | 2007 | 2009 | 2013 |
| President | 64 | 63 | 55 | 23 | 25 | 30 | 7 | 6 | 12 |
| Church, religious organizations | 42 | 48 | 48 | 17 | 21 | 25 | 12 | 10 | 10 |
| Army | 31 | 37 | 43 | 30 | 33 | 34 | 20 | 16 | 13 |
| State security, special services | 24 | 31 | 36 | 27 | 33 | 32 | 18 | 13 | 14 |
| Regional authorities | 18 | 21 | 32 | 35 | 39 | 40 | 33 | 24 | 21 |
| Government of Russia | 19 | 34 | 30 | 41 | 40 | 38 | 26 | 14 | 25 |
| Local authorities | 16 | 19 | 27 | 31 | 38 | 42 | 41 | 31 | 26 |
| Federation Council | 12 | 22 | 24 | 37 | 35 | 39 | 22 | 16 | 22 |
| Procurator (Prosecutor) | 16 | 21 | 26 | 28 | 37 | 41 | 26 | 21 | 18 |
| State Duma | 13 | 21 | 25 | 41 | 42 | 44 | 33 | 21 | 26 |
| Media | 27 | 28 | 24 | 35 | 49 | 50 | 14 | 16 | 19 |
| Courts | 17 | 21 | 21 | 28 | 38 | 44 | 27 | 25 | 22 |
| Militia/police | 12 | 17 | 18 | 35 | 42 | 46 | 38 | 31 | 27 |
| Trade unions | 9 | 16 | 18 | 21 | 26 | 34 | 28 | 29 | 26 |
| Political parties | 7 | 7 | 12 | 27 | 38 | 46 | 36 | 36 | 33 |

Source: 'Doverie institutam vlasti', Levada-tsentr, 7 October 2013

# Bibliography

This list is limited to books and does not include the Russian language titles and relevant English-language pieces from periodical literature referenced in the endnotes to each chapter. With a few exceptions, the list is limited to titles published during or after Medvedev's term as president.

Adamishin, Anatoly, Richard Schifter, *Human Rights, Perestroika, and the End of the Cold War*. Washington, 2009.

Aggarwal, Vinod K., Kristi Govella, eds. *Responding to a Resurgent Russia: Russian Policy and Responses from the EU and U.S.* New York, 2011.

Alekperov, Vagit, *Oil of Russia. Past, Present, and Future*. Minneapolis, US, 2011. (Alekperov is president of LUKoil).

Allina-Pisano, Jessica, *The Post-Soviet Potemkin Village. Politics and Property Rights in the Black Earth*. Cambridge, 2008.

Allison, Roy, *Russia, the West and Military Intervention*. Oxford, 2013. (Chatham House)

Aslund, Anders, Sergei Guriev, Andrew Kuchins, eds. *Russia After the Global Economic Crisis*. Washington, 2010.

Babchenko, Arkady, *One Soldier's War in Chechnya*. Boston 2008. Translated by Nick Allen.

Bailes, Alyson J.K. et alia, *The Shanghai Cooperation Organization*. Stockholm, 2007. SIPRI Policy Paper, 2007.

Balmaceda, Margarita M. *Energy Dependency, Politics and Corruption in the Former Soviet Union: Russia's Power, Oligarchs' Profits, and Ukraine's Missing Energy Policy, 1995–2006*. London, 2008.

Balzer, Marjorie Mandelstam, ed. *Religion and Politics in Russia: A Reader*. New York, 2010.

Barany, Zoltan, *Democratic Breakdown and the Decline of the Russian Military*. Ithaca, NY, 2008.

Barysch, Katinka, ed. *Pipelines, Politics and Power. The Future of EU-Russia Energy Relations*. London, 2009.

Bennetts, Marc, *Football Dynamo: Modern Russia and the People's Game*. London, 2008.

Black, J. L., *Into the Dustbin of History. The USSR From Coup to Commonwealth, August-December 1991. A Documentary Narrative*. Gulf Breeze, FL, 1993.

——*Russia Faces NATO Expansion. Bearing Gifts or Bearing Arms?* Lanham, MD, 2000.

——, *Vladimir Putin and the New World Order. Looking East, Looking West?* Lanham, MD, 2004.

Black, J.L., Michael Johns, eds. *From Putin to Medvedev. Continuity or Change?* Manotick, ON, 2009.

Black, J.L., Michael Johns, eds. *Russia After 2012. From Putin to Medvedev to Putin – Continuity, Change, or Revolution?* London and New York, 2013.

Blank, Stephen J., ed. *Prospects for Russo-United States Security Cooperation.* Carlisle, PA, 2009. (US Army College)

Blank, Stephen J., *Towards a New Chinese Order in Asia: Russia's Failure.* National Bureau of Asian Research, Special Report #26, March 2011.

Blank, Stephen J., *Civil-Military Relations in Medvedev's Russia.* Carlisle, PA, 2011 (US Army College)

Blank, Stephen J., ed. *Can Russia Reform? Economic, Political, and Military Perspectives.* Carlisle, PA, 2012. (US Army College)

Blank, Stephen J., ed. *Central Asia after 2014.* Carlisle, PA, 2013 (US Army College)

Blum, Douglas W., *National Identity and Globalization. Youth, State and Society in Post-Soviet Eurasia.* Cambridge, 2008.

Colton, Timothy J., *Yeltsin. A Life.* New York, 2008.

Blyakha, Nataliya, *Russian Foreign Direct Investment in Ukraine.* Turku, Finland, 2009. (Pan European Institute Electronic Publication, 17/2009)

Brown, Archie, *The Rise and Fall of Communism.* New York, 2009.

Bunce, Valerie, Michael McFaul, Kathryn Stoner-Weiss, eds. *Democracy and Authoritarianism in the Postcommunist World.* London, 2009.

Casula, Philipp, Jeronim Perovic, eds. *Identities and Politics During the Putin Presidency. The Foundations of Russia's Stability.* Vol 92 (Soviet and Post-Soviet Politics and Sociery, SPSS). Stüttgart, 2009.

Chebankova. Elena A., *Russia's Federal Relations: Putin's Reforms and Management of the Regions.* Abingdon, UK, 2010.

Chebankova, Elena A., *Civil Society in Putin's Russia.* London, 2013.

Chunan, Anna L., *The Social Construction of Russia's Resurgence: Aspirations, Identity, and Security Interests.* Baltimore, 2009.

Cohen, Ariel, *Kazakhstan. The Road to Independence. Energy Policy and the Birth of a Nation.* Cambridge, MA, 2009.

Cohen, Stephen F., *Soviet Fates and Lost Alternatives: From Stalinism to the New Cold War.* New York, 2009.

Cooley, Alexander, *Great Games, Local Rules. The New Great Power Contest in Central Asia,* Cambridge, MA, 2012.

Dejevsky, Mary, *Russia.* London, 2009.

Dimbleday, Jonathan, *Russia: A Journey to the Heart of a Land and Its People.* London 2007.

Diuk, Nadia M., *The Next Generation in Russia, Ukraine and Azerbaijan. Youth, Politics, Identity and Change.* Lanham, MD, 2012.

Dunkerley, William, *The Phoney Litvinenko Murder.* New Britain, CT, 2011.

Dutkiewicz, Piotr, Dmitrii Trenin, eds. *Russia: the Challenges of Transformation.* New York, 2011.

Easter, Gerald M. *Capital, Coercion, and Postcommunist States.* Ithaca, NY, 2010.

Gaddy, Clifford, Barry Ickes, *Russia's Addiction: The Political Economy of Resource Dependence.* New York, 2008.

Gaidar, Yegor, *Collapse of an Empire. Lessons for Modern Russia.* Translated by Antonina W. Bouis. New York, 2008.

Galeotti, Mark, *The Politics of Security in Russia.* Farnham, UK, 2009.

Garrard, John, Carol Garrard, *Russian Orthodoxy Resurgent. Faith and Power in the New Russia*. Ithaca, NY, 2008.

Gessen, Masha, *The Man Without a Face. The Unlikely Rise of Vladimir Putin*. New York, 2012.

Giuliano, Elise, *Constructing Grievance. Ethnic Nationalism in Russia's Republics*. Ithaca, NY 2011.

Glazunov, Mikhail, *Business in Post-Communist Russia. Privatization and the Limits of Transformation*. London, 2013.

Goldman, Marshall I., *Petrostate: Putin, Power and the New Russia*. Oxford, 2008.

Gomart, Thomas, *Russian Civil-Military Relations. Putin's Legacy*. Washington, 2008.

Gower, Jackie, Graham Timmins, eds. *Russia and Europe in the Twentieth Century*. London, 2007.

Gower, Jackie, Graham Timmins, eds. *The European Union, Russia and the Shared Neighbourhoods*, London, 2013.

Gustafson, Thane, *Wheel of Fortune: The Battle for Oil and Power in Russia*. Cambridge, MA, 2012.

Hahn, Gordon M., *U.S.-Russian Relations and the War against Jihadism*. New York, 2009. (A Century Foundation Report).

Harding, Luke, *Mafia State: How One Reporter Became an Enemy of the Brutal New Regime*. London, 2011.

Hass, Marcel de, ed. *The Shanghai Cooperation Organization. Towards a Full-Grown Security Alliance?* Clingendael, Netherlands, 2007.

Henry, Laura A. *Red to Green. Environmental Activism in Post-Soviet Russia*. Ithaca, NY, 2010.

Herper, Marcel Van, *Putinism. The Slow Rise of a Radical Right Regime in Russia*. London, 2013.

Hill, Fiona, Clifford Gaddy, *Mr. Putin: Operative in the Kremlin*. Washington, 2013. (Brookings Institute).

Helleweg, John, Alexandre Latsa, eds. *Putin's New Russia*. Washington, 2012.

Herrara, Yoshiko M., *Mirror of the Economy: National Accounts and International Norms in Russia and Beyond*. Ithaca, NY, 2010.

Hoffman, David E., *The Untold Story of the Cold War Arms Race and Its Legacy*. New York, 2009.

Hoffman, David E., *The Oligarchs: Wealth and Power in the New Russia*. 3rd edition, New York, 2011.

Howard, Glen E., ed. *Volatile Borderland. Russia and the North Caucasus*. Washington, 2011. (Jamestown Foundation).

Jafalian, Annie, ed. *Reassessing Security in the South Caucasus. Regional Conflicts and Transformation*. Oxford, 2011.

Judah, Ben, *Fragile Empire: How Russia Fell In and Out of Love with Vladimir Putin*. New Haven, 2013.

Klebnikov, Paul, *Godfather of the Kremlin. The Life and Times of Boris Berezovsky*, New York, 2000.

Krickus, Richard J., *Medvedev's Plan: Giving Russia a Voice but Not a Veto in a New European Security System*. Carlisle, PA, 2009. (US Army College)

Krickus, Richard J., *The Afghanistan Question and the Reset in U.S.-Russia Relations*. Carlisle, PA, 2011. (US Army College)

Kuhrt, Natasha, ed. *Russia and the World. The Internal-External Nexus*. London, 2013.

Laurelle, Marlène, *Russian Eurasianism: An Ideology of Empires*. Washington, 2008.

Laurelle, Marlène, ed. *Russian Nationalism and the National Reassertion of Russia*. Foreword by John Dunlop, London, 2009.

Laruelle, Marlène, *Nationalism and Politics in Contemporary Russia*. London 2010.

Ledenova, Alena V., *How Russia Really Works*. Ithaca, NY, 2006.

Ledeneva, Alena V., *Can Russia Modernize? Sistema, Power Networks, and Informal Governance*, Cambridge, UK, 2013.

Lipman, Maria, Nikolay Petrov, *Russia in 2020, Scenarios for the Future*, Washington/ Moscow 2011.

Liuhto, Kari, ed. *EU-Russia Gas Connection: Pipes, Politics and Problems*. Turku, Finland, 2009. (Pan-European Institute Electronic Publication, 8/2009).

Lo, Bobo, *Axis of Convenience: Moscow, Beijing and the New Geopolitics*. London, 2008.

Lucas, Edward, *The New Cold War: Putin's Russia and the Threat to the West*. London, 2008.

MacFarlane, S. Neil, *Post-Revolutionary Georgia on the Edge?* Chatham House Briefing Paper, London, March 2011.

Mankoff, Jeffrey, *Russian Foreign Policy: The Return of Great Power Politics*. Lanham, MD, 2009.

Matlock, Jack F. *Superpower Illusions: How Myth and False Ideologies Led America Astray – and How to Return to Reality*. New Haven, 2010.

McFaul, Michael, *Russia's Unfinished Revolution*. Ithaca, NY, 2002.

Medvedev, Dmitry, *Natsional'ye prioritety: Stat' i vystupleniia*, eds. G. Pavlovsky, K.V. tanaev, Moscow, 2008.

Medvedev, Dmitry, *Novaia politicheskaia strategiia v Poslanie Prezidenta Dmitriia Medvedeva*, eds. G.O. Pavlovsky, K,V. Tanaev, Moscow, 2010.

Menshikov, Stanislav M., *The Anatomy of Russian Capitalism*. Washington, 2007.

Mickiewicz, Ellen, *Television, Power, and the Public in Russia*. London, 2008.

Monaghan, Andrew, ed. *The Indivisibility of Security: Russia and Euro-Atlantic Security*, Rome, 2009. (NATO Defense College Forum Paper).

Monaghan, Andrew, *The Russian Vertical: the Tandem, Power and the Elections*. Chatham House. Russia and Eurasia Programme Paper REP 2011/01, London, June 2011.

Murphy, Paul J., *Allah's Angels: Chechen Women in War*. Annapolis, MD, 2010.

Nygren, Bertil, *The Rebuilding of Greater Russia: Putin's Foreign Policy Towards the CIS Countries*. New York, 2009.

Ostrow, Joel M., Georgiy A. Satarov, Irina M. Khakamada, *The Consolidation of Dictatorship in Russia. An Inside View of the Demise of Democracy*, Westport, CT, 2007. Foreword by Garry Kasparov.

Oushakine, Serguei Alex, *The Patriotism of Despair. Nation, War and Loss in Russia*. Ithaca, NY, 2009.

Paik, Keom-Wook, *Sino-Russian Oil and Gas Cooperation: The Reality and Implications*. Oxford, 2012. (International Institute for Asian Studies)

Pape, Ulia, *The Politics of HIV/AIDS in Russia*. London, 2013.

Papkova, Irina, *The Orthodox Church and Russian Politics*. Oxford/Washington, 2010.

Patico, Jennifer, *Consumption and Social Change in a Post-Soviet Middle Class*, Stanford, 2008.

Pilkington, Hilary, et alia, *Russia's Skinheads*. London, 2013.

Pouliot, Vincent, *International Security in Practice: The Politics of NATO-Russia Diplomacy*. New York, 2009.

Pukhov, Ruslan, ed. *The Tanks of August*, Moscow, 2010. [on the Georgian War]

Remington, Thomas F., *The Politics of Inequality in Russia*. Cambridge, UK, 2011.

Richards, Susan, *Lost and Found in Russia: Lives In a Post-Soviet Landscape*. New York, 2010.

Roberts, Sean P., *Putin's United Russia Party*. London, 2013.

Robertson, Graeme B., *The Politics of Protest in Hybrid Regimes. Managing Dissent in Russia*. Cambridge, UK, 2011.

Roxborough, Angus, *The Strongman. Vladimir Putin and the Struggle for Russia*. London, 2012.

Rueschmeyer, Marilyn, Sharon L. Wolchik, *Women in Power in Post-Communist Parliaments*. Washington/Bloomington, 2009.

Saari, Sinikukka, *Promoting Democracy and Human Rights in Russia*. London, 2010.

Sakwa, Richard, *Gorbachev and His Reforms, 1985–1990*. New York, 1990.

Sakwa, Richard, *The Crisis of Russian Democracy: The Dual State, Factionalism, and the Medvedev Succession*. Cambridge, UK, 2011.

Serio, Joseph D., *Investigating the Russian Mafia. An Introduction for Students, Law Enforcement, and International Business*, Durham, NC, 2008.

Sherr, James, *Hard Diplomacy and Soft Coercion. Russia's Influence Abroad*. London, 2013 (Chatham House)

Shevtsova, Lilia, *Lonely Power. Why Russia Has Failed to become the West and the West is Weary of Russia*, Moscow/ Washington, 2010.

Shevtsova, Lilia, *Change or Decay. Russia's Dilemma and the West's Response*. Moscow/ Washington, 2011.

Shlapentokh, Vladimir, Anna Arutunyan, *Freedom, Repression, and Private Property in Russia*. Cambridge, UK, 2013.

Shulgan, Christopher, *The Soviet Ambassador. The Making of the Radical Behind Perestroika*, Toronto, 2008. [on Aleksandr N. Yakovlev]

Simons, Thomas W. Jr., *Eurasia's New Frontiers: Young States. Old Societies, Open Futures*. Ithaca, NY, 2009.

Soldatov, Andrei, Irina Borogan, *The New Nobility. The Restoration of Russia's Security State and the Enduring Legacy of the KGB*. Washington, 2010.

Starr, Frederick, Svante E. Cornell, eds. *The Guns of August 2008. Russia's War in Georgia*. New York, 2009.

Stefes, Christoph H. *Understanding Post-Soviet Transitions: Corruption, Collusion, and Clientelism*. New York, 2006.

Sutela, Pekka, *The Political Economy of Putin's Russia*. London, 2012.

Sutyrin, Sergei F. *Internationalization of Russian Economy: Threats and Opportunities in Time of Crisis*. Turku, Finland, 2009.

Svanidze, Nikolai, Marina Svanidze, *Medvedev*, Moscow, 2008. (only available in Russian)

Taylor, Brian D., *State Building in Putin's Russia: Policing and Coercion after Communism*. Cambridge, UK, 2011.

Treisman, Daniel, *The Return: Russia's Journey from Gorbachev to Medvedev*. New York, 2011.

Trenin, Dmitrii, Pavel Baev, *The Arctic: A View From Russia*, Moscow/ Washington, 2010.

Trenin, Dmitri, *Post-imperium: A Eurasian Story*. Washington/ Moscow, 2011.

Tsygankov, Andrei P., *Russophobia: Anti-Russian Lobby and American Foreign Policy*. London, 2009.

Umland, Andreas, ed., *The Nature of "Neo-Eurasianism": Approaches by Alexander Dugin's Post-Soviet Movement of Radical Anti-Americanism.* Armonk, NY, 2009.

Way, Lucan, Steven Levitsky, *Competitive Authoritarianism. Hybrid Regimes after the Cold War.* Cambridge, UK, 2010.

Wegren, Stephen A., ed. *Return to Putin's Russia: Past Imperfect, Future Uncertain.* Lanham, MD, 2012. 5th edition.

Wishnick, Elizabeth, *Russia, China, and the United States in Central Asia: Prospects for Great Power Competition and Cooperation in the Shadow of the Georgian Crisis.* Carlisle, PA, 2009. (US Army College).

Zavisa, Jane R. *Housing the New Russia,* Ithaca, NY, 2012.

Zon, Hans von, *Russia's Development Problem. The Cult of Power.* London 2008.

# Index

Abkhazia 133–36, 169n8
ABM Treaty 132, 163
Adaev, Aslan 53
Afghanistan 141, 149, 157, 159, 167, 168, 187; *see also* wars
Afonin, Yuri 69
Agency for Strategic Initiatives (ASI) 27–28, 105
Agrarian Party 69
agriculture *see* economy
AIDS *see* healthcare
Ajaria 133
A Just Russia Party 26, 27, 28, 47, 69, 70, 78
Akhmadov, Ilyas 53
Akulin, Dmitry 202, 211n114
Albright, Madeleine 167
alcohol abuse 181, 185–87
Aleksashenko, Sergei 74
Alekseeva, Lyudmila 70
Alfa Group 102
Al-Qaeda 53, 55, 58–59, 153, 168; *see also* terrorism
Alferov, Zhores 100
Algeria 122
All-Russian Civic Congress 70
All-Russia People's Congress 27–28, 71
Andropov, Yuri 10n9, 191
Anheuser-Busch Inbev 186
Arab Spring 120, 161
Arby's 125
Arctic 120–21
armed forces 163–69; military concept 164, 167; military exercises 168; missile defence dispute 132, 148, 153. 156–57, 166–67; *see also* corruption
Armenia 98, 122, 140, 143, 164
arms reduction/control 166; Intermediate-Range Nuclear Forces

Treaty (INF) 154, 163; Strategic Arms Reduction Treaty (START) 154, 155, 157, 158, 159, 163–64; Strategic Offensive Reduction Treaty (SORT) 163
Asia-Pacific Economic Cooperation (APEC) 98, 149, 155
Association of Southeast Asian Nations (ASEAN) 145
Astemirov, Amzor 56
Austria 115, 117
automobile industry 123–24
Azarov, Mykola 113–14
Azerbaijan 115, 133, 137, 140, 143

Bagapsh, Sergei 133, 138
Bakiev, Kurmanbek 157
Balkans 132
Baltic States 97, 136
Baluevsky, Gen.Yury 139, 165
Bangladesh 149
banking *see* economy
Barrett, Craig R. 100
Barroso, Jose Manuel 115
Barshchevsky, Nikolai 69
Basaev, Shamil 51, 54
Bastrykin, Aleksandr 200, 201
Bates, Larry 121
Baturina, Yelena 24, 179, 202, 211n114
Belarus 91, 122, 143, 151, 164
Belkovsky, Stanislav 103, 198
Belousov, Andrei 107
Belov, A. *see* Potkin, Aleksandr
Belykh, Nikita 69, 70, 86
Berezovsky, Boris 10n18, 14, 37n6, 51, 91
Beslan atrocity 44, 53–54, 55
Beyrle, John 136, 154, 160, 169n13
Biden, Joseph 155, 159

bin Laden, Osama 55, 58
Blair, Tony 118
Blake, Robert 142
Blavatnik, Len (Leonid) 119, 129n97
'blue bucket' campaign 200
Boehner, John 160
Bogdanov, Andrei 12, 69
Bokhanovsky, Leonid 122
Bolivia 122
Bombardier, Magna 123, 124
Boos, Georgy 47
Borodin, Andrei 202, 211n114
Borovoi, Konstantin 33
Bortnikov, Aleksandr 58
Bout, Viktor 158, 159
Bratsky Forestry Co. 6
Brazil 143; *see also* BRIC(S)
Brezhnev, Leonid 5, 10n9, 191
Brezhnevism 5, 30, 36, 48, 83, 192
BRIC(S) 92, 93, 105, 121, 131,
    143–46, 149
Brown, Gordon 119
Browder, William 159, 162
Bukovsky, Vladimir 2, 5, 12
Bulgaria 114–17, 123
Burjanadze, Nino 138
Burns, William 156
Bush, George W. 97, 135, 136, 153, 158
Buzin, Andrei 74

Canada 96, 120, 123; *see also*
    Bombardier, Magna
Capital Federal District (Moscow) 35
Carlsberg beer 186
Caucasus Emirate 52–53, 55, 59
Central Asia 132, 142, 150–52
Central Electoral Commission (CEC) 4,
    12, 34
Chaika, Yury 196, 198, 200, 102, 203
Chapman, Anna 157
Chechnya 47–48, 50–52, 54;
    *see also* Kadyrov, Akhmad; Kadyrov,
    Ramzan; wars
Cherepkin, Viktor 32
Cherkesov, Viktor 193
Chernenko, Konstantin 10n9
Chernogorov, Aleksandr 107
Chernomyrdin, Viktor 7
'chicken wars' 110, 156; *see also*
    agriculture
children 173n96, 188–89; orphans
    162–63
China 48–49, 105, 118, 133, 203; and
    BRICS 105, 143–46

Chirikova, Yevgenia 82, 177
Chubais, Anatoly 69, 100, 103, 105
Chuichenko, Konstantin 201
Churov, Vladimir 12, 30, 77, 79, 84
CISCO Systems 102
Civil Force 69
Civil Platform 87
Clinton, Bill 97
Clinton, Hillary 79, 80, 155, 157, 161,
    163, 167
Collective Security Treaty Organization
    (CSTO) 136, 141–43
'coloured' revolutions 72, 81, 132, 190
Commission for Modernization and
    Technological Development (CMTD)
    99–100, 102, 106; *see also* Skolkovo
    Innovation Centre
Committee for National Salvation 71
Common Economic Space 98, 123, 142;
    *see also* Eurasian Union
Commonwealth of Independent States
    (CIS) 13, 34, 131–32
Communist Party of the Russian
    Federation (CPRF/KPRF) 12, 17, 26,
    45, 47, 63, 66, 67–69, 72–74, 75, 78,
    86, 202
Communist Party of the Soviet Union
    (CPSU) xii–xiv, 191–92
Concern Kalina 125
Constitution, Russian (1993) 6, 11, 42,
    63, 214
Conventional Forces in Europe Treaty
    (CFE) 163
Cooperation and Partnership
    Agreement (PCA) 163; *see also*
    Partnership and Cooperation
    Agreement
corruption 37, 54, 77, 107, 140, 179,
    191–206; *krysha* 6, 192; in business
    198, 204; in education 199; in
    government 197–99, 200, 201–3, 204;
    in law enforcement 193, 195, 198, 203;
    in military 165, 196, 199, 204;
    National Plan 194, 196; National
    Strategy (2008) 195, (2012) 194–95,
    198, 204
Council for Economic Modernization
    (Putin) 107
crime 71, 104, 198–99; *see also*
    corruption
Crowley, Philip J. 173n84
Customs Union 91–92, 97–98, 113–14,
    123, 142
Cyprus 104

Czech Republic 113, 155, 156
Daimler 123, 199–200
Delyagin, Mikhail 71, 75
democracy 67, 73, 102;
  *see also* sovereign democracy
Democratic Party of Russia
  12, 69
Democratic Platform 6
demographic issues *see* population
demonstrations *see* protests
Demushkin, Dmitry 71
Denisov, Andrei 147
Deripaska, Oleg 74
disasters: human (accidents) 180, 183,
  186, 207n23; natural 108–9, 180, 182
Dmitriev, Mikhail 29
Doctrine on Food Security 107–8
Domodedovo airport 25
drought 108–9
drug abuse 168, 185, 187
Dudley, Robert 118–19, 120, 121
Dugin, Aleksandr 75
Dunkin Donuts 124
Dvorkovich, Arkady 23, 26 101

Eastern Siberia Pacific Ocean Pipeline
  (ESPO) 118
economy 91–130, 138, 180–81;
  agriculture 107–11; banks 92–94, 96,
  125; debt 93; foreign investment 93,
  103, 104–5, 182, 199; inflation 93,
  176; national champions 23, 91, 93,
  99, 176; privatization 97–7, 106–7;
  recession 92–97; 'shock therapy' 99;
  tax collecting 91; *see also*
  modernization; Reserve Funds; energy
education xv, 176, 199
Egypt 122
elections 214; general 2–4; regional 47;
  rigging 47, 79–81; rules 3, 34, 63,
  78–79; *see also* political systems;
  presidency; State Duma
emigration 149
energy 92, 111–23; electricity 180–81,
  182–83; gas wars 112–17, 129n89;
  hydro-electric 180; LNG 117, 119;
  nuclear power plants (NPP) 117,
  122–23, 147; pipelines 92, 113–20,
  121–22, 148; *see also* oil and gas
  industry; Rosneft; Transneft
Equatorial Guinea 122
espionage 157–58
Eurasianists 75, 99, 149; *see also* Dugin,
  Aleksandr

Eurasian Economic Community
  (EurAsEC) 91–92, 98, 132
Eurasian Union 98, 123, 142, 150
European Court of Human Rights
  (ECHR) 86
European Security Treaty (Draft)
  165, 214
European Union (EU) 22, 114, 115, 137

Far Eastern Development Agency 49;
  *see also* Siberia
Federal Assembly 43
federal districts 43, 46, 62
Federal Financial Monitoring Service
  (FFMS) 1
Federal Migration Service 101, 184, 185
Federal Security Service (FSB) 22, 46,
  56, 58
Federation Council 44–45, 62
Federation of Russian Car Owners
  (FAR) 74
Fiat 123
fires 108, 180, 183
floods 108
Ford Motors 123–24
foreign policy 131–75; Russia's relations
  with: China 140–52, 160, Georgia
  131, 132–40, India 143–46, 147, 148,
  Iran 159, 161, Japan 145–46, Ukraine
  111–17, 132, United States 131, 132,
  148, 151, 152–63 (reset 155–56, 160);
  *see also* individual countries
Foreign Policy Concept (Medvedev)
  102, 131, 165
Foreign Policy Concept (Putin) 142
Foreign Policy Doctrine 156
France 167
Fridman, Mikhail 119, 129n97
Frolov, Sergei
Fukushima NPP 123
Furman, Dmitry 194
Fursenko, Andrei 26

G-7 144, 171n34
G-8 93, 131–32, 214
G-20 92, 94, 154–55, 214
Gadhafi, Moammar 168
Gaidar, Yegor 69
Gakaev, Khuseyn 56, 58
Gas Exporting Countries Forum
  (GECF) 122
Gates, Robert 159
Gazprom 7, 26, 100, 106, 111ff
General Electric 102, 124

General Motors 123
Georgia 52, 115, 164, 166;
    *see also* foreign policy
Georgia Dream Party 140
Germany 104, 120, 122, 167
*glasnost* 36, 99, 103, 192
Glikin, Maksim 215
Gogol, Nikolai 181
Golikova, Tatiana 16, 189
Golos 79
Google 102
Gorbachev, M.S. xiii–xv, 5, 6, 21, 25,
    29–30, 31, 36–37, 73, 83, 85, 99, 103,
    153, 155, 186, 195, 186, 191–92, 195
Gordeev, Aleksei 18, 47, 107
government *see* political systems
governors *see* regions
Gozman, Leonid 83
Gromov, Boris 345
Gryzlov, Boris 64
Gusinsky, Vladimir 14, 91

healthcare 35, 50, 176, 179, 183–89;
    HIV/AIDS 187, 188; life expectancy
    185, 207n33; *see also* alcohol abuse;
    drug abuse
Hewlett-Packard 199
Hitler, Adolph 68
housing 35, 177, 179
Hu Jintao 121, 147, 148
human rights 71
Human Rights Bureau, Moscow 184
Human Rights Council, Russian 189, 191
Hungary 117
Hyundai 123

IBM 124
Ilim 6
Ilyumzhinov, Kirsan 47
images, Russia in the West 132, 135–36,
    137, 140, 153, 159, 195, 214
immigration 71, 184, 189; *see also*
    migrant workers
Independent Democratic Party of
    Russia 73
India 122, 123, 133, 145, 147, 148, 149,
    151; *see also* BRIC(S)
Information Science for Democracy
    (INDEM) 70, 194
infrastructure 93, 123, 124–25,
    179–81
Inmark 125
Innogorod *see* Skolkovo Innovation
    Centre

Institute of Contemporary Development
    (INSOR) 21
International Monetary Fund (IMF) 46,
    92, 143, 145, 214
Investigative Committee *see* law
    enforcement agencies
Iran 122, 123, 149–50, 153, 155,
    157, 161
Iraq 145, 161; *see also* wars
Ishaev, Viktor 49
Islamicists 52–54, 55, 57–59;
    *see also* terrorism
Islamic Movement of Uzbekistan 55
Israel 81
Italy 167
Ivanishvili, Bidzina, 140
Ivanov, Anton 6
Ivanov, Sergei 1, 7–8, 31, 204, 205
Ivanov. Viktor 187
Ivanov, Vitaly 17
Ivashov, General Leonid 27

Jackson-Vanik Amendment 157, 159,
    162, 173n77
Japan 121, 145; Kuril Islands
    145–46, 159
John Deere 124
Jordan 122
Jumanbekov, Jenisbek 56

Kadyrov, Akhmad 54
Kadyrov, Ramzan 46, 47–48, 50–51,
    53–54, 56; *Kadyrovtsy* 50–51
Kagarlitsky, Boris 9
Kalina Cosmetics 125
Kanokov, Arsen 54
Karzai, Hamid 141, 149, 167
Kasparov, Gerri (Garry) 2, 5, 34, 66, 69,
    70, 76–77, 80, 81, 88n21, 178, 194
Kasyanov, Mikhail 2, 5, 12, 27, 37n6,
    74, 81, 82
Kazakhstan 91, 101, 115, 151–52
Khamiev, Rinet 32
Khazbulatov, Khamzat 124
Khimki Forest 177–78
Khloponin, Aleksandr 46, 57–58
Khodorkovsky, Mikhail 7, 14, 27, 32,
    91, 118, 162, 193
Khrushchev, Nikita 191
Khudainatov, Eduard 120, 121
Khudyakov, Aleksei 72
Ki-Moon, Ban 143
Kirill, Patriarch 34
Kissinger, Henry 155

Klepach, Andrei 95
Kokoity, Eduard 133
*Kolskaia* 183
Komsomol 68–69, 88n15
Kornberg, Roger 100
Kosovo 133, 134, 138, 145; 'Kosovo
    Effect' 134, 138; Kosovo Liberation
    Army (KLA) 134
Kozak, Dmitry 7
Kozlov, Aleksandr 47, 107
*krysha see* corruption
Kryshtanovskaia, Olga 22, 78, 103–4
Kudrin, Aleksei 21, 24, 25, 26, 29, 32,
    82, 85, 86, 94, 95, 120, 193, 196
Kurianovich, Nikolai 12
Kuril Islands *see* Japan
*Kursk* 183
Kyrgyzstan 67, 98, 115, 151–52, 157

labour 35, 177–78, 184; pensions 35,
    178; unemployment 20, 43, 177–78;
    wages 179; *see also* protests
Latynina, Yuliia 28
Lavrov, Sergei 119, 133, 147, 152, 155,
    157, 160, 167, 168
law enforcement agencies 22, 195, 201;
    Investigatory Committee 81, 193, 195,
    198, 203
League of Voters 84–85
Lebedev, Platon 162
Lenarcic, Janez 81
Lenergo 200
Lenin, Vladimir Ilych 38n20, 47
Liberal Democratic Party of Russia 12,
    27, 66, 78; *see also* Zhirinovsky
liberals/liberalism 69–70, 73–74, 75,
    80–82, 86, 105, 213
Libya 25, 122, 144–45, 159–60, 168
Lieberman, Avigdor 81
Limonov, Eduard 27, 66, 67, 71, 75,
    76, 81
Lithuania 122
Litvinenko, Aleksandr 51, 140
L'Oreal SA 124
LUKoil 94
Luzhkov, Yuri 23–24, 47, 67, 178, 179,
    182, 202

McCain, John 154, 158, 160
McConnell, J. Michael 153
McDonald's 124
McFaul, Michael 101, 160, 161
Magas, Emir 56
Magna Co. 123

Magnitsky, Sergei 159; Magnitsky Bill
    160–61, 162
Makarov, Gen. Nikolai Ye. 165–66
Marxism-Leninism 68, 69
Massachusetts Institute of Technology
    (MIT) 105
Matviyenko, Valentina 45
media: Russian 13, 14, 16, 34, 48, 62,
    66, 73, 75, 79, 80, 86, 106, 132, 154,
    157–58, 163, 214, 215; Western 34, 51,
    60n20, 70, 79, 80, 86, 132, 135–36,
    140, 157–58, 178
Medvedev, Aleksandr 121
Medvedev, Dmitry: biographical 5–9;
    and corruption 6, 15, 20–21, 35, 36,
    50, 193–204; and democracy 13, 18,
    21, 67, 72, 87, 105; election
    campaigns 11–15, 81–87; family 5;
    'Go, Russia!' 21, 98–99; as liberal 13,
    15, 26, 213; and modernization 15,
    18–20, 21–22, 36, 65, 98–107, 120;
    popularity 17, 20, 24–25, 30, 67, 200;
    pre-presidency career 1ff; and reform
    72, 73–74, 78, 82–83, 84, 85, 87, 214;
    supporting Putin for president 29–30;
    *see also* National Priority Projects
Memorial 66
Merkel, Angela 122
Mezentsev, Dmitry 32
Microsoft 102
middle class 31, 67, 81, 189
migrant workers 184, 189
migration: internal 44, 184–85, 189;
    out 185; *see also* emigration,
    immigration
military *see* armed forces
Miller, Aleksei 115
Milov, Vladimir 16, 70, 82
Mironov, Boris 27
Mironov, Sergei 2, 26–27, 32, 33, 45, 64,
    74, 195
missile defence *see* armed forces
Mitrokhin, Sergei 27, 69, 74
Mitsui 124
modernization 98–107, 200;
    *see also* economy
Moldova 98, 163
*Molodaia Gvardiia* 23, 157
'Motherland: Common Sense'
    *see Rodina*
'Motherland: National-Patriotic Union'
    *see Rodina*
Movement Against Illegal Immigration
    (DPNI) 71

Mujahedin Jamaat 55
Myanmar 149

Nabiullina, Elvira 16, 26, 124
Nabucco 115, 117
Naftohaz 111
Nagorno-Karabakh 139
Naryshkin, Sergei 1, 20, 31,
    195–96, 204
*Nashi* 22–23, 34, 77, 202
National Bolshevik Front 71
National Bolshevik Party 27, 71, 75
national champions *see* economy
National Priority Projects 8, 13, 16,
    35–36, 107, 176, 205
NATO 22, 25, 55, 72, 132, 137, 142,
    145, 163–65, 166–69, 174n112;
    expansion 132, 140, 153, 155, 163–64,
    168; Membership Action Plan (MAP)
    134, 139, 140; NATO-Russia Council
    (NRC) 164, 165; training exercises
    138, 168
Navalny, Aleksei N. 27, 34, 79, 84, 202
Nazarbaev, Nursultan 152
Nazarov, Aleksandr 201
Nazism 71
Nemtsov, Boris 2, 16, 34, 66, 69, 74, 76,
    81–82, 86
Nepal 149
Nevsky Express 55
Nigeria 122
Nogaideli, Zurab 138
Nokia 102
Non-Government Organizations
    (NGOs) 80, 140, 189–91
Nord Stream 115
North Atlantic Treaty Organization *see*
    NATO
North Caucasus 46, 50–59
Northern Distribution Network (NDN)
    159, 167
North Korea 122
nuclear power *see* energy
Nurgaliev, Rashid 57–58, 196, 200, 203

Obama Administration 139
Obama, Barack 132, 138, 147, 154–55,
    158, 160, 167, 214
oil and gas industry 93, 111; BP (TNK)
    118–21, 200; Chinese National
    Petroleum Corporation 118, 121; ENI
    (Italy) 117; Exxon Mobil 119, 121;
    gas wars 112–17; Petroleos de
    Venezuela SA 120; Ruhr Oel 120;

Shell 119, 121; Total (France) 119;
    *see also* energy
oligarchs 14, 91, 177, 192
Olympics (Sochi) 58
Onishchenko, Gennady 186
Oracle 104
Organization for Economic
    Cooperation and Development
    (OECD) 20
Organization for Security and
    Cooperation in Europe (OSCE) 34,
    77, 152; Office for Democratic
    Institutions and Human Rights
    (ODIHR) 77, 81, 84
Organization of Oil Exporting Countries
    (OPEC) 122
Orlov, Aleksei 47
Orlov, Oleg 66
Orthodox Church *see* religion
Other Russia 34, 70, 75, 82
*Otlichnitsy* 78
Owen, James 119

Pakistan 147, 149, 151, 159
Palin, Sarah 154
Panfilova, Yelena 203, 206
Parliamentary Assembly of the Council
    of Europe (PACE) 13, 32, 34, 56,
    77, 137
Partnership and Cooperation
    Agreement (PCA) 137
Party of Social Justice 69, 70
Patriots of Russia 78, 79
Patrushev, Nikolai 51–52
Pavlovsky, Gleb 29
People's Freedom Party (PFP-
    PARNAS) 27, 75, 77, 82–83, 86, 202
Pepsi Cola Co 124
*perestroika* 99, 103, 192
Petrov, Yury 195
Peunova, Svetlana 32
plenipotentiary representatives *see*
    presidency
Podberyoskin, Aleksei 70
Poland 97, 109,136, 155, 156
political systems 11–61, 72–74; 'Against
    All' 3, 77; municipal filters 84;
    political reform 49ff, 63–65, 66–67,
    77–78, 82–83, 84, 85, 86–87; *see also*
    Federation Council; presidency;
    protests; regions, governors; State
    Duma; Tandem
Politkovskaia, Anna 140
Ponomarev, Lev 70

population 35, 42–43, 176, 183–84, 185, 189
Poteev, Col. A.N. 158
Potkin, Aleksandr 71
poverty 176, 184, 189
Powell, Colin 132
power vertical see *Vertikal*
Pozner, Vladimir 86
presidency 11–15, 17, 72–74; elections (to 2008) 2, 12–15, (to 2012) 20, 30–31, 32–35, 78; plenipotentiary representatives 43, 46; Tandem 9, 11–41, 63–64, 103–4, 213–14; *see also* political systems
Presidential Economic Council 107
Primakov, Yevgeny 8–9, 49, 131–32, 146, 164, 214
Prokhorov, Mikhail 27, 32, 33, 34, 82, 83, 87
protests 32–33, 57–58, 66, 67, 70, 72, 76–77, 79–81, 82, 86, 177–79; Bolotnaia Ploshchad 33, 81, 86; Strategy-31 66, 75, 76; Triumfalnaia Ploshchad 67, 70, 178
Public Chamber 13, 28, 37n8, 85, 195, 201
Pussy Riot 85–86, 90n72, 159
Putina, Lyudmila 3
Putin, Vladimir: as conservative 26, 103, 105; and corruption 6, 192–93, 194, 204–5; demonization 140, 158, 160; and economy 96; and modernization 28, 103, 106; popularity 2–3, 17, 20, 24–25, 3, 33, 140, 200; Putinism 3, 33, 213; and reform 179

Qatar 122

racism 71, 184
Radical Left Front 86
railways 109–10, 123, 124, 181–82
Rasmussen, Anders Fogh 142, 167, 168
regions 42–61, 182–83; governors 18, 43–44, 47–49, 50, 84; plenipotentiary representatives *see* presidency
religion 42, 153; Islam 50–59; Orthodoxy 42, 85
Remnick, David 192
Renova Group 100
Republican Party of Russia 86
reserve funds 92, 93, 94–95, 96; National Prosperity Fund 92, 95, 176
Rice, Condoleezza 135, 136
Right Cause Party 69, 78, 79, 83

roads 181–82, 186
*Rodina* 70, 75
Rogozin, Dmitry 71, 164–65, 167, 204
Romania 117, 156
Romney, Mitt 162
Romodanovsky, Konstantin 185, 189
Rosatom *see* energy, nuclear powerplants
Rosatomstroieksport 122; *see also* energy, nuclear power plants
Rosneft 26, 94, 118, 120, 121
*Rosoboronexport* (Russian Arms Export Agency) 92
Rossel, Eduard 47
*Rossiia Molodaia* 23, 72
RUSAL 94
Russia, Forward! 76
Russian Corporation of Nanotechnologies (ROSNANO) 100, 105
Russian Federation 42f
Russian National Democratic Union (RNDS) 74
Russian Technologies 124
*Russkiye* group 71
*Russky marsh* (Russian March) 71
Rutskoi, Aleksandr 37n2
Ryabkov, Sergei 156
Ryzhkov, Vladimir 34, 74, 81, 86

Saakashvili, Mikheil 133, 134–37, 139–40, 154
SABMiller 186
Sachs, Jeffrey 99
Sakwa, Richard
Sarkozy, Nicolas 136, 147, 177
Satarov, Georgy 70, 194
Sayano-Sushchenskaia power station 48, 180
Schröder, Gerhard 122
Schwarzenegger, Arnold 104
Sechin, Igor 26, 113
Sedov, Col.-Gen. Aleksei 55
Serbia 7, 115, 117, 159, 169n7; *see also* Kosovo
Serdyukov, Valery 2, 164–65, 166, 174n103, 197
Shanghai Cooperation Organization (SCO) 34, 55, 56, 92, 117, 132, 141–42, 147, 149–50, 151
Shaymiev, Mintimer 46
Shcherbakov *see* Poteev, Col. A.N.
*Shchit Moskvy* (Shield of Moscow) 71
Shenin, Oleg 12

Shoigu, Sergei 35
Shuvalov, Igor 19–20, 95
Siberia 48–49, 111, 118, 119, 152
Siemens 124, 199, 200
Siguler Guff 102
*siloviki* 19, 22, 26, 37, 72, 106, 192, 202, 213
Singh, Manmohan 150
skinheads 3, 71, 185; *see also* racism; xenophobia
Skolkovo Innovation Centre (Innogorod) 22, 27, 35, 49, 100–103, 104, 105, 127n46, 156, 157
Skrynnik, Yelena 18, 107, 111
Slavic Union 71
smoking 187–88
Snowden, Edward
Sobchak, Anatoly 5–6, 86
Sobchak, Kseniia 86
Sobyanin, Sergei 24, 25, 202
social issues 43f, 176–79; *see also* labour
Solidarnost 69, 70, 74
Sollers 123–24
Sorochkin, Aleksandr 199
South Africa 145; *see also* BRICS
South Korea 104, 122
South Ossetia 133–36, 138, 169n8–9
South Stream 115–17
sovereign democracy 99
Soviet Union *see* Union of Soviet Socialist Republics
Sri Lanka 151
Stabilization Fund 92, 93
Stalin, J.V. 68–69, 133, 204
Starbucks 124
State Council 65, 94, 180
State Duma 62, 65, 72–74, 81–84, 85; elections (to 2003) 3, (2007) 3–4, 14, 63, 64, (2011) 30–31, 32–33, 48, 64, 74–79
Steinmeier, Frank-Walter 135
Stepashin, Sergei 23, 192
Storchak, Sergei 193, 196
Strategic Arms Reduction Treaty (START) *see* arms reduction/control
Strategic Offensive Reduction Treaty (SORT) 163
Strategy-31 *see* protests
Sukhoi 123, 147
Surkov, Vladislav 22, 31, 66, 83, 99, 102, 103
*Svyataia Rus* (Holy Rus) movement 85
Syria 145, 161

Tagliavini, Heidi 137
Tajikistan 98, 151
Taliban 52, 55, 141, 168–69, 187
Tandem *see* presidency
TAPI 118
Tatarstan 46, 183
Taziyev, Ali *see* Magas, Emir
terrorism 25, 51–59, 183; *see also* Al-Qaeda
terrorists 51–59, 161, 168
Tibet 148
Timakova, Natalia 16
TNK-BP *see* oil and gas industry
tourism 124
Toyota 123, 124
Trans-Anatolia Pipeline 117
Trans-Balkan Pipeline 117
Transmashholding 123
Transneft 118, 121
Trans-Pacific Partnership 98
Transparency International 197, 201, 203; *see also* corruption
transportation 124, 181; *see also* roads
Trenin, Dmitri 23, 26
Trinidad and Tobago 122
Troika 131, 146–48
Turkey 115, 117–18, 122, 151–52
Turkmenistan 115, 117, 151
Tymoshenko, Yulia 112, 113, 114

Udaltsev, Sergei 34, 71, 75 81, 84, 86
Udugov, Movladi 52
Ukraine 98, 132, 164, 166, 214–15; *see also* economy; energy, pipelines
Umarov, Doku 52–53, 55–57; *see also* Caucasus Emirate
unemployment *see* labour
Unified Energy System (UES) 100, 179
Unilever PLC 125
Union of Right Forces (SPS) 69, 83
Union of Soviet Socialist Republics (USSR) xiii–xvi
United Civil Front 74, 82
United Democratic Movement 69
United Labour Front 75
United Nations 131, 134; UNICEF 50; United Nations Security Council (UNSC) 138, 148, 150
United Russia Party 2, 16, 21, 26, 28, 35, 47–48, 62, 64, 65–67, 69, 72–74, 78, 103–4
United States of America 101, 137; *see also* foreign policy

Ushakov, Yury 154
Uzbekistan 151

Valdai Discussion Club 30, 77–78
Vasilevskaia, Yeva 16
Vekselberg, Viktor 100, 119, 129n97
Venezuela 122
Verheugen, Gunter 97
*Vertikal* 13, 18, 179
Veshnyakov, Aleksandr 12
Vietnam 145
Vilsack, Tom 156
Vneshekonombank 94
Volodin, Vyacheslav 31
Voloshin, Aleksandr 7
*vospitanie* xv

wars: Chechnya 132; Georgia 52, 97,
    132–40, 154, 165–66; Iraq 132, 145
Wen Jiabao 147, 149
Wendy's (Wenrus) 125
Wimm-Bill-Dann Foods 124
women 16, 18, 73, 77, 78
Wood, Robert 170n20
World Bank 46, 92
World Health Organization (WHO) 50
World Trade Organization
    (WTO) 20, 97–98, 134, 153,
    156, 159, 203

xenophobia 71, 179, 184–85;
    *see also* racism
Xi Jinping 147

Yabloko 17, 27, 33, 69, 73, 74,
    78, 88n19
Yanaev, Gennady 37n2
Yanukovych, Viktor 113, 114
Yashin, Ilya 70, 74, 76, 79, 81
Yavlinsky, Grigory 2, 27,
    32, 69, 82
*Yekaterinburg* 183
Yeliseev, Ilya 6
Yeltsin, Boris 5, 6, 7, 9, 10n8, 11,
    13, 14, 62, 67, 103, 132, 153,
    192, 214
Yevkurov, Yunus-Bek 54
Young Russia *see Rossiia Molodaia*
Yurgens, Igor 22, 85, 86, 215
Yushchenko, Viktor 112, 113

Zakaev, Akhmed 52, 56–57
Zhirinovsky, Vladimir 2, 5, 12, 27, 32,
    33, 45, 64–65, 70, 74, 81
Zhukov, Konstantin 69
Ziazikov, Murat 54
Zubkov, Viktor 1–2, 20, 26, 108
Zyuganov, Gennady 2, 5, 12, 26, 31, 32,
    33, 34, 64, 68–69, 74, 81

For Product Safety Concerns and Information please contact our EU representative GPSR@taylorandfrancis.com Taylor & Francis Verlag GmbH, Kaufingerstraße 24, 80331 München, Germany